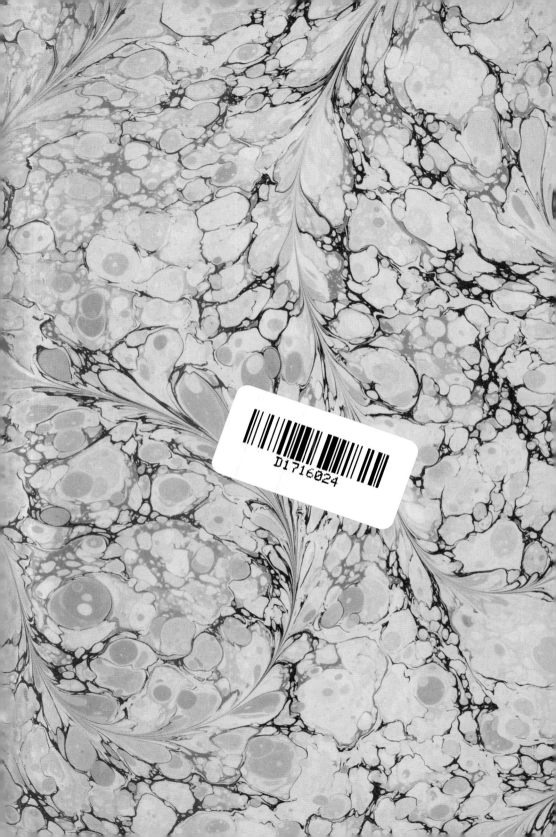

the interrogator

Also by the Author
FIGHTER ACES OF THE LUFTWAFFE
(with Trevor J. Constable)

FIGHTER ACES OF THE U.S.A.
(with Trevor J. Constable)

the interrogator
the story of Hanns-Joachim Scharff
master interrogator of the Luftwaffe

Raymond F. Toliver

Schiffer Military History
Atglen, PA

ACKNOWLEDGMENTS

The author and the interrogator Hanns-Joachim Scharff wish to express unlimited appreciation to those who assisted in the preparation of this book. Trevor James Constable, coauthor on several previous books about fighter aces, gave unstintingly with advice and editorial assistance, as did Scharff's longtime friend, the late Frank Dunnebacke, and Michel E. Oliveau Jr. Many others, too numerous to name, cooperated to the fullest, and our warmest personal thanks are hereby extended to each one, and a special thanks to the ever helpful Kurt Schulze and Edward Schroeder.

Book Design by Robert Biondi

Copyright © 1997 by Raymond F. Toliver.
Library of Congress Control Number: 96-72252.

All rights reserved. No part of this work may be reproduced or used in any form or by any means—graphic, electronic, or mechanical, including photocopying or information storage and retrieval systems—without written permission from the publisher.
The scanning, uploading and distribution of this book or any part thereof via the Internet or via any other means without the permission of the publisher is illegal and punishable by law. Please purchase only authorized editions and do not participate in or encourage the electronic piracy of copyrighted materials.
"Schiffer," "Schiffer Publishing Ltd. & Design," and the "Design of pen and inkwell" are registered trademarks of Schiffer Publishing Ltd.

ISBN: 978-0-7643-0261-9
Printed in China

Schiffer Books are available at special discounts for bulk purchases for sales promotions or premiums. Special editions, including personalized covers, corporate imprints, and excerpts can be created in large quantities for special needs. For more information contact the publisher:

Published by Schiffer Publishing, Ltd.
4880 Lower Valley Road
Atglen, PA 19310
Phone: (610) 593-1777; Fax: (610) 593-2002
E-mail: Info@schifferbooks.com
Web: www.schifferbooks.com

For our complete selection of fine books on this and related subjects, please visit our website at www.schifferbooks.com. You may also write for a free catalog.

We are always looking for people to write books on new and related subjects. If you have an idea for a book, please contact us at proposals@schifferbooks.com.

PREFACE

In the early 1950s, while doing the research for a book later titled *Fighter Aces of the U.S.A.*, many of the aces I interviewed had been POWs in Germany. Almost to a man they commented that their interrogator at the Luftwaffe interrogation center at Oberursel had been a first-class gentleman named Hanns Scharff. Some swore he was an officer dressed in enlisted clothing, some said he was a member of the aristocracy, and all said he was one of the most intelligent of all men they had ever met. Then I was told that he was a Luftwaffe enlisted man with the rank of *Gefreiter* (the equivalent of corporal).

This really whet my curiosity, so I began a long and almost fruitless search for him. I wanted to hear his side of the story and try to determine what it was that made this man the Luftwaffe's most successful interrogator. I was told by one source that he lived in Germany, and another told me he had passed away shortly after the war.

The logjam broke, however, when I read an article in the *Air Force Magazine*, authored by an ex-POW named Royal D. Frey. The story mentioned Hanns Scharff and stated that he lived in the Los Angeles area. Now, I lived in Encino, a suburb of Los Angeles, so I picked up the San Fernando Valley phone book and there he was! He lived in the Hollywood Hills area, just twelve miles from my home. A quick phone call, and Hanns's wife, Sabine, was asking me who I was and if Hanns knows me. That phone call was the beginning of this book and of a friendship that flourished as long as he lived.

Scharff's life story, and in particular his experiences with American fighter pilots from the 8th and 9th US Air Forces who had been downed and captured by the Germans, was so gripping that my other writing projects were pushed aside.

The Interrogator

While it was a self-satisfying accomplishment to see this book published, the most rewarding part was acquiring the friendship of Hanns Scharff. I have tried to catch the essence of his speech and grammar (European grammar) throughout the book and hope I have succeeded.

Auswertestelle West was established in 1941 as the principal Air Force intelligence center for the whole of the Western theater of operations. Its main purpose was to obtain operational information through the interrogation of captured air crews, and through evaluation of documents and other materials recovered from crashed enemy aircraft.

The center was located at Oberursel and is often mis-called "Dulag Luft," and it may have actually functioned under that misnomer until the true "transit camp" was established at Wetzlar and officially called Dulag Luft. Dulag Luft actually translates into "transit camp."

Oberstleutnant (Lt. Colonel) Killinger was the commandant of Auswertestelle West beginning in 1941 and was responsible for the growth of the camp from a very small operation in 1941 to the important center it finally became. In 1941 it had a small staff of about fifty, with only four interrogators, and only 400 to 500 POWs passed through at that time. To illustrate the constant growth of the operation, it should be noted that in 1942 about 3,000 POWs were interrogated. In 1943 over 8,000 POWs passed through, and in 1944 more than 29,000 Allied airmen were processed.

The number of interrogators also had to grow in order to handle this increasing workload. In 1943 there were thirty to forty interrogators, and in 1944, sixty to sixty-five interrogators and about 550 total personnel in all departments. The departments included interrogating, evaluation, press, radio listening, broadcasting, photographic, reception, and sanitary.

The Interrogator was originally published in 1978 by Aero Publishers of Fallbrook, California. Mr. Ernest Gentle, the president of Aero, was as impressed as the author by Mr. Scharff and has also developed a friendship with him. Sadly, Aero went out of business, so Schiffer Publishing is bringing this new edition of the book to the public. This new edition, published in 1997, has been revised, corrected, and updated and reflects many experiences that have taken place since the first edition. Literally hundreds of ex-POWs have contacted Scharff and the author since the book was published, praising once again and saluting their honorable captor. To a man they have expressed a desire to meet him again or to write or telephone him. Scharff has a right to feel very special, and it all happened because he was gentle and believed he could get more information from an interrogatee through kindness rather than through bullying and threats. He was professional in his approach to his job, and he always got the information he was seeking from each POW.

Major (later Lieutenant General) Gerald W. Johnson, United States Air Force, 56th Fighter Group, one of America's top fighter aces, was downed and captured

Preface

by the Germans on 27 March 1944. During interrogations at the Luftwaffe Intelligence and Evaluation Center at Oberursel, Johnson left with the impression of Scharff as an unswerving and loyal soldier, and an alert, correct, and polite gentleman-officer.

Obtaining no useful results, the interrogation officer tossed the 56th Fighter Group file folder to Johnson. This file contained not only the history of the group but also the life story of this very prisoner, even his mother's maiden name. As Johnson turned the pages, he was muttering with each turn, "This breaks my heart!"

CONTENTS

Preface 5
Foreword 10
Prologue 11
Introduction 12

Chapter 1	Come In, Please..	16
Chapter 2	How to Become an Interrogation Officer........	20
Chapter 3	Playboys of the Air......................................	29
Chapter 4	Fighters behind Fences................................	49
Chapter 5	Wits as Weapons	80
Chapter 6	Remarkable! Most Remarkable!...................	114
Chapter 7	Worthy of Imitation.....................................	154
Chapter 8	To Err Is Human..	200
Chapter 9	Unwept, Unhonored, Unsung	229
Chapter 10	Ehr, Lehr, Wehr	251
Chapter 11	Love's Labor Lost	279
Chapter 12	End of the Rainbow.....................................	287
Chapter 13	Epilogue	315

Appendix... 324
Glossary 339
Index 342

FOREWORD

In 1946–47, when I wrote about my wartime experience as a Luftwaffe interrogation officer, I was a lonely man. I had lost my wife, my children, my home. I was jobless, ill, and disillusioned. I had lost much more: Faith, Love, and Hope.

I wrote my story in English, the way I used to speak during the war, but I had no intention of publishing any of it. Indeed, I never had the intention to go to the United States of America and settle there. But the extraordinary circumstances that had brought me into close contact with most of the finest American fighter aces lingered on in my mind, and, so to speak, in a strange way the ring began to close itself. It had started when I was stripped of everything I possessed, at the gate of the prisoner-of-war camp after I, myself, had been captured. The American guards ordered the German soldiers to leave everything behind they were carrying. Rucksacks, greatcoats, blankets, bundles, briefcases; everything was thrown onto a big heap, while the guards were constantly shouting in a funny German accent: "Ihr kriegt alles neu!" I did not believe their words, saying "You get it all new!," and little did I know that they really meant what they were saying. But it was true: "I got it all new," not only the greatcoat and the blanket, but everything else I had lost. Not immediately though, no, no—it took some 20, 25 years, and everything I got new was even bigger and better.

Tolle lege, tolle lege: Take and read!

HANNS SCHARFF

PROLOGUE

There are no words that can express the magic of that wilderness / That wilderness away up high / Where banks of clouds float softly by / And hide the problems of earth below but then . . .you know / If you have flown.

To those who sail the sky above / Comes peace of mind and understanding love / There is no bitterness in the sky / As gently earth and clouds drift by / All is beautiful, serene / You know exactly what I mean . . . If you have flown!
—Anon

I never saw a man who looked with such a wistful eye upon that tent of blue which prisoners call the sky, and at every wandering cloud that trailed its ravened fleeces by.
—Oscar Wilde
(from the *Ballad of Reading Gaol*)

INTRODUCTION

This is an important book.

Important because of the person who is its principal subject. In the midst of war, one of the most inhumane of human activities, we learn of a man who retains his humanity. The lessons that we derive are inescapably ennobling.

It is said that if you keep your head while all about you lose theirs, then you don't understand the problem. Some do keep their heads even while understanding full well. Hanns-Joachim Scharff kept his. He retained a sense of personal human responsibility toward those over whom he wielded almost total power. As we learn in this book, he methodically and deliberately treated his prisoners with respect and dignity. Nevertheless, while so doing, he did not neglect the wartime purpose of the interrogator's task. These two purposes seem to be mutually exclusive. Yet, here we have proof that solution of the paradox can be found by an exceptional human being.

In fact, this is not one book but two books intertwined. It is the personal story, originally written in diary form, of the wartime experiences of Hanns Scharff. That diary was never intended to be other than a family archive for his children and grandchildren. The extraordinary coincidences by which it became an important part of the first edition of this book (published in 1978) are explained by author Ray Toliver.

The other book is by Ray Toliver, about the extraordinary success of Hanns Scharff as interrogator of American fighter pilots. Because of his encyclopedic knowledge of fighter pilots worldwide, Toliver knew Scharff by reputation long before he met him.

How did Hanns Scharff come to be an interrogator? What qualifications did he have for this job? The answers are (1) by pure chance (or was it fate?) and (2) he had no specialized training whatsoever for the role of interrogator.

How did he become the phenomenally successful interrogator?

My conviction is that his early education, and the development of his personal value system, permitted a profound appreciation of life and understanding of his fellow man. In the chapter titled "Ehr, Lehr, Wehr," we gain insight into his beliefs about the characteristics of the complete individual. Truly a Renaissance man. Thus equipped, and with the advantage of captor over the captive, he was quasi-irresistible as interrogator.

When he was drafted into the German military, Hanns Scharff had no idea that he would become an interrogator. Through a series of surprising and implausible coincidences, that responsibility seemed to have sought him out. Was this predestined fate? Or the workings of pure chance? Hanns often pondered this dilemma. Whatever the answer, it is clear that he was instantly propelled from the role of simple soldier to the position of interrogator, which permitted him almost unlimited power.

How was he to exercise that power? That was, for the most part, subject to his personal whim. The choice was his: whether to choose linen to dress wounds, or nails to crucify. We learn how he exercised that power from the eloquent testimony of many American fighter pilots who were interrogated by him.

The world is a better place because of Hanns-Joachim Scharff.

This introduction was written by Hanns Scharff's friend Michel E. Oliveau Jr.

DEDICATION
to SABINE

and to Hanns-Felix, Hanns-Christian, Hanns-Claudius, and John Robert, the four sons of the interrogator Hanns-Joachim Scharff, each the apple of his father's eye. This book is further dedicated to those stalwart, loyal, and brave unfortunates who are or have been prisoners of war. Their unswerving faithfulness to principles and country have cost them their happiness, health, and even their lives. THESE ARE THE MEN AND WOMEN WHO KNOW THE MEANING OF TRUE CHARACTER. This book is also dedicated to all my friends around the world.

H-JS

1

COME IN, PLEASE

Hide not your talents, for use they are made. What's a sun dial in the shade? —Benjamin Franklin

"Come in, please. I am your interrogator." With these words, Germany's master interrogator welcomed each captured Allied fighter pilot into room 47 at the Luftwaffe Intelligence and Evaluation Center, Auswertestelle West.

The center, located just 7.5 miles (12 km) northwest of the center of Frankfurt/Main, Germany, was the collection point for all enemy airmen captured by the Germans in World War II. By directions from the highest Wehrmacht headquarters, once an enemy was captured and determined to be from an enemy air force unit, he was to be transported as soon as possible to this evaluation center, where the Luftwaffe interrogators would question the prisoner of war (POW).

Interrogations usually took a week to four weeks. Once the inquisitor determined that he had all the information he could get from the POW, he would release him for transport to the Dulag Luft, which was a sort of distribution center located in a park in the center of Frankfurt/Main. Later, after being bombed by the Eighth Air Force Fortresses and Liberators, Dulag Luft was moved to Wetzlar, about 33 miles (52 km), as the crow flies, north of Frankfurt/Main. There was some suspicion that the Luftwaffe moved Dulag Luft to Wetzlar because the big letters "POW" painted on the roof to ward off Allied bombings might serve to protect the very important optical and other industry located at Wetzlar. From the Dulag Luft,* POWs were sent on to permanent camps called *Stalag Luft*. (*Dulag Luft is short for *Durchgangslager*. It means "through-going camp." *Stalag Luft* is short for *Stammlager*. It means "permanent camp.")

Auswertestelle West came into operation during the Battle of Britain. Douglas Bader, the famous "Station Master of Tangmere," was interrogated at a small restaurant located about halfway between Oberursel and Hohe-Mark before being

Chapter 1: Come In, Please

THE LUFTWAFFE'S MASTER INTERROGATOR
This photo shows Hanns-Joachim Scharff just a few days after he was conscripted into military service.

sent on to Colditz Castle in Saxony, a permanent prison camp for British, Poles, French, Canadians, Australians, New Zealanders, South Africans, Americans, and Dutchmen. This restaurant later became the quarters for the guards who worked at Oberursel. The evaluation center at Oberursel consisted of about fourteen buildings, the largest one a U-shaped building that had approximately 150 solitary cells and was surrounded on three sides by a security fence. This building was known as "the Cooler." Twelve of the other buildings served as the headquarters, supply quarters, Red Cross quarters, interrogation quarters, catchall quarters, officer's quarters, ladies quarters, noncommissioned officers (NCO) quarters, and enlisted quarters. The fourteenth building, located in the forest that surrounded two sides of the complex, was the home or quarters of the camp *Kommandant*, Lt. Col. Erich Killinger.

The interrogatees who arrived at Oberursel were all Allied airmen who flew from the United Kingdom or Africa and Italy. Russian airmen were sent to a separate evaluation center, so none were questioned at Auswertestelle West.

The interrogators at Oberursel were men who had earned their red certificates as interpreters at one of the *Dolmetscher Kompanien*, interpreter schools, and had been assigned to Auswertestelle West. None had been trained in the interrogation of POWs, but each was qualified with an excellent knowledge of his enemy's language and a fair knowledge of his country or homeland and was well educated and worldly wise. Some wore officer's rank and some were enlisted ranks. Hanns-Joachim Scharff, Germany's master interrogator in the view of many, is the central character in this book. He resided in Johannesburg, South Africa, when WWII broke out in 1939. He had lived there for eleven years and was the director of the overseas division of Adlerwerke, an industrial giant in Germany, manufacturers of automobiles, airplanes, King-Tiger tanks, typewriters, and many other items used in peace and in war. Married with children, he and his family had returned to Germany in the summer of 1939 on a company vacation, only to be caught up

The Interrogator

VILLA JAHN AND TEXTILE MILL AT GREIZ
Scharff's grandfather owned this mill. He was instrumental in establishing the wool industry in Passaic, New Jersey. The villa is surrounded by trees at the upper right. The hillside (*at left*) covers a gigantic cave used by employees as a bomb shelter during the war.

in the whirlwind of Hitler's Blitzkrieg. Scharff's exit visa was revoked and he found himself, at the age of thirty-two, pressed into service in the German Wehrmacht. That was the beginning of his career as an interrogator.

Poker Face or Stone Face were nicknames given to Hanns Scharff by British, American, and South African POWs at Oberursel. His serious demeanor belied a warm heart. Hanns-Joachim Scharff, interrogator-to-be, was born in 1907 in East Prussia. His father, Hanns-Hermann Scharff, was an army officer who quit the army to join his father-in-law as a partner in a textile factory in Greiz, south of Leipzig, Germany. Eyes fixed to the future, Father Hanns trained his three sons, Hanns, Eberhardt, and Wolfgang, in textiles, so that they would be prepared to carry on the business.

Hanns's mother, Elsa, née Jahn, was the daughter of Christian Jahn, cofounder of the Botany Woolen Mills of Greiz and Passaic, New Jersey. When World War I came along, Hanns's father rejoined the army and lost his life following a battle on the French front in 1917. He had won the Iron Cross (I and II Class), the Reuss Cross, and the Hanseatic Cross, all for bravery in combat. Elsa, Hanns's mother, lived fifty-four years as a widow, passing away at the age of eighty-six.

The Scharff family lived at Villa Jahn in Greiz, perhaps the largest home in the city. Hanns began formal training in textiles upon reaching his teens. Three years of textiles and weaving was followed by a year in merchandising and

Chapter 1: Come In, Please

marketing. Next he spent a year in Hamburg, where he studied exporting. This led to a year in Johannesburg, South Africa, for experience in sales, but he was so successful in his job there in the Adlerwerke Foreign Office that Adlerwerke promoted him to director of the overseas division. Several years elapsed before he got back to Germany on other than short visits, and he was at Greiz when WWII started. Greiz, a city of about 40,000 inhabitants in 1939, once more became the home of Hanns Scharff. Greiz is the oldest principality of Reuss and in its rural setting provided bountiful fishing and hunting. As Scharff says, "Fit for a Prince!" Small game, big game, trout streams, ducks, geese, deer; all were plentiful in the area, and, by a stroke of luck, it was one part of Germany left practically untouched by the war. Unfortunately, it was East Germany.

The Jahn/Scharff textile industry flourished until the end of WWII and even when occupied by American troops the first few weeks after the war ended. The prosperous business came to a screeching halt on the very day the Americans hastily evacuated Greiz (as well as all of Thuringia and Saxony) in accordance with the terms of the agreements with Great Britain and the United States, which turned Eastern Europe over to communist Russia. The Soviets moved into Villa Jahn, and it became known as "the Soviet Pioneers Clubhouse."* (*In 1990 the Soviets abandoned the Villa Jahn. Its future is unknown.)

At home in Greiz, Hanns Scharff was notified that he was to be drafted into the army, and after reporting he was assigned as a *Panzergrenadier*. His career, as it unfolds from grenadier to interrogator of American fighter aces, is a dramatic tale strewn with intrigue, deception, psychology, ingenuity, and fortune. His story of how he became known as Germany's master interrogator is unique.

Scharff is the interrogator who managed to get every pilot he questioned to give him the answers he had to have. In many instances the prisoners of war being questioned never realized that their words, small talk or otherwise, were in one way or another of great value to Germany's war machinery. One American ex-POW puts it this way; "Hanns Scharff could get a confession of infidelity from a nun!" Another puts it more succinctly: "I suppose he got something out of me, but to this day I haven't the least idea what it could have been." Another writes: "What did he get from me? There is no doubt he got something from me. If you talked about the weather or anything else, he no doubt got some information or confirmation from it. His technique was psychic, not physical."

What is this magic spell or formula used by Hanns Scharff that makes the POWs talk even though they are conditioned to remain silent? Let us listen now to his narrative, broken only where necessary for clarification and better understanding.

2

HOW TO BECOME AN INTERROGATION OFFICER

The journey of a thousand miles starts with a single step.
—Chinese proverb

All you have to do to become an interrogation officer in the army is to stand, on a gray and dull early February morning, in front of your fog-veiled barracks on the outskirts of Potsdam and listen to the frightful farewell speech and endless chain of admonitions of your captain. He tells you that with his command of "Forward March!," you will take the first step of your long-lasting and already long-feared journey to the Russian front.

Others are luckier, of course, and go south to sunny Italy and even Africa, or west to live like God almighty in France, or north, where they say the food is really good and plentiful and, because of the long nights, there is not too much duty. But *you*! You are just about to be told to leave for the icy, infinite, dreadful East. The train is already under steam, and you soon have to be smart and quick to stake out a cozy "*Hommes Forty*"* full of straw and, although you are not after just two months' training fully acquainted with the conditions of such trips for fresh-baked panzer recruits, you will have a horror growing within you every minute and every inch it takes you farther away. (* *Hommes Forty*: a covered railroad wagon for carrying goods in peacetime but in wartime used to carry forty men or twelve horses.)

There you stand, a new-made grenadier with 170 pounds of luggage to carry, a gun, ammo, steel helmet, bayonet, spade, gas mask, mess kit, knapsack, and whatnot. Your breath steams, your knees feel weak, and you freeze despite three suits of underwear wisely donned that morning. You are over 6 feet tall and therefore stand second in the first row. Your friend the movie architect whispers behind you that he could stand the strain of standing hours at attention no longer and would die before getting started for sure.

Chapter 2: How To Become An Interrogation Officer

PANZERGRENADIER-TO-BE AND HIS DAUGHTER
Photo taken three days after Scharff's induction.

You think of your wife and two little sons, not very far away. In fact, only 20 miles away in Berlin. Until yesterday they did not know that you were to be sent off beyond all bounds. You yourself did not know! Only when the sergeant major told you and your buddies of the granted permission, an exception, to telephone to your family for the purpose of coming to see you once more, you had strange forebodings what it meant. After wasting hours at the beleaguered telephone booth, you finally contacted your wife, and she said no! No, she would not come to see you off!

"Russia! Crazy! Absolutely crazy!" No, she would rather try to speak to somebody about it. To whom? To somebody!!

Poor little wife. Who . . . to whom could she speak? She had not yet met any influential person in Berlin. She hardly knew the town and not even the language to speak to a somebody! Besides, if your wife, a Britisher, comes from South Africa for the first time in her life to Europe, and the people there have nothing better to do than start another war—and she finds everything odd and new surrounding her, you will understand that she will try to the last possible moment to have it her own way. Ah, the lowest rank in the whole German army would not listen to her. Well . . . listen, perhaps, but laugh at her ideas, simply laugh. What a pity she did not come to say goodbye.

Your fingers, which hold that icicle of a gun, begin to freeze badly now, and you wish the captain might come to an end. You notice by his raised voice that he intends to conclude his exhortation. At this very moment a motorcyclist passes the guards at the opened gate. He rushes around the corner at terrific speed and stops nearby. You observe his red shoulder straps, denoting he is from headquarters.

The Interrogator

He dismounts and runs to the office, returns after a few seconds, and approaches your sergeant major. You and your buddies watch the sergeant major take a sort of telegram from him, read it, and pass it on to the captain, who has just finished his speech. The captain reads, looks along the line of soldiers, then suddenly calls your name and orders you to report to the office. You are transferred from this very hour to the Dolmetscher Kompanie Nr. XII (Interpreters Company 12) in Wiesbaden!

"The whole battalion! Right turn . . .Quick march!"

In less than a minute you stand all alone. Your buddies are on their way to the vast East. You are no longer a panzer grenadier. You are an interpreter now. While you wind yourself through a maze of military red tape, you wonder all the time just whom your wife might have spoken to.

How to become an interrogation officer, eh?

Well, that is still a long, long way off!

Now you have to return to the quartermaster all that wonderful new equipment you received just yesterday. Armed now with nothing but a gas mask, which you will lose on the way in any case, you have to take the next train to Wiesbaden. An express train, of course, which covers the 400 miles within twelve hours. Because you are a good soldier, you miss this express until you have ample time to go meet your family in Berlin. Your wife expects that. She is entitled to see you for a day because she managed your transfer. Yes, indeed, she persuaded a general! A general—please don't be so inquisitive—a general from headquarters in Berlin. How?

"AN OLD ASSAULT CHIEFTAIN SENDS HIS LOVE."
Hanns's father, Hans-Hermann Scharff, penned that message on this photo sent home in 1916 in WWI. He was wounded a few days later and died in a hospital a year later.

Chapter 2: How To Become An Interrogation Officer

Oh, well, she walked straight into his office. The guard? Pshaw! You see, she had put her new hat on.

Time is really up, and you have to take that express to Wiesbaden. You do like your new uniform, although it makes you feel bitter if you think of all the cigarettes you had to slip to the quartermaster. You do like it, although there is no medal or distinction of rank, not yet, but you feel you are going south and you are going to be an interpreter. Your gas mask you have already lost.

You cannot be expected to know where on God's Earth this Dolmetscher Kompanie XII is located, and the best thing to do in Wiesbaden is to ask right at the railway station at the military information office. Their knowledge of all military units is thorough, but of an Interpreters Company 12 they have never heard before. It is, at the same time, utterly impossible that you or your wife's generous general has made a mistake. Your transfer papers state with military clarity what outfit you are to join, but are minus the information as to where this execrated bunch of intellectual soldiers is buried. If the information booth of military police at the Bahnhof is unable to dig it up among the numberless host of units, and if you too do not know what to suggest, you are dispatched to the first panzer grenadier battalion they can find. There you will be kept, and disregarding your ability to speak English, you'll be trained as a common cannon fodder soldier for the Russian front, from which hell itself is a step up!

Cursing the swear words you were taught during the last two months does not help! Think of a way out of this new, pretty predicament! Why is the one panzer grenadier outfit worse than another? Here duty begins at 0500 hours instead of 0600 like in Potsdam. Training takes one hour longer in the evening, and it is harder and more exhausting. Food, any soldier's main outlook next to leave, is less. AWOL is the only way to town. There is no little English wife to help you, and no bigwig from headquarters this time.

What a pickle! But relax a moment; you must know of an episode of my younger days:

It was the third year of WWI when my father, a regular officer in the old Prussian army, was mortally wounded near Soissons. He must have had a premonition, some days before his last battle, that he would never see his three much-loved sons again, and he wrote a letter addressed with these words: "To my boys. For personal perusal at their sixteenth birthdays."

I was only ten at that time and had to wait six years till I found among my birthday presents the envelope containing my father's letter to me. He gave a long account of his happy life, and finally he worried, like every father in the whole wide world will do, about the future of his children. The letter thus ended with the earnest adjuration that should one of his sons ever feel in need of fatherly advice and counsel, they might faithfully consult his two best friends in the regiment. These were Majors Ledebur and Postel. My father then died as a soldier bravely in battle.

The Interrogator

Those two friends did survive the war. Their names were quite familiar to me, although I had no need for help, so no personal contact was ever established. I tried to keep cognizant of their whereabouts because they had been my father's friends. As soon as the war was over, Herr Ledebur went to Hamburg and Herr Postel, who had advanced to lieutenant colonel, became a syndic of a large textile trust in my hometown through the solicitude of Grandfather. He retired after many years of successful work to live in Wiesbaden. I had forgotten about him and would have doubted whether the old gentleman was still alive.

Suppose your father had written such a letter to you. Suppose, further, you forgot all about his two friends recommended to you as guardians. You would feel as if you had dropped from the clouds if you had gone to town on your first free Sunday afternoon and, visiting a restaurant to find some relief from your misery, had spotted a folded newspaper with this arresting headline;

"GENERAL POSTEL WINS HIGHEST AWARD FOR BRAVERY." Postel? Postel! . . . that name George-Wilhelm Postel!* (* General George Wilhelm Postel, Kdr. I.R. 364, was decorated with the Ritterkreuz on 29 September 1942 and the Eichenlaub on 28 March 1943 and was the fifty-seventh winner of the Swords [Schwerter] on 26 March 1944.)

All that had vanished in the last twenty years returns to mind vividly. Your eyes fly over the paper. Yes, this general is the son of the old WWI gentleman Lt. Col. Postel, and it says he lives right here in Wiesbaden! You snatch up a telephone directory. M . . . N . . . O . . . P . . . Po . . . Por . . . Pos . . . POSTEL, LT. COL. There he is! A retired lieutenant colonel. *Oberstleutnant*!

"So, you are the son of my old friend?" says a deep, pleasant voice. "Come around and see us; yes, right away, if you wish."

After you have expressed a thousand and one questions, you beg your new-found ally for one great favor. To him, an old imperial officer, your story seems quite fantastic. Naturally he will help you. Oh, yes! He knows the commanding general personally. He plays awhile with him every Monday. In fact, tomorrow! He will see him in the morning. Yet, he cannot conceive how a simple soldier can be kept by some wrong unit and why neither a sergeant major nor a captain will not listen to reason. "You are, so to say, a wrongly directed parcel. We shall put matters straight." That evening, after the bugle's retreat call, you climb the fence around the camp with more agility. In expectation of coming developments, you sleep well. In the morning, shortly after 0900 hours, you are not really surprised, although you must pretend to be, of course, at the excitement caused by a telephone call from the commanding general personally. All of a sudden that beastly sergeant major wants to become your best friend, and he escorts you to the captain.

"For heavens sake, Private, you should have reported to the Dolmetscher Kompanie XII in Mainz long ago! Go quickly! Go at once! Is there anything you need from us? Have you enough supplies of victuals? Perhaps I had better explain how such a misassignment like yours could occur. Long ago a squad of interpreters

Chapter 2: How To Become An Interrogation Officer

PUNCHING HOLES
Hanns-Joachim Scharff's first assignment was as a file clerk in the 12th Army Headquarters. His job: punching holes in pages to be filed.

were attached to this battalion. Then they became an independent company and were moved to Mainz. They are not fighting soldiers, you know, and I feel sympathetic toward you because I think you have the stuff to enjoy fighting our arch enemies on the Soviet front. I am sorry, but you are, to coin a phrase, a misdirected parcel. By the way, are you perhaps a relative of the commanding general?"

You laugh, but not visibly or audibly, over the newly coined phrase.

As you leave that base, you wonder: Is that how to become an interrogation officer?

No! Certainly not, but by a long string of coincidences you have taken the initial steps toward that career.

The *Dolmetschers* in Mainz all look alike. Everyone wears the same field gray uniform. Most of them are privates, and a few are noncommissioned officers. But oho! If you talk to them you will find out who they really are: *messieurs*, mynheers, signores, sahibs, gospoda and effendis, gentlemen and just plain guys, baases, and *bwanamkuba*s. You find among them university professors, teachers, lawyers, journalists, globetrotters, factory directors. In fact, they are all types of men of high intellectual standard and multilingual training, with the exception of our *Kompanie* den-mother type, the sergeant major.

The work is pleasant. Although you live in barracks, as any other soldier does, you are almost solely occupied with scientific studies. Your captain makes lots of

The Interrogator

the decisions, and it is he who determines you will join the English-speaking section, not the American! Morning lectures, therefore, are about British military organization. Boring and stodgy, this will never be an asset to your wits. In the afternoons, you are free to visit the town of Johannes Gutenberg, the writers' good friend who invented the printing press. You go there solely in the interest of your scientific studies because you must consult books and sources at the huge municipal library. Yes, in its proper light it is called "Cafe Corso."

A commission of five masterminds carefully examines your English, your perfect knowledge of an Allied armored division, and your ability to describe torsional steel rods used for independent wheel suspensions. Your knowledge of the Monroe Doctrine as the political creed of the average American is also tested. Your officers, moreover, want to know your opinion of the significance of olive oil in Mediterranean countries during the Middle Ages. You also have to know how to halt British horses. Don't think for a moment either that you can roll your Rs, saying "brr" as we do in the German language. The British horses wouldn't understand you, since "brr" is a German word meaning "whoa!"

Soon you begin to appreciate that German businessman who was asked, after living in England over forty years, how he liked Great Britain. "How can a German like a country where ginger beer is a drink and daddledo is a language?" he replied.

When your section walks through the streets to attend shooting practice, it is amusing to see the townsfolk crane their necks as we march along singing, "Rrroll me over, in the clover." After four weeks, nevertheless, you tire of playing soldier so much, and you think of nothing else but furloughs and favorite dishes. Ha! You win a great reputation as the man who commands the largest variety of limericks too. Then one fine morning in the spring, your captain tells you in sharp tones and with finality of his decision to send you to headquarters in Wiesbaden. They have requested a well-educated man who can touch-type, and with this captain's decision, Fortuna had pointed her finger at you.

Off you go again! Pack your kit bag and catch the next train into Wiesbaden. Since you don't belong to any special military unit there, you are quartered in a private hotel just like a civilian. What luck! The day before you left, you were promoted to lance corporal, and that night, right below your window, hidden in a jessamine bush, trills a nightingale, the first you have heard in all your life!

Unbeknown to you, you have just taken an important step toward your appointment as an interrogation officer.

If you say, ruefully, that you manufacture little round holes at the headquarters, it sounds stupid, but punching holes is how you get started. The trouble with you, though, is you expect too much from Providence. True, you are a selected man, and not everyone is tactful; not every corporal knows how to behave in a castle overcrowded with high-ranking staff officers. However, the error on your part was to picture yourself an important person in such noble surroundings. You mounted

Chapter 2: How To Become An Interrogation Officer

that high horse too soon. Yes, much too soon, even when you were on the train en route to Wiesbaden. You should have chatted amiably with that very kind-hearted old lady who gave "this poor soldier" some strawberries. You lost your cool and were too easily irritated when she asked why simple soldiers had to wear gloves on such a warm day. You must have more tolerance of your fellow man.

Now, at headquarters, your job is to write names on cards for the registry, and then you punch holes in the cards. From morning to night you punch holes . . . holes in those damn cards. You operate a machine that punches two holes at a time, and you cannot help but think you'd rather be out at the Cafe Corso getting an ice cream soda. Good soldiers, however, must never question the why or the what-for of an order; theirs is simply to do or die.

Everything still has two sides! All right, you punch holes, but after six o'clock, when you leave this castle in the evenings, can't you promenade in the world-renowned parks of Wiesbaden? Don't you even direct your steps to the theater or the concert hall? Think back! While back in Mainz, did you have friends like the Postel family or did you have a waiter in the barracks obeying every wink of yours?

Your pride may hurt a little that you, in private life a well-to-do merchant, now have to punch holes, punch innumerable apertures into paper. What difference does it make, though? Isn't this one hell of a lot better than trying to punch innumerable holes into enemy tanks near Stalingrad or Murmansk? You do love your wife, too, don't you, even though she is very self-satisfied for getting you chosen as an interpreter. You should be satisfied, too, regardless of how dull your work is. To do the same thing day after day becomes too tiresome. Not that you execute your work carelessly, oh no, but you are thinking too much. Soon you even pun about punching and find you are a puncher; you punch peradventure. I'd rather be a cowpuncher, though.

After one month, you total up the hours you spent creating little paper flakes. How many cards have you perforated? You also think of your private income from business back home, and finally you come to the conclusion that each one of these holes is costing five pfennig . . .very expensive. A nickel a hole! Now calm down and take it easy. If the army or the State is so rich it can pay five cents a hole, a nickel for each little round piece of paper, let it. Their money is wasted. You are just wasting your time.

Perhaps you should have been more careful and tactful when you answered your adjutant one day when he asked how you liked your work. You should not have mentioned your calculations about a nickel a hole. Who can foresee that your serious contemplations would make him laugh as if he had never before heard a better joke.

Nobody will hold against you your inability to anticipate the consequences of your enlightenment, either. Be it that the adjutant intended to amuse the BIG BOSS one evening at the club, or be it that he tried with a little wit and great conceit to be sarcastic; he told him the story of a lance corporal at headquarters who makes holes in paper costing a nickel apiece. God's mills grind slowly but surely. The Old Man's mill is sure but fast. Next morning you had to appear before him. Contrary to all expectations, he was friendly and understanding. He just didn't appreciate corporals figuring out costs that were none of their business. An air of goodwill prevailed, however, when I told him my tale.

"So you speak English, eh? I will tell you something, corporal. The army has the privilege of attaching each year three of its interpreters to the Luftwaffe interrogation center at Oberursel, near Frankfurt/Mainz. The next class starts in July, and you will be one of those in the class."

Author comments: According to the Letter of Privilege in the Office of Heraldry in Dresden, the Scharff family carries, since the sixteenth century, a coat of arms depicting on its shield a white rose and a red rose. Shakespeare narrates in *Henry VI*, part I, act II, scene IV:

Plantagenet: "Let him that is a true-born gentleman and stands upon the honor of his birth; if he suppose that I have pleaded truth, from off this briar pluck a white rose with me."

Somerset: "Let him that is no coward and no flatterer, but dare maintain the party of the truth, pluck a red rose off this thorn with me."

3

PLAYBOYS OF THE AIR

The seeking for one thing will find another.
—Irish proverb

Whatever new military base you may go to, lance corporal, you will have first of all to meet a sergeant major. Not so in Oberursel! The tramcar brings you from Frankfurt am Main right to the huge camp. Civilian passengers are helpful to direct you to your new domicile. They all seem to be well acquainted with the intelligence center. "That is where the enemy airmen are interrogated."

You enter the camp grounds by the lower walk and want to inquire which one of the buildings and barracks is the head office. Best to stop at the first barrack and find somebody there to tell you. Whooppee! It's full of girls! Not girls stuffed into ugly uniforms, but pretty, charming, and handsome young ladies, most of them attired in light and colorful summer apparel, some with very short shorts. How complacent they are to a stranger! The prettiest, the most charming of the gallinaceous family, that tall, slender, shoulder-long-haired blonde with the tennis racquet under her arm inquires after your requests, discreetly overlooking your bashfulness.

"If you are to stay here we will become neighbors since the barrack for privates and lance corporals is next door to ours. Leave your luggage there and then it will be best for you to report to the deputy commander's office first thing tomorrow morning."

No sooner said than done. You dump your kit bag at the next barracks, one of four in a row. The rooms are plain but comfortable, the bed extremely soft, and the three new buddies, all privates first class, are obliging and helpful. At dusk you have to close the outside shutters of your window to comply with the strictly observed blackout orders. The lion-maned girl opposite your room is just about to do the same. She nods at you with a friendly smile.

The Interrogator

"BIG CHIEF" HORST BARTH
As a former merchant marine radio officer who spoke excellent English, the Luftwaffe drafted him and had him establish a radio listening post at Pewsum, and one later at Wissant. He and his men listened to radio transmissions from England. Soon outranked, he was transferred to the interrogation center at Auswertestelle West, Oberursel.

Next morning a tremendous surprise overwhelms you at the deputy commander's office. Without much ado, he, a major, overlooks your parade ground salute and ushers you into a chair. Can you trust your eyes and ears? He addresses you as "Mister," not as a corporal, but as a MISTER!

"We are glad to have you here, and I thought it might be to your advantage if you work your way through all our departments. May I suggest, therefore, that you start at the office of the COR? Very well! Call on me from time to time, whenever you like, without invitation, to tell me how you are getting along. You are always welcome. Now, you'll find the COR in the next building but one from here. Good day and good luck, Mister Scharff."

Soft words do more than hard blows. Mister? Sir? Interpreter? Interrogation officer? What a break!

COR may as well be Chinese to you? However, you soon find a door marked COR and enter it. There are many mystery CORs in the room, soldiers and girls, all busy writing. The chief COR tells you to report to the sergeant major. Of course you have to be embodied in the muster roll. The sergeant major, should you not know by now, is a man who takes you tenderly in his arms. He is fond of all outsiders. For soldiers who are attached to his unit only for a limited time, he shows his affection by wanting you, the parasite, to sweep the floors. Never you fear, though. No small sergeant major can do you harm. Fate wanted you to be one of the CORs.

Fortune is fickle. COR stands for Camp Office–Reception. It is the camp receiving office.

Chapter 3: Playboys Of The Air

Your work there is not only to sort out hundreds of names on little cards alphabetically, but also to *punch more confounding, cursed damnable holes!*

For one solid month you remain in a trance, and those who know something of your English and your knowledge of Zulu and Afrikaans feel sorry inside for you. Think how much understanding you could have utilized as interpreter for the benefit of the POWs. Your strongly cultivated Anglophile sentiments are astir in you, and it becomes your profound desire to be helpful to your wife's cousins, as she likes to call them. The spirit of always being on the side of the underdog, as you were taught in the English countries, is wide awake in you.

Ideas like these may sound queer to your German companions, and it may even be risky for you if you state that British hospitality has left such an impression on you that you will not overlook or neglect an opportunity to repay even though it is wartime. Ten years in England and Africa have presented you with innumerable friends, and although the two peoples are at war, there is no reason to forget the debt of gratitude for an extremely happy decade of your life. You would have been surprised, at this stage, had you known how beneficial for your work your determination was to be. You had opportunities later to observe how interrogators let themselves be influenced by their personal feelings in the treatment of prisoners. If an interrogator had been unsuccessful professionally or socially in the country

AMERICAN COLONEL EINAR AXEL MALMSTROM
The CO of the 356th USAAF Fighter Group, Malmstrom was shot down and captured on his 58th mission. His interrogator Hanns Scharff arranged for Malmstrom to visit a nearby Luftwaffe fighter unit, where he was allowed to take off in and quickly land an Me 109, escorted by the commander of the Luftwaffe unit, of course.

The Interrogator

in which he had lived as a guest, he would enter his interrogation work with a negative outlook.

Your new lucky break comes straight through the door, impersonated in a German girl from Southwest Africa, now a typist in the camp. Good humored, with similar convictions to your own, she has heard of your presence and simply comes to say "Hullo" to an old African acquaintance. She asks you for evening tea and obtains special permission to invite you to her room, a delightfully furnished cozy boudoir shared with another English-speaking girl. She is the one whose smiling nod at the window the first evening had made you think of her perhaps a bit more than is militarily permissible.

A man must be a man. A soldier a soldier. Strong, rampant, fearless, ready to battle—to fight not men and machines alone but also unpleasantries of life. The chance to beat your discomforts comes to you spontaneously; you need not lift one finger. Could the warm eyes of the lovely face framed with the golden waves speak to you? Had her laughing mouth repeated its smile at you and said, "I might be able to help you, Punch!?" Did she think of you perhaps a bit more than is permissible?

So it was she who talked to the deputy commander! Well, the most natural thing for any private secretary to say to her chief when he pondered finding a perfect-English-speaking man to be the assistant in the fighter interrogation section is that she might know the right one; now, Captain Horst Barth, head of the Fighter Section, nicknamed "Big Chief," is your new boss. Barth scrutinizes you from tip to toe and puts you to work. Does it matter if you have to start from the bottom again? If you have to draw boresome diagrams of USAAF organizations? What about it if you have to sit in a room and read the results of interrogations and sometimes watch while a POW is being interrogated? What about it?

You have one overwhelming impression: should you ever come into the position where you would interview a POW yourself, you should do it in a calm and friendly way. Not to bully, threaten, swear, or shout.

Soon, this will come true through a dreadful disaster.

Your new buddies are all old cronies of "Big Chief" Barth, all from his old radio-listening organization called a "Y" Company. There is "Blackie" Schwartz, Kaspar, Schroder, and Weyland. Schroder happens to be the most congenial of all of them. As the discoverer and owner of the world-famous *Ichthamol* ointment, he is a wealthy man.

Author comments: Two more interesting people belonged to Big Chief's circle. First there was "Shorty," who was stationed in Paris as the liaison man for the "Y" group. Scharff's duties required that he be in almost daily communication with Shorty.

Then, there was young Baron Eberhard von Danckelman, who was stationed down in the Mediterranean on the Isle of Crete. Hauptmann Horst Barth had chosen the baron as godfather for his daughter Dagmar. Eberhard's cousin, the Baroness

Chapter 3: Playboys Of The Air

"NICE FIGHTER!"
Malmstrom (bareheaded) smiles as he quipped, "Very light and maneuverable with only five minutes of gasoline and no ammo, but a damn good fighter! May I fly it back to England?" Scharff stands to the left of Malmstrom.

GRASSHOPPER RIDE
Malmstrom had been flown from Oberursel to Eschborn airbase and back in this Fieseler "Storch."

The Interrogator

Sabine von Danckelman, will play the most important part in the later life of our protagonist Hanns Scharff; Scharff met Baroness Sabine in the United States, and they were married in Los Angeles in 1958.

Hanns Scharff continues: At that time—winter of 1943–1944—USAAF fighter pilots were still a novelty at the camp at Oberursel. The two interrogation officers in charge of the USAAF Fighter Section, Weyland and Schroder, had trouble killing time because only one or two Yankee fighters would be brought in each week. Yet, they clamored for an assistant to help prepare their cases, and you were selected. This gave you a chance to witness the beginning of what we called "the invasion of the fighter colonels." The "invasion" started when the USAAF's Colonel Martin had some bad luck. He was a group commander of one of the USAAF's first Mustang-equipped outfits, and he had briefed his pilots that they should make use of the psychological effect the appearance of the new P-51 must have on the enemy. In head-on attacks, they should continue straight on toward the German plane, not budging or giving an inch. The oncoming Luftwaffe pilots would lose their nerve and pull up or try to break away.

"Then, boys, after them! You have the tactical advantage, so keep them going."

This principle of not giving way was also observed by a German squadron leader. Even a child can figure out what happens when two stubborn bulls meet head on in the air. Crash! The impact occurs at a speed difficult for anyone to imagine. Not every child can figure out how both pilots managed to float to the ground in their parachutes, though. Both airplanes could be put into matchboxes, the two representatives of the same bullheaded idea; the tough colonel and his tough opponent were put into hospital beds with broken arms and legs, plus bruises and lacerations, but otherwise unhurt. All witnesses to the midair collision, Americans of the 354th Fighter Group and Luftwaffe *Gruppe* buddies, were

YEARS LATER, MALMSTROM'S SON VISITS SCHARFF
Einar Malmstrom's son James visited Hanns Scharff at Los Angeles, California, on 13 March 1978.

Chapter 3: Playboys Of The Air

CRASH OF DESTINY
This Fieseler "Storch" crashed and killed several of the Auswertestelle West interrogators, vaulting Hanns Scharff into the position of interrogator of the USAAF fighter pilots from the 8th Air Force, flying from England.

convinced their leaders had met their deaths. Colonel Martin's arrival at Oberursel from the hospital at Hohe-Mark, just walking distance from your camp, was the beginning of your really intimate contact with the USAAF.

At this time comes your big lucky break. Oh boy, you will never forget the sensation you created in the camp when you did something nobody had thought of doing before, and nobody, at the same time, could be told about it.

Your job as assistant interrogation officer requires you to enter the names of the latest arrivals into the "Ins" column of the ledger, and late one evening as you do this, on May 5th, you enter the name "Col. Malmstrom, Thunderbolt pilot, 356th Fighter Group." Another participant of the "invasion of the fighter colonels." You throw down your pen on impulse and walk over to the cooler, knock on the door of number 17A, and visit the newcomer. You brought along some snacks, and now he sits on the edge of his cot, eating buttered bread and cheese. He is a tall, blond man and looks just like his name.

Although you are just an army private first class, you must not let yourself be influenced by his rank, race, or creed. Yet, you must pay a colonel a slight bit of extra attention. You are staunch to your principles and devote your visit entirely to comfort him a little. Both of you feel, after you have bid him good night, that captivity need not necessarily be only a depressing atmosphere.

Good for you, too, that you are such a wizard with your Leica camera! You don't think our leader Horst Barth, the "Big Chief," would have asked you to join him and some of his friends at a party at a nearby Me-109 base for any other reason, do you? There at Eschborn base you will be able to take some nice pictures

The Interrogator

FENCING MUST BE A FUN SPORT
Horst Barth was one of the outstanding fencers in Germany prior to WWII. Barth is shown here covered with his own blood following a fencing duel.

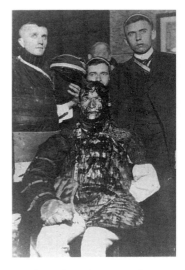

of him with some of the famous "Ace of Spades" (Jagdgeschwader 53 "Pik-As") squadron members.

"What did you say? You met a captured colonel last night?" The Big Chief raises his eyebrows at your thought. "Nice guy, eh? *But take him along to the party too?* Well! Give him a treat? Hmmmm. Never have I heard of such a suggestion before, taking an enemy pilot with us to meet our Luftwaffe aces. But, come to think of it, why not?" You relax, since it is obvious the boss is intrigued with the idea after all. "Yes, our own fighters would probably be happy to meet a gallant foe on the ground. Indeed. Why not? Go fetch him and the others."

Fighter pilots are the playboys of the air. On the ground they gamble, sing, drive fast cars, tell stories, wear large wristwatches, and wear dark glasses. Sometimes they drink a lot. They are not sailors so spin no salty yarns, but the more they drink, the more enemy planes they shoot down. Tall stories indeed!

At a real playboy party with a foreign guest, a *Dolmetscher* is in great demand, so that they may talk to the guest in words rather than just with their hands, as fighter pilots are inclined to do. No one can explain why it has to be that men must fight first in the air like mad and afterward become the best of friends. The harder the tussle in the air, the faster the friendship. Not enough chivalry can be shown, not sufficient appreciations are said. "And would you kindly translate to the colonel that I should regard it an honor if he would allow me to take him for a joyride in a 109? He will!? Thank you; come on, let's go now!" Einar Malmstrom was allowed to fly the Me-109. Of course, it has only thirty minutes of gasoline, not enough to get to the Channel, but he makes a takeoff, some acrobatics, and a nice landing. You take pictures with your Leica of this strange comradeship. Of course, the *Kommodore* flew right behind . . .with loaded guns.

Chapter 3: Playboys Of The Air

Fighter boys are playboys. They play with great intensity. Sometimes their lives are short.

"Goodbye, Colonel Malmstrom, glad to have met you. Keep your chin up and good luck to you. *Hals und Beinbruch!* May you return to your home well. And so long, Big Chief. By the way, we would like to have some of those photographs as souvenirs, and if any of your gang wants a joyride with us, come back tomorrow and we will be glad to oblige."

You are lucky. You are extraordinarily fortunate to have your first three-day pass granted the next morning, and you prepare for your furlough. Colonel Einar Malmstrom is being transferred to Dulag Luft at Rothschild Park in Frankfurt and then on to one of the *Stalag Luft*s. You ask the Big Chief if you can escort him along with his Luftwaffe *Feldwebel* (sergeant) guard to the railway station in Frankfurt. Permission is granted, and the Big Chief assigns us a big, black chauffeur-driven Mercedes. We ride like it is peacetime to the station. He boards the Berlin Express, a luxury train, first-class compartment. As the train starts to pull out, you compulsively walk along with the coach while Einar lowers the window, stretches his hand out, and says,

"Thanks for having treated me like a gentleman!"

You now go on your furlough thinking war is hell, but soon forgetting it in your own thoughts and deeds. Furloughs come all too seldom and seem to be over before they have really started. You have to go back to work.

Vicissitudes of life await you upon your return. This time, warm eyes look at you almost horrified. She is the first to cross your path and therefore is the one who must inform you first.

"Schroder is dead and Weyland mortally injured! The fighter ace at Eschborn took them for a joyride the day after you left; he crashed with them and is dead too." Their Fieseler "Storch" had crashed into some trees.

Farewell playboys!

Lance corporal! You are hereby transferred from the army to the Luftwaffe and commissioned to take over the duties as *Vernehmungsoffizier*, interrogation officer, for the USAAF Fighter Section immediately. The orders are clear and simple.

You are now an interrogation officer.

Author comments: Horst Barth, the chief of the Fighter Interrogation Section at Auswertestelle West, is a legendary figure of his own. A student at the German university in Leipzig, Barth became one of the outstanding fencers in the dueling fraternities. His victories and defeats were well documented by photographs, and his photo album was as popular with the POWs at Oberursel as were the few movies they were allowed to attend. Photos showing Barth in various stages of disrepair, including a temporarily severed nose and other slices and slits about the face, gave some of the Americans their first knowledge of the aristocratic past of old Europe. Fencing can be a deadly game!

The Interrogator

"H" COMPANY AT PEWSUM
Barth's listening post operated from this ancient building at Pewsum.

T.W.O.z.b.v. SECRET POST AT WISSANT
Barth's listening post operated from this building on the Channel Coast.

Chapter 3: Playboys Of The Air

In the early 1930s, Barth joined the German Merchant Marine as a radio operator, traveling between European ports and the Caribbean on a banana boat. As the German military began to burgeon in the mid-'30s, Horst recognized the need for radio technique development and joined up. Having some ideas of his own, this learned man developed for Germany a capability of monitoring and interpreting radio transmissions emanating from the United Kingdom. This had far-reaching effects during the war.

After some successful experiments, the Wehrmacht had him set up a station in northwestern Friesland near the village of Pewsum, 15 km north of Emden. Germany's most famous and romantic pirate, Klaus Stoertebecker, had made Pewsum famous by building a castle tower there and headquartered his gang of robbers in the vicinity. History has it that Klaus eventually so angered the people of Hamburg that a price was put on his head. Soon afterward, the Hamburgers had a special necktie party, with Klaus playing the leading role. Horst Barth, who loved the Caribbean and its lore, enjoyed the romance of Klaus's background and his own covert operations and shortly had one of Germany's most secret and effective war weapons in full swing. By mid-1938 the new listening post was able to monitor expansions of Britain's potential for war, both defensive and offensive. As headquarters usually do, they tended to downgrade the importance of the news from Pewsum.

After the occupation of France, the Pewsum gang was moved to Cap Gris-Nez, to a base called Wissant, and the Luftwaffe had its first radio-monitoring system to be used in directing fighter aircraft on intercepts. Most of the Luftwaffe fighter units participating in the Battle of Britain had *Kommodoren* who put no faith in the supposition that men sitting in a windowless radio shack at Gris-Nez could tell them when the enemy was taking off over in England . . . and where to go to meet them. Kommodore Major Adolf Galland was no exception!

Horst Barth, this magician of the ether waves in WWII, passed away in August 1984 at his home in Westphalia. During my visit with him in 1983, Barth gave the author this account of those WWII days:

"While it is true that Major Galland at first condemned me and my boys to hell because we seemed to have exact knowledge of what was going on between the Channel coasts up in the air, it surely was a great help to the fighters in action and to the Jafü (*Jagdfliegerführer*) at his control center. It did mean, too, that my job meant I had to have quite a bit of control.

"I cannot ever forget the wild, sparkling eyes of Major Galland when we first met in the control room of Jafü 2 and I could confirm the victories of his squadron. He was terribly annoyed, I know that I could not confirm them all. I had friends then, but also I was called "the police of Jafü" because they knew I was looking over their shoulders.

"Galland's own words were 'I'm a fighter and free-hunter. I've got good eyes and find my opponents by myself! I do not need another controller who tells me where to fly and fight!'

The Interrogator

"So far, so good. I, by no means, would have argued, for fighters are far more independent than heavy-bellied bombers, and in their decisions they want to be completely free. I know all that by experience, having flown in He-111 scout planes.

"But Major Galland was really mad, mostly because the Jafü general backed me up. You see, I had proven that I could give the control center exact pictures of the English opposition and strength. Our operation functioned so that in our mind, in our imaginations, we were looking at the RAF radar screens and could almost see the WAAFs push the little figures on the ops room tables.

"'Indianer' was our code word for enemy fighters, and we knew what their ops rooms were telling them because *we knew all the code words*. By listening on our radios, we heard their operations orders such as takeoff, rendezvous points, altitudes, speeds, map references, and finally the commands of their leaders in flight. All was in code words, but we could read it as if it were plain English. I still remember some of them: GOLF COURSE meant LeTouquets, BIG WOOD was St. Omer, and when they talked on the air in action, we would hear 'Pipsqueak on! Hallo Woodie!' (he was calling Gp. Capt. Woodhall). Any trade in sight?' Then . . .'Are they building up over there??' 'GOLF COURSE!,' then 'GAINING ALTITUDE! FIFTY PLUS! TWO O'CLOCK! BANDITS! HUNS ABOVE,' and so on. The RAF had such a good radar installation and good D/F and ops rooms, but we could use their know-how and whereabouts for our own purposes. Sometimes we wished we were personally among them, so beautiful sounded their voices over the air. (So we really liked our enemies instead of hating them.)

"We were a modest little unit with a modulated name or title; T.W.O.z.b.V., meaning Telefonic Weather Investigation Service on Special Assignment! This was just a poor camouflage, since all weather investigators are suspicious characters, but no one knew the exact meaning of our title. Secrecy was so tight that only military persons from colonel's rank and higher were authorized to visit us.

"Galland, having listened to my arguments, uttered that he had never before heard of such a unit as ours, but he was now interested. I suggested that all fighter leaders listen to my frequency and advice. They were thankful for our support and knew my assistance was well meant, and did not intend to wrest any control or responsibility from them.

"Galland would give us a try. He would take off with his number two, his Katschmarek, and look for trouble, as he often did, but I was to be responsible for that party and keep an eye on him for the next half hour. Fair enough?

"He took off, and almost instantly the English on the other slide scrambled two fighters. First they just alerted the two fighters but a few minutes later scrambled them into the air, probably just because they were anxious for a fight. I had a good contact and listened as the RAF gave orders directing their pilots toward a position in the sun. Position reports were made, and then . . .'Right Ho!' There was the tally-ho! I warned Galland and told him to look into the sun. The

Chapter 3: Playboys Of The Air

engagement . . .and then some minutes of excitement in English when they commenced an excited search for two baled-out pilots down in the Channel.

"That ended the disagreement between Galland and myself. When he had pancaked, he came over to the place I had set up my special apparatus on the terrace of a farmhouse, and held two fingers up, indication that he had scored a double. 'Guess you saved my life,' said Galland. 'I didn't see those darned Injuns until you called!'

"Yes, I knew they came out of the sun because their directions and radio messages interpreted in my mind that way, and when they called their tally-ho I knew Galland could not have made a saving turn in time had he not been warned. Also, I knew the RAF was searching for two downed fighter pilots, so it was easy to confirm Galland's two kills. We talked things over and decided the flight leaders would listen, so I could place them in the sun. Everybody in the fighter units was convinced that T.W.O.z.b.V. was good for all the boys fighting for Germany and their own lives.

"We lost our camouflage soon because the visitors and big brass came in droves and asked thousands of questions. They all wanted to see the magic tricks. The most prominent visitor was the ponderous *Reichsmarschall* himself, "Iron Hermann" as we called him then. He tramped into the little village with a surrounding cavalcade of brass-shining generals. Someone must have told him about the remarkable, noteworthy little unit that knew how to find all the "Injuns."

THE LATE HORST BARTH
Horst Barth (*right*) invited author Ray Toliver to the Pipsqueakers reunion at Boppard on the Rhine River on 14 May 1983. The Pipsqueakers were the members of the radio-listening post in WWII. Barth died in August 1984.

The Interrogator

FIGHTER LEADER AND FIGHTER DIRECTOR
Oberst Adolf Galland, then *Kommodore* of JG 26, and Horst Barth, who then operated the radio-listening post at Wissant, discuss the capability of radio intercepts to direct fighter interceptions. Galland was dubious at this time.

"WO IST DIESE T.W.O.z.b.V.?"
Below: Reichsmarschall Hermann Göring visited Horst Barth's listening post at Wissant because he, too, could not believe RAF opponents could be located just by listening to their radio transmissions. Two escorting generals eagerly point the way to the secret operation house.

Chapter 3: Playboys Of The Air

"Where is this T.W.O.z.b.V.?" he roared like a stag, and all the generals raised their arms in unison and showed him the direction. I'll send you the photo of this historic moment!

And then the invasion of my homely radio shack.

The little staircase sounded as if it might break down under the heavy steps of such weighty VIPs.

Let me tell you about my little interrogation center.

"Yes, we interrogated the air waves, so I was an interrogator long before I went to Oberursel. The ops room was on the first floor and was very small, so it was easy for me to survey. In this room were five operators sitting at desks on the right side, while my desk, with a very big 1:50,000-scale map on the wall behind it, was on the left. Every operator had a special receiver, earphone logbook, pencil, and loudspeaker. Plus his magnificent experience! Each one had his special frequency to monitor. I had all the phones that connected me to the fighter control rooms.

"The loudspeakers squeaked and I listened, sifting out the important information, translating and interpreting the info as it came in, almost never taking my eyes off that map, except to look into a rearview mirror so I could see whenever an operator raised his arm, signaling he had important data coming in. I evaluated the data quickly, then passed my instructions on to the airborne pilots or to their control centers.

"Göring arrived. We were very busy, since some planes were in an action, when I heard Iron Hermann coming up the stairs. The din sounded like elephants in a porcelain shop, and I yelled, 'Gentlemen! Quiet! There is a war on! A dogfight!'

"The Fat One evaluated the situation instantly and pushed the golden marshal's baton into the belly of the nearest general, a field marshal, and made them all go back and stand by the wall and the door. "Silence!" he bellowed, and you could almost hear a pin drop except for the loudspeakers squeaking. Then he tiptoed through the little room to one of the operators, who looked at him interestedly, finally removed the cigar from the corner of his mouth, and stared.

"Indeed, Iron Hermann was something glorious to stare at! Unbelievable! I myself thought it must be a dream. One could not help but look at him in astonishment. There before us stood our commander in chief, resplendent beyond words, like a monument! He wore a light silver-gray uniform of the finest cloth, double breasted, no medals except the Great Cross of the Iron Cross, his personal and exclusive medal, hanging at his neck. He had on yellow riding boots with golden spurs . . .yes, spurs! His cap had a golden hat guard, which he wore down under his chin (who knows what a storm he awaited?).

"Göring took the earphones from the operator and listened for a few moments. 'I don't understand a single word! And I know English too! They are all twaddle and muddling it up with those code words. This is blither and no radio discipline

The Interrogator

at all! Well . . .never!!' Here Iron Hermann was complaining about the RAF for not making it easier for us.

"How can you make sense of that prattle?" he asked us.

"Well, for trained men it is not confusing, so it was routine for my men to make sense of it. The air battle soon ended, and shortly the planes began to come back and pancake at nearby bases. Some waggled their wings at us, signifying they had scored a victory. We listened to the British rescue forces going out after downed airmen in the channel.

"The Big Boss came to my desk and leaned across my shoulder, the Great Cross dangling against my cheek. Clapping me on the back hard—it nearly knocked me out of my chair, he said, 'Fine! Wonderful! That was great! How come I never heard of your unit before?'

"Before I knew what I was saying, I answered . . .'I wonder, too, sir. Since 1938 and 1939 I have made numerous reports to headquarters about this listening-in business.'

'So? Well! I'll ask some pointed questions when I get back! I promise!' "With that he turned about, raised his baton for silence (a monument again): 'Gentlemen, what I have seen and heard here has deeply impressed me. This is the most

THE STATION MASTER OF TANGMERE
Wing Commander Douglas R. S. Bader, the famed legless RAF fighter leader, was shot down by a Luftwaffe pilot. Horst Barth interrogated him. This photo, taken in 1956 at an airbase in England, shows Bader speaking to the officers and wives at the 20th USAF Fighter Wing headquarters.

Chapter 3: Playboys Of The Air

WINGCO BADER AND OBERST HUTH
Some historians claim Oberst Huth held a pistol in his left hand while talking to Bader. This picture clearly shows Huth did not have a pistol; he was holding gloves.

WINGCO BADER IN COCKPIT OF ME 109
Oberst Huth and interrogator Barth are interested observers as Douglas Bader sits in the cockpit of an Me 109. Bader's plea for permission to shoot a few "circuits and bumps" in the German fighter was turned down by Adolf Galland.

The Interrogator

"WE'VE CAUGHT A BIG FISH!"
With those words, Galland was informed the Douglas Bader was now a POW. Bader was brought to JG 26 HQ for a visit. *Left to right*: Johannes Seifert, Schmitt, Galland, Meinardus, Pappi Causin, Bader, Horst Barth (with hands in the air).

important unit in an air battle, especially important to the Jafü. I thank all you men here.' Turning to the general in command of technical forces, Martin, he said, 'All these men are promoted! This is at least sergeant's work. Why are they all just privates?'

"He was informed that this is an intelligence unit with specially selected men. Most of them had lived in foreign countries; they had no military experience or training, but they had good brains and high IQs. Göring departed full of enthusiasm, saying, 'That is the way to win this war, with men like these.'

"Our unit grew and grew, after his visit. New men arrived and some of our best men left for other bigger jobs. We became a *Kompanie* and soon became a regiment. High-ranking officers took over command. I lost interest, as might be expected. General Kammhuber became the top man, and everyone soon called the ops rooms '*Kammhuberische Kino's*.' *Kino* means 'cinema.'

"Now, about Wing Commander Douglas Bader. I knew him long before he came to Europe by bailing out of his fighter, not in person but by his radio voice and tactics. He was no secret to us. He was kind of a VIP (Very Interesting Pilot) like our Galland, Mölders, Lutzow, Oesau, and the like.

"I had listened to his combat, his bailout, and then I informed our headquarters to search for him, not knowing whether he had survived or not. When the report

Chapter 3: Playboys Of The Air

came in that he was found, was wounded and in hospital at St. Omer, I was ordered to look after him as long as he was on the Channel coast. Though I had my own work to do, I became quite a helping angel to him. Then he made a most fantastic, risky, and artistic attempt to escape from the second floor of the hospital . . . and this with two artificial legs!!

"Bader was free for one night, and when he was again picked up—from beneath a haystack—he grinned at me, much relieved. 'Oh! It's surely good to see *you* again!' he exclaimed. I'll bet it was good, because I spoke English and because the German big shots were not happy at all over all the trouble he had caused everyone with that escape. They admired his spunk but were not happy with him at all.

"After giving him his spare legs and a couple of letters the RAF had delivered during an air raid, and after giving him a meal of bacon and eggs we had spared from our own rations, we gave him a hot bath and a nice big French bed to sleep on his own adventures. He was then transported *Heim ins Reich* to Oberursel and eventually to permanent POW camp at Colditz Castle.

"I am sure my *Abwehr* friend and I saved Douglas Bader a lot of inconveniences while he was on the Channel coast. In fact, the night after he was sent to Oberursel, a company of SS arrived. Their orders were to find the escaped Bader *by all means!* What this meant at the time was clear enough!

"One day I escorted some POWs to Oberursel for interrogations and took a look at Dulag Luft. There I met the *Kommandant* and his staff, and I soon realized I had followed the call to Auswertestelle West. I became the chief of fighter interrogation and wireless operators, which was the technical side of the job. I was my own master again and very happy. There I met Hanns Scharff.

"I needed a special type of man as an assistant interrogator, and somehow Hanns Scharff was the man who came before me and got the job. He was exactly what I wanted, fitting my description of an interrogator. An interrogator, to my mind, should be a man who fights without weapons, fences without a sword, fights only with his brain. He must be a very curious man . . . and we Saxons are notoriously curious. We question everything. Also, he must be a gregarious man. They do carry their heart on their tongue, if you know what I mean. They won't sit singly at a table for four, glaring at people to frighten them away. No, a natural inquisitor will invite others to sit with him and talk in friendly fashion. I soon found out that Hanns was this type of man. He came out of a good patrician house in Greiz, Thuringia, was a businessman in South Africa, and spoke of our homeland with warm heart, and he certainly had recognized the idiom in the language. Scharff was a man I could like, and so I hired him as my assistant.

"My feelings during the war are very simple to describe; I'm sure the same is true of Hanns. We were all human beings, and we respected our opponents as brave and honest soldiers who were carrying out military orders. We all had our noses in the mud and knew many real dangers. Yes, we were lucky to live through the war and the first couple of years after.

The Interrogator

"We used no trickery on the POWs, and at that time I was very much aware that I balanced (and so did Hanns) on a thread, on a tightwire, so to speak, for there was a Gestapo *Kommando* unit right next to our Auswertestelle West camp, watching our every step. One wrong move would have meant losing my valuable head!

"We were a very good team at Oberursel, had a lot of fun and gags, and Hanns could perform sleight of hand and magic tricks. He could wake up the dullest of parties with his humor. I think that even most of the POWs who passed through Oberursel discovered it was not nearly as bad as they had expected it to be, and even enjoyed being safe and alive there, in spite of this misfortune of their having been shot down and captured.

"Well, let Hanns Scharff tell you all about it . . . he is a great storyteller. My motto:

"FAIRNESS AND HONESTY WILL ALWAYS PAY OFF!"

Sincerely yours,
HORST BARTH

Author comments: Horst Barth befriended the famous western movie star Tom Mix, who starred in 170 or more films over a period of twenty-four years. Mix had served in the Spanish-American War as well as the Boer Wars in South Africa. In Oklahoma he served as a marshal and a sheriff. As a genuine cowboy he had a special talent with lariats, rifles, and handguns. When Grauman's Chinese Theatre in Hollywood invited him to cast his image in cement in front of the theater (where it may still be seen), Mix asked his friend Horst Barth to make the handprints, while the rest of the image is true Tom Mix.

4

FIGHTERS BEHIND FENCES

Drop by drop fills the tub.
—French proverb

HANNS SCHARFF continues: Bright sunshine, shimmering war air covers the gentle slopes of the Taunus mountain range. Between mighty beech trees, pines, and chestnuts stand the ruins of the ancient watchtowers, ring walls, and castles bearing witness to Roman enterprises of yore. Built more than two thousand years ago, the Limes is a long line of fortifications, supply depots, and lookout towers. This Maginot Line of the Romans stretches from the Rhine River to the Danube River and, here, runs along the mountain ridge. On its highest peak, the Feldberg, just 8 miles from the encampment, appears the new, huge, modern communications tower. Two big, square mirrors of convex shape are mounted on its roof, and likewise a pair are on one of the barracks at Auswertestelle West. This mirror-reflection system is a new way of optical-telephonic communication. Half a century ago, the Boer generals employed a similar means in the South African War; they knew the Bible by heart and would transmit book, chapter, and verse numbers, and the receiving party knew what the verse said and acted accordingly. With this "new" system we get information much more rapidly.

Earlier you were taken through the steps necessary for you to become an interrogation officer. Being in the right place at the right time was part of it, but also necessary was the proper education and bilingual ability. You must have earned the "Red Certificate" to be a full-fledged *Vernehmungsoffizier*, which has been placed inside your passport or identification booklet.

Now, may I show you over the camp? Let me lead the way and explain to you the composition of this famous and only interrogation and evaluation center of the Luftwaffe. You must know that every enemy aviator who is captured, whether in Germany or in an occupied country, from Norway down through France or Italy,

The Interrogator

SIXTY-NINE PLUS TWENTY-FIVE
Reichsmarschall Hermann Göring points to the 94 victory marks on the rudder of Adolf Galland's Me 109 fighter. Galland scored a total of 103 aerial victories before war's end, and many of his opponents passed through Oberursel interrogation center en route to a *Stalag Luft* prison camp.

Chapter 4: Fighters Behind Fences

rescued from the English Channel or plucked from the waves of the North Sea or fished out of the warm Mediterranean, will be brought to this place for questioning. It makes no difference whether he is taken prisoner at the front lines or whether he comes dangling down from the sky in the most remote location, nor does it matter if he is disguised as a civilian in France or merely mistakes one of our nice Luftwaffe airfields for his own base in Britain and landed on the wrong side; he comes to Oberursel. Russian personnel are excluded. They go someplace else, since we have nothing to do with the East.

That explains why our next-higher echelon of command, as a part of the Leading Staff of the Luftwaffe, with its headquarters near Berlin, is called Foreign Air Forces West (Fremde Luftwaffen West). Our camp is called Evaluation Center West (Auswertestelle West). The western category included, besides Americans and Tommies, the Poles who were serving with the RAF, the Free French, Greeks, Norwegians, Canadians, Australians, New Zealanders, and South Africans. It mattered not what type of aircraft they were flying—bombers, fighters, transports, reconnaissance. It mattered not whether they were strategic, tactical, or marine fliers.

Later I will show you how even seemingly useless pieces of scrap, items of personal property of airmen killed in action and sometimes burned beyond recognition, will be accurately registered and can be useful to us. The most important information comes to us from the POWs themselves.

The most essential branch at Auswertestelle West is the Interrogation Department, where information is accumulated by questioning prisoners. However, equally productive is the BUNA Department, which gathers information through booty. Downed enemy planes, or the remains of them, are thoroughly investigated by the Technical Department. A so-called press department, with many experts, is very important, too, since they accumulate and correlate data in their Yellow Card Registry, the Wireless Interception Detachment, the Squadron History Unit, the Victory Credits Registry, and a reception office. Finally, there is a map room, with its precise plots of the current military situations. Valuable information is gleaned from their display of conditions, positions, and general state of affairs. As a result of this intelligence-gathering combine, the courier who travels daily to Berlin with his top-secret luggage carries very important documents, the results of the findings of this organization of intelligence agents here at Oberursel.

Oh, yes! I must not forget counterintelligence! An American military dictionary defines counterintelligence as that phase of intelligence covering all activity devoted to destroying the effectiveness of inimical foreign intelligence activities and to the protection of information against espionage, personnel against subversion, and installations or material against sabotage.

Well, if ever you need a hearty laugh, naturally inaudible, go there and study the measures taken by those wiseacres to protect us from enemy espionage or to prevent prisoners from escaping.

The Interrogator

All in all, a few hundred officers, soldiers, and girls are at work here. They are busy building a gigantic jigsaw puzzle by fitting together carefully and cleverly the plain and pell-melled pieces of information. Their work may be likened to the sagacious construction of the missing parts of a complicated mosaic.

Everybody here, except the sergeant major and a handful of Russian POWs working as gardeners and handymen, speaks more or less good English. You will notice some King's English. You might also hear the nasal drawling speech of the southern American or hear the Cockney who drops his "haiches."

Next to a Canadian lumberjack you can meet a professor of Indology. Two English words dominate the unusual vocabulary, here, though, and they are "cooler" and "briefing." They have become parts of the German language. The word "cooler," it is said, made its way here via Africa, where prisoners could cool down in captivity. Briefing came to be used because it was so much shorter than the German term *Offiziersbesprechung*. Looking deceptively like a museum, our most entertaining section is the Camp Officer's Reception Bureau. Before we inspect the COR. let us take a look at that long building next to it, the one with all those windows. This is the Interrogation Barrack. In there are about fifty officers, each with his own quarters or office. No, he does not sleep there at night; it is just his little cubicle-like office where lieutenants, captains, majors, and colonels chew their pencils.

This first office on the left is for the department chief, who is also the deputy commander. He wears two hats, so to speak. He is Major Junge, a WWI ace, a record flier, good natured, extremely polite, a complete gentleman. He is also a connoisseur of all vintages of wines.

The adjoining rooms are occupied by the interrogators of the "bus drivers of the sky," the bomber crews. These rooms are divided into two sections, a USAAF and an RAF section. Next come the supercilious dandies with crossed propellers on their lapels, the Department of Technology. After them are the overbearing navy liaison officers, followed by another group of investigators, those harmless grand daddies of the flak units. By the way, do you know what has been planted all around our cities, shooting upward but hitting nothing? Asparagus. Our flak! Oh, come now! Please don't look at me in surprise. We do have our little jokes occasionally, but better be careful for there are also some Gestapo agents attached to this camp.

Well, after the guileless granddads from the antiaircraft units comes "Division South." They question all captured airmen from the North African, Greek, and Italian theaters of war. Through those doors there must pass, for instance, all POWs from the 12th and 15th Air Forces. Finally we come to the "Y" department, where about a dozen smart lads from the Signal Corps, all experts in wireless communications, are situated. They have separate sections for RAF fighters, RAF night fighters, and USAAF fighters from 8th and 9th Fighter Commands.

Seeing all these officers makes me realize that though I know my work best, it is not going to be an easy task as a lance corporal among brass. Many of them,

Chapter 4: Fighters Behind Fences

especially those who have traveled the tortuous roads of the world, will have little patience with you, although they will regard you as their kind, will be courteous, and will treat you as a chum, but some may soon begin to envy your youth and vex you.

Mind be alert! Here comes the chief of security and counterintelligence. He is an old and fat captain, and you must salute him with terrific vigor; else he kicks. His symbol should be a man on a bicycle. He kicks downward at everything below him. Higher up, he bends his back and bows his head.

"Hey! You, man! Corporal is it? Where did you learn how to salute?"

"In Potsdam, Herr Hauptmann!"

"That must have been at a training school for street cleaners and not for soldiers! Look sharp, *Gefreiter!*"

That was Captain Offermann. He hoots at the low ranks, but you should have seen him talking to the commandant after another prisoner had escaped. Not long ago, an agent from the British Secret Service, disguised as an enemy flier, got away and actually sent him a postcard to tell him he had returned safely back to London. In private life, Offermann is some sort of a missionary, and he likes to conduct church services for wounded POWs, yet he does not hesitate to impose upon them and hurt their feelings in the very same breath. Beware of him!

There! Look at that American bomber sergeant being led by the guard to the interrogator. Doesn't he look like a good-natured teddy bear in his coverall jumpsuit? One can easily see how glad he is to have saved his bacon. Bailout from a B-17 Fortress must be a frantic experience in the turmoil and din of battle.

RESULTS OF A MIDAIR COLLISION
This P-38 "Lightning" and an enemy fighter tried to fly in the same airspace at the same time. A very capable American pilot landed it in friendly territory.

The Interrogator

Yonder! The tall English flight leftenant being led back to his cell from the night-fighter department. How smartly he salutes at the door, yet how calm, solemn, and collected. And over there! An American Blackie. He would make an ideal night fighter, since in the dark of night you would not see a thing unless he smiled. Nothing but teeth!

"Good day, Herr Professor Bohner! Yes, here's the new interrogator in the American fighter section, owing to the disaster at Eschborn.

"He is touring the camp to familiarize himself some more. What does BUNA mean, sir? *Beute- und Nachrichten-Auswertung*, which means information through booty? Ha! Thought it was a Japanese word, possibly in memory of your lectures at the military academy in Tokyo." Maps and more maps! Some torn, some burned, some very gory with mud or blood, all marked with colored lines and spots and Xs, folded and wrapped in cellophane pockets. Paybooks, mess hall tickets, short-snorter bills, tramcar tickets, letters, newspapers, photographs. Everything imaginable comes out of the airman's pockets when he is captured. With great interest, we watch a sergeant from the ack-ack assort numerous little passport photos.

"And therefore as a stranger, give it welcome. There are more things in heaven and earth, Horatio, than are dreamt of in our philosophy."

Booty expert Herr Nagel, one of Germany's ablest specialists in literature, particularly in Goethe and even more so in Faust, and once a Heidelberg University lecturer, enjoyed quoting Hamlet every time he found a certain item among the POWs' effects. Enemy airmen carried five small photographs, like passport photos, neatly protected in cellophane wrapping, showing themselves in civilian clothing. They always gave us an important clue.

As long as his airplane was flying, the average American aviator would never fully acquaint himself with the idea of how to evade and escape captivity in case he should be shot down. His War Department took everything into consideration on his behalf, providing him even with trouser buttons that could be cut off and used as compasses. Maps were printed on soft silk for him to find his way in enemy country. Twenty useful sentences in nearly every European language were at his command in a small folder. One sentence said *"Ich liebe Dich"* in German and *"Je t'aime"* in French. I love you. The American aviator was provided with a small hacksaw made of the finest steel to cut the iron bars of his cell. To be able to pay his expenses, he was supplied with a variety of foreign currency. Since he could not walk into an enemy restaurant, it made him carry food, a water disinfectant, and a stimulant against sleepiness. He had a morphine syringe ready in case he became injured. His War Department was a very good war department, because it worried all the time how to help him on his difficult way out of the land where the sauerkraut grows.

That War Department was so good that it could visualize how an unshaven man could immediately arouse suspicion, so it presented these escapees with a dwarf's razor and a sweet little dwarf's soap stick, although it sat over there in

Chapter 4: Fighters Behind Fences

Washington, DC, far away on the other side of the Atlantic Ocean. It went even further. It said to itself that if the Huns still have their ridiculous fascination for travel papers, identity cards, certificates, and safe-conduct passes, we must give our stranded airmen a chance and the means to possess such papers.

Now, any of the many French underground organizations that were helping Allied airmen escape could supply all these papers, but the little passport-sized photographs of the bearer were something else again. The underground had no facilities at all for making them (this was long before the Polaroid camera, of course), so the airmen came supplied with them. Back at their bases in England, each airman had been given a set of five pictures of himself in civilian clothes, pictures to make him look like a French peasant or civilian. Every air station in England had its own photographer.

These photographs! Each airman must pose in civilian clothing, and, quite naturally, none had mufti with them in England, so the photographer at each base thoughtfully collected one civilian suit, one shirt, one necktie. He dressed each airman in these same clothes, and the photo was placed in the escape kit.

Likewise, the photographer always used the same background in the pictures. Also, each photographer had his own particular way of cutting and trimming the final prints. That is what makes it possible for a German ack-ack sergeant to say without fail, the moment he looks at a confiscated escape-kit picture, which military unit the subject in the photograph belongs.

He loved to work out his scheme systematically, and soon he knew all the suits, shirts, and ties, striped or checkered, in Wattisham and Debden, Mount Farm, and Biggin Hill. He was able to classify by memory each bomber and fighter unit within the whole of the United Kingdom after just a quick glance at the picture.

In private life he was a professor, but now, as a flak sergeant, he quotes Shakespeare every time a prisoner brings him five new photographs for his large collection. Ah! Our doctor Bert Nagel is a whiz!

In looking through this BUNA Department with me, I want you to understand what an important role all these apparently meaningless articles play in the intelligence game. The enemy brings them to us either by carelessness or by *force majeure*. A sure bet is that every one of them who forgets to throw an old mess hall ticket away before launching on a combat sortie has read a book on espionage and counterespionage, has watched a movie or heard a radio program on the subject, or has listened to countless intelligence briefings in his squadron, and they all know how dangerous and revealing such carelessness can be. Yet, he will find an excuse for himself, rationalizing why he and he alone happened to have that insignificant piece of paper on him. Also why he did not have time to swallow the flimsy, the very secret orders for this last mission of his. They were even printed, those flimsies, on thin, sweetened rice paper so they would be palatable.

If, for instance, you will turn your attention to these huge file cabinets filled

The Interrogator

with mess hall tickets, to give you an example of only one of numerous subjects available to us, you will realize how easy it is for us to classify these papers so that we can determine where its bearer is headquartered and from what base he operates. Here, this mess sergeant in England always makes the same "x" in red pencil. This one here uses a rubber stamp, and that one makes a pencil mark. Once the fact is established, in most cases initially by too much talk by the prisoner who spills the beans about who and where the mess sergeant is based, it is easy for any interrogation officer to check on a newcomer POW, or to convince the POW of his superb knowledge. The prisoner can never be in a position to judge whether his answers are of any importance. There are just too many at the interrogator's command to surprise his prey with beforehand-gathered information, so he will always win.

All of the results of this search work are to be found in the so-called *Lagenzimmer*, a special information room where you are at liberty to inquire into the current situation, right down to the smallest Smithsonian detail.

How about an airman who carefully destroyed every bit of information carried from his home base? He even changed out of uniform into mufti and is disguised as a Frenchman. He threw away his dog tags and, when caught, remembers only his name, rank, and serial number.

Well, I don't care what he has done before or even what he may forget or who he may be. Within a very short time he will give me all the information I need without the use of extreme or brutal methods. Barbarism is not necessary. I will collect, as you may see, a stifling amount of information and evidence beforehand, and by its display along with persuasion mainly appealing to common sense, I will make him tell me things I have not heard before.

I know that statement sounds like boasting or bragging, my friend, but please do not believe that I might triumph over an enemy frivolously.

The strongest character, the most unyielding soldier, is exposed to violent psychological strains by the bare fact of captivity. It exerts powerful pressures on the mind and spirit of a man who knows he is innocent of any wrongdoing. Try, therefore, to find a psychological explanation for this deep mystery known by every soldier in captivity. This unfathomable "barbed-wire psychosis" does things to a man that have nothing at all to do with fear or discomfort or anger. The POWs core, or soul, is eroded by this psychosis, which distorts his conception of the world and the humans who share it with him.

This suddenly realized fact of confinement under duress hits Americans harder than anyone else, since these young men are not only brave but also have a deep-seated passion for freedom and liberty of the mind as well as of the body itself. The captured American is instantly weighed down with a feeling of guilt, even though his capture is not his own fault at all but the fault of the motor that quit on him in midair, or the fact that a bullet from a Messerschmitt or Focke-Wulf has crashed into his cockpit.

Chapter 4: Fighters Behind Fences

COL. EVERETT W. STEWART, USAAF
Commander of the 355th Fighter Group, Stewart was never captured by the Germans, but Frau Biehler of the Squadron Histories Section at Oberursel had this photo and a full background file on him in case he came into German hands.

He feels guilty because he knows he is on the sidelines from now until the end of the war and that he cannot be in there fighting with his pals. This mental anguish finally makes him vulnerable. The man who pays no heed to the warnings of his intelligence officer does so because he feels, even subconsciously, incapable of any infamy. He detests treasonable conduct. It will remain an anomaly, therefore, that a prisoner will even unconsciously surrender secrets to his enemy of his own free will or from inclination, or by instinct, whatever motive he may have had. An example (fictional name, true facts):

Blond, tall, healthy Richard Price Jr., uncomplicated, broad minded but taciturn, good hearted but discreet, passed his primary and basic flying courses without difficulty. Eighteen months had elapsed since the tests to determine his physical qualifications before he started his flying training. Hopping about in primary trainers like the PT-17 and the basic trainers like BT-13s and AT-17s was great fun, but he was just getting ready for the bigger fighters. After three more months of flight training, he received his commission as a second lieutenant in the US Army Air Corps just two days before his twenty-first birthday on 5 May 1943. His orders would not be effective until his birthday, however, and so he sat comfortably and full of vigor and expectation in the Advanced Flying School's Officers'

The Interrogator

Club at Kelly Field, Texas. He had received his wings today, plus a new serial number, which was 0-678 543. His old enlisted number, 6276597, which he held as a flying cadet, was committed to the ash can forthwith. His new number, O-678 543, was destined for much use in the future. The *O* part indicated his officer's commission. New papers, dog tags, a new uniform, and a new station followed his acquiring this new number. So did a couple of months of training at a CCTS (combat crew training school) with a new fighter group and a couple of unpleasant days waiting at some fort in New York. Then, on a nice, warm, and sunny summer day, his whole unit boarded the SS *Queen Elizabeth* and they embarked for Europe—and destiny.

So long, Dad and Mom, don't you worry about me! Keep your chin up, darling. I won't forget you over there! Goodbye, sweet homey shores! For you I shall bring back with me the Air Medal and Silver Star, the DFC, and, if it must be, the Purple Heart. Come on, chums, let's worry about kings and aces, or boxcars instead of Jerry submarines. Make hay while the sun shines. Yea! Real old Scotch! And put on some music!

Britannia surely does rule the waves! But, ugh, that Greenock is an old and ugly place. They seem to be far behind the times here in Limeyland. It's good to get away from those foggy and cold riverbanks of the Clyde and down to East Anglia. In fact, it's good to be stationed near London, near Picadilly Circus and the Café de Paris. Soon you will be on another mission over Germany, Richard. Watch out for the ack-ack alley, then, as you cross Happy Valley. And watch for the Hun in the Sun!

To hell with those boring lectures by the nutty intelligence officer. What is all this bunkum for, anyway? Others may get shot down, but never I, Richard Price Junior, from Dallas, Texas. Never! I have my rabbit's foot right here, and besides, there isn't a Jerry fighter pilot good enough to get me. No siree! Day after tomorrow we are scheduled for another escort mission over Hunland, another milk run. But no more drinks now. I wonder what happened to the Luftwaffe. *Wo ist die Luftwaffe!* Not one single Jerry fighter have I seen yet. No Abbeville Kids. No Hermann Göring Boys. No Yellow Noses. *Wo ist die Luftwaffe!* I came over here to become an ace, and they aren't cooperating. Not even any worries about flak, either; they can't shoot that high, although the Fortresses seem to enjoy staying down there in the middle of the bursts just to challenge those Heine gunners. Only old man SNAFU can get me, and he is far away.

No, he is not! The foe introduces himself by making little tiny oil dots on the windshield of Dick's fighter. After a while, he is more conspicuous—he makes the oil pressure drop a little, and a few minutes later the oil temperature gage goes up a few degrees. Dick now begins to worry and turns back toward England, led by his element leader. Suddenly the rev counter shows a decrease in rpm and the engine has a funny sound to it, occasionally. The Channel and England are far away, and the engine is losing power. Then the foe, old man SNAFU, appears in

Chapter 4: Fighters Behind Fences

full and the engine seizes, the propeller standing stock-still and the only way for Dick to keep flying is to drop the nose and glide. SNAFU causes Dick to radio to his leader: "I'm finished, sir. Tell my gal down at Picadilly I'll see her sometime." He opens his canopy, unfastens his seat belt and harness, turns the beautiful fighter over on her back, and falls free, tearing his oxygen mask and helmet off because he forgot to disconnect the oxygen hose and radio plugs.

Seven, eight, nine, ten—the parachute opens with a plop! A forest below, a river like a broad silver band, a dear little girl back home; why did I joke about a girl at Picadilly? The DFC . . . gone, ace . . . gone; green fields and brown ground. Earth . . . hey, hey!

Thank heaven! Not a scratch!

Meist all Chrity, Dick, where the hell are you? What river was that wide silvery ribbon? Boy! Was I clanked up!

Hat's off to Dick's efforts! Swimming across the Rhine River in uniform is not easy and is no joke. Then he walked miles and miles. He stole milk in tiny quaint villages at night, and he speared some trout in a brook at sunrise. He tasted snails for the first time in his life. He slept under bridges during the daytime and walked at night until he noticed by the change of names and the spelling on signposts that he had crossed the German-French border. Still, he knew he was not safe . . . yet. He marched on, aiming for Rouen, using his silk maps, from where he knew he might be able to cross the Channel to England. Just now it was high time for him to change into French peasants' clothing so he could talk to one of the girls working in the fields. If he could get one separated from the rest, she just might understand his *beaucoup Français.*

Aha! Exactly as I have pictured all mademoiselles, Dick thought, as she beckoned by whirling her black curls and smiled charmingly. Oh boy, he said to himself, from now on everything will be all right. And this little girl did know all the *comme ci–comme ca*; she took him to some friends who hid and dressed and fed Dick to the best of their capabilities. Owing to the fact that his hosts belonged to an underground organization, Dick quickly turned into a genuine farmhand; at least his new passport said so. They made him up as a French farmhand, using the nice escapee passport photo he carried with him from England.

Eventually, Dick was lucky enough to make arrangements to be shipped to England within a week's time. He paid all his expenses with GI escape money, which had come in very handy. He left Lucille, the daughter, most of the remainder of his money because he would have no further use for it now.

Home, back home! *Toute suite!* And the tooter the sweeter!

"If I may suggest, Herr Kriminal-Kommissar, not to arrest such members of the underground organization who help the Allied airmen escape to Great Britain."

"Are you mad? How also can the Gestapo allow an enemy partisan organization to function against German interests under our very eyes?"

"Sir, if we have these partisans arrested and executed, Herr Kommissar, we

The Interrogator

THE HUN IN THE SUN
Where is the Luftwaffe? Check six, pal, because he is usually there. Adolf Galland, *Kommodore* of JG 26, scored 103 aerial victories on the Western front and accounted for many of the Allied pilots who appeared at Oberursel.

give ourselves the trouble to search for new channels through which the fliers will return to England. More partisans take their place with new ideas. This way we know what they will do."

"Hmmm. All right then, just shadow them and see that none of them get away. In fact, I'll pass my new idea on up to headquarters!"

One can hear the gurgling waters, the small waves slapping against dock and boat hulls, but it is impossible to see it yet in the first soft shimmers of twilight. The boat will leave in just a few minutes, and hazy figures are running to one spot. Dick is there. He is surprised how many American buddies he finds here, all with the same anxious wish to get back to England to fly again! About twenty-five men are together now, and not one is recognizable as a member of the USAAF. All troubles and worries are over! Freedom, pals. Bon voyage! High spirits!

It did not strike our young friend, as he stood at the bow and was the first one who had the opportunity to observe oncoming motorboats emerging in the darkness, that he might lose this newfound freedom in just a few more seconds. Just when he felt sure he had won the game, he needed several terrifying moments to conceive the meaning of those words, *"Hande hoch!,"* which boomed loud and clear in the morning stillness. He lifted his arms overhead with a deep sigh. *C'est la guerre!*

In spite of their French passports, twenty-two of the men claimed to be Allied airmen and requested they be treated as soldiers. Sixteen were judged, by their accents and mannerisms, to be American pilots, and according to high orders, they were, as disguised fliers caught trying to escape in France, to be turned over to the Luftwaffe interrogation center at Oberursel without delay.

Chapter 4: Fighters Behind Fences

Sorry for you, Dick. Your efforts were great and your spirit good, but not every time does the better man win.

Lucille and Gustave earnestly tried to help you. Never were they aware of the threatening shadow of the Gestapo. The more they tried to help unfortunate fugitives, the less likely they themselves were to be arrested. The French unwittingly rounded up the escapees for us!

Some people have their own ideas. He is a humble Luftwaffe corporal, here at Oberursel, a merchant now in uniform but a wizard on numbers and dates. Young, well mannered, and conscientious, Herr Gomman is the inventor of a system that has taken many a POW by surprise.

Now, my friend, let me show you how his system works. Gomman will give me my first lead about this newcomer, Second Lieutenant Richard Price. By the time I call Price in for interrogation, I will have a heap of information about him, I am sure. Let us give Gomman a telephone call. Exchange? Please connect me with Yellow Card Registry. "Herr Gomman? *Guten Tag!* Would you please give me some information on USAAF number 0-678 543?" He said I should wait a minute. We will see what he can tell us about that Lt. Price. "Hello? Advanced Flying School at San Antonio, Texas? Commissioned lieutenant May 5, 1943? A fighter pilot? Good, and thank you very much, Herr Gomman."

How Gomman does it, I really cannot say. He gets his very accurate information from a system of yellow cards worked out under his direction from data collected by many foreign agents. He has the serial number of every USAAF officer, from the low numbers of the old-timers to the high numbers of the newest commissioned men, the numbers of the regulars as well as of the reserves, the West Pointers and the flying cadets. He will give you readily all the information he has assembled concerning each number. Nevertheless, he is very secretive about how and where he gets all this data. His system is a secret.

Some people have it their own way!

Tap, tap, tap, tap—it's a monotonous and ominous sound, sometimes growing louder as it approaches, sometimes quieter as it recedes in the distance. It is a noise in the corridor outside Dick's cell room. He lies on his hard bed after a fitful and sleepless night, listening to the footsteps of the guard on duty. The cell is small and there is just enough room for a bed plus a wooden stool and small table. The soundproofed walls are whitewashed, and the only window is made of opalescent glass, a milky pane that allows the light to come in but does not allow anyone to see in or out. If the occupant of the cell room wishes to see outside or even get out to have some fresh air, he must get special written permission from the interrogation officer and give it to the duty guard.

An electric light and a heater in each cell room are operated only from the corridor, just beyond the cell door. A tiny iron handle inside the cell releases; out in the corridor, a red-painted piece of sheet metal that signals the guards. It's similar to the turn indicator mounted on British automobiles. The guard must be

The Interrogator

in a good humor to answer the call in any big hurry. There are washrooms with shower baths and toilets at the far end of the passageway. The guards carefully avoid letting POWs meet there, and it seems an endless coming and going every day until all 250 inmates are attended to.

Our newly arrived 2nd Lt. Dick Price has overcome his first excitement but not his apprehensions. He has cooled down in his solitary confinement, although he still feels bitter about how he was fooled yesterday upon his arrival at Auswertestelle West. You have to go through this mill twice, he says to himself, if you want to be properly prepared for all these damned tricks Jerry pulls on you. Some squarehead had received them and then led them courteously into the prison barrack, where he told them to put *everything* they possessed on some tables. "Don't try to hide anything! Anything we find later will be confiscated and not returned to you. *Verstehen?*

Dick's turn came and he put his passport on that table, also the picture of that charming girl back home that he would never forget, some cigarettes (Boy! How he hated to part with those!), a pocketknife, a pencil, and a handkerchief.

"The wristwatch too," said the Luftwaffe soldier nearby.

"I protest!" answered Dick rather bitterly. "That is my own private property."

"*Jawohl!* Don't worry," he was assured. "It will be returned to you the moment you leave this camp."

The man noted each item of booty on a slip of paper, marked it all with the number 21A, had Dick sign the paper, and stowed the lot in a paper bag.

"Was that all you have?" the man asked.

"Yes!"

"Come with me to the search room now."

"Okay!"

"Now, take off your boots!"

Silence, but the boots are removed.

"Your jacket and your shirt!"

Silent compliance.

"Your socks and your pants!"

They came off without hesitation or comment.

Dick was amazed to see his searcher draw one of those tiny American escape compasses from his pocket and start systematically passing it over all his clothing. When the needle vibrated vigorously near his belt, right where his own compass was hidden, he merely gave the Deutscher a wry grin. "You win," he mumbled.

The German cocked his eye a bit, smiled back at Dick in a friendly way, shrugged his shoulders, and said in a soft, natural tone, "Never mind. A compass? Now give me your money, please."

Dick had already been allowed to put his shirt and jacket on, and his hand, for a split second before he caught it, jerked upward toward the pocket flap on the jacket.

Chapter 4: Fighters Behind Fences

Now, thinking it over back in his cell, Dick could kick himself for having been the victim of his own perplexity. Those pound notes and dollar bills could have remained his, but since he had not declared them they were confiscated. Hell's bells! He would rather have given them to Lucille instead of financing the Reichsbank with them. Maybe he could have played poker with them in prison camp or even have found them handy in an escape sometime. This lowdown tricky son of a bastard had cut right into the pocket flap with a razor.

Still annoyed, Dick finds some consolation in the thought of how he rejected all the questions that the reception officer asked him last evening. I know this friendly approach, Dick thought, and he flatly rejected the proffered cigarette. The German looked disappointed but prepared to fill out the questionnaire.

"Name?"
"Richard Price Junior."
"Rank?"
"Second Lieutenant."
"Serial number?"
"Oh dash 678 543."
"USAAF? RAF? Come now, you can tell me."
"Sorry, I cannot tell you," after some hesitation.
"Are you a bomber or a fighter?"
"Name, rank, and serial number, sir!"
"When were you shot down?"
"Sorry, I cannot say."
"All right, where did you come down?"
"Name, rank, and serial number."
"What is your home address?"
Dick thinks about this before he finally replies, "Sorry."
"Won't you change your mind and have a cigarette?"
"Okay, I will, thank you."
"Where are your dog tags?"
"I lost them."
"What is your military squadron number?"
"I will tell you no military information.
"Who is your next of kin?"
"Sorry."
"What type of aircraft did you fly?"
"Sorry."
"How can you expect me to be satisfied with this 'Sorry, I cannot tell you' of yours?"
"My orders say nothing but name, rank, and serial number."
"Are you in good health or do you need a doctor's services?"
"Sorry, I cannot ans— . . . I, well, I am all right."

The Interrogator

"Why do you wear civilian clothes?"
"I tried to evade."
"Where from?"
"Sorry, I cannot . . ."
"Have you any buddies in this gang?"
"No."
"All right, then, sign right here and take a cigarette, if you like."

Dick took a cigarette, disdainfully, signed on the dotted line, and smartly saluted the retiring German interrogator, feeling pleased with himself since he felt he had won the first round. Yet, he would like to know what the German's note on the back of the questionnaire meant. The officer had written: *21A sagt nur Rang, Name und Nummer. Hartnäckig, ungefällig, starker Raucher, keine dogtags, Civil, vielleicht Jager?*

The last two words, which meant "perhaps fighter," caught the eye of the executive officer as he perused the reports that evening. Lt. Price had been assigned to room 21A because he would be further interrogated by the USAAF Fighter Section—Scharff. The rest of the penciled comments merely stated that his name, rank, and serial number were all he would say, plus stubborn, displeasing, strong smoker, no dog tags, civilian. The fighter specialist would treat him as a true example of POWs from the USA. Major Junge initialed the report.

Tap, tap, tap—Aha! The guard again.

Click—snap!—my door? What now?

Breakfast. Two slices of black German army bread with some ersatz butter and coffee. Lukewarm coffee! Ugh! This is terrible. The coffee is ersatz too, dammit. Bet the bread is ersatz; it tastes and looks like sawdust, by golly.

"Hey! Take this crap back and warm it up!"

Snap! Click! The door was locked shut, and did that guard have a wry smile on his face as the door went shut? Ah, hell. Maybe all is fair in love and war after all.

Now, the next step is a very interesting department that is of great assistance to interrogators in their task of accumulating data. It bears the name Squadron Histories, and it will enlighten us about the smallest detail of all Allied units flying against Germany. Frau Biehler is a tireless, obliging, and proud manageress, and she should be. She has many assistants, and still she knows nearly every answer to your questions, by heart. She will draw for you a complete diagram of each air force from any country, of units stationed in Africa, England, or wherever. She knows the names of the air force commanders and their staffs. She can supply you with photographs of air bases and has file clippings of late news of the respective enemy units. The interwoven connections of military organizations are no enigma to her, except the one about the US Navy, which grows like a banyan tree with every one of his subordinate branches reporting to the chief of naval operations. But ask her about the number of victories or medals of an Allied ace, and she will

Chapter 4: Fighters Behind Fences

PERMANENT STAFF AT OBERURSEL
Artist Schafer drew this montage showing Camp Commandant Killinger leading the orchestra.

tell you. This lady is very efficient. If somebody notifies her of a change in stations of some squadron, it gives her more pleasure, it seems, than if she were invited to a dance.

As we are ushered into her office, she jumps to her feet and meets us halfway.

"Certainly, I'll be happy to lend a helping hand, Herr Scharff. Would you like to have me show you around and tell you how we compile and systematize the information that we hope will be of help to you? First, sit there and let me tell you from beginning to end that there is nothing easier to do, and anyone could do it. I have three main sources as informers. In the first place I study all interrogation

The Interrogator

reports every day. I find lots of new facts there that are worthwhile recording. These file cabinets here, arranged by colors and by country, contain full particulars on almost all military organizations.

"Take this one on my desk, for instance. A South African fighter group serving in Italy. A recent report by a POW describes details of its airfield near Foggia, and it mentions squadron members. I have this knowledge entered into the file, and the next time Herr Hanemann squints at it, he most probably will find there the nickname of the man he is just about to worm out of his secrets.

"Here is another example, this time about a night-fighter squadron in England. Our press department has sent me newspaper clippings and photographs from the *English Illustrated News*. Squadron Leader Gibson is awarded the Victoria Cross, and he and some of his companions are received by the King in Buckingham Palace. This famous destroyer of the Edertal Dam may be one of our newcomers tomorrow, who knows? Our news readers make themselves sick reading the latest daily papers from all over the world, and their scissors cut conformable to politics, military subjects, and economics. You should go and see Herr Major von der Esch and his peerless press service at your convenience.

"This red file illustrates the complete history of an American bomber group. Oh, yes, you are fighters, I must remember, but I will use this bomber file as an illustration. Professor Bohner's BUNA Department supplied a list of dead airmen identified by their dog tags, which were saved from some burned-out wreckage. We will make notes of their fate because quite often you interrogators can induce POWs to loosen a bit by supplying them with information about what happened to their squadron mates. You see, I am in agreement that prudence is better than strength. There are no tricks to this business here, just facts. I see you have a question?" Frau Biehler looks at me for my query.

"Frau Biehler, what can you tell us about a stubborn fighter pilot from the USAAF named Richard Price?"

"Well! Stubborn, is he? We'll just ask our expert on photographs about it." A little tinkle on the phone, and yes, Herr Nagel has his fake French passport, and the photo points right straight to the 355th Fighter Group at Steeple Morden. Okay?" We nod.

"Now, Frau Biehler, please let me see that famous green file you have of General Doolittle's Eighth Air Force. I wish to see the 65th Fighter Wing, 355th Fighter Group information. Thank you."

She takes the file from one of her cute assistants and turns a few pages.

"355th? Here you are. Yes, it has perhaps the entire history of Lt. Price's squadron. When it was commissioned, where it first started training, what date it arrived in Scotland aboard the SS *Queen Elizabeth*, where it is stationed now. Is it important to you that it was activated at Orlando, Florida, as late as 12 November 1942? And here is a good picture of their air base at Steeple Morden, showing runways, hangars, houses, Quonset huts, mess halls, barracks, antiaircraft

Chapter 4: Fighters Behind Fences

emplacements, the headquarters, the officers' club too. See here, these are the names of the commander and his deputy, the staff officers, the intelligence officer, supply and maintenance officer, pilots, and ground crews. We have lots of data about this group, even technical data. They first flew P-47 Thunderbolts until late March, when they converted to P-51 Mustangs. The squadron codes are WR for 354th sq., OS for 357th sq., and YF for 358th sq. Here are the colors of each squadron too. That photograph shows the CO's plane with the name of Sunny. He calls his wife Sunny, one of the POWs has reported, and you'll find that right there, see? Their hottest aces are Hovde, Henry W. Brown, and Haviland, and we have a file on them and their buddies just in case they come to be our guests.

"Now here are the squadron secret radio call signs and respective frequencies. These next few pages give particulars on each and every mission they have flown since their first one on . . . let's see . . . 14 September 1943. We even have their losses, POWs, deaths, and furloughs. I have an idea that you will update the losses column after you talk to Lt. Price. Here are the victories they have claimed, and here are the decorations, and the nicknames of the men. Can you imagine a nickname like "Badass"? His name really is "Badavas." And how do they get "Jonesey" out of a nice Polish name like Szaniawski? Americans!

"Just read it and you will know as much as Jimmy Doolittle knows about his own Air Force, if not more. You want to check that file out for a while. All right, just sign this voucher and I will have it sent to your office . . . is it number 47?"

At your service, gentlemen. Please come again."

I know a lot about 2nd Lt. Richard Price, now, but something is still missing. His background is all here; it will be easy to fill in any blank spots, but I am bothered about several things. What was his number on his Mustang? What was his mission? How did he have to leave his plane? Where did it fall? When exactly? Who shot him down? For all that information, we need to find his crashed plane. To throw light on that clue, it is necessary to visit Herr Model, the sergeant and Lord Great Master of the *Abschusskartei*, the recorder of the Victories Registry.

Evidently, Herr Model is a good hand at that business, and his name guarantees, so to say, a model department. His arms reach far and his telephone wires to everywhere when an enemy airplane has come down on European soil. He can account for Flying Fortresses, Spitfires, Liberators, Mosquitos, Mustangs, Thunderbolts, Lancasters, Lightnings, Tempests, Dakotas, Wellingtons, and anything else, blown to pieces, burned, drowned under water, or landed by force, mistake, or deliberately.

Who keeps this kettle boiling? Luftwaffe fighter squadrons, frontline army units, occupation forces, police squads, Boy Scouts, *Burgermeisters*, hausfraus. Anyone who sees a plane fall must report it, and Herr Model scrupulously classifies all announcements in accordance with his system. It is fabulous!

Every plane, wrecked or not, will be numbered, and it does not matter whether the crew survived or not, not at this time, anyway. His scale of notation consists

The Interrogator

of a few capital letters and a couple of ciphers for each enemy plane. The capital letters reveal the theater of war or operation, the type of aircraft, and its country of origin. The ciphers disclose the number of planes accounted for of this type. For instance, "J-678" means *Jager*, or fighter, number 678.

Herr Model types up a neat little paper slip, marks it with his letter and number as it is called in, and pins it on the wall of the *Lagezimmer*, alongside the map of the mission in question. The pilot's name and, in case it was a bomber, the names of the crew, are left blank and will be filled in by the interrogator the moment he establishes the fact that plane and crew belong together. Vice versa, if there is a crew and no airplane; the number will remain in suspense. After the interrogations are finished, the interrogator completes Herr Model's neat little slip of paper and fires it back to Model, who chalks up another filled square, another mission accomplished, another addition to his collection.

In our case, we have the man but not the plane. First consultations of the victory registry denote five aircraft, all fighters, which cannot be tied to any specific pilots. We must look further.

Two of the five can be tracked down by their still-recognizable squadron letters, but they belong to the 4th and 361st Fighter Groups. This merely means we have not caught those two pilots yet. One of the remaining three can be discarded, since it was a P-38 and we know that the 355th Group has Mustangs. The last two have been found several days and weeks ago, and they were assigned identifiers KUE-J506 and KUE-J 512. Both were Mustangs and the pilots were missing. Both were smashed to smithereens and burnt. One came down on April 15th in northern Germany, and the other one near the Rhine River on May 2nd. Which is which? Which one belonged to 2nd Lt. Richard Price Jr., USAAF 0-678 543? "Herr Model, what can we do to solve this puzzle?"

"Why not try the radio monitors, Gefreiter Scharff?"

The Wireless Observation Section of the Signal Corps might be able to help? Let's see. The "Y" soldiers, these radio men, listen to every word said on the enemy aerial frequencies, including plane to plane and plane to ground, and they write it down or record it all. Since many pilots are vociferous, garrulous, the radio men have filled file after file with voluminous typewritten messages, and it will all be there if we can just find it. We want two dates, only, so maybe they can trace it for us from the *Funklage* they have created.

Here! On May 2nd a message reads: CATSPAW RED FOUR TO WHITE ONE. BALING OUT—ENGINE TROUBLES. Time: 1132 hours. Frequency 500 kc.

It checks. 355th. "Give me the telephone, quickly!"

"Herr Kaspar, what USAAF unit uses 500 kc, please?"

"That frequency is used by USAAF Fighter Group 355, and their call sign is 'Catspaw.' Squadron letters are WR."

By Jove! This is Dick's last speech in the skies! So now we can mark his questionnaire with Herr Model's number KUE-J 512. Price's plane is the 512th

Chapter 4: Fighters Behind Fences

victory or "found on base" USAAF fighter in the North European theatre of operations.

I am almost certain the name Model derives from modesty; that is, if moderateness conceals unusual intense diligence.

Nowadays, not too many men work in the fields and meadows; either they are at the front fighting or they are laboring in the big armament factories, or they serve in the last call-up levy. Only elder grandfathers consigned to armchairs are still at home. Even the youngest are taken away from their schools and pushed into the Home Defense flak battalions. Women and girls are left to do the homework and heavy work, along with a sprinkling of French and Russian POWs.

The women and girls screamed as they saw a silver bird tumbling like a falling leaf from the sky, and they tried to run to shelter in a nearby woods, but before they had taken a few steps the plane thundered into the ground, metal parts and white smoke spraying all directions, and instantaneously an immense fireball rose into the sky, accompanied by the black smoke of gasoline and oil.

The old and tottering country policeman came as fast as he could to listen to the excited women, "Ho, ho! Keep calm, girls. Did you see a parachuting airman? No? Then you must not go near the wreckage, because a body will be badly mangled and burned there. No sight to see." No, not a trace of a pilot or parachute had been seen.

The ancient warrior scrawls out his report to the *Burgermeister* of the quaint, runty, Rhenish village who, when he reads the report, calls on the telephone to a Luftwaffe base not far away, a flak battalion, and the captain notifies his headquarters and before long a car with two Luftwaffe technical inspectors arrives and they begin to examine the sad jumble that had been a beautiful silver bird, a Mustang. They quickly confirm it was indeed a Mustang, but that is all they can tell. Searching the surrounding fields in an ever-enlarging circle, they look at each part, wing parts, a machine gun, then one finds the gun camera, and it still seems to be intact. It is carefully tagged and then wrapped and dispatched to Oberursel.

At Oberursel, a man from BUNA receives it and asks Herr Model for an identification number. Model looks in his big registry book and sees that wreck is number KUE-J512, and the camera is tagged accordingly. The BUNA man then takes the camera to the photographic-developing laboratory technicians, who are always eager to see what pictures people have been taking, expecting the Folies Bergère or some such thing, perhaps.

Since gun cameras in fighter planes are coupled with the machine guns in such a manner that when the pilot presses the gun trigger or firing tit, the camera starts operating too, the 16 mm movie camera takes pictures to show what the guns are firing at. The lab technicians come out now, a disappointed look on their faces. The film is blank; it has not been exposed, indicating that the guns had not been fired before the crash. I am not disappointed. I know that Mr. KUE-J512, in number 21A, had not fired a single shot on his last combat sortie.

The Interrogator

Lunchtime! Tap, tap, tap, tap comes the clicking heels of the guard in the corridor, bringing food to the cellmates.

"Hey Fritz! Yes, you! Come here!"

"*Jawohl, Herr Leutnant. Was ist los?*"

"*Du nix* like American?"

"*Ich nix* like *Soldat. Nix amerikanisch Soldat; nix* English *Soldat, nix deutsche Soldat.*"

"*Du* will *geben* more chow? More to eat—*essen?*" "*Essen. Ja, ja! Du haben viel.*"

"*Viel? Nein! Das ist nix was.*"

"*Ich haben Ration wie Du und nix* more."

"*Du geben* more? Okay?"

"Okay, *ich will geben aber nix haben. Du haben viel essen*, plenty, *verstehen?* Red Cross *geben du* plenty. *Amerikanische* Red Cross, understand? Plenty *zigaretten, Schockolade,* uniform, pullover, *Schuhe,* SOCKS, blankets, *viel, haben viel.*"

"Yes, Fritz, but when . . . ?"

"Oh! *Wenn?* In Permanent Camp. *Das hier nix lang* stay in Auswertestelle West. *Du finish mit Offizier Du gehen* in Permanent Camp. *Du haben viel,* plenty *essen und Geld und* gin rummy. *Du* never *haben* it so *gute.*"

"Fritz, how many POWs in cooler? *Combien, wieviel, nummer?*"

"*Ja? Korridor* A has *funfzig.* B. C, each *funfzig.* Main wing *haben ein hundert. Das macht zweihundert funfzig. Verstehen?*"

Dick nods. "All single . . . solitary?"

"*Ja, das muss sein.*"

"Why. What for? *Warum?*"

"*Ich weiss nicht.*"

"Can I have a bath? A shower *mit* soap?"

"*Bad? Ja! Du musst haben von Offizier* okay."

"Can I read *ein buch, ein* magazine?"

"*Buch? Ja! Ja! Musst haben von Offizier* okay."

"Can I write . . . *er schreiben von America.* Home?"

"Oh, *Ja! Aber* permission *von Offizier.*"

"Look, Fritz. All these POWs coming down the corridor. *Wo gehen?*"

"Ah! POW *fini mit Offizier und gehen* Permanent Camp. *Du gehen* soon? Now I go work. *Guten Tag!*" The German clanged the door shut.

Click—snap! Pap, tap, tap, tap recedes in the distance.

"So long, Fritz. Nice guy."

Dick is by himself again, but he remains standing by the iron door, and it is not difficult to hear the German army interpreter, the D.v.D. on duty, address the crowd that marched down the corridor a few minutes ago. They are off to camp Dulag Luft. Dick listened carefully: "Prisoners of war! You will all leave here in

70

Chapter 4: Fighters Behind Fences

a few minutes to go to permanent POW camps. The officers will go to one camp, the enlisted to another. Before you leave here, I will return to you all your private property that was taken from you upon arrival here. I wish to point out that according to regulations, property that has been confiscated and that has been carried on your lists with a red 'C' includes all military or GI property and includes army wristwatches, compasses, bowie knives, and such. Also, any private knife with a blade over 2 inches long has been confiscated. Your private money is not confiscated but has been sent on to your permanent camp, where it will be given to you. You are going to travel by ordinary train with coaches reserved for you. My orders are to instruct you not to sing on the way, since you might annoy German travelers. Spitting is prohibited. Your senior officer of this group is Major Grant. Also I have to warn you not to try to escape during this journey, and the guards have orders to shoot without warning anyone who attempts to run away. Now, get a move on."

Every day such groups of departing POWs were addressed by the interpreter on duty in the same manner. Dick's cell was situated nearby, so he heard the spiel several times. He thought that since others leave, it was only a matter of time before he, too, would be on the way out. But were they going out because they had talked? Spilled their guts? Well, he would be here until the end of the war, or his own end, whichever came sooner, because he would never talk. Cooler or no cooler.

It is twelve o'clock and time for the officer's daily briefing, the most interesting part of the day, perhaps. Each day at 1215 hours, Lt. Col. Killinger, our commandant who was navy in WWI, addresses his officers and gives us a true picture of the current military situation. He will have a general discussion on principal matters and finally will suggest so-called "open" questions or unsolved problems from us. You will find him a superb speaker, and he knows how to keep a discussion interesting and alive. His austerity of character does not infringe his fine sense of humor, and his vitality coupled with worldly wisdom makes him demand the execution of his orders always one grade better the higher the rank. He won fame and admiration during WWI by escaping from Siberia. The Russians had shot him down early in 1915 and kept him in a dark and rat-infested cell of the famed Lublianka Prison for weeks, finally deporting him to far eastern Siberia. He got away and managed to get to Manchuria and to Japan in a most frightful escape. From Japan he went to the United States and was shown great hospitality and respect for his courage. They helped him press on to neutral Norway. From there it was only a short step to report back to his duty station in Germany. The Iron Cross First Class was his reward. He wrote a book about his harrowing and exciting experiences, and he will remind his officers even today not to be carried away by personal feelings during interrogation of prisoners.

Yes, it is very likely that you meet the man here who dropped the bombs on your home. There are but few of us who have not yet felt the burden of this war. In almost every family, somebody was wounded or lost or killed but never let a prisoner of war feel it!

The Interrogator

Here we are, my friend. Come with me to the left side of the semicircle of these waiting officers. That is the Fighter Section's usual place. Oh, oh! Here comes some trouble! Captain Offermann is the security officer, you know.

"Wait outside! How dare you bring this man in here! You know perfectly well that no strangers are admitted to officers' briefing!"

"Special permission for attendance was ordered by the CO!"

"When?"

"This morning."

"How?"

"Verbally and by telephone."

"All right! Take your places."

"Thank you, Herr Hauptmann."

"Tell me who the personal staff of the commander is," I hear your voice ask in the hubbub going on in the room.

Well, in the first place there is the deputy commander, Major Junge. You know him already, but he is extremely polite to friend or foe. He is the man who attempted to break the record between Berlin and Tokyo in 1938, but he and his plane fell into the South China Sea. His life and the lives of his two copilots were saved by an American colonel named Miller, who later was shot down over France while leading a USAAF bombardment group. He evaded and was eventually caught by the Gestapo at the Spanish border. Now he is here at Oberursel, and you must meet him and hear his story.

Now, here they come! At the left of Oberstleutnant Killinger is his adjutant, Leutnant Bottner, in private a brilliant lawyer and rabid tennis player. Over on the right of Major Junge is the executive officer, Major Böhringer. He was a wealthy factory owner and expert piano player, an adorer of the classic masters. That's about . . .

"Achtung!"

The assembly has sprung to attention. Killinger strides in, erect and proper, and stands front and center. For a few moments his eyes scan the room unfalteringly, noting, no doubt, who is and who is not present. Then in a calm and self-confident voice he begins the daily briefing.

"*Meine Herren, Die Lage*! The military situation of the last twenty-four hours shows heavy bombing in daylight of oil refineries throughout Germany. Type of bombs: incendiaries and blockbusters. Remarkably accurate bombing at Leuna and Brux in spite of our intense smoke screens. Antiaircraft defense was severely hindered by our own smoke. Ground observation reports there was no fighter escort with the bombers.

"Two separate night attacks on Frankfurt and Kassel. Type of bombs: mostly incendiary plus some medium-weight bombs. Considerable loss of civilian houses and large number of people have been killed. Sixteen bombers were shot down by flak and night fighters.

Chapter 4: Fighters Behind Fences

"Victories: sixteen four-engined bombers at night. Seven victories reported by Flak and Night Fighter Command. Daytime low-level attacks on airdromes situated around Berlin by USAAF long-distance fighters. Twenty-one losses on the ground. Victories: eleven. Enemy fighters attacked through cloud cover even though the cloud bases were only 900 feet. How did they do that? We must find out! Simultaneous attacks on shipping off the Norwegian coast and near the Greek islands. Fighters were equipped with rockets. We lost three ships carrying bauxite. Victories: six.

"Air combats of Luftwaffe with enemy tactical air forces in the south; four losses, no victories.

"New airbases in England are slowly being garrisoned by new 9th Air Force squadrons.

"Gentlemen, any questions? Yes, Professor Bohner?"

"Sir, flimsies and maps obtained from POWs show a definite scheme for escort fighters to protect their bombers particularly effectively when they are over the targets, and according to a certain schedule. At the same time, we have definite proof that the fighter groups supposed to rendezvous with the bombers over the target are not always there. Perhaps our own fighters are diverting their attention and that would explain the Fortresses arriving without fighter escort."

"Major Waldschmidt?"

"I can confirm Herr Professor Bohner's statement as questioning of bomber POWs revealed their anxiety to meet with the escorts. If our fighters had met the bombers over the target unescorted, they could have made devastating attacks, even spoiling the bombardiers' aim. I wonder why our fighters were not there?"

"Our fighter units had been ordered not to take off."

Killinger continues:

"The liaison officers of the navy should inquire during interrogations about the tactics used for rocket attacks on our shipping. Find the weak points and suggest countermeasures."

"The knowledge of the enemy fighters' navigation under weather conditions such as at Berin yesterday should be investigated thoroughly by the fighter interrogators today. We also need information about the new bases and units in the 9th Air Force, down to the smallest details. I come now to open questions. Work on these some more, please. First: What orders are the Allies giving to their tactical group leaders about attacking railroad trains? Many, many civilians are killed in strafing attacks, and we must know if the enemy airmen have special orders to shoot at locomotives only on passenger trains, or at the coaches too. Second: What is the significance of the shooting of ten-straight white tracer bullets in combat? Third: When do incoming escort fighters discharge their belly tanks? At sight of the enemy or after contact? This question is of special importance. No more questions? Thank you, gentlemen."

"Get there—and get back!" That is the prayer of a little girl kneeling before her bed, pressing a photograph in her hands.

The Interrogator

Do you like this poster? You see, this is the way Americans teach their people to be aware of and guard against our work. These rooms you are now seeing are the museum of our counterintelligence offices. Look at the insignias of all the enemy armies, navies, and air forces and note the distinctive marks of the various squadrons. Here is the leather jacket of the controversial "Murder Incorporated" USAAF bomber crew, which, instead of instilling fear in the hearts of Germans, has painted a picture of gangland mafia-ridden Chicago for all Europeans who see it. A collection of waterproofed silk maps of Germany, Holland, Belgium, France, Spain, Italy, Denmark, Sweden, Norway, and Switzerland. Another accumulation of GI escape money in little waterproof cotton bags: guilders, francs, belgas, pounds, lire. Puny compasses hidden in pencils, smoking pipes, uniform buttons, earplugs, rings, and whatnot. Steel saws, bowie knives, daggers and daubs, switchblade knives, helmets, caps, heated suits, heated shoes, uniforms, medals, ribbons, and wings, Horlick's concentrated food tablets, stimulants, dinghies, parachutes, cameras, goggles, pistols, ammunition, cold-meat ration tickets, dog tags, ID cards, bibles, paybooks, ration cards, orders, codes, flimsies, lucky charms, Varga pinup girls.

If one desired to do so, one could change in here in a matter of minutes into any type of soldier of any country, and if you were keen to turn into an American, we could even provide you with American chocolate, Chiclets, and chewing tobacco.

To top off one's knowledge of our enemies, we will go one step further and end our inspection of Oberursel's intelligence center with a visit to the map room, the *Lagezimmer*. There are many soldiers and girls busy here preparing a huge map of western Europe, showing each mission flown by the Allies each day. All interrogation reports relating to a singular mission are correlated and bound together in a rather voluminous book. This office resembles a public library with its reading and map room, where students and faculties read and search in silence or whisper with the attendants.

"May we see the map for the second of May, please?"

"Yes, certainly. Right over there in the register. It goes by dates."

We fumble for a moment then . . . Aha! May two! Uh huh! Daytime attack by USAAF Eighth Air Force . . . Happy Valley . . . the flak-infested Ruhr. See this big black arrow? It denotes the course of the Fortresses inbound. There are the times they took off in the UK, time coasting in at the Dutch shoreline, time over the German border, time over target. Small green arrows at each side indicate escort fighter units. We now know what target was primary and which one was their alternate target, and they are marked in red pencil. Interceptions by our fighters are shown here in time, and each place a plane was shot down is noted geographically and shows on the map in the form of two crossed swords. The black arrow, that fat one there, breaks into several points after H and Z points, the target, and shows the courses the bombers and fighter squadrons flew back to England. H = rendezvous point. Z = target.

Chapter 4: Fighters Behind Fences

Let us see if we can find that shavetail's spot of disaster. Yes, right here we see a small green cross on the right bank of the Rhine River. There is the time of crash . . . 1132 hours. Now if you needed to know which bomber group he was escorting, you could go through the records for that day and find out. However, even Shavetail Price did not know what bomb group he was escorting, and it makes no difference to us, so let's not waste a moment on trivial matters now.

What time did he leave his base at Steeple Morden? Marked in green at his base location on the map near Cambridge is a time . . . 1015 hours. That is the time his CO led the group off. I can just hear Colonel Everett Stewart radioing back to his boys, "Okay, gang. It's a piece of cake, but you guys dress it up and fly like the pros you are. Guy that gets the first Heinie today gets free drink for a week at the bar!"

Stewart is a brilliant pilot and leader, and I am looking forward to meeting him when his turn comes to visit Oberursel.

What was Lt. Price's flying position in the formation of fighters? Well, he was a wingman, like maybe Green 16, but that's not important. His squadron was on the left side of the bombers. I know because the flimsie we took as booty said "355th FG. Left of bombers over target."

What were the weather conditions over the target that day? Right here it shows it was an unusual day for May in Germany. Perfectly clear. From the altitude of the bombers, the pilots and bombardiers could probably see Monchengladbach, Aachen, Hagen, Hohenlimbourg, Iserlohn, and Kassel without squinting an eye.

Now, do you think we are prepared to talk to 21A, Lootenant Price? I love the way these Americans stretch out the "loooo." Makes the blokes right angry, and they insist on being called leftenant. Last week one bloke told an American he had just blotted his copy book for referring to him as loootenant. Made my day! Let's go back to 47 and call our stubborn friend in, shall we? What's happened? Here comes a frothing guard. Suppose someone escaped?

"Sir, I am a guard at the cooler, and I have been told to get this information to you immediately. The POW in 21A has been trying to communicate with the POW in 22 by tapping Morse code on the wall between them."

"Thank you. Did you catch what they said"?"

"Negative, sir. That Morse code is Greek to me. *Ich spreche deutsch.*"

"Thank you. You are a good man." I think this Loootenant Shavetail Price is a character. He is never going to give up. Too bad for him that the Merlin engine in his Mustang gave up the ghost; otherwise he would probably have developed into a most worthy opponent.

Into each cell of the A-wing of the cooler, a sensitive microphone has been cleverly hidden with much ingenuity. The softest whisper of any one of the inmates, fifty of them, can be heard in the reception room, where our monitor is installed. Of course, the inmates do not know for sure that we are listening, but some think we are, so mostly our listeners hear only such rude sounds as belches and farts,

The Interrogator

THROUGH THESE PORTALS...
Some of the finest fighter and bomber crews of the Allied forces passed through this gateway to the cooler at the interrogation center based at Oberursel.

THE COOLER!
This is the building called the "cooler" at Oberursel. It was a jail that had a large number of solitary cells, and nearly every flier shot down by the Germans spent a few days in this facility while being interrogated.

Chapter 4: Fighters Behind Fences

and occasionally some wiseacre makes a long speech to Hitler or Göring, who he is sure is personally monitoring every word he utters. Sometimes we go away from listening to such a tirade with tears in our eyes from laughing so hard. Once we had tears from listening to the most tender love scene of a young captain talking to his wife that I have ever heard. It was most revealing to hear an enemy flier so filled with worry and love for his pregnant wife, and everyone of us who listened wondered why we were fighting against such warm and compassionate people. War is really HELL!

Now we must get to room 47 quickly. That long barracks is a mess hall and a movie cinema in the evenings. Sometimes we take a POW there to see the movies just to give them a change in venue. Shut up, Bowser! Yes, we have watchdogs, which look very ferocious. They are to make the POWs think twice before trying to scale our fence. The dogs are quite harmless but are very ferocious looking, don't you agree? They lick your hand, and if they find a piece of sausage therein after breakfast, you have a lifelong friend. The prisoners, however, think they are bloodhounds and do not know their bark is much worse than their bite.

Corporal Kaltenhauser, Doctor of Jurisprudence, fills two jobs here. With one ear he listens to all BBC transmissions, and with the other he listens to the whispered conversations of the POWs in Wing A. His big radio set is for BBC, his jack plugs for Wing A.

"Corporal, connect us with room 21A, please."

"Oh, yes, I can hear knocking, but what does it mean?"

"Well, he is using Morse code. Very slow business because you have to pound out each letter, and without a pencil to write them down you forget the letters." Dit-dit-dit-dit—dah-dah-dah—dit-dah-dah. "What is he saying?"

"Hell, I wish I could understand Morse too. Herr Doctor, can you read what he is sending?

"Yes, sir. He just said 'How long U here?'" Dit.dit.dit.dit.dah—dah.dit.dit—dit.da—dah.dit.dah.dah. "Four days."

"Now?"

"Just a moment. He said 'Leaving?,' and the answer was 'Don't know.'"

"Talk?"

"Never."

"American?"

"Yes. B-17. You?"

"Mustang."

"Escape?"

"No good."

"Try again?"

"Me too."

Silence. We know enough. "Thank you, Doctor Kaltenhauser."

The Interrogator

Germany's triumphs in its wars have been achieved by a high degree of organization. The system that assigns to each individual his place and function in such a vast and complex mechanism secures effective cooperation only at high cost. In some respects, it sacrifices personal self-reliance and individual initiative, which are attributes and characteristics generally found in the American army. But here you find the exception to the rule. The fine mechanism would run idly if the interrogator lacked the capacity to supply it constantly with new power and motivation from his deep well of individual resourcefulness. In summing up the mountain of beforehand-gathered evidence, he must realize that his vital work really begins only when he surprisingly displays facts that undermine the morale of his adversary step by step.

"Operator, connect me with guard post 9 at the cooler, please."

"*Wache!* Please bring no. 21A to interrogation at room 47."

Stubborn, intransigent, displeasing fake-civilian Richard Price Jr., who has no dog tags, likes to smoke, but sticks to his orders to say nothing but name, rank, and serial number, is on his way to me for interrogation.

Actually, he is Second Lieutenant Price, USAAF, 0-678543, from the 355th Fighter Group at Steeple Morden, Essex, England. He was commissioned at San Antonio, Texas, on 5 May 1943. Just one year later, on 2 May, he flew as Tail-End Charlie or Green 16, covering the left side of the bomber stream with the mission of supplying escort protection over the target area, which was the Ruhr valley in Germany. On account of engine trouble, he abandoned his P-51 Mustang, marked WR Star P, before he reached the target area. Then he called on the radio, just before bailing out. He landed on the ground by parachute about 1145 hours, and he managed to evade capture. The wreckage of his plane was identified. Price had not fired a single shot. His military training is known. He will be reported as missing in action (MIA) to his next of kin by his squadron CO Jonesey Szaniawski. He wants to write home, and he wants to escape.

He may be stubborn, displeasing, but the fact remains he is a brave and loyal fighter pilot, even behind bars and fences.

I am a soldier.

I have received orders.

I am afraid, little praying girl, that I have to do the utmost, until the war comes to an end, to prevent your soldier from getting there and back.

Author comments: The use of Morse code for communications between POWs in separate cells was a chancy thing, simply because it is an international code and easily understood by anyone trained in radio CW transmissions.

POWs facing long-term incarceration always developed a much-faster and more-difficult-to-break code, since Morse code requires every letter and number to be tapped out. The American POWs in Vietnam perfected such a code, one that was short and snappy and could be tapped or even coughed, and one that the enemy captors were never able to break.

Chapter 4: Fighters Behind Fences

Quite naturally, nearly every ex-POW makes the confident claim that "Scharff certainly never got anything out of me, or, if he did, it was so unimportant that I did not know it."

However, as Scharff pointed out, the seemingly innocuous items such as order flimsies, maps, mess hall tickets, log books, escape photos, in fact, the very stitching in clothing indicating the location of the escape compasses . . . every idiosyncratic peculiarity or mannerism of a POW told the German intelligence officer some portion of a story or supplied confirmation to the mosaically composed knowledge of the enemy.

5

WITS AS WEAPONS

The force of words can do whatever is done by conquering swords.
—Euripides, 480–406 BCE

It is advantageous to study the files before bringing the prisoner into the interrogation office. Imagine oneself in the position of the POW. What would you try to hide? Most important, though, there must not be the slightest personal repugnance toward the home country of the prisoner or toward the man himself.

An interrogation is composed of three phases. At first, all that matters is to get the POW to talk, to break him in, as the camp vernacular describes it. We know that according to each adversary's natural personality and temper, each of the following will play a most significant part in his reactions; surprise, ambiguity, uncertainty, ignorance, and, as a consequence of insufficient, inaccurate intelligence training, an overrated sense of duty and honor. Common sense and a highly developed moral perception of responsibility also will influence his reactions.

Second, we must cause the POW to reveal military secrets, *if he knows any*, possibly without perceptibility. Third, the interrogator must write up an evaluation that is truthful and useful to higher-ups, so they may use it as a basis for decisions. Like a test pilot's report, it would be quite useless if the pilot could not write a report that was meaningful and understandable.

Neither commandant nor department chief had issued any rules or regulations governing how the questioning of POWs should be conducted. Control of an interrogation depended, therefore, solely on the temperament and insight of the officer in charge, an undertaking in which he received no specific training. Methods varied between individuals to a considerable degree. Results were paramount. Success was judged by the quality of the reports rendered.

Back at the time I was still COR's "Punch," I became witness one day to how one of our interrogators, Bauer, drove a totally frightened POW into a corner of

Chapter 5: Wits As Weapons

"OLD SOLDIERS NEVER DIE!"
Lt. Col. Claude Stokes of the Royal Flying Corps wrote that message to his family in England in 1917. Shortly after, he was shot down by one of Richthofen's pilots of Jasta 11. Hanns Scharff married Stokes's daughter Margaret before WWII.

the room by his mad roaring. Had I not said to myself then, should I ever be in a position to direct an inquiry, I would act in the opposite way? My desire stemmed from my sentiment to be on the side of the underdog who refuses to give up and who adheres in soldierly fashion to his allegiance. Much later it became evident to me that this impulse, if genuinely held and pursued, makes the hardest and most unflinching interrogatee vulnerable.

Often I felt the difficulty of reconciling service to my country with sympathetic emotions for my enemies. The call of duty, however, appearing to me as capital law, kept my course certain. Reprimands, nevertheless, came quite frequently from the counterintelligence people for excessive affability toward "those air gangsters." On the other hand, I always had protection from my appreciative commander. He was the man who had been captured in WWI and personified the corps d'esprit of the old army. The traditional chivalry of fighter pilots was strongly alive in him. He knows I have a British wife, and he also knows, I think with regret, that because of this, the suspicion of espionage was cast upon me and cost me twenty days in exile.

"An *old assault troop chieftain sends you his love*," wrote my father on his last picture. It shows him as a frontline soldier, in France in the trenches. He wears the Iron Cross First Class that he had won for bravery in the face of the enemy.

"*Old soldiers never die*" read the words under the last picture of my father-in-law, the lieutenant colonel who was a squadron leader in the Royal Flying Corps. He wears the Distinguished Flying Cross, won for bravery.

I like to look at both these pictures standing now, side by side, on my writing desk. They bring back the solemn instant, many years ago, when at my wedding

The Interrogator

in South Africa, guests of various nations raised their glasses to pledge the silent toast that a captain of the King's African Rifles had proposed in honor of the two fathers' supreme sacrifice. It makes me treasure in memory the noble spirit of Germany's Ace of Aces, the Red Knight, Baron Manfred von Richthofen, who had defeated the father of my wife in gallant aerial combat. They recognized each other by their squadron insignia, and when the German saw his opponent going down, he landed next to him and brought him, heavily wounded, into a field hospital. The Red Baron took brotherly care of and brought chocolate, cigarettes, and even some champagne to the squadron leader as he lay dying. He was with him at the end.

My own father died of his severe wounds on almost the same day in a remarkable coincidence!

Of all good bonds connecting me with the family of my wife and her country, the praise and honor done to the conqueror of her father had been the first and most impressive deed, perhaps destined to unfold its virtues now.

Now, back to the story of the USAAF's Lieutenant Price, an imaginary officer being used as an example to explain proceedings at Oberursel.

"Come in, please!"

"*Kriegs-Gefanagner Nr* 21A!"

"*Danke, Posten! Sie konnen gehen!*" The guard had just delivered war prisoner number 21A to me, and I thanked him and told him to return to his post.

"Step into my office, Mr. Price, or is it Lieutenant Price? Allow me to introduce myself: I am Gefreiter Hanns Scharff, and I am assigned to be your interrogation officer. Be seated, please, and let me explain to you what the procedure will be.

"Help yourself to one of those 'West Point' cigarettes, there, and please don't think that I am giving you a doped cigarette if you feel a bit dizzy after the first few puffs. That happens to every smoker who stopped smoking for a while. We had this West Point brand especially made in Holland for you guys, according to your taste, we hope. I imagine, though, that you would prefer your own brand. Unfortunately, I am unable at this moment to supply you with your own favorite type, but you will, I hope, be able to draw your POW rations from the American Red Cross and get some. What is your favorite cigarette? Lucky? Camel? Chesterfield?"

"Sorry, sir, I am Lt. Richard Price, 0-678543."

"Yes, I know that, of course, but your orders won't do over here. Do you think I would dare take the responsibility upon my shoulders in admitting you to a POW camp without first having established that you are who you say you are? Even if you had your dog tags, which I see from this questionnaire are lost, I would want more proof of your identity.

"I have seen too many false dog tags in this show already to believe in them anymore. But let me ask you something else. You say you are a second lieutenant. An American, I presume? In this case you should be acquainted with the army's

Chapter 5: Wits As Weapons

Stars and Stripes newspaper? Now I am very fond of the 'funnies,' the comic strips, especially Terry and the Pirates. Unluckily, one issue is missing, and although I have all the recent ones, perhaps you can tell me what happened to Terry in the one that is lost?" I fumbled in my desk drawers for the old issues.

"Don't bother to look for it, sir. I can tell you nothing but my name, rank and . . ."

"All right, Dick, you may have it your way, but I can foresee how we two must argue for a long, long time until I have your case cleared, and I think it is a lot of wasted breath. Naturally, I know what your orders are, and since you not only want to obey them but also wish to follow your own conception of morale, I might as well tell you where you stand."

"Sir, I stand on the grounds of the Articles of the Geneva Convention. They say that I have to give you my name, rank, and serial number and that I can refuse to answer all other questions!"

"That is your own contention, Loootenant. I am of a different opinion. Paragraph 77 of my copy stipulates more details. Read it, if you like. Among other items, it requires you to give me your home address. May I ask you for that?"

CLAUDE STOKES, RFC
Stokes earned his wings in Rhodesia in 1913 and was killed in action in WWI. His daughter became Scharff's first wife.

MANFRED FREIHERR VON RICHTHOFEN
Leader of Jasta 11, Richthofen became the top fighter ace of WWI with 80 victories. His unit was credited with the victory over Hanns Scharff's father-in-law, Claude Stokes.

The Interrogator

"Sorry, sir."

"Well now, you would, I am sure, be glad to let your folks at home know that you are a POW and well and uninjured. Equally certain I am that you would like to receive some mail from home like thousands of other POWs do. Why you should not, I cannot see, and how you will ever write home without addressing your letters, I cannot understand."

"Again, I am sorry I cannot tell you."

"There are more questions you should answer; just look at all these squares I have to fill! What is your religion? Are you in good health? Who is your next of kin? When and where were you taken prisoner? What military unit do you belong to? What is your age? Now, I don't even know whether you are a soldier, and, if you are, you must belong to some unit. In that case you surely had dog tags and you would wear a uniform. Alas, you do not. Do you really think answering those silly questions would be telling military secrets? Be reasonable! There is no law on this whole earth requiring me to send you to a POW camp and accept you as an honorable combat soldier, entitled to his rights, entitled to the privileges offered by the International Red Cross. Are you curious about those postcards there on my desk?" I had seen his eyes wandering over to them more than once.

"Don't strain your eyes, Mr. Price. Go on, have a look. They are written by American fighter pilots to their folks back home. You may, even if you do not pretend to be one of them, know some of their names? They will leave here soon, but the more time I spend with you, fruitlessly, the less time I have to devote to getting them ready for transport to a POW camp."

"Sorry, sir, I can't oblige. Name, rank, and serial number! That is the way it has to be with me, and if I have to stay here with your fleas in the cooler till the end of the war, I will."

"Oh, I know you will not stay that long. But supposing you do, how long do you think that will be?"

"I don't know, sir."

"Of course not! But I do. In fact I can tell you the exact time the war will be over. When the British are beaten down so much they submit to eating rats, and we Germans: ersatz rats!"

Dick Price was still smiling after my joke when a young girl messenger appeared, bringing me the day's mail. There was a letter for me and a parcel for me, and I asked the lieutenant's permission to read the letter since I could not resist opening the news from my family. While he smoked—yes, he now accepted every offer of a cigarette and looked at the pictures of my wife and children that had slipped out of the letter onto my desk—I read the letter and then opened the package.

Before I say what the contents were, I must state that my wife can make the finest Boston Baked Bread between Capetown and Hamburg, and she had baked this soldier's delight especially for me. My stomach reacted instantly when the bread came into sight, and I was ravenously hungry. A good soldier is always

Chapter 5: Wits As Weapons

hungry, I think, and POW Dick Price was hungry too. In fact, I feel quite sure all our POWs were hungry all the time, whether they had just eaten or not. Young men all seem to have a hollow leg where they store food for later digestion.

As soon as the beautiful cake was unrolled from its waxed-paper wrapping, we tried a slice. My thoughts wandered home, and I'll bet Dick's thoughts did also. We had a second slice. Dick seemed to like it, and I definitely did. We had some more. My wife was not a member of the intelligence team, but she baked the best Boston Baked Bread I had ever eaten this time. Before long, Dick and I had finished it all, and we carefully picked up and ate every loose crumb.

"Lieutenant Price, your comment about fleas in our cooler was not very nice. Really, are they back again? You accuse me of something bad, but surely you do not hold me responsible. Believe me, we fumigate the place once a week. I am aware how horrible it is to be continually harassed by the little brute. Tell you what—I'll give you written permission to take a daily bath if you'll promise not to blame me for those fleas. After all, they are not German fleas, they are Allied subjects brought here by your compatriots. I have none in my own quarters at all." Dick smiled. The cake had relaxed him, it seemed. "Well, thanks for the bath permission. But don't get me wrong, sir; I still cannot tell you anything but name, rank, and serial number."

"Oh, stop that! I would not ask you to spill a military secret in exchange for a shower. You may also read books all you wish, and I am going to give you special permission to have your window open whenever you want. And if you want to shave every day, the guards have the necessary tools."

"Thanks, sir."

"Don't mention it. Now take my advice and don't stay here at Auswertestelle West too long; that is, unless you are knowledgeable about some military secrets of extraordinary value. Now I know you will not have any of those secrets, but I have to make sure. That is my job, you know. Would you, for instance, consider the letters painted on your fighter a secret?"

"Yes, I would not and cannot divulge them to you."

"Why? In my opinion, one does not paint a secret on an airplane in huge letters that can be read from a long distance away, even from the ground, if no one is supposed to know what they are. Why that display if secret?"

"Can't say."

"Do you perhaps think it is a secret that 8th and 15th USAAF is fighting a war against Germany? If so, *Stars and Stripes* would not be allowed to print things about it, would they?"

"All I can tell you is name, rank, and . . ." However, Dick's rather tight smile had now relaxed a bit and was wider.

"And now, Dick, all I want from you, talking straight from the shoulder and eyeball to eyeball, is some dope to put in these squares on this form. When and where will the Allied invasion of Europe take place? Wait! There is, quite naturally,

The Interrogator

some doubt in my mind that General Eisenhower shares this interesting secret with you."

"Look here, sir, I am just a soldier and I obey my orders."

"OK, Dick, I meant no disrespect toward you. What I was trying to convey was the ridiculousness of this situation in which we are. I must identify you as a good and proper American army officer . . . or rather, you must identify yourself." Noticing how the interrogatee's stern expression had eased off just ever so little, I quickly applied one of my favorite jokes, an invention of mine that had never failed up to this time.

"If you maintain that you are Lieutenant Price, 0-678543, then I must reintroduce myself to you. My real name is Colonel Hanns Bullshit, and my number in the Luftwaffe just happens to be 20,000!"

"Ha! Baloney! Nice trick," says Richard as he reaches for another cigarette, "but it won't work, Colonel B."

"Oh, no, my friend; no trick at all. See here, I have my dog tags here to prove it." I opened my shirt and removed the dog tags from around my neck and handed them to him.

"Colonel B. Number 0-20,000! Right! But I better just call you Hanns." "Please, do, Dick," I replied, reclaiming the dog tags but noting that Dick's attitude had visibly changed from stubbornness to a fine shade of amenity. Outwardly he appears relaxing; inwardly, bewilderment ripens.

ANXIOUS POWS ARRIVE AT THE INTERROGATION CENTER
The future looks bleak for these American fliers who have been captured and are arriving at the interrogation center at Oberursel. Scharff took this photo from his office window.

Chapter 5: Wits As Weapons

"I can't make heads or tails of this, Hanns. Here I know I am Lieutenant Price, but I have no dog tags to prove it. There you are with dog tags proving you are Colonel B, yet I know you are not. Something very phony going on here."

"Yes, of course. Phony and funny, yet very serious. Look over here at my guest book, Dick. See here what one of your famous Eagle Squadron pilots has written:

DULAG-LUFT, "DER KOOLER"
OFFICE OF DER INTERROGATOR

Interrogator: "How do you do? Who are you and how did you get into Germany?"

Young Fighter Pilot: "I am an American officer; my name is K. G. Smith. My rank is captain and my serial number is 0-885 251. Here is my proof, my dog tag."

Interrogator: "Oh, yes! Allow me to introduce myself, and here is my dog tag to prove it—COL. BULLSHIT, 0-20,000, Johannesburg, South Africa."

"In other words, Dick, he admitted that he found himself in the very same situation as you do now, a position in which any intelligent individual must see its absurdity. Right?"

Price's curiosity catches him off-guard almost completely. He laughs openly and points again to the dog tags.

"Good show, Colonel B. May I look at the guest book some more?"

"Certainly! But first, I think this entry will interest you even more. In this book I have entered all the names, ranks, dates, squadrons, groups of all POWs passing through my office. Please note that there is not one fighter pilot who has not stated his squadron and group."

"No! Here is one who left his squadron number blank!"

"Of course! He was a colonel and commander of a group. He may have flown with a squadron the day he had his bad luck, but actually he is assigned only to the group, not a squadron. Right?"

"Right! Still, according to our intelligence briefings, these guys have all broken with their loyalty codes. They should have told you only the three identity items: name, rank, serial number!"

"Oh come, now, Dick! In the first place, every one of them is just as good and conscientious a soldier as you claim to be. Second, they are not traitors because not one told me a real military secret. Furthermore, they had to get out of Oberursel sometime. You don't think I invented these squadron and group numbers or grabbed them out of thin air, do you? Like a magician? And Dick, you don't think you can leave here being the only one with the spaces for the squadron and group left blank, do you?"

"Well, Stony Face, I learned from your guest book what these other POWs call you; all I can reiterate is name, rank, and serial."

"Dick! You might at least tell me what type of plane you crashed or bailed out of. We need the information in order to identify some abandoned planes we found lying around the countryside."

"Sorry, I just cannot do it."

"Well, *Stars and Stripes* makes no bones about it, do they? Read."

ZEMKE GROUP BOOSTS "KILL" TOTAL TO 508

AN EIGHTH AIR FORCE BASE: July 5: Col. Hubert Zemke's Wolfpack outfit, highest-scoring fighter group in the ETO, marked the 4th of July by shooting down 17 German aircraft, boosting its total to 508 kills in the air. It became the first pursuit unit in the theater to destroy more than 500 enemy aircraft in aerial combat.

The group boasts 38 aces and the leading U.S. fighter pilot, Lt. Col. Francis E. Gabreski of Oil City, Pa., who is now credited with 28 enemy planes in the air.

"You are not supposed to know all that!"

"Yet, I do, Dick. Right there in *Stars and Stripes*, and I or almost anyone else can read about it. Secrets? Maybe your great Colonel Zemke and the top-scoring ace, this Francis Gabreski, will both come walking through that door one day. They will be very surprised, like you are, that I know these small details. They would be even more surprised if they heard how I obtain my information, I am sure."

Dick swallowed hard. "Oh well, famous men like them are known equally well on both sides. They can't help that, but I do not recall *Stars and Stripes* ever having given me any write-up, so there is no information for you on me, is there? Only the three idents you get from me."

"Okay! I want to tell you a true story, Dick, so listen carefully. You can verify the facts just as soon as you get into one of our permanent camps, where you will meet this colonel and his buddy. I hope this example helps you understand why you must identify yourself. Not long ago, one of your well-known fighter aces, a lieutenant colonel named Jonesy Szaniawski, was downed, and when he bellied his plane in he found himself surrounded by a large number of our panzers, our tanks. Of all places, he had landed right on the practice grounds of the panzers.

"His buddies, flying overhead and watching his forced landing, covered his escape by strafing some of the tanks. They also burned his airplane. The colonel, being an athletic type, was bent on escaping, so he ran up a hill trying to reach a nearby woods. However, our panzers were a bit aggravated about the strafing they got, pursued him, and started shooting at him with their big guns and everything else they had. There is no fighting against such fearful odds, and the panzer boys soon took him as their prisoner and forwarded him here according to the standing orders about captured fighter pilots.

"When arriving up here, he turned out to be a very cheerful and pleasant man, a tough fighter in the air but a refined man on the ground. He did not mind discussing general matters of no significance, but he was always on guard, just as you are."

Chapter 5: Wits As Weapons

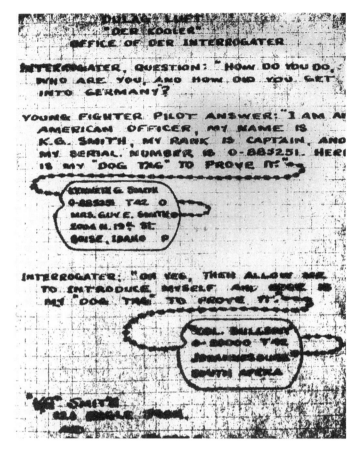

PAGE 17 OF SCHARFF'S GUEST BOOK
Capt. K. G. Smith of Boise, Idaho, was one of the Eagle Squadron pilots who came to visit Scharff at Oberursel. He soon discovered that military dog tags do not suffice for identification purposes because Scharff had one too. Smith made this entry in Scharff's guest book.

"Excuse my interruption, Hanns, but did he give you his group and squadron number?"

"No, he did not. I knew it long before he came in, well known as Jonesy is with his score and that nickname. However, interrogation was over very quickly with him, since we had jokingly agreed that he was unable to tell me when and where the invasion would start. We argued the old and thrashed-out point as to whether name, rank, and serial number would be sufficient for any POW to identify himself as an honorable combat soldier. Just then I heard a commotion outside and stepped to that window to see a group of about forty civilians being marched

The Interrogator

into the grounds. They were guarded by police, not by Luftwaffe soldiers. They stopped right here below my window, lined up in three rows, backs toward me.

"'Here, come to the window, Colonel, and take a peep.' Jonesy came over and looked out too. I continued: 'Odd crows like this come in here almost daily, and they all claim to be from some Allied air force. Yet, by appearance, they look like peasants or workmen, even like spies! They have, I know beforehand, no dog tags and no papers to identify them as soldiers, and all they can remember is name, rank, and serial number. They were caught probably by Gestapo agents somewhere along the Channel coast while being transsshipped back to the UK. Now tell me frankly, Colonel, and let me remind you beforehand that not all you chaps are well known over here like you are; would you say all those men are soldiers? Place yourself in my position, please. Would you take the responsibility and the risk to admit that motley crowd into a regular POW camp, where they would enjoy all the rights and privileges guaranteed and provided by the International Red Cross for combat soldiers?'

"The colonel looked, slightly bewildered, at the guys in French berets, some with their trousers halfway up to the knees, some in Dutch wooden fisher shoes, one in a skiing costume, and one in an old German army greatcoat. Indeed, it was a colorful and spectacular crowd, not the least resemblant of military soldiers. 'Colonel,' I asked him, 'do those chaps look like American fliers to you?' I waited only a moment.

'Hell!' he replied. 'Not very much. I don't think I would.'

He froze a moment then suddenly shouted with excitement.

'Look there! One of my buddies is in that gang!'

'Which one,' I asked.

'The one fourth from the right in the front row.'

'What is his name?'

'Kosinski. First Lieutenant Kosinski!'

'Same squadron and same group as yours?'

'Yep!'

"Well, I begged Colonel Jonesy to be patient for a while, and I went to my files to see what we had on Kosinski. Kosinski had fortunately been mentioned in a newspaper article, too, but I had to know if it was the same Kosinski or whether Jonesy was trying to pull the wool over my eyes. Then I returned and took the colonel into a room directly behind the man in the ranks out on the parade grounds. I opened one pane of the window and yelled as loud as I could. 'First Lieutenant Kosinski!'

"As if struck by lightning the fourth man in the front rank spun around to locate the voice. I ordered the guard to have that man sent to room 47 and, along with Lt. Col. Jonesy, awaited the arrival of the decrepit individual who looked like a peasant, acted like a spy, and who, hoping he would not be shot as a spy, wanted to change his identity to one of a common soldier POW very quickly.

Chapter 5: Wits As Weapons

"Now I ask you, Dick, is it unworthy of a merited soldier, after having plummeted safely from heaven into such an ordeal, to shed a tear when he finds his colonel and buddy waiting for him in prison camp?"

"I spared all routine work and red tape for this *falsch* 'spy' because this colonel, this Jonesy, had identified him. They left together for the permanent prison camp within a number of hours. You will, as I said, meet both of them there and can talk to them about this, and will you also be so kind as to give them both my best wishes? Too bad for you, Dick, that you do not have a colonel at hand who will speak for you and rescue you from your own mess." The lieutenant seemed a mite disturbed.

"There is a difference," he ventured. "You already knew the colonel's group and other details. In my case you do not, and I cannot tell you."

"Lieutenant Price! My shavetail friend! Let us suppose, for a moment, that instead of being the flier I think you are, that you really are an American spy or British spy! We caught you, and you have no dog tags. You insist on the three identity answers. You leave it entirely up to me to decide whether you're a spy who will be shot or soldier who will live. If I were the spy, I would claim to be a soldier exactly as you are doing. Yes?"

Lt. Price's muscles in his jaws visibly tightened. I could see the wheels and cogs in his thinking apparatus were at work. Casually I continued, slowly, softly, convincingly, "I suggest you tell me just enough to prove that you are what you claim to be, not a spy pretending to be a soldier. Maybe you should tell me the number of your outfit and perhaps some technical things about your airplane that a spy would not know about? I know it already, but a spy would not, so you will not be spilling any beans, I assure you." Price stared at my right ear as if something was on it, but said nothing.

"Lieutenant, please don't make it difficult for us."

"I have nothing whatever to say, sir."

I smiled at Price. "Well, perhaps tomorrow you will have thought all this over. The sooner you get out of here, the better for you. *You know that?*"

Now he stared at me in utter surprise.

"Yes! The sooner the better!" I almost yelled vehemently.

There was a pause and I waited until Dick started to speak, but I interrupted him, not wanting to give him the chance to talk just now. I wanted him to think, not talk.

"And in the meantime, is your health good? Do you need a doctor for anything at all?"

"No."

"Okay, good afternoon, Lieutenant. Until tomorrow!" I saluted him and called the guard to return him to his cell. Slowly, almost imperceptibly, Dick's attitude had been changing; the stubborn atmosphere had softened. Our parting had been almost a friendly one at that.

The Interrogator

HOW DOES IT WORK?
General Jimmy Doolittle and General Jessie Auton query Col. Dave Schilling and Col. Hubert Zemke (*far right*) about the new external fuel tanks, which will extend the range of American fighters. Next to Zemke is Gen. Tooey Spaatz. When the fighters extended their range, more American pilots came to Oberursel as POWs.

357th GROUP ACE AT EASE
John L. Sublette sits on the fireplace mantle at Leiston, England. Sublette scored 8 victories. Scharff had a full dossier on Sublette and other members of the group.

Chapter 5: Wits As Weapons

(Reader, please note here that I would not call any officer by his first name or nickname, or even *Looo*tenant, except that Dick was not sure of my rank, and being friendly with him was getting results.)

There was a reason other than the Geneva Convention Rules for the Americans to instruct their pilots to give out only name–rank–serial number. Again and again the intelligence officers at the English bases emphasized in their lectures how important it would be for any squadron member falling into enemy hands to leave the Luftwaffe evaluation center as quickly as possible. Any man remaining there more than a few days could only be regarded as suspect and might even find himself the subject of a court-martial when he was eventually repatriated.

The thought behind this American doctrine was simple. A POW, it assumed, who remains there for over a week is being kept by the Germans on account of his willingness, or stupidity or ignorance, to talk too much or to reveal secrets. The more he talks, the longer he will be milked by the enemy. The less he would say, on the other hand—namely three answers only, the more rapidly we would discard him as useless, sending him out to a regular POW camp promptly.

This was the wrong attitude for the Americans to take, and it played right into our hands. I made use of it to urge all interrogatees to avoid a long stay at Auswertestelle West. From our German point of view, the situation was reversed. *The talkers were done with very quickly and sent on.*

I can account for only one single incident of a prisoner offering information soon after his arrival. He was quickly processed and done with and promptly sent on his way in two or three days. After all, it would take only a few hours to get all the information he had, once the man was ready to talk.

I can also remember hundreds of loyal soldiers who put up terrific struggles, day after day and week after week. A man who tenaciously clung to his instructions, holding out in his forlorn post, was regarded by us with great respect. In many cases, unreliability should have been the charge against those prisoners leaving Oberursel too quickly, rather than against those staying with us, as the Allies believed.

I personally did not interrogate all prisoners. Many were assigned to departments other than mine, as, for instance, the Bomber Interrogation Section. Conditions there were different. One interrogator there would not question all ten men of one plane's crew. He might select the pilot and the navigator, or whomever he might choose, and send the remainder straightaway to a permanent camp, just to make room in our limited cells for new arrivals. This was particularly true when our Luftwaffe shot down sixty daylight bombers and several more planes landed badly damaged, and we were swamped with new prisoners. We often had great numbers of fighter pilots arriving, too, but nothing on the scale of the bombers with their big crews.

Let us take our hats off to those who chose to go the long and hard route at Auswertestelle West.

The Interrogator

There are lots of things on a POW's mind while he is lying on his hard straw mattress in his cell after a restless night. The sergeant in charge of the library at the cooler had telephoned me to say that Lt. Price had chosen James Hilton's *Goodbye Mr. Chips*, but I doubt if Dick enjoyed it very much. He had read the simplest lines three times, but his thoughts would wander off. He would skip a few pages and try to get interested, but he just could not concentrate. He is unquiet, restless, tossing and turning. How he would like to have the ammunition to fight back against my convincing arguments. Imagine his thoughts:

"That damn guest book! The phony dog tags . . . What is your home address and the number of your military unit and the letters on your fighter?

"Hell yes, I want to write home and I want my family to know I am a POW and am alive, and I want my unit to know it, too, but if all I can give is my name, rank, and serial number without being court-martialed later on for treason, how will anyone ever know? What shall I do?

"That newspaper clipping about Zemke! This colonel Jonesy! A spy? Goddamn, how could anyone take me for a spy? But maybe, from Hanns's point of view . . . The sooner out of here, the better, he had said. What was he trying to tell me? He seems like a good head, not at all what I had expected, and has not threatened nor has he put toothpicks up under my fingernails or put presses on my gonads. Haven't seen a cruel German yet, so maybe we Americans are propagandized too? All my buddies have given him their squadron and group numbers . . . I saw them in the guest book and they were exactly correct, no attempt to mislead Hanns there. I even saw Lt. Hecht's name in there, and we all thought he had bought the farm. So glad to know he's alive. But my squadron and group numbers, my fighter plane number? My mission? No! Nope! Never! Nein! That's out of the question. What happens to a West Pointer when he becomes a captive? Does that oath he takes about never lying or cheating or tolerating people who do continue right into the enemy camps? Will have to check that one out some day with a West Pointer . . ."

Dick, I think I know the trend of your thoughts, and I am going to destroy your illusions. I am going to break your resistance completely. First, I wanted to make you think out the principal problems concerning your current situation. That is the reason I refrained from disclosing any part of the information I already have on you. Having put my key of psychological technique into you, I am now going to turn that key and unlock you . . . open your lock.

Come on, now, let's fight it out! One on one, so they say.

We saluted each other as he came in. I never use that German Heil Hitler salute but give a salute that all German soldiers give to each other, and it is almost exactly like the American soldier's salute. Then we shook hands, which is an ingrained German custom. I invited Dick to have a chair, and a cigarette, then smilingly began:

"Well, Lieutenant, you can stop worrying about whether we might mistake you for a spy."

Chapter 5: Wits As Weapons

A sigh of relief escaped him even though he tried to hide it. However, he was still wary. I leaned forward from my chair and with a slight wink continued: "Tell me, Dick, has Curly Brown ever gotten himself straightened out about that time he walked across the ceiling?"

Dick's facial muscles tightened and his eyes narrowed ever so slightly. It was a yarn of late date about some of the 355th pilots. Frau Biehler had it in her files. An earlier prisoner had spun the yarn innocently, since it had merely been a practical joke, but we had noted it down for use on such occasions just as this one now. "Hanns, I don't know anyone named Curly Brown."

"Good heavens, Dick!" I said laughingly. "You from the 355th and haven't heard that tale? Come now, maybe you've just forgotten it. Curly jingled there in the officers' club at Steeple Morden one night and slept in a chair. Bill Cooper and Mike Jones took his shoes off and made your chief steward, old Sniffy Megaw, bring them some shoe polish and a ladder. They blacked the soles of his shoes, climbed the ladder, and made footprints up one wall, across the ceiling, and down the other wall. The last I heard about it, Curly has begun to believe he really did walk across that ceiling when he was snockered. Does he still think so?"

"I'll be damned, Hanns; how did you know that story?"

"Well, Dick, you won't believe it, but I have a direct line to Pinetree. You wouldn't know where that is, though. A little place north of London where Jimmy Doolittle has his 8th Air Force headquarters."

"BIG CHIEF" BARTH AND FAMILY
Horst Barth poses with his wife and his son Bodo. As Hanns Scharff's boss, Barth was quick to realize that Scharff was truly a wizard at inquisitions.

The Interrogator

The lieutenant had not blinked an eyelid when I told him this, and the only thing he had done when I mentioned his unit as the 355th was a slight contraction of the pupils of his eyes. I firmly believe the pupils of a person's eyes tell more secrets than any other part of the human body. I continued, since I now had his undivided attention:

"Your 8th Fighter Command in that air force consists of fifteen groups divided into three wings, which are the 65th, 66th, and 67th. To which wing does the 355th group belong?"

"I'm not saying, Hanns."

"All right, I'll tell you. To General Auton's 65th."

"Could be. Could be."

"Do you know a Colonel Arthur G. Salisbury and do you know what his position in the headquarters might be?"

"Never heard of him, Hanns."

"That Steeple Morden is a lousy place to live, by the way. Almost as bad as Colchester. These Limey fireplaces look cozy, but they never warm you properly . . . unless you are bundling, of course. And in that red brick building . . . Wow! And your O Club in a fancy Quonset hut must be freezing, too, because the brick fireplace at one end of the library isn't enough to heat it. Even the pot-bellied stove in the game room can't hack it, I'll bet. And that ancient gramophone you have there makes me wonder if you guys can stand such distorted music. Sickening just to think of it. I would prefer to hear Al Peterson sing his Texas songs to that."

"You would, eh? Well, Pete won't sing any more for us, since the last time I saw him he was going down in flames, and no one saw him get out. I liked that gutty guy."

"Dick, he did get out, but he can't sing for a while because he is pretty badly burned about the face. Our medic says he will be all right again but will need quite a bit of skin transplant. You can see him later, if you like."

"I can? Honest? Alone? That's swell!"

"All right, that can be arranged, but he is too bandaged up to do much talking. Tell me, did you two guys train together?"

"Sorry, Hanns, I cannot tell you that."

"Then I guess it's up to me to tell you the answers. No, you did not train together. He is just a young replacement boy who does not even know that you graduated from the Air Corps Advanced Flying School at San Antonio as a fighter pilot in May, the 5th of May 1943."

Eyes, facial muscles, posture, face coloring; all changed very slightly as Dick was perplexed and gasped: "Yes . . . er . . . Hanns!"

"He did not come over on the *Queen Elizabeth* with you and the group, either, but I am sure he hated Gourock and Greenock on the Clyde River as much as you did?"

Chapter 5: Wits As Weapons

Dick now almost roared in laughter, nervous laughter, because I noted his hand trembling slightly as he lighted another cigarette. "What else do you know about me, Hanns?"

"Who is asking the questions here, Lieutenant? Am I not the interrogator and you the interrogatee? Let's not get the cart before the horse or I'll lose face here at Auswertestelle West. Now! Tell me the date of your last mission, please."

"Do you know it, or is this a game?"

"Of course I know it, but I want you to tell me. Got to fill squares."

"How do I know that you know?"

"Well, I'll write it on this piece of paper . . . there . . . and you tell me . . . then look at the date I have written down. Fair enough?"

"It's a deal!"

"Well?"

"It was the second of May."

"Look at the date. May second, right? And to make it easier for you, I will tell you what time you took off from Steeple Morden, too. It was at 1015 hours, and then you bailed out at 1132 hours on your way in to the target, without having fired a shot from your guns, your 50s. Your P-51 Mustang was marked WR Star P, and the engine quit on you over the Rhineland."

"How the hell could you know where it quit!?" Price asked sharply.

I laughed and leaned back in my chair, slapping my knee gently. "Ah, but you were lucky it quit so near the Rhine River and you could find a hiding place and later escape into France. You were just unlucky with your V-1650 engine. It's a rare thing for a Mustang engine to quit in flight, or so it seems to us here. By the way, how's Captain Charlie Blair from Texas doing? We hear he is one of the hottest throttle jockeys in the 355th and can really make a Mustang sing."

I really wanted no answer, so almost without hesitation I continued on, letting my complete familiarity with his identity and his experience sink in. "Be glad, though, that you did not get as far as Happy Valley, where you were to rendezvous with the Fortresses. Too much flak there, and they would have picked on you when you dropped out of formation. You were to give the bombers left-side cover, and you were Tail-End Charlie, remember? What flight were you in?"

"D Flight, dammit. Don't you know?"

"Naturally I do, but I have to check thoroughly because you have given the impression here that you are someone other than Lt. Price. D Flight of the 354th squadron, 355th Group. Your Mustang serial number? I doubt if you would remember that, Dick, but here it is right here, 42-108950. We can tell from serial numbers just how many have been manufactured, since we know the starting number for each annual series. How D Flight was the red flight that day and you were 'Red Four.' Your squadron call sign, what was it?"

"That really is secret, Hanns."

"Well, no secret at all. It was Catspaw! You called, 'Catspaw White One, this

The Interrogator

is Red Four . . . bailing out now, engine trouble!'"

"You son of a gun, Hanns! You got that too?"

"I think you boys have more trouble memorizing your call signs than we have, because we write them down each time they are changed, whereas you have to forget one and use another so often."

Dick shook his head from side to side. "Incredible! I'll believe anything you tell me now, Hanns. I think you must have had an exquisite training in the intelligence field. Of course, we have heard many romantic stories about the amazing and mysterious German spy system, and I would not be surprised if you named someone in my own outfit as one of your agents. When do I get the booze and the girls?"

"Excellent deduction, Lieutenant. One thing you Americans do causes us some confusion, though. There is a 357th Squadron in the 355th Group, you know, the OS markings, but there is also a Mustang outfit called the 357th Group over at Leiston. The CO is a Colonel Donald Graham, and there are some hotshot aces there. One is a guy called Kit Carson. I hope to get to meet him, since I hope he is related to your famous explorer of the same name. Also one is John England, and I hope to see him, too, since I admire England, the country, and it will be fun to make his acquaintance. Look at the names of pilots in the 357th Group! Foy, Broadhead, Bochkay; Storch is a real German name! Dregne, Karger, Sublette, Yeager, and Kirla! I am quite fascinated by those names. But when you go home again, will you speak to your war department about using the same numbers for different organizations? It would help us a lot if they would refrain from that practice, I assure you.

"Now, my friend, I think I can fill all the squares in this questionnaire without you having to spill any secrets at all. What is your home address, so we can tell them you are okay, and you can write home yourself?"

"2204 Main Street. Dallas, Texas, in care of my parents, Mr. and Mrs. Richard Price Sr."

"You better slide up here to the desk and write the postcard to them yourself. They'll be glad to hear from you because the USAAF has already reported you as 'missing in action,' Dick."

"Thanks. Would it be okay if I wrote two cards?"

"Go ahead. The other one to the nicest girl in the world?"

"Yes! You are a grand guy, Hanns. It's too bad you are on the wrong side!" Dick was now in a happy mood, acting perfectly natural, relieved and free of most of his troubling thoughts. He wrote his two messages while I filled out the twenty-odd squares in the questionnaire. Presently I suggested with a friendly smile, "Lieutenant, what say, now that we are all through with the interrogation, that we go for a walk. It's one hell of a fine day outside, and I know you must be getting sick of that cooler. There is some very pretty countryside around here, and you should see it before you head out on the next transport for Dulag Luft and a POW camp."

Chapter 5: Wits As Weapons

SPRINGBOK CIGARETTES
South African lieutenant Deryck Birch was captured and brought to Hohe-Mark hospital badly wounded. Scharff walked over to the hospital to visit him and brought him a pack of cigarettes.

"Great! I'd love some fresh air! You mean . . . ?"

"Will you give me your word of honor as an officer not to try to escape during the time you walk with me? It saves me from having to take a guard along, or a gun, and I couldn't shoot you anyway."

"All right. You have my word of honor as an American military officer."

"Good, then just sign this slip right there, please, which I will return to you when we come back. After we are back here, you are free to plan any escape you have been thinking about, because you will no longer be my responsibility."

Dick laughed heartily. "OK! I promise to hold in abeyance my escape at least until I am out of your jurisdiction, Hanns. By the way, I am hungry as hell, and if we leave now I'll miss chow call in the cooler. Lousy food down there, but better than nothing, and I'm hungry."

"Don't worry about that. We will dig up some food along the road. You know I would not let you starve. Besides, the food outside might be better than it is inside, this time of year. Potluck, you know."

Perhaps it is a little difficult for you to comprehend the profound effect all this chatter had upon the junior Richard Price. But then, of course, you have to be twenty-one years old, a prisoner of war who has been in a sort of solitary confinement for days, and suspected of being a spy or an intelligence agent eligible to be shot, before you really understand the pressures on him. He had obeyed his orders exactly. He had been firm in his determination not to answer even the most innocuous or plausible of questions, even to the extent that we might become convinced he really was a spy.

The Interrogator

We had him taped from early on. I knew the answer to every question except his home address beforehand.

We strolled out through the country lanes. Under the circumstances, in the face of my obvious friendliness and my simple manner of forgetting for a little while that we were military enemies, it was quite impossible for the lieutenant to walk along in complete silence. The manners he had been taught in a pleasant home back in America prevented him from that sort of glumness, and so he began to talk a little about himself. Oh, not military matters at all, but about the trees and shrubbery we passed, about the birds that were singing in a thicket nearby, about a castle on a nearby hilltop, about the roaming prairies of Texas.

We passed an anthill in the woods, and I stopped and threw my handkerchief over the top of it, covering just the top, thinking it might amuse my new friend to see what would happen. As a little boy roaming through the forests, I had watched how the disturbed ants attacked the handkerchief. They would, I knew, sting it and eject a strong acid, which, if brought close to one's nose, smells very much like smelling salts.

We bent down and watched the tiny creatures running hither and thither, some just excited, others charging and snapping at the cloth. Was instinct ruling their behavior or was it intelligence? Were they ruled by one all-encompassing thought or did they act as individuals? We discussed it quite a while.

"Observe these here, Dick. They seem to be clearing the entrance holes of the debris and destruction I caused with my hand. Very much like our own air raid precaution squads."

"I would say they act more like soldiers."

"Why? Because they are running off with the eggs?"

"No, I meant that they act as if they were under orders."

"Hmmm. Do you think their queen is an absolute potentate?"

"No, more like a president, like we have, because their home seems well run, their social life well organized, so they must have a sense of colonization. They have friends and enemies . . . see, watch those two!"

"Dick, you Americans are so sheltered! I beg to differ with you. If it is a question of organization, a dictator would be their ruler. I think I can see they have a caste system. See, there are slaves . . . right there is a batch of them. There are minor workers, like those over there, who may be apprentices or youths too young to shoulder the heavy loads, and I see specialists such as this one here who does an intricate operation and then hands the finished product to a worker to transport to the interior of the anthill. I'll swear that gang lined up doing arms drill are soldiers. Look at that . . . just like shoulder arms as they move those blades of grass in unison! And I'd say those helter-skelter ants are the individualists. They most likely just scramble hither and thither watching everyone else."

"Man! What an imagination you have, Hanns. I can see why you are in intelligence work now. You see so much deeper than most people. In fact, you make me think that Americans have a tendency to be very shallow people. But about

Chapter 5: Wits As Weapons

these ants; we don't know whether they are a democratic race or a fascist race—probably the latter since you say they have slaves."

"Ho, ho! Do you mean to admit Americans were fascists before your famous Abraham Lincoln freed the slaves?" I hesitated for a long moment, since he did not reply. Then I continued, "Darwin states that in England their ants do not enslave other species, but it is reported that in America a colony of bellicose red ants will foray upon a colony of black ants for the purpose of enslaving them. That has been observed frequently."

"Oh, yeah? Malarky! Our American ants have freedom of speech, freedom of religion, freedom of gathering, freedom of press and politics!"

"Sorry, Dick. No offense. Could they be communists? The ants."

"Come to think of it, they must be. Note that they are RED ants. Yep! They are dominated by a collective system, don't you agree?"

"You like organization, I can see. Do you like the idea of Bolshevism?"

"Hell no! Jeez, Hanns, you know that without asking!"

"Neither do I, Dick. Equalization just does not work out. Comes the revolution, we'll all be revolting! Right? Mediocrity is the result of communism as I see it. Everyone is brought down to the level of the lowest common denominator, so that no one is better than the other. Secrecy proliferates, since the most capable and smartest must be kept out of sight. Listen! Our own propaganda forced a slogan down our throats for years, mainly in wintertime, which said: "Nobody shall freeze! Nobody shall starve!" The slogan was well meant, but the people answered: "You see, we are not even allowed that anymore!""

This seemed to tickle Dick's funny bone, as he laughed heartily. "We have the same kind of stories, too, of course. He told one about Roosevelt, but it was too subtle for me to catch the point, and I was too embarrassed to acknowledge I did not understand it, so I laughed along with him. We discussed political events and economic conditions in America. I listened as the voice of the average enemy spoke, unhindered and quite frankly. As we meandered along a path, we came to a little coffee house secluded in the woods, and we went in and I ordered cheese rolls and tea for both of us. There was no sugar or lemon or cream for the tea, but it was hot and tasted delicious to both of us. We hated to go back to Auswertestelle West, he to the cooler and me to room 47.

This little incident was the origin of a long series of political interrogations at Oberursel. Just because I had noticed how easy it was to get Americans involved in arguments reflecting on political and economic outlooks, differences, and conditions, I led many other POWs along this path, annoying the ants and obtaining interesting information. From that day on until the end of the war, those ants must have wondered why they had to rebuild their castle over and over again just because some captured POW and his unarmed Jerry escort had passed by.

On the way back, I told Dick some more yarns about his group, his buddies, and his base, just chinning along with no pretense that any of it was important. I

101

The Interrogator

talked about his CO, who had married an English girl, and about the new fur-collared leather flying jackets some of the American bomber crews were sporting now. He took it all in and sometimes could not keep astonishment from showing on his youthful face. Well, of course he knew nothing at all of BUNA or Sgt. Nagel.

I kept in the background the three critical questions that had been brought up at officer's briefing. They concerned the shooting of white tracer bullets, orders about strafing ground targets, and the discharge of the long-range belly tanks from the fighters. I had thought it best to convince Dick first that our information already was so complete that nothing he could tell us would be news, and, to be honest, I had not yet decided how I should phrase each question so that he would not clam up again. This display of intimate acquaintance with his affairs and his friends was, to him, altogether dazzling and shocking, and he was thrown off balance, I'm sure.

In his own expression, Dick was not sure which end was up anymore. Instead of beaten with truncheons, seduced by women and wine, he was walking along a quiet woods talking to a pretty good skate of a fellow for a Kraut. This Heinie already knew all there was to know about the 354th, the 355th Group, about Mustangs, and about Lieutenant Price from Dallas. What was all this stuff about secrecy, tight lips, say nothing but name, rank, and serial number? Hell's bells! This Kraut wasn't even asking questions anymore.

AXE THE AXIS
Lt. Peter E. Pompetti, USAAF, had five victories when German flak ended his quest for top honors in the 78th Fighter Group. Scharff enjoyed Pompetti's sense of humor, a humor that lasted right up to his death on 25 April 1985.

Chapter 5: Wits As Weapons

At this point, knowing full well what Dick was thinking, I used another very simple bit of psychology. Conversationally, and as if we were just continuing our discussions about the different ways of life between Americans and Europeans, I mentioned the logistics problems the Americans were having operating off English bases. All were true and known to us, and to him, and then I slipped the real McCoy into him casually.

"It is too bad America did not have more experience in working off English bases, since it sometimes overloads your industry back home, such as they now have run out of the chemicals they use to make red tracer bullets. Those white ones you fellows are using in your dogfights must be rather hard to follow with your eyes, so you have to shoot a whole string of them; ten, twenty, even fifty of them."

You see the point. The lieutenant may be excused, I think, for not seeing it. For hours I had been telling him things about myself and about himself and his outfit, all of them very factual. I did not know the truth about this critical point, so I made this statement offhand and he impulsively wanted to set me straight on it, just as he had been doing in our discussions about American habits versus German habits.

"Ha! You're nuts, Hanns; they haven't run out of much of anything back home. White tracers are just our own way of warning ourselves. When ten of them or any big batch of them shows up, you know you'd better start heading for home pronto because you have just shot out your last ammo. The guns are empty."

I ignored his answer, outwardly by changing the subject to a more trivial subject, like central heating as used in the USA, but my mind was thinking how valuable this bit of info would be to our own fighter pilots. When they would see those white streaks, they would know the enemy plane was now defenseless.

I intended to disseminate that information just as soon as possible.

The long walk after solitary confinement had an unexpected effect on Dick. Where the trees were thickest, he suddenly begged me to be excused for a moment so that he could answer a call of nature. I trusted him and noted that a thoroughly experienced American Indian on the warpath could have taken a lesson from Dick on how to make oneself inconspicuous in less than a second. Before I fully grasped what was coming off, he was gone and there I was, left alone, my prisoner and ward seemingly evaporated into thin air.

At first I could think of nothing but a rather appropriate nursery rhyme:"*Ein Mannlein steht im Walde ganz still und stumm,*" then I visualized our cockeyed security officer thoroughly enjoying my court-martial for letting a POW escape. Finally, because there was now nothing I could do about it, I began to philosophize about the value of the "word of honor" of an American officer. If I run after him and he is not trying to escape, it would be shockingly embarrassing to him. He might take my obvious attentiveness for distrust of his word. I did not want that to happen. If, on the other hand, he had escaped, I was a fool for not taking countermeasures to prevent his escape while there was time to do so. I made the decision to believe in his word of honor, and so I had sat down on a nearby rock beside the path and sweated out the next five minutes.

Lieutenant Price reappeared with such artlessness that I felt pretty awkward for having doubted even for a moment the promise of an honest American boy.

Hohe-Mark! Situated in the middle of the beautiful forest, surrounded by a huge and well-groomed park, lies a modern, clean sanatorium. It used to be a castle belonging to a Russian czar who took health cures in the thermal springs at nearby Bad Homburg. Later it became a therapeutic asylum for people with disturbed minds. Even the door handles bent downward gracefully, cheating anyone out of using them for suicide. There is no hook, no nail, no catch. The window glass is shatterproof.

This infirmary now serves as one of the Red Cross hospitals for wounded prisoners of war from the various air forces.

I salute the sister of mercy who opens the park gate for us, and Dick follows suit. Most of the sick boys in the American ward know me quite well. Some are playing on their harmonicas when I come in, and I wonder if they knew I was coming because they play my favorite, "Anchors Aweigh!" Over there is the young South African lieutenant from Johannesburg who has a badly wounded leg. He still wonders how the hell I was able to present him with a package of real South African "Springbok" cigarettes on his birthday. Deryck Birch is his name.

Friendly Oberarzt Ittershagen, our Luftwaffe medical doctor in charge, whom POWs like Stark and many others will vividly remember all their remaining lives, is as good at orthopedic surgery as he is the games of poker and bridge. He is a master of all these skills.

There are also a number of American and British officers and men on the permanent administrative staff, and everything runs smoothly.

"You can witness here," says the senior Allied officer, an RAF group captain from Bermuda, "the actual results of efforts by the American Red Cross and St. John's!" On his desk stands a picture of the Royal Couple of England, with acknowledgment for his professional skills.

At the German office, some orderlies and NCOs fight with the usual military red tape, files, papers, duplicates, inkpots, and telephones. Most of the registered cases suffer from severe burns, shock, or broken bones.

"Herr Doktor, this is Lt. Price, an American pilot. He asks for permission to say hullo to a personal friend of his, Lt. Peterson."

"Ja, ja! Granted! But not more than five minutes, and Peterson is not supposed to move his face or talk."

I took Dick to A1 and left the two boys alone. While waiting, I chanced a quick hand of gin rummy with RAF air vice marshal Ivelaw-Chapman, who wore his left arm in a weird wire contraption for the past six months. I didn't know his

Chapter 5: Wits As Weapons

flying record, but if he fought with his guns as well as with cards, it must have been hard for us to bring him down.

Dick soon returned, his pockets filled with cigarettes and candy. He was thoroughly happy. My funds were exhausted, and I thought it was time to leave. Or it may have been that I thought Dick might be in the right mood now to talk business with me.

We wandered back alongside a little mountain brook and watched the trout shooting upstream to evade our frightening shadows. Not long ago a discharged belly tank had fallen into the woods, and our silly, scared country folks had put up "DANGER" signs to warn strangers of this awful enemy bomb resting peacefully against the trunk of an old tree. I realize that there must be something sardonic in human nature to enjoy a cheap laugh at somebody's ignorance.

Dick examined the monster and said, "Germany must be full of these."

"You ain't kiddin'!" I said in my best American. "But we prefer them to blockbusters. Did you throw this one down, Dick?"

"I don't think so. You can find mine farther north around Dummer Lake." Coming straight to the point, I asked him, "Don't you guys get yourselves into trouble at times dropping them too soon?"

"Yes, we do. Lots of stories going around about the arguments between Eighth Bomber Command and Fighter Command."

"Oh, I know about that," I said, although I really was a bit surprised, "but those bomber jerks aren't too clever anyway."

"Naturally they want us to hang on to the damned things until every drop of fuel is out of those belly tanks. Means we can stay with them longer and give them fighter protection longer. We are not permitted to go below 18,000 feet; we are not allowed to drop the long-range belly tanks unless we engage in a fight. You know that."

"Certainly I do, but if you wait to engage before dropping them, it's already too late, isn't it?"

"Well, yes. We actually jettison them after sighting the enemy and considerably before engaging, since we need to increase our speed."

"I know. But no more worries since the Luftwaffe is now hiding."

"Indeed! What happened. *Wo ist die Luftwaffe?*"

"You devil, Dick! You do speak German!"

"Just that one sentence. Every one of our boys know the words *Was ist los mit die Luftwaffe?*"

"You have to come down to the deck," I invented quickly, "where the 20 mm flak also has something to say in the matter."

"You would like that, wouldn't you! Too many of our boys have already gotten themselves into trouble by doing just that. Just because they want to increase their victory string by counting planes destroyed by ground strafing. Eighth Air Force has issued a memo stating that headquarters will credit a victory on the ground

The Interrogator

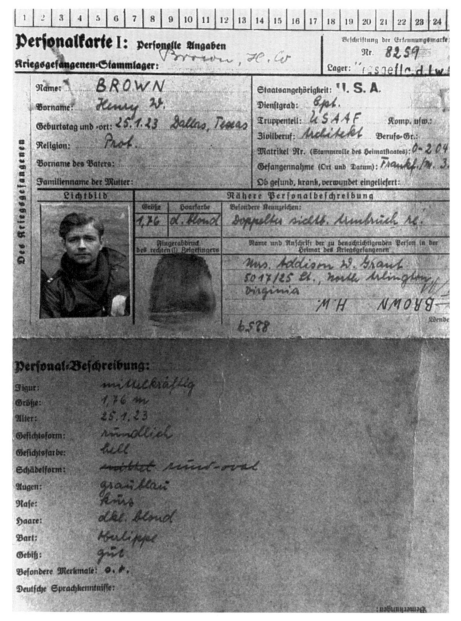

LUFTWAFFE POW PERSONAL DATA CARD
All POWs had to have an identification card filled out by the Luftwaffe interrogation center. This one was concerning Henry W. Brown, 354th Squadron, 355th USAAF Group. Brown had fourteen aerial victories before his career was terminated.

Chapter 5: Wits As Weapons

by strafing the same as a plane destroyed in air-to-air combat. Our boys are eager to fatten their scores with the easy kills on the ground. Of course, at most German airbases the flak makes strafing very dangerous for us, but it sure is a hell of a lot easier to score a victory on the ground. Takes a lot of skill to get them in the air, and guts to get them on the ground."

"You're telling me? I've had most of the strafers right here at Oberursel. You'll be meeting them soon at a *Stalag Luft*."

"When am I leaving this place, Hanns? I think I'd rather stay right here with you. OK?"

"I have put you on the list for the next transport, Dick, and it will probably leave the day after tomorrow. Say! Would you like to go to the cinema with me tonight?"

"Thanks, that oughta be swell! Tell me, Hanns, Al Peterson seems worried about something. Do you know what is bothering him?"

"Yes, I think so. We found all his papers concerning his mission on him, since he was in such shock and agony he could not think straight. He cannot talk even now; we got all the info on him from his maps and flight plan. I am sure he would not have told me anything had he been able to talk, though. You know what? You haven't told me anything either!"

Dick looked at me candidly with his clear blue eyes, and we both fell silent in thought. I tried to picture one of our youngsters being interrogated in England, and I found no solution to the perplexing problem concerning the questioning of a POW on either side. War is terrible.

After our very enjoyable visit to the cinema, I felt certain Dick was now ready to answer my third question. We had met a small number of other allied POWs there, escorted by guards or interrogators, officers and sergeants of bombers crews, a Canadian, an Australian, an RAF flight leftenant. Otherwise, the crowd consisted of Luftwaffe camp soldiers and some girls and civilian men.

The film proved to be a masterpiece of photography. It was a full-length feature of the 1936 Olympic Games in Berlin, and Dick pounded my shoulder as he almost went into a frenzy over seeing Jesse Owens get three gold medals, and Glenn Morris of Fort Collins, Colorado, win the ten-event decathlon. In one event, Americans got first, second, and third, and Dick was ecstatic when the three star-spangled flags were hoisted all at once.

"How would you like a cool glass of German beer, now?" I asked Dick as we filed out of the cinema building.

No argument from him, that was for sure. We went to my office, and the steward from the officer's mess brought us some. Too late, I realized I had made a mistake. Dick barely tasted it, and I could read his mind; he wondered if the women were next. You see, the intelligence officers on the other side always briefed the pilots that the Germans would try to get them drunk, at least merry and talkative, then bring on specially trained fräuleins who would get everything out of them, including any secrets.

The Interrogator

POMPETTI MEETS SCHARFF AGAIN
Almost two years before his death, Peter Pompetti came to Encino, California, to see Hanns Scharff again. In September 1983, ace Pompetti asked Scharff again and again, "What did you get from me?" Scharff tried to put his fears to rest by saying, "Nothing of importance."

It would be senseless, at this point, to explain to Dick that if any interrogation officer brought a woman into the picture, he would face a serious trial. Such tactics were strictly *verboten*! In fact, such arrangements could have been most helpful at times, but it was taboo for a German girl to be seen talking to a POW, by strict government order. But now I could see Dick was wary.

"Dick, your S-2 for intelligence, Captain Berger, told you to expect wine, women, and song, no doubt, but I am sorry we cannot oblige."

"Yes, he stressed those points, and I wondered when you were going to get around to that." He looked disappointed!

"Well, perhaps tomorrow evening we'll go out for some wine and song, but the women and interrogations will be missing from our party. We'll make it a farewell party for you. Okay?"

"I would not mind if the wine is good."

"You have my word for that, Dick."

Just then, through the door adjoining my office with the next one, my fellow interrogator and faithful buddy Otto Engelhardt emerged. He was a learned scholar and my splendid assistant, and everybody called him "Bill," or "that Wild Canadian Bill," which tells the story of his prewar overseas experience. We were extremely well tuned in toward each other, and without question and

Chapter 5: Wits As Weapons

answer he knew immediately whether he was disturbing or needed for assistance.

"Howdy!" he said to Dick in his own ingratiating style. He was a real nature boy, and one of his pet themes was how to make a fire in a rainstorm. He also knew the secret of how to make sourdough bread and how to fell a large tree. Every night, I'm sure, he would dream of his little spread and house in the Canadian wilds.

I signaled to him to look into the top drawer of my desk, and he casually sauntered over and opened it and instantly knew what I wanted to talk about. A small photograph lay there, an enlargement of some enemy gun-camera film showing a low-level attack on a train.

Two hours later I was convinced that a new phase of war was upon us. Dick's stories and some obvious deductions clearly showed the change. In fact, prior to the time that he was shot down, some weeks ago now, his outfit had instructions to keep above 18,000 feet over the Continent except during an actual aerial engagement. Now the situation had altered, and Dick did not know it yet. Previously, only certain fighter squadrons were allowed to strafe ground targets. The remainder of the fighters had to stay up high near the bombers they were escorting, and dare not chase enemy planes very far away from the Fortresses. Now it was obvious to us Germans that Fighter Command had won its argument that there was almost no reason to stay up high anymore. The war was becoming very boring to the fighters, so they should be allowed to strafe targets of opportunity after the bombers had turned for home and were not being attacked by the Luftwaffe. Nowadays the fighter squadrons came down low to hunt anything on the ground that moved, and they penetrated deep into German territory. Was this a prelude to D-day?

Now, my chief, Horst Barth, poked his head around the corner of the doorway, and I was glad, since I could use him to help relieve any tensions Lt. Price must have felt. Barth was an excellent impromptu guitar player, and he willingly fetched his guitar. For half an hour we four sat and sang songs in low, soft voices. "Home, Home on the Range" left all four of us misty eyed. The song always has the same effect on me as "Lili Marlene": "Under the lantern by the barracks gate . . . ."

We called it a night. The guard came and escorted Dick back to his solitary cell. Captain Barth took his guitar home, and Wild Bill mumbled that he was going to hit the hay. *Gute Nacht!*

As soon as I was left alone, I carefully wrote out a transcript of my conversations with Lt. Price that day. I knew it would make interesting reading for our aviation people, and that within twenty-four hours, people in our headquarters and other high places would be studying my report. Duty was done. On the way to my quarters I became conscious of the song . . . ringing again and again through my mind: "where seldom is heard, a discouraging word . . . ."

The next two days I had half a dozen more chances to talk with Lt. Price. I never asked him any more questions, and we simply told yarns. He had a natural

The Interrogator

impulse to match every one, I could tell. During those two days, I dictated more than a dozen new pages of anecdotes and little tidbits about personalities of the 355th Fighter Group to my secretary. She, in turn, would hand them over to Frau Biehler for her squadron histories. Our files were brought up to date so that we could talk about current things and happenings when the next pilot from the 355th fell into our hands.

"Dick, this is your bus to take you to Dulag Luft, the distribution center. Good luck to you in the tough times ahead of you. Although we met under difficult circumstances and our tasks and goals were adverse, I respect you as an individual and an enemy officer. I like you as a man. Here is a little souvenir to take home with you to remember our relationship, and I wish you well."

"So long, Stony Face. Thanks for the courteous treatment and your generosity, and I hope you'll come to Dallas some day and I'll treat you to some real country-fried chicken!"

"Goodbye, Dick." No hard feelings.

Author comments: Hanns Scharff has just presented an example of the hidden workings and inner mechanisms of the use of wits as weapons at the intelligence and evaluation center of the Luftwaffe. Lieutenant Richard Price Jr. was an imaginary character, but every incident happened in true life at one time or another with many of the POWs who were processed through Auswertestelle West. Use of the fictitious Richard Price name was made in order to prevent embarrassment to any of the actual POWs concerned.

Springbok cigarettes: The young South African lieutenant from Johannesburg who was so surprised when he awoke in Hohe-Mark hospital on his birthday in 1943 to discover a fresh pack of Springboks and a happy-birthday note on his side table left his address in Hanns Scharff's "Guest Book." A letter to him from the author in 1976 reached him, although he had moved from Johannesburg to Scottburgh, near Natal.

Lieutenant Deryck W. Birch, ex-SAAF, was happy to respond to the author's query in the following manner:

"First I would like to say how pleased I am to know where Hanns is living. I still remember quizzing him when he said he had lived in Jo'burg before the war, asking him about certain places and such. Little did I realize that he was actually interrogating me at the same time.

"I was absolutely amazed that he had managed to obtain a supply of these cigarettes after the war had been underway for five years, and when I asked him about how he acquired them, he never did give me a direct answer. No wonder he was considered "the Luftwaffe's master interrogator"!

Author comment: Scharff explained to the author that some German civilians who had been interned in South Africa had been rather mysteriously repatriated to Germany in 1944. They had been allowed to carry with them all the cigarettes they wished. One of them came to see his old friend Hanns Scharff and brought

Chapter 5: Wits As Weapons

FLAK GOT CARE TOO
Raymond C. Care of the 4th Fighter Group went down near Celle, and his next stop was Oberursel and Scharff's office. Care was an ace with six victories, and Scharff knew all about them.

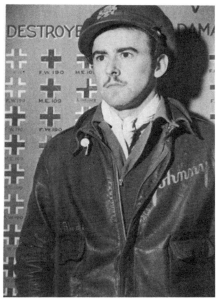

CAPT. JOHN T GODFREY
This ace had 16.33 victories at the time he fell into German hands. He graduated from Scharff's interrogation class and signed out on 27 August 1944 en route to a *Stalag Luft*.

a carton of Springboks as a present for him. Since Scharff had acquired a taste for another brand, he saved the Springboks and gave them away to the various South African POWs.

Lt. Deryck Birch continues:

'After transitioning to Martin B-26 Marauders, I joined Number 13 Squadron at Telegra, Italy. I was a copilot, and on our third mission we dropped our bombs on a target at Pescara. We came in from the sea, and the flak was fairly heavy. After dropping the bombs, the pilot leading us, we were flying no. 2 position and for some unaccountable reason turned inland directly into the heaviest flak area. We took a direct hit in the bomb bay, which severed the elevator and rudder cables. The plane pitched into a steep dive. My seat belt was unfastened, since I had just returned from the rear of the plane and had just sat down in the copilot's seat when we were hit. I was thrown forward very hard into the instrument panel. I thought for sure this was it, and I lost consciousness.

"Next thing I knew was when I felt a strong wind on my back and legs and then realized my feet were trapped and were holding me in the cockpit of the disintegrating aircraft. Then somehow I was loose and I fell free and saw bits and pieces of my plane falling right along beside me. I felt dead tired, all my energy was gone, and it was a tremendous effort for me to find the ripcord on my parachute and pull it, but I did and the chute jerked me up short as it opened. As I drifted down, I saw another chute below me, but I did not have the strength to try to steer mine toward it. I could hear dogs barking, and in just a few seconds I hit the ground among some trees in an orchard.

"Some Italians surrounded me and stared at me. A few moments later, some armed Fascists came running, and one pointed his gun at me, talking away sixty to the dozen while pointing at my wristwatch. Damned if I'd let him have that, so I took it off and put it in my mouth. After more jabbering and a long consultation, they were disappointed to see some German soldiers running toward us. Obviously the Germans had run a long way, but they took charge and sent the Italians over to get a stepladder, which they used as a litter to carry me, since I could not walk due to my injuries. They put my parachute under my head as a pillow.

"It seemed that they must have carried me several miles before reaching their military truck, parked on the road. They drove me to a German outpost, where an English-speaking German officer told me, "For you the war is now over!" I was in great pain and did not appreciate his remark at all. Soon they drove me for another hour, stopping at two hospitals who refused to take me in. The third hospital took me though.

"Surgery was required, and afterward I awakened to find myself in a cast from the top of my chest to the bottom of one leg and halfway down the other leg. Next day the two German guards who had picked me up in the orchard came to visit me and brought me the half-wing insignia that our observer had sewn on his uniform. They told me the entire crew, except for me, had perished in the crash.

"After a series of moves to various hospitals in Italy, I eventually was sent to Metz, France. General Patton's tanks began to approach, so I was evacuated and eventually arrived at Hohe-Mark hospital. The Springbok cigarettes and my meeting Hanns Scharff soon followed."

Author comments: Gestapo *(*Geheime Staatspolizei, or Secret Police) was not a military unit so was not bound by the Geneva Convention Rules. It was a natural action for interrogators to tell Allied prisoners that if they could not prove they were military men, they must be turned over to the Gestapo for questioning. It took more than the usual name–rank–serial number responses to prove a military connection. The problem arose when Allied evadees were captured wearing Polish or French clothing with absolutely no military identification on them. When turned over to the Gestapo, they were given every opportunity to prove their military status, and if they could not they were generally considered to be spies and were summarily executed.

In mid-1944, approximately 150 Allied personnel were in the hands of the Gestapo and had given enough evidence that they might possibly be military but not enough to be convincing. The Gestapo bundled them into freight cars and

Chapter 5: Wits As Weapons

shipped them off to the Buchenwald concentration camp. Investigations continued, and most of the men were confirmed as military and were eventually shipped to regular prisoner-of-war camps. Several had died at Buchenwald due to typhus, pneumonia, pleurisy, or other ailments, which were common under such conditions as existed in the camps.

6

REMARKABLE! MOST REMARKABLE!

What can the enemy do when the friend is cordial?
—Bismarck

SCHARFF continues: As long as wars have been waged on this earth, captors have taken the right to question captives. As long as POWs are interrogated, they will talk. No patriotism, no self-control, no logic gives any man enough strength to repel relentlessly pressed attacks utilizing accumulated combinations of facts and circumstantial evidence. The methods of wringing these words from a POW may differ widely, from genuine affability to gruesome brutality, but the result is the same.

The first and foremost problem facing any soldier who falls into enemy hands, once he has survived, is what to say or what not to say when being questioned. Since it is not the fault of the POW that he is at a disadvantage, all there is left for him to do is make the most of his misfortune. Every soldier on either side is prepared and trained beforehand for just such an eventuality.

Each prisoner will say something. One will say more, another less, but all of them are bound to the iron rule never to disclose military secrets. How can a soldier determine how far he can go when he is being called on to answer questions? In my own opinion as an experienced interrogator, it is absolutely impossible for any interrogatee to know what his limits are. Therefore, it has become almost universal that intelligence officers will instruct their charges never to give out more than name, rank, and serial number.

Can this demand be fulfilled? Can this military order be complied with, or should it be disregarded? Perhaps only those who have been POWs or interrogators are qualified to answer that question.

My experiences show quite clearly that the higher the rank, the less a prisoner felt himself bound by the three identification answers.

Chapter 6: Remarkable! Most Remarkable!

This was true on our side as well as on the Allied side. Naturally, the higher the rank, the higher the grade of education and judiciousness. With this greater intellectual power goes a general superiority and ability to master a difficult situation. I present this perception as the true explanation of why most officers allowed themselves, even felt entitled, to speak more freely. With their superior conception of responsibility, they proved their capability for better judgment.

To my mind, American military intelligence knew much more about these facts than the German, and their training was better than ours, but they, too, did not know enough to find the right solution. Experiences in Korea in 1951–1954 and in Vietnam in 1960–1976 provide evidence supporting this conclusion. *Name, rank, and serial number cost many a POW his life in those conflicts, yet what they knew and could say was insignificant as far as secrets were concerned.* Our German intelligence training officers realized the impossibility of carrying out such theoretical orders under practical circumstances, and since they did not wish to allow German soldiers who were captured by the enemy any flexibility, they sought the easiest and most uncomplicated way, ordering them to be mute, to say nothing at all. This also was the safest approach.

In the same way, American soldiers were indoctrinated very thoroughly back in America at the training bases and reindoctrinated in England. Many of them still carried illustrated pamphlets, issued by the US War Department, when we captured them. These told them how they should behave if they fell into our hands. Of course, one finds almost everywhere people who like to look up in their reference books "What to do now!" just like a cook in the kitchen with recipe books.

GERMAN INTERROGATIONS DIFFERED FROM THOSE IN VIETNAM
Col. George E. "Bud" Day was shot down over North Vietnam and spent 67 months as a POW. He won the Medal of Honor for his steadfast resistance to the cruelties being meted out to him and his fellow POWs by the North Vietnamese.

The Interrogator

"Joe Doaks and Hanns Kraut are just alike! There is no difference between Doaks and Kraut," said a surprised West Pointer colonel in our prison one day, setting into the right perspective one of the most essential facts. This same colonel wrote:

"If the intelligence officers knew another fact, they would have taught their men that the Germans already had a blood and urine test of every Allied soldier before he was captured."

Now that is not true, of course, but neither were most of the things they taught their soldiers concerning what to expect if they fell into German hands. Their business was to be well informed about us, but mostly they gave inaccurate descriptions about what was going to happen during interrogation. The old story of wine, women, and song was a common belief among our guests, and some of the POWs were actually eagerly looking forward to that kind of persuasion. At the same time, it was wrong to create wittingly or unwittingly the impression that rough treatment was ahead. I think I can say that in all cases of which I have knowledge, if any rough treatment was handed out it was because the POW tried to escape or in some other way brought it upon himself by his own actions.

As a result of the adverse propaganda concerning the German war machine, they often expected torture, mistreatment, degradation, and other severe punishment applied just to make them talk. This frame of mind was heightened as the prisoners imagined the retribution they might suffer, since as they were transported to Oberursel they had opportunity to observe firsthand the wreckage and devastation for which it suddenly occurred to them they might be held responsible.

As a result, the Allied indoctrination and propaganda played into our hands. Alas for them, they were told little or nothing of what I call the *barbed-wire psychosis*. They also were unfamiliar with our traditional "officer class" attitude, which we maintained with great punctilio in our interrogations: I know that such things are romantic and a little ludicrous in this day and time. Modern war is such a grim business that each side must take to itself any advantage it can possibly get. We felt, even when we chose our point of view, that we were being perhaps a trifle naive. This very thing turned out to be another strong factor in our ability to make pilots talk to us in the prison at Oberursel. Nevertheless, name, rank, and serial number; nothing else! And yet there was another point equally stern . . . *DO NOT TELL ANY LIES!*

Author comments: In this chapter, Hanns Scharff speaks of the Korean and Vietnamese Wars, so a word is appropriate here concerning North Vietnamese interrogation methods.

US Air Force major George E. "Bud" Day, pilot of an F-100F Super Sabre, was shot down by ground fire over North Vietnam on 26 August 1967. He was immediately captured but, despite a right arm broken in three places, escaped from his captors six days later and evaded the enemy for two weeks. Within sight of freedom, Day was captured again and was not released until five years later. He

Chapter 6: Remarkable! Most Remarkable!

is now a colonel and has been awarded the top award, the Medal of Honor, for his bravery far beyond the call of duty.

Day's published memoirs* reflect his own eyeball-to-eyeball character, and just one page of it will be quoted at this point (*Day's book *Return with Honor*):

Colonel Day's story:

"Rodent (the name I had given my interrogator because he reminded me of a rat) had a couple of his hooligans wrap a set of ropes around my back and underneath my armpits. They pulled the ropes up very hard, and I found this position very painful as they tried to make my shoulder blades touch together and my elbows touched. Rodent then said, 'I am going to force you to tell me the answers!'

"'I'm compelled by my Code of Conduct to give only name, rank, and serial number. I was injured bailing out and cannot remember.'

"'I will make you remember, colonel!' One of his hoods put a stick in the ropes and began twisting it like a captain's wheel, and my arm joints tried to pop out of the sockets. Circulation was stopped and my hands puffed up like two huge, swollen sausages. Fancy the pain, possibly like passing a kidney stone or acute appendicitis, as the muscles in the chest tear apart. I was surprised that my broken arm, still in a cast, was the least painful. Now the SOB applied pressure for short periods of time, on and off. I weathered that torture session.

"It became clear that if this dreadful torture continued it was going to be impossible to adhere to the Code of Conduct. A man incoherent from pain, semiconscious, might babble anything . . ."

What is this set of rules called the Code of Conduct? Although it was not signed until after WWII by President Eisenhower, the general principles applied during WWII. The Code of Conduct was law, as far as the American combat soldiers were concerned, in the Korean and Vietnam Wars. These rules governed the behavior of all American combatants. Here they are:

CODE OF CONDUCT
FOR MEMBERS OF THE ARMED FORCES OF THE UNITED STATES
I am an American fighting man. I serve in the forces which guard my country and our way of life. I am prepared to give my life in their defense.

1.I will never surrender of my own free will. If in command I will never surrender my men while they still have the means to resist.

2. If I am captured I will continue to resist by all means available. I will make every effort to escape and aid others to escape. I will accept neither parole nor special favors from the enemy.

If I become a prisoner of war, I will keep faith with my fellow prisoners. I will give no information or take part in any action which might be harmful to my

The Interrogator

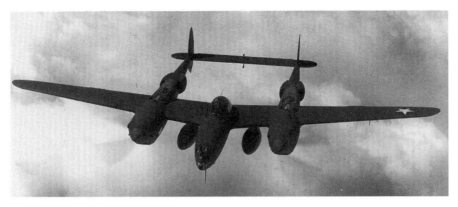

LOCKHEED P-38 "LIGHTNING"
The P-38 was outclassed by the Luftwaffe's Me 109 and the Fw 190 due to its slow rate of roll. Many USAAF pilots were shot down while flying the P-38.

comrades. If I am senior, I will take command. If not, I will obey the lawful orders of those appointed over me and will back them up in every way.

When questioned, should I become a prisoner of war, I am bound to give only name, rank, service number and date of birth. I will evade answering further questions to the utmost of my ability. I will make no oral or written statements disloyal to my country and its allies or harmful to their cause.

I will never forget that I am an American fighting man, responsible for my actions and dedicated to the principles which made my country free. I will trust in my God and in the United States of America.

(The above Code of Conduct is an executive order signed by President Dwight D. Eisenhower, commander in chief of the Armed Forces of the United States.)

ARTICLE 104, UNIFORM CODE OF MILITARY JUSTICE
AIDING THE ENEMY
Any person who
 aids or attempts to aid the enemy with arms, ammunition, supplies, money or other things; or
 without proper authority, knowingly harbors or protects or gives intelligence to or communicates of corresponds with, or holds any intercourse with the enemy, either directly or indirectly shall suffer death or such other punishment as a court-martial or military commission may direct.

ARTICLE 105, MISCONDUCT AS A PRISONER
Any person subject to this chapter who, while in the hands of the enemy in time of war . . . for the purpose of securing favorable treatment by his captors acts without proper authority in a manner contrary to law, custom or regulation, to the

Chapter 6: Remarkable! Most Remarkable!

SHORTLY BEFORE THE DISASTERS
Gen. Jesse Auton (*center*) talks with 4th Group aces Duane Beeson and Henry Mills, who were shot down a few days later. Mills finished his interrogations by Hanns Scharff on 3 March 1944, and Beeson signed out 13 April.

"WHEN WE GET THESE TWO, THE WAR IS OVER!"
Interrogator Scharff showed this photo to another POW, saying that Don Gentile (21.83 victories) and Donald J. M. Blakeslee (11) would surely drop in soon. Neither did.

detriment of others of whatever nationality held by the enemy as military prisoners . . . shall be punished as a court-martial shall direct.

The Germans also had a code of conduct. It was published in the form of ten commandments and was printed on the inside cover of every German soldier's identification and paybook. Here they are:

10 COMMANDMENTS OF THE GERMAN SOLDIER
FOR CONDUCT IN WAR.

1. The German soldier fights chivalrously for the victory of his people. Cruelties and unnecessary destructions are unworthy of him.

2. The combatant must be in uniform or identified with a specially introduced emblem recognized from afar. Fighting in civilian clothes without such an emblem is forbidden.

3. An enemy who surrenders shall not be killed, not even the terrorist or spy. They will receive fair punishment through the courts.

4. Prisoners of war shall not be mistreated or insulted. Arms, plans, and notes are to be confiscated.

5. Nothing shall be taken of their personal effects.

6. Dum-dum projectiles are forbidden. Regular projectiles are not to be altered.

7. The civilian population is inviolable. The soldier is forbidden to loot or to wantonly destroy. Historical monuments and buildings serving religious service, the arts, science, or charity should be respected. Payments in kind and service of the population can be demanded only on higher order and with proper compensation.

8. Neutral territory shall not be included in the combat zone by trespassing into, flying over, or shooting at.

9. If a German soldier is captured, he has to state his name and rank if asked to do so. Under no circumstance is he allowed to reveal the membership of his unit and the military, political, economic situation on the German side. Neither promises nor threats should tempt him to do so.

10. Violations of the above orders are punishable. Violations of rules 1 and 8 by the enemy are to be reported. Retaliatory measures are allowed only if ordered by the high command.

Obviously, the American code of conduct as well as the German code of conduct were often ignored during the war due to the exigencies of the service, war escalations, and the circumstances existing at the moment. Most Americans, due to our way of life, have no idea nor can we imagine the hardships and tortures that are imposed on prisoners. It seems that mankind, when put into a position of authority, too often loses the sense of balance and fairness and become disciplinarians without limitation.

Chapter 6: Remarkable! Most Remarkable!

HANNS SCHARFF continues: "Gentlemen," said Oberst Killinger at briefing one day, "tonight an inspection will take place by Generalmajor Schmidt, commander of the Luftwaffe 2nd Corps Area. His staff will be with him, and I request all personnel work overtime, to be in their offices, especially the interrogation officers, since the Herr General may wish to observe or even interview some prisoners of war personally."

At about eight o'clock that evening, I could hear many steps and much heel-clicking and chatting of voices approaching along the well-lit corridor outside my door. Casually the camp commander opened my door slightly and peeped in, saying as if surprised:

"Excuse me, please, just now saw your light was on. So you are still busy, Gefreiter Scharff!"

He ushered the general and his adjutant and some lesser staff officers into the room with the remark that perhaps Herr General would like to see one of the best horses in the Oberursel stable at work. All the visitors wore those rank-heavy white- or red-striped trousers and much braid.

I jumped to attention and reported as is required in the presence of a commanding general. "Private First-Class Scharff, sir, working on interrogation of captured members of 8th Fighter Command, 8th US Army Air Forces."

As usual, I was now asked generalized questions, and I answered them...Age? Where from? How long in the Luftwaffe? Why not decorated yet? And so forth. Through my mind passed the fairy tales one reads and hears; Herr General should have taken the Ritterkreuz or Knight's Cross that adorned his neck and bestowed it upon me on the spot. Instead, he just reached over and took one of my "West Point" cigarettes from my desktop, turned, and motioned for everyone to be seated. It looked like we might be in for a long session.

His eyes swept sharply across my littered desk before finally halting at the Varga pinup girl seductively posed there on one corner. Then his eyes moved on to disapprove of an untidy heap of *Stars and Stripes* on a shelf behind me, before finally noting the large map on the wall.

Herr General liked maps; I could see that, since his eyes crinkled into a smile as though he had just seen an old friend. Decorated with little strategic and tactical flags and colored pins, the map looked as though it contained a lot of very important information. I wondered how soon he would ask about the one at 39 Heerstrasse in Berlin, and what I should tell him if he did. After his silent eyeball survey, however, he asked me only how I conducted my interrogations. He added that he had read some and heard about others, and his curiosity was aroused. Would it be disturbing to me if I interrogated a POW in the presence of him and his staff?

Though I nodded that it would be feasible, my stomach growled a complaint about what the general would say if I brought some young lieutenant in here, interrupting his solitary dinner most likely. That would make any POW uncooperative. My stomach hinted I'd probably lose my stripes.

The Interrogator

JACK RAPHAEL AND DON BLAKESLEE
4th Group fighters Raphael and D. J. M. Blakeslee met each other again at Tustin, California, in 1992. Raphael met Hanns Scharff while a POW in WWII, but Blakeslee did not.

My aim now was to explain that there was no mystery in gathering information from the fighter pilots, that anyone could ask first routine questions followed by open questions, and that anyone could be present, providing he did not mind being bored stiff (now I did not say exactly "bored stiff" to the general) by hearing nothing but name–rank–serial number and seeing a POW stare at nothing but my right ear for half an hour or so.

Herr General wanted to see it done from scratch, so from a list on my desk of today's new arrivals, a POW was selected at random, and he was one who had not had his first interview yet. The sergeant of the guards on duty at the cooler was ordered by telephone to send POW number 183 to room 47. The high-ranking staff officers stretched out their legs and lit up more of my West Point cigarettes, making quite a fuss over the taste and aroma. "Ah! *Amerikanische! Sehr gute!*"

There was a knock at the door a few minutes later, and the guard, when called to enter, nearly broke the bones in his heels and shoulders trying to do a snappy "Present Arms!" in the face of all the brass in the red-striped trousers. His about-face was comical as he left the room, because he was so self-conscious.

There stood in the doorway a half-sleepy, half-surprised American second lieutenant who, after some moments of hesitation, saluted curtly, his eyes looking everyone over, trying to lock on to the culprit who wanted to talk to him. He knew from all the braid that there were some very high ranks here, and I could see he was filled with foreboding. I rose from my chair and returned his salute, introducing myself as his interrogator; I asked him not to mind the encounter with this collection of big-wigs, and to be seated comfortably.

Chapter 6: Remarkable! Most Remarkable!

Lo! It looked like a disaster. I had run up against an invincible foe, immutable and intrepid! With his eyes fixed on my right ear, he would repeat his name, rank, and serial number over and over again. Though it was contrary to my own interests, I began to admire this fellow who was so irreproachably imperturbable in defending himself, yet in such a chivalrous and soldierly manner.

Questioning and single-sided arguing had long become tedious, and half an hour must have passed. The general and his staff were losing interest since they were unimpressed. Then suddenly the young lieutenant abruptly stands, turns, and walks to stare out the window, crossing his arms behind him in a military "at ease" stance. He looks out into the dark night, then begins to talk of his own free will. First slowly, then quicker and easier he gives his name, rank, and serial number, then continues. He tells us where he was stationed, when he took off, what his mission was, his call sign, his squadron and group numbers, his plane numbers and type, how he was shot down, where he was captured, everything. All of it came so easy that my hair was almost standing on end.

The general and his followers look on with awe. I can read their thoughts: What is the secret trick of this interrogator? Has everybody noticed how he made this obstinate bull of an enemy speak? Are his arguments so convincing? Can no one resist him?

"Your excellency, permit me to suggest that you take a short break now, after which it will be more productive for me to continue the questioning alone?"

"Yes, my lad, by all means! By all means! Amazing! I understand and we shall leave now. Before I do, I must congratulate you on your most lucid and exquisite manners with which you have conducted this interrogation. Remarkable! Most remarkable! What I have heard and read of you is true! You shall be decorated! Now, auf Wiedersehen!"

Salute! Salute! Click of heels. Snap of door. The camp CO looks back quickly in wonderment as he is the last one out of the door.

My American opponent still stands at the window. No doubt he had seen all in the reflection in the pane. Arms crossed behind him, slowly he turns . . . until he faces me and his face breaks into a broad, generous, and friendly smile.

"Say, sucker, have I helped you out of the mess you were in?"

Who, I asked myself, would ever reprimand this POW for having told lies to his inquisitor?

Surprise, often as a result of a strange coincidence, played a very important role in successful interrogations. However, surprise is not a biased element in favor of one side only. It works both ways, and therefore it backfired and cut me short on occasion too.

What do you do with a POW who was once your tailor in Berlin? Years later, here he is frantically waving at you from a huge crowd of newly arrived captives just brought in from the Greek theater of war.

The Interrogator

"Look!" he says imploringly. "I ran away from Hitler in 1938 and I was going down to Palestine where I got mixed up with a British fighting unit. Now here I am right back where I started from. Hanns, can you help me start up a little tailor shop here in the camp?"

What can you do with a fellow like that?

A number of Brigadier General Elliott Roosevelt's "photo-recce" boys, from the 27th Photo Reconnaissance Unit (PRU), attached to the 8th Air Force, fell into my lap. One of them brought his fully loaded cameras to us intact, through no fault of his own, and our own photo lab developed the film for us. The pictures, lots of topographical shots and landscapes, did not concern me so were duly handed over to BUNA for evaluation. One picture, though, caught my fancy, so I kept it out. The pilot had taken a few test pictures just before taking off from his base at Mount Farm in England. This picture I like so much showed the tip of one of his propellers and a good general view of the flight line. Directly in the foreground on the left side was another P-38 Lightning, with all details and markings clearly discernible. Its number was 963.

Farther in the background were hangars and buildings, P-38 after P-38 and a couple of Spitfires, all neatly lined up along the parking ramp. Right in the middle of the foreground was an army jeep with a mechanic working on it. I had this picture enlarged to about half the size of my desktop, and I mounted it on the wall under my map. Soon I had forgotten about it, and it finally reentered my mind only when I noted the name of an American first lieutenant among the new arrivals. I had heard his rather strange name someplace. Prokop!!

I went to the registry office and looked in their books, and it came up quickly that this man and his plane could be found in the file on the 27th PRU operating from Mount Farm, under the command of Colonel Homer L. Saunders until January 1944, then under the command of Lt. Col. George A. Lawson until mid-February and under Lt. Col. Norris E. Hartwell until May. Now, though, it was under the command of one Lt. Col. Clarence A. Shoop, whom we were currently adding to our dossier file in anticipation of a potential visit in spite of the fact he was a much renowned and revered pilot and leader.

The 27th Squadron file convinced me I had met this young recce pilot before, yet I knew my only acquaintance was by photograph. I took the Mount Farm airbase photo from its hiding place under my maps and put it upside down on my writing desk and called for the newcomer.

We exchanged the usual courtesies and I made a little welcoming speech in a serious tone, although right from the beginning I meant it as a little joke. I told him that I knew perfectly well who he was, where he came from, and what his missions were, and that I knew perfectly well that he did not know any military secrets. However, I was obliged to question him, so I had only one single question to ask him, and if he should answer it satisfactorily, I could call off all the rest of the unpleasant interrogations. He nodded eagerly.

Chapter 6: Remarkable! Most Remarkable!

"It is very important," I said as I uncovered the photo and pointed to it, "what is the name of that mechanic working on that jeep!"

My honorable friend scrutinized the photo in bewilderment. He immediately recognized Mount Farm, of course, and naturally he did not know the name of the mechanic. I saw the muscles of his jaw slacken, and he knew the jig was up. He saw through my cunning game. There it was, a great photograph of his own airplane number 963, obviously taken on his next-to-last mission right there at Mount Farm! What a sensation! What a spy system! (Interrogators at Auswertestelle West also had built up dossiers on Brig. Gen. Elliott Roosevelt and two of his senior officers, Colonels Harry T. Edison and Wayne E. Thurman.)

His compliments to the fantastic German intelligence work!

My highest respect belongs to an 8th Air Force fighter jockey who, one fine, crisp winter morning, bailed out directly over our intelligence center of all places! In nearly all other cases, it took days and sometimes weeks before a captured enemy airman could reach us for interrogation. This usually gave them plenty of time to get mentally psyched up for the ordeal.

This one was still hyped up with the adrenalin flowing freely in his veins and, stimulated as he was, should have been easy prey for us. I saw him falling in his parachute as he came down through the clouds. I had seen his Mustang spinning like a top, and then his white parachute blossomed behind it. I picked up my telephone and within seconds was in touch with Oberursel Police. When the officer on duty there confirmed that the airman was being watched likewise by his officers,

STRONG-WILLED MOZART KAUFMAN
Capt. Mozart Kaufman, USAAF, held out, saying no more than name, rank, and serial number until interrogator Scharff asked him how many states were in the United States. Kaufman knew the jig was up because he was from the 48th Fighter Group.

The Interrogator

and a man had been dispatched by motorcycle for his reception, I requested that he be brought immediately to me.

Only about fifteen minutes later a cold, drenched, exhausted but unhurt and excited young pilot stood before me. To all questions I fired at him from left and right, he declined to answer. In the state he was in, he did not feel like talking; he wanted to get those wet clothes off, get warm, and calm down a little bit first. Finally, in complete frustration and irritated through and through, he pointed his finger at me and said, albeit with crinkles at the corners of his eyes, "Stop it! If you don't stop houndng me I will go right straight back where I came from! You hear?"

I couldn't let him go straight back where he came from, but he certainly won my admiration.

The foundation for a fruitful interrogation can sometimes be laid by utilizing an unforeseen opportunity too.

Any history written about the US Army Air Forces in World War II would be incomplete if the Eagle Squadrons remain unmentioned. These "Red-Nosed Boys" of "Double-Winged" fame had become the 4th Fighter Group at Debden, England, in General Jesse Auton's 65th Wing in the 8th Fighter Command. They were such a proud outfit that one of them who became our guest wrote a postcard from prison

HIS DEEP VOICE WAS HIS SIGNATURE
US Army captain Silvernail took the wrong road and was captured by the Germans. A forward air controller whose call sign was "Sweepstake Two," Silvernail was identified immediately when he spoke to Scharff.

Chapter 6: Remarkable! Most Remarkable!

to his group CO, saying, "They know all about us over here, Boss, and they respect us. Paint 'em ALL-RED, Sir!" (he meant that the P-5 Is should be *all* red!).

Strangely enough, a new type of flying jacket with a little black-fur collar had been issued to these members of America's most daring fighter group for some unknown reason. Strange, I thought to myself, and I set out to discover the reason. Later on, nearly every air force officer had one, and before long a number of German pilots also were wearing them, but for a period of four weeks or so those clad in that specific type jacket could only be one of the erstwhile Eagle Squadron boys. That fact led to one of my fruitful interrogations.

Canadian Bill and I, outwardly distinguishable only as two privates first class, walked one day from the mess hall to our living quarters and had to pass near a crowd of about fifty new arrivals. POWs, neatly lined up in threes awaiting orders to be committed to the cooler. In the first row stood two Eagles with their fur-collared jackets. I exclaimed to Bill at audible distance and with genuine certainty, "Look, Bill! Two fighters from the 4th Group!"

Not a head was turned nor was an eye blinked, but the jaw muscles told me we left behind us two totally perplexed fighter pilots.

You would be perplexed, too, if as a civilian in peace time you traveled across the ocean to some remote village such as Graustark or Lower Slobovia on a Cook's Tour and two humble baggage carriers would point you out and say nonchalantly, "Ah! Two traveling salesmen from the Argentine Corned Beef Company," if that's where you were from.

I tried to set up interrogations in advance, before certain fliers were downed.

The war was over before I forgave General Jimmy Doolittle for having grounded "Silent" Don Blakeslee, the leader of the noted 4th Group, and that gentleman of the air, Don Gentile, both of whom we awaited with great expectations but never captured. I had their pictures hung up on the wall in my office, had nice dossiers prepared, knew their background and accomplishments by heart... I would have given them a fine reception, for sure. In fact, should I ever bump into one of them anyplace on earth, I would recognize them, although I will have to go beyond earth to meet Gentile, since he was killed in the crash of his airplane at Andrews Air Force Base in Maryland on 28 January 1951.

Wild Canadian Bill had met his master, a captain from the 9th Tactical Air Force. He had been downed and captured by frontline troops in France, and there was no lead anywhere as to where he had flown from or to which unit he belonged. Wild Bill mentioned to me that he had a very stubborn case with a Jewish American pilot and that he was getting nowhere with him. The POW, sitting in his solitary cell, had read through all the books in our tiny library and was now complaining there was only Hitler's *My Struggle* left to read. Sporty and good humored as he was, he told Bill that he had to kill time somehow, and so he asked for the book and read it. "*Mein Kampf* was a golden experience." His sarcasm was not unnoticed.

The Interrogator

To terminate his overlong visit, I decided we should go ahead and ship him out on the next morning's transport to Dulag Luft, even at the risk of never knowing which unit he belonged to.

We were having a beer party that night, and since I would like to meet this young captain, I suggested that Bill invite him to come along.

I sat beside the pilot and soon realized it would take longer than I could afford to give to make him talk at all, so I made up my mind to let it go at that, to let the better man win.

As the evening wore on and we were telling jokes and limericks, in no way aiming to discuss military problems, I suddenly recalled an oft-repeated joke. It was a silly trick to ask an American how many states there were in the United States. Forty-eight, of course, but then I would give them pencil and paper and ask them to name them all. We knew that almost everyone could name thirty-five to forty of them, and we continentals always thought it very funny they could not name all forty-eight. Sometimes we would express our doubt that the man was truly an American, and suggest he might be masquerading as one. At the right moment, I caught his attention once more and rather ostentatiously said to him:

"Herr Hauptmann, I have come to the conclusion that you really are from the Middle East and are not an American at all. Now every American knows how many states there are in the USA. Do you."

"Why, every child knows that!"

"Sure? Well, captain, tell me and convince me."

"No! No, you are putting me on, Hanns. Preposterous!"

"So! You now admit you don't know! You are a prevaricator. You simply do not know, and perhaps you are a spy!"

"All right, Hanns. I know. Forty-eight! See?"

I acted rather stupid, quaffing my beer in a big gulp, and reaching for my pen and paper. I went on with my foolish joke. "OK, captain, write them all down for me and I'll believe you."

The captain smiled, since he knew he could not recall all forty-eight. "Hanns, you have a wonderful way about you. Do you always get what you want? Put that stuff away, and instead, may I just write in your guest book? Somehow I knew that you had it figured out where I came from."

He took pen in hand and made one of the nicest entries in the book, which reads as follows:

Hanns—You are slick and sly.

(How many states are in the Union?) but you make a wonderful party companion.

Capt. Mozart Kaufman, 48th Ftr Gp. [Author: Mozart Kaufman lives in San Anselmo, California.]

To most captured airmen it seemed incredible that the enemy interrogation officer could have a file at his command in which nearly every single word

Chapter 6: Remarkable! Most Remarkable!

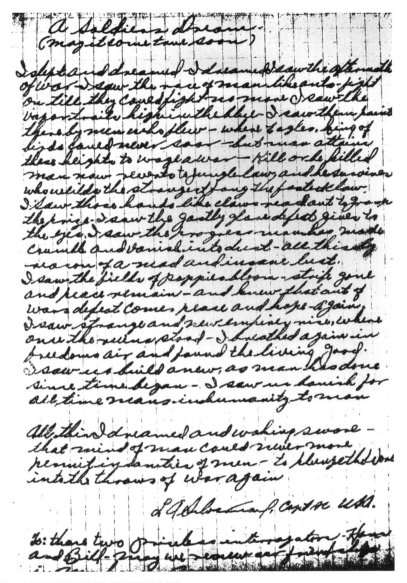

PAGE 26 OF SCHARFF'S GUEST BOOK
Captain L. A. Silvernail wrote "A Soldier's Dream" into Scharff's guest book upon release from interrogations.

The Interrogator

spoken in the air from plane to plane or from base to plane or vice versa was carefully noted. This was logged in a book telling the exact minute and second of the conversation, what was said, and the frequency used. "Listening in" or monitoring operations were being used by both sides, so I did not really understand why POWs were always so surprised that every word they had uttered over the radio was down in our books. We thought it quite valuable information because we could always tell what unit was in action. Soon we knew individual voices, plus various tactics, because we found out that not all leaders flew the same way.

Yet, once I was flabbergasted when interviewing a newcomer because he became so muddle-headed as I casually remarked that he'd better steer clear of his commanding officer should he ever see him again, and he stared at me with wide-open eyes as I repeated to him a remark he had made on the radio in his moment of despair. The incident happened like this: He flew Tail-End Charlie, Blue Four, top cover on an escort mission, and he had stayed a bit far back while intently looking at some specks in the sky too far away to identify. Two of our Messerschmitt 109s, watching his formation from a safe and apparently unobserved distance because they did not want to fly into the hornet's nest, saw him lag behind and realized this was the opportunity they had hoped for, seized the initiative, and struck Purple Heart's corner with all the fury they could muster.

Of course, Blue Four panicked when the surprise bounce occurred, snap-rolled his plane, and lost control. The group leader, flying above him as White One, obviously knew Tail-End Charlie was a wink uneasy since he was a new and inexperienced youngster, so he was keeping an occasional check on him. The Luftwaffe assault came furiously fast, so all the group leader could do was to try to calm him over the radio and dispatch some planes to chase after the already retreating German 109s.

"Blue Four! Blue Four! Steady, steady there . . .there's nothing to worry about; your plane will fly okay, recover from the spin now . . .steady!"

The youngster, still scared out of his helmet and his plane riddled by bullets, tried to straighten out his plane and recover from the spin, but no soap. He punched the mike button and said firmly, "Steady, hell! They got me right by the ass, you SOB!"

He let the stick go, let the canopy go, and bailed out. "And you have all that in printing?" he asked me, almost terrified as I showed him the teletype-written message.

"Goddamn!"

One of the "F Kompanies," a listening post monitoring the radio channels with their earphones, was stationed at the top of the Feldberg, near our intelligence center, and another was at Treisberg, also in the Taunus range of mountains. Naturally, every soldier on duty there spoke excellent English, and with time their ears became accustomed to certain voices. They heard a voice so often that it was easy for them to say that this or that particular voice, which used to be heard on

Chapter 6: Remarkable! Most Remarkable!

FAMOUS LAST WORDS
America's top fighter ace over Europe, Francis S. Gabreski, said, "One more sortie and I'll go back home and marry Kay." But one more was one too many. His P-47 propeller hit the ground while strafing, and a few days later he appeared in Scharff's office as a POW.

one specific frequency, now calls on a different wave length and uses another call sign. Just as easy as it is for you to recognize the voice of an acquaintance over the telephone, such as your girlfriend, your mother-in-law, your stockbroker, they could keep track of voices on the radio.

Nonmystical as this is, our POWs at Oberursel thought it was so very cunning and very secret. Their bases changed call signs and frequencies every so often. They thought it was one of the most secret secrets of the whole war. Actually, such periodic communication changes gave them far more of a headache than it did us, their enemy.

We were certainly not supposed to know, but we were in possession of complete lists of the changes long before the date they were to become effective.

Our radio monitors were particularly enamored of one Allied operator who had an outstanding, low, sonorous voice, distinctive. He, we soon discovered, was a fighter pilot and a captain in the 9th Air Force who was sent to the front to operate a forward air controller's radio. This meant he was with the troops and advised pilots of the 9th Air Force flying overhead where to drop their bombs and where to strafe in support of the ground troops.

The Interrogator

A FRUSTRATED AMBITION
Lt. Royal D. Frey, USAAF 20th Group pilot, was certain he was destined to become the world's greatest fighter ace. A bad engine on his P-38 and German flak put an end to that objective. Frey lost the nice new flying jacket in Germany.

    This captain was an air force liaison officer, and since liaison officers in this capacity did not fly, we never expected to see one at Oberursel. However, this man took a wrong turn down a road in his command car one morning and drove straight into the German lines. Before he could fathom what was wrong, he was disarmed and captured, complete with van, radio transmitter and receiver, guns, maps, boxes of cigarettes and chocolates, . . . and driver. It was near Diedenhofen-Thionville.
    Our army troops who captured him saw he was air force, so they transshipped him to Auswertestelle West. I liked his even-tempered manners and his habitual way of organizing his thoughts in detail before uttering them in his pleasant deep voice. We passed the anthills as I ventured to take him on an outing into the forest and up to the mountaintop where sat our listening post. There we found the men who had so often listened to his callings before his capture.
    Most of them were privates and noncommissioned officers and, since they were quite secluded, were always eager to get a break in their monotonous lives. Though I had not forewarned them or prearranged this visit, we were very heartily welcomed into the inner sanctums. Introducing my guest, he had hardly boomed his "How do you do?" when a chorus of the men screamed in utter amazement, "Sweepstake Two!" (His name was Captain L. A. Silvernail, and he wrote "A Soldiers Dream" in my guest book.)
    The words put him in a state of utter amazement, too, because "Sweepstake Two" had been his call sign at the front!
    The last, really the last, bottle of cognac was hurriedly brought forth and opened, since the mountain lads wanted to honor the man from the other side. At the risk of a stiff court-martial, we slipped him into the receiving room and

132

Chapter 6: Remarkable! Most Remarkable!

20th FIGHTER GROUP COMMANDER
Luftwaffe fighter pilots had the knack of shooting down the Allied formation leaders, so many group and squadron COs came to Oberursel. Col. Cy Wilson of the 20th Group was no exception. Scharff says he was a tough and noble opponent.

he had the unique experience of listening to the talk of his own replacement on his own frequency . . . from the wrong side. We wanted to let him take the microphone and say "hullo" to the new lad manning "Sweepstake Two," but thought better of it.

One day I was called by the department chief and asked to rush out as many prisoners as I could because the rooms were urgently needed for an influx of new arrivals. I began to work again after office hours. That evening just before dinner, I had assembled all my fighter group files on a work table, then went to eat, locking the door behind me. Tidily arranged according to air forces, five groups to each wing, each wing in a different color, and each group file marked with its respective number in this fashion: 8th USAAF Fighter Command, 65th Wing, 4th Group.

In my hurry to go eat, I forgot to clear that table or cover the files. The table stood near the entrance door. When I returned from dinner, I called for the next prisoner and had quite a shock when he stood in the doorway, saluted me, half turned to face my table where my *secret* files reposed, and silently selected one of them. With the file of his own group in his hand, he stepped over to my desk, behind which I stood speechless, and, standing once more at attention, reported with the perfect natural assurance of a foregone conclusion who he was! Either he took it for granted that this procedure was the customary one, or he knew I was in a hurry.

Another helpful enemy, unwittingly cooperative, was a first lieutenant who, without the slightest hesitation, answered every question I asked. I did not have to do any trapping or preliminary work.

The Interrogator

Again it was one of those rush jobs, and I did not intend to devote much time to him since I was fully involved with the interrogation of two very important colonels who had fallen into our web, Col. Cy Wilson and Lt. Col. Francis Gabreski.

Contrary to my usual procedure of fully investigating a case before calling the POW into my office, I called this young first lieutenant in spontaneously. All I could see from his name, rank, and serial number was that he had graduated from West Point and was a regular officer. Again, I was the one to be surprised. He was based at Wattisham in England in a newly arrived P-38 Lightning group, and I had never heard of his outfit before. There was really no need to ask about it because he told me everything himself. Sometimes he interrupted his own sentences, saying, "Of course, you already know all this." I would nod affirmatively although I was becoming more and more startled as he talked.

While talking to him, I picked up the phone and, on the direct line to Paris, asked my friend "Shorty" of the Signal Corps about the call signs of the new group, the 474th, and he confirmed what my friend the POW had just told me.

The phone call caused the young lieutenant to have some doubts about just what I did know, or maybe it was just plain curiosity, but he suddenly asked if I really did previously have knowledge of what he had been talking about. For an answer I called Wild Bill and requested he go downstairs and bring me the registry's file on the 474th Fighter Group.

"Certainly!" said Bill, "That old stuff . . ."

Bill returned shortly and handed me a file marked 9th USAAF, 474th Fighter Group, and then he chatted a while with the prisoner. But Lieutenant Mills watched me carefully as I perused the file, which actually looked well worn by much thumbing. I read, deeply concerned for several minutes . . . the blank pages . . . which Bill had hurriedly placed in the new file.

"All is correct," I said at last, "but how the heck did you know I had all this poop on you in here?"

"Well, I figured that if Axis Sally knows every detail about us, you must know it too. Hell, she called us on the radio the very day the 429th Squadron arrived at Wattisham, the 5th of May, and I think what she said was 'Welcome, boys of the 474th Fighter Group at Wattisham and Moreton. We have been waiting for you!' Then she told us a lot of things about ourselves, which were correct, so why should I be secretive with regard to something that is public knowledge, and you send it out on the radio?"

"Sure! Sure! Why should you?"

My instant attempts to solve this mystery of Axis Sally's broadcast failed. I was reassured that no other source for the supply of information to the shortwave radio stations existed other than our own Auswertestelle West, for military information anyway. However, several following prisoners swore to have heard Axis Sally's words too.

Chapter 6: Remarkable! Most Remarkable!

Author comments: Axis Sally had actually received an intelligence report that had passed through Auswertestelle West but had fallen through the crack, as papers are wont to do in the battle of red tape. She knew and broadcast that the 474th Fighter Group had been trained in the US under the command of Colonel Clint Wasem, and that it moved to England in February and March of 1944, with headquarters at Moreton. The group's three squadrons were the 428th, 429th, and 430th. The group had flown its first mission on 25 April 1944 and until 6 August had operated out of England, helping in the preparation for and later participating in the invasion of Normandy. On 6 August the group moved onto the Continent to Neuilly, France, and to St. Marceau, France, on 29 August. First Lieutenant Mills had flown on 5 September while the headquarters was at St. Marceau.

Scharff's confusion that the 474th was a new unit into England is best explained by that it was really a new unit on the Continent, having been in England for the previous five months.

In order to get a viewpoint from our side, the American side, of Auswertestelle West, the author has contacted several of the American fighter pilots who were captured by the Germans and interrogated by Hanns Scharff. Their stories are pieced into this book at various points apropos to the story by Scharff.

A young USAAF lieutenant, Royal D. Frey, was one of these pilots who tasted the hospitality of Oberursel. He most graciously consented to give the author the details of that visit.

Author comments: Royal D. Frey in early 1944 was a second lieutenant, flying with the 55th squadron of the 20th Fighter Group, stationed at King's Cliffe in England. On 11 February his P-38 had one engine quit over Germany, so he aborted the mission and started back toward home plate at a somewhat reduced airspeed. A German ack-ack (flak) battery tracked him and fired six shots into the air. Frey saw five bursts and felt the sixth. His Lightning burst into flame, and he burst out of the cockpit into space and soon opened his parachute.

P-38-10-LO, serial number 42-67855, left a long, black trail of smoke as it plunged toward the ground. It crashed 2 miles east of the village of Ludinghausen, about 15.5 miles south of Munster. The pyre of smoke rising into the air signaled the last of Lieut. Frey's ambitions to become the world's greatest fighter pilot ace. When he left RAF Wittering that morning, he had been convinced he was destined to replace Eddie Rickenbacker as the top American ace, and he might even surpass the famed Baron von Richthofen as the world's number one ace. Instead, that damn Allison engine had thrown a monkey wrench into his plans, and now he was destined to go a different route in life; his altered plans would take him to Oberursel, where he would become one of Hanns Scharff's prize pupils.

Lt. Frey takes over the story here: "I arrived at the Frankfurt railway station after dark, escorted by an elderly military gentleman guard who knew very little English. I felt sympathetic toward him because he had lost his wife and daughter in an RAF night-bombing raid near Düsseldorf.

The Interrogator

ESCAPE PHOTOS
Paul A. Conger of Hesperia, California was Gabreski's wingman during most of his combat over Europe, still he had 11½ victories of his own. Here are his escape photos which he kept wrapped in a cellophane packet. Professor Doctor Bert Nagel at Oberursel could instantly identify the coat and tie used by the 56th Group pilots from these photos.

PAUL CONGER'S ESCAPE PHOTOS
Paul A. Conger was Gabreski's wingman during his first combat tour and ended up with 11.5 victories. Prof. Dr. Bert Nagel at Oberursel could instantly identify 56th Group pilots from these escape photos because they all wore the same shirt and tie.

"It was the 11th of February, and at noon that day American heavy bombers had unloaded on Frankfurt, a 500-pounder dropping through the glass dome over the Bahnhof waiting room. As my guard and I walked from one track over to the trolley line to get to Oberursel, the workers were still carrying out the mangled bodies of women and children. I really got scared at this point as I saw the crowd looking me over in a hostile manner. There was no mistaking that I was American, and I thought the moment of truth might be at hand. I envisioned myself being strung up on one of those light-pole stanchions in the terminal. The elderly man who was my guard would be ineffective in fending off a determined crowd.

"However, no one bothered us as we stood waiting for the trolley, although a beautiful young German girl came up and talked to my guard. She was going to Oberursel, too, and I was really impressed since she looked exactly like Claudette Colbert of the movies.

Chapter 6: Remarkable! Most Remarkable!

"We arrived at Oberursel and walked up the hill to Auswertestelle West, the intelligence and evaluation center, where I was turned over to the post guards. They took me to a room, where they ordered me to remove everything from my pockets. Next they confiscated all US military items, including military issue clothing. It happened that I was flying that day, wearing my tanker's pants and jacket, and lost them at this time, but they allowed me to retain my officer's green shirt and pants and my GI shoes. Normally I would have been flying in my battle jacket, but I think it must have been at the cleaners that day, or perhaps it had been so cold I opted to wear the tanker's jacket. My escape compasses had been sewn into my battle jacket, so I did not have to worry about them finding that. After this episode was over, they marched me over to the building where the solitary cells were located. They called this building 'the cooler.'

"The cooler had small cells with frosted windows, and an excelsior-filled mattress. I was exhausted and lay down the minute the guards closed and locked my door, falling asleep instantly. Don't know how long I slept, but I awakened chilled to the bone . . . freezing. On the inside of the cell was a knob, which, when turned, dropped an arm out in the hall, allowing a knocker to fall against the door, signaling the guard that the POW inside wished to see him. I turned the knob and soon the door opened, and by sound and sign language, I told him I was cold.

"Ja, ja, ja!" He turned and left, locking the door behind him.

"I fell asleep again when I felt warmth coming into the cell, and again I did not know how long I slept. When I awakened I thought I was being parboiled! It must have been 120 degrees inside. I rang for the guard again. When he came, I semaphored that it was now too hot and then looked at his wrist watch. It was 12 o'clock, and I thought it was noon and realized I was very hungry, so I motioned to him that I wanted to eat. That caused him to jabber away at me, and he left in a huff. I found out it was midnight, not noon at all, and so I slept fitfully and hungrily.

"The next morning he came and led me to the latrine. I washed my teeth by scrubbing them with my finger, which was a little better than nothing, really. Then back to the cell, where they soon brought me some breakfast. Terrible! Coffee made of roasted tulip bulbs and some very sour, smelly German black bread. It was the pattern of things to come.

"That afternoon sometime, I was led over to room 47, where I met my interrogator Hanns Scharff. Standing behind his desk dressed in Luftwaffe blue, he could have been a colonel or a PFC, because I did not know German rank insignia. I did not know what to expect, and when he courteously greeted me and asked me to be seated and offered me a cigarette, which I did not take because I did not smoke, I admit I was caught off base because I fully expected to be bullied and threatened and perhaps even tortured. I filled out the first three squares in his questionnaire—namely, name, rank, and serial number—drew a diagonal line through the rest of the page, and signed my name at the bottom. Scharff looked at me with disappointment written across his face, then turned and picked up a file folder marked '55th Fighter Squadron, 20th Fighter Group.'

"Scharff scanned through it, handing me some pages to read myself, and reading others to me. I was impressed with his command of the English language but answered none of his questions. He knew everything, though, even where I went to college and my mother's maiden name. He wanted me to confirm some of the items in his file and warned me that until I could positively identify myself as an American soldier, there would be the suspicion I was really a spy feigning to be a soldier, and I could get myself shot as a spy. Rather convincing arguments.

"After some sparring back and forth, a good-looking girl waltzed into the room with some cookies on a plate. My thoughts went back to the briefings the 20th Intelligence Officers had given us at Wittering and King's Cliffe that the German interrogators might try to ply us with booze and perhaps even good-looking women, and I thought that if this gal was the start of that routine I'd sing like a canary for them, even though I was a dumb second lieutenant and did not know very much. Well, maybe I could make up enough in my imagination to satisfy them. But Hanns never offered to set me up, so that was the end of that. Struck out again!

"Sitting or lying on that little bed was all I had to do between interrogations, and I thought it was a terrible waste of talent for the world's greatest fighter pilot just to lie there, so I began to look forward to the interrogation sessions with Hanns Scharff. It seemed mighty ludicrous for the potentially hottest fighter ace since Rickenbacker to languish unhappily in a cell when not being interrogated.

"Hanns Scharff was a smooth talker who exuded confidence as well as Continental grace and charm. His high bearing and demeanor denoted his aristocratic lineage, and his English, which came across as Oxford, combined with all the other outward appearances, told us POWs that we were dealing with *a real sharp cookie*! He used all these attributes to the utmost too. We were not supposed to give more than name, rank, and serial number, but this guy would say things to irritate you in his all-knowing manner, and you would impulsively pop off and smart-aleckly correct him or defend the USAAF or your family or whatever. Probably this was one of his tactics! He told me once that he got some information from every interrogatee. After the war, I asked him what he got out of me. He replied, "Not very much!" Maybe he was being the gentleman that he is, but I have always worried about it anyway, thinking I might have given him a lead someplace when he had my dander up. However, as a second lieutenant, I knew nothing anyway!"

Author comments: The author owes a debt of gratitude to Royal D. Frey. While researching and writing *Fighter Aces* (1965) and *Horrido!* (1968), both coauthored by Trevor J. Constable, I interviewed numerous American fighter aces, and many of them referred to Interrogator *SHARP* at Oberursel. Actually, they meant *SCHARFF*. Having flown many B-25 Mitchell bombers and numerous noisy

Chapter 6: Remarkable! Most Remarkable!

fighters during WWII as a test pilot at Wright-Patterson AFB in Ohio, I have lost some hearing and am slightly bone deaf. Frey's article about Scharff in the June 1976 *Air Force Magazine* brought Hanns Scharff and me together. My heartfelt thanks to the late Colonel Royal D. Frey.

Hanns Scharff continues: Have you ever heard the Russians sing? I like it because they sing so beautifully. But have you ever heard Russian POWs shouting and screaming when they take a shower bath? Knowing that they were actually enjoying themselves, I laughed about it, but they sounded as if they were murdering each other.

In the cellar of the building below the cooler, we had our showers in one big room, and once each week the Russian handymen, about twenty of them, had what sounded like the time of their lives. The yells and shrieks could be heard afar, and everyone knew from all that racket that it was Saturday afternoon. The din made me wonder if it was as much a luxury to them as it sounded. Did they bathe in wooden tubs before the fireplace back home, or just swim in the horse trough? Or did they bathe at all?

Perhaps only a learned psychologist can explain why nearly all men let off steam in the steaming bath. You will do it, and I do it too, but we usually sing or hum or whistle a quiet tune, at least moderately. Other peoples express their joyous emotions differently. Come to think of it, there have been thousands of reports

BOMBERS HAD LARGE CREWS
The USAAF B-17s and B-24s carried crews of 10 or more aboard. When the bomber streams grew, Oberursel was inundated with interrogatees.

The Interrogator

WERNER PLACK AND SON "PUTZI"
German wine merchant and friend of Anheuser Busch, Plack once had his nose broken in a fistfight with Walter Winchell. Plack was celebrating a German victory before the US entered the war. Winchell did not like anything German except their automobiles.

POLISH POW AT OBERURSEL
A wing commander in the RAF, this Polish officer signed a photo to Horst Barth with these words: "To my best friend who put to use very much the heart during my first days as a prisoner war. Always with love, W/C 5/11/43."

that all the Russians who were prisoners of ours in WWII were tried by courts-martial in Russia when the war ended, and all were sentenced to several years of penal servitude in the Gulag Archipelago in far eastern Siberia, and I'd almost make a wager that it was because they had tasted the luxury of a weekly bath in the German prison camps. Maybe?

I have witnessed war dance celebrations of the Kaffir tribes in Africa and was present at Indian wedding ceremonies. They were nothing to compare with the hubbub and commotion of twenty Soviet soldiers in a shower bath. They screech and scream and slap each other's bodies like they were positively mad. They never had it so good!

Right above the shower room were the cells of the cooler. A young American lieutenant had just begun his irksome prison career in one of them, and he was so terrified of the assumed torturing that he called the sergeant of the guard, the warden, and actually begged to be led without further delay to the interrogation officer. Perhaps I could not describe sufficiently the noise those Russians made in

Chapter 6: Remarkable! Most Remarkable!

the showers, but it really did sound as if they were torturing and killing each other. I rather imagine many a POW, hearing that racket and later escaping any brutality at all, went on to Dulag Luft honestly congratulating themselves that they must have performed satisfactorily before the interrogator, because they escaped those torture pits down in the basement.

His face a chalky white, the young lieutenant stood before me resolute and prepared for the worst.

"Sir, I will not be beaten! I'll die if you torture me! I am prepared to make a statement right now. Where are your questions, and what do you want to know?"

I did not laugh about the Russians anymore.

Since so many American and British fighter pilots were shot down over France, especially when the Americans first started fighter operation out of the UK and later after the invasion, we often sent one of our interrogators, Leutnant Haas, over to Paris so that he could interrogate POWs as soon as possible (ASAP) after their capture. We found it generally much easier to question them and get cooperation if we could talk to them while they were still clanked up after their downing, rather than in several days or even weeks. Time was on their side, since they were able to gather their wits about them and generally prepare themselves for the ordeal they knew they were about to face.

Lt. Haas had mastered French as well as the English languages and therefore was an extremely valuable inquisitor because he could work with American, British, and Free French captives, as the case required. There in Paris, Haas met one of my friends in the German Foreign Office, one Herr Werner Plack, who had attained a degree of notoriety in the American press since he had been called everything from "Master Spy" to "a smart cookie from Hollywood, California." Plack had owned a wine business in Hollywood and due to his business, his shrewdness, and his outgoing personality had known nearly all the big movie celebrities on a personal basis before the war.

Once upon a time, it was just at this time, a young American bomber pilot was scheduled to leave the US for combat duty in Europe, and it was his last night in the States. The giant USO (United Service Organizations) was hosting a big party for the departing gladiators in Los Angeles, and this young B-17 pilot and most of his buddies were being feted. He, lucky and handsome boy, danced with one of the most beautiful of the film stars present. He was envied by his squadron buddies.

But this young bomber pilot was apprehensive about going to war and was overly quiet, so quiet he may not even have appreciated the great honor this movie actress was bestowing upon him. She had noted his fine physique, his movie-star looks, and his serious eyes, and perhaps she thought, "Here is one who is not a wolf. I could bestow all upon him."

As they danced, he spoke hardly at all, and when she thought his mind might wander, regardless of where, she carried the conversation to him. Shy, preoccupied, whatever, he left it up to her to do the talking.

The Interrogator

In the way that one tells a parting pal to give his best regards to a remote friend, she asked him that should his path ever cross with that of the famous wine merchant and illustrious gentleman Werner Plack, who was German and was back over there on the other side, to say "hullo" for her. He had been a key figure in her rise to stardom.

Over there in Paris on a rare sunny afternoon, not long after the lieutenant had been the envy of every other stud in the bomber group, the air raid sirens began their warning shrieks to tell the Paris inhabitants to seek cover because the American bombers were coming, and it was hard telling what they would call military targets this time. Herr Plack, a brave man who did not like wasted motion, said to hell with those damn sirens, since he had no time for air raid shelters, so he just stopped his open sports car on the Champs-Élysées and walked to a small clearing that would give him a good view of the bombers overhead, playing Russian roulette with the flak guns ringing Paris.

Every time there was a flak burst very close to a Fortress, half the population breathed a sigh of relief and the other half said, "Ah! Enfer!" Suddenly there was a smoke ball right on the wing of one of the scores of airplanes flying almost wingtip to wingtip in a beautiful formation. Torn, the airplane violently rolled out and away from the rest and fell into a fateful plunge to earth like a badly winged pheasant, spilling its human cargo haphazardly right above the Montmartre. Most of the crew made the jump in time, one of them descending very near Plack. For a landing place, this pilot picked the rooftop of a movie theater, and my friend Plack ordered some gendarmes to capture him and deliver him to his car.

They soon returned, holding between them a good-looking American lieutenant who was all right physically but quite speechless due to all the excitement. Things took quite a change when the civilian asked him to take a seat in his car and introduced himself as a member of the German Foreign Office.

"Of course," he said. "I have to hand you over to the Luftwaffe, but having lived a long time in the States and knowing that you won't enjoy yourself as much in my home country as I once did in yours, you better come with me to my apartment and have a quick drink with me."

At Herr Plack's apartment, his charming German / Southwest African wife greeted them. Plack poured the Scotch, and the American did not feel quite so much a prisoner.

"What is your hometown in the States?" asked Plack.

"Nevada, I mean Reno, sir."

"Reno! I am a member of the Fortune Club in Reno! Darling, please bring the album and show him my photographs of Werner Plack's Life in Reno."

"Excuse me, sir," stammered the American. "Did you say you are Werner Plack? I am supposed to say hullo to you from a friend of yours in Hollywood, from a film star . . . from . . ."

"Here is to her!" said Plack, raising his glass, "for auld lang syne!"

Chapter 6: Remarkable! Most Remarkable!

FRIENDLY OPPONENTS
This photo was taken during an afternoon outing to the Georg von Opel hunting lodge in the Taunus. South African Philippe Loock and Scharff's assistant Walter Hanemann wistfully consider Loock's comment that he would rather have met Scharff in Johannesburg, South Africa.

If one fares on sea back and forth from Africa to Europe, one learns many a cunning stratagem. I met numerous clever entertainers on these voyages, who showed and taught me various hocus-pocus games and tricks. After a few years I had scraped them together into quite a nice repertoire of my own.

Don't think, madam, that I would saw you in halves, and don't, good sir, believe I could make you invisible . . . but I can betray your eye. I am able to muddle your mind, and I will make you grab the very playing card, out of a pack of fifty-two, that I want you to take.

If anyone had told me that I would utilize the trick of forcing a card at Oberursel, I would have considered myself a candidate for the nut mill. You see, everything happens logically and step by step. In the first place I won a reputation for achieving extraordinary interrogation results. Then I made a name for myself by making every prisoner talk, and finally, everyone knew my favorite proverb, Aristotle's famous saying: "Always something new comes from Africa."

Something new often had to be applied during interrogations, too, especially where everything had gone wrong. Several times I was called on to help other interrogators who had run into a dead end while questioning some particularly recalcitrant POW. Through this practice, I came into contact with a few bomber pilots, some Polish officers, a Free French fighter pilot, a couple of South African colonels, some RAF types, and a Negro captain up from Italy. Since I was not at

The Interrogator

home in their fields, as I was in my own 8th and 9th USAAF Fighter Commands, it was always a strenuous task for me.

One day I was informed that an RAF squadron leader had been badly handled by one of my colleagues, not physically but by way of wrong questioning techniques. Since it was thought he might have some data that would be of value to us, I was asked to give it a go. The only thing we knew was that he came from RAF 321 Squadron, but he did not know that we had even that information. I planned to build my case on that.

As the first step, I received the squadron leader in my office and patiently listened as he registered a long complaint about being abandoned in the calaboose. My colleague, having been at the end of his wits with this stubborn man, was reluctant to release him to go on to Dulag Luft because he was an important POW, but my colleague also just left him cooling his heels in the cooler for day after day. The squadron leader was now ill tempered and getting more so daily. After he had lodged his complaint, I pledged my word that I would arrange his immediate release. I stated that I already knew all he would know of important military consequence since it was overtaken by events so was no longer of any value to us. We had acquired the answers from elsewhere. Then I invited him to afternoon tea at the officers' mess, where we could relax, and called over to have his private property returned to him immediately. This was to confirm in his mind that he was indeed going to depart. Then he went back, shaved, had a good shower, and was brought to me to go have tea.

Captain Barth was also invited, and I asked him to carefully avoid any reference to military matters in our conversation. Barth agreed that all he had to do was, after about two or three hours of light banter and insignificant conversation, suggest that I perform some card tricks for the amusement of the POW squadron leader.

Tea, toast, buns, butter, honey, and milk . . . Ah! It was good to taste these long-missed delicacies. Plus a little sweet French Benedictine, just a little glass of it . . . and soon the air was blue from our cigarette smoke in the pleasant air of tranquility.

Natural harmless conversation ripples along like a merry brooklet in the springtime. Topics about dry fly fishing and even classical music can be stretched out as long as desired, just to avoid the slightest touch on any military subject, anything to create a feeling of confidence and certainty. This induced lull in security was to slowly but surely diminish all vigilance.

Another table nearby was left by its occupants, somewhat messy with two decks of cards, some tallies, cigarette butts, and empty glasses. They had been playing bridge. Casually, Captain Barth reaches over and liberates the cards and, with his best winning smile, begs me to kindly do a card trick or two for his amusement. He is so persuasive that even the major is interested in seeing a sleight of hand or two, and I cannot resist. Right away I perform the smartest of all my

Chapter 6: Remarkable! Most Remarkable!

tricks just to establish a high esteem. My audience of two marvels at my magic, and the major visibly shows his relaxed enjoyment. This was so much better than being stashed away in the cooler.

The second trick I performed, I asked the major to draw three cards from the pack, and we lay those three down on the table in front of him, facedown. Then I ask him to turn them faceup, one at a time, beginning from the left.

As he turns them up, I exclaim, "Three . . . two . . . one! Look! Did you think of your squadron number as you turned them over?"

"Yes, I did," he says quickly and firmly. "That's it!"

He grabs my hand and shakes it, and I had the feeling he was a bit doubtful yet relieved too.

"Hanns, what a character you are! Did you do that or did I? Anyway, what a marvelous trick! You are a hell of a fine fellow!"

When I wrote a long report that night about all that I had learned from the major, which was a lot since the card trick triggered his cooperation at that very point, I began to feel 100 percent sure that I was a character, all right, but I did not feel 100 percent sure that I was such a hell of a fine fellow.

Wars, we know, have made our earth seem smaller; in fact, so small that people from faraway places must meet with seemingly dead certainty. When countries shut themselves off from the rest of the world during wars and block their borders, it becomes even more interesting to the individuals of the opposite sides to encounter each other as if drawn by magnets.

After my hot South African days, I had come north and spent my first winter Christmas in a tiny and forlorn village in the Austrian Alps. New Years Eve I was in my hotel room when the door opened and one of my best friends stepped in, thinking it was his room. He had just completed his tenth trip around the world and had just checked into the hotel from Canada. He had not the foggiest idea that I was in Austria, never dreaming I had left South Africa. When we recovered our senses from the complete surprise, he told me of another incident. He often traveled to New Zealand, and an English friend had entertained him with lavish hospitality. His English friend had a large estate and a fleet of cars, one of which was a big yellow Chrysler sedan.

The chauffeur always called it the "Flying Banana" and had taken my friend on many a pleasant drive through the beautiful countryside around Wellington. Then came the war, and my pal, a civilian during the war, passing a group of Allied prisoners who were marching along the road, was nonplussed to hear a voice cry from among them: "Hey! Remember the Flying Banana?"

The chauffeur! A renewed acquaintance under most unusual circumstances. Small world!

If one wishes to be exact in explaining how Herr Walter Hanemann became the interrogation officer for the POWs from the 12th and 15th Fighter Commands, which operated out of North Africa and Italy, it is necessary to describe our first

The Interrogator

meeting. If he had not chosen my bed to sleep in while I was absent on three days leave, we might never have met or known each other. Returning from a visit home, I found a visitor in my cot, a stranger to our outfit who had grabbed the only empty bed he could find in the night. Now he submitted to my rights to it, although he could have claimed possession was nine points of the law or some such footle.

He had lived in America, learned to fly there and married there, and had been on a visit to his fatherland when the war started, the same as had happened to me. He had participated in the Polish and French Campaigns as a Stuka pilot and was wounded so was sent to the rear to become the interpreter at Dulag Luft in Frankfurt. This was the processing or distribution center for POWs in transit from our camp to a permanent POW enclosure, one of the *Stalag Luft*s. Then Dulag Luft was destroyed by an Allied air raid, with only one POW killed. This resulted in Dulag Luft being moved to Wetzlar, which was about 50 miles away from Frankfurt.

Walter Hanemann and I became good friends, and subsequently we visited each other often. One day he telephoned me that he had gotten into some sort of troubles with his superiors on behalf of some prisoners and was to be transferred. Of course, it was understandable that he might get into trouble, since he had lived very happily in America for some years and he liked Americans, so it was very difficult for him to avoid being accused of mollycoddling POWs. With our Lord's help and Captain Barth's help, he was assigned to me for the purpose of becoming an interrogation officer. After I coached him a few days, he caught on to my methodology quickly and took over the interrogations of the 12th and 15th Fighter sections of the USAAF and the South African air force.

My scholars and understudies usually adopted my own system of inquiry, even to the extent of using some of my own phraseology. His perspicacity enabled him to quickly conduct interrogations skillfully without any help. We worked together in close cooperation, exchanging on an almost daily basis the experiences of our routine work and our personal views. For this reason I was able to participate in some of his most remarkable events. Before telling you about them, I will tell you about a South African intermezzo:

My dentist had made me wish that the American 8th Air Force bombers might list his torture chair as the primary target for the day, and I left his office with mixed feelings for the tramcar terminus. I waited in front of the Schauspielhaus for the Oberursel tram, and there I saw three different lots of POWs being guarded by soldiers as they awaited the tram to the intelligence center.

There were ten Americans, obviously the complete crew from a downed bomber, three British airmen, and one single prisoner. All were carefully being kept separated by the guards. When the streetcars arrived, the guards put the Americans in the first car, the British in the second, and the single POW in the third. I chose to ride in the third car and managed things so that I ended up standing out on the platform right next to the prisoner.

Chapter 6: Remarkable! Most Remarkable!

This POW was clad in a khaki uniform and coat, without any insignia, and my curiosity about him was aroused. I looked him over and he looked me over, then I asked him where he hailed from.

"A place nobody here has heard of, or knows," he answered abruptly.

"So? I have a fair knowledge of geography. Maybe I know it."

"It's no use," said this stranger. "I have been asked a thousand times, and people just shrug their shoulders."

"What country?"

"South Africa."

"Oh? I do know a little about that country. What town?"

He looked at me mockingly. "Joburg!"

"Joburg!" Now every true Johannesburger calls his city "Joburg" because he never has time for such long words. From my breast pocket I took out my silver cigarette case, a beautiful caisson given to me by a South African friend as a souvenir. I had taken a memorable motor trip around Basutoland with them, starting at Joburg and ending there again, and they had a map with our route engraved on the cigarette case. In true Afrikaner custom, the word "Joburg" was engraved on it. I just put my finger under the word and showed it to the Joburger.

His guard was swill up, and he suspiciously asked me if I knew any of the suburbs. "Yes, Rosebank, Parktown, Houghton, Orchards, Westcliffe, Berea, Fordsburg here; pardon me, please. Have a cigarette. I am pleased to meet a Joburger again."

He declined my offer and turned to look out the window, silent for the whole hour it took to get to Oberursel. There we had to part.

Walter Hanemann interrogated him, of course, since he fell into Hanemann's category, and when that was completed, I asked the Joburger to go for a walk with me past the formicary of the ants and over to the hospital, where he could see one of his wounded buddies. He spoke freely to me now because he knew who I was and I knew who he was and I was acquainted with his family. My friend with the "Flying Banana" had played many a set of tennis at his parents' home too. As for his strange behavior on the tram, he apologized. "I figured that your famous German intelligence net had phoned up from Italy, where they caught me, and had told your outfit to send an unconstrained, relaxed, but highly specialized agent from Joburg to meet me accidentally along the way for just such an extraordinary yet seemingly unintentional interrogation. You have a reputation for cleverness, but this time it really was accidental that we met."

Murder Inc. A new stream of grist for our propaganda mills began flowing when some bomber crews were shot down, and they were wearing jackets with the words "Murder Inc." painted on the backs. Our official propaganda voices were continually trying to incite the public by making out American pilots as terror fliers, air pirates, air gangsters, or whatever, but actually there was very little

The Interrogator

response from German civilians or soldiers, in spite of the heavy losses and damage due to the bombing raids. Until Murder Inc. came along.

The man in the street wavered in his opinions when he could see with his own eyes how those generous American travelers of peacetime had turned into murderers in wartime. Now they even labeled themselves with big white letters on their backs, turning many German heads toward them and many people's minds against them. There were only a few Germans who really understood the harmless, figurative meaning of this hoax. Distinctive and funny to the wearers and other Americans, but to foreigners the jacket logo left an extremely bad taste in their mouths.

Author comments: Murder Incorporated was the nickname given to Boeing Flying Fortress B-17F, serial number 42-29858, assigned to the 508th Squadron, 351st USAAF Bombardment Group, Eighth Air Force. (Oddly the Boeing family, makers of the Boeing Fortress, came to America from a village near Hagen, Hohenlimburg. In Germany, the name was spelled Boing. In the first World War, Anthony Fokker of the Netherlands built a fighter plane and tried to sell it to his country and what later became the Allies. Turned down, he sold the Fokker planes to Germany.)

On 26 November 1943, Boeing's Murder Inc. developed an engine problem, and the crew had to fly a spare bomber on a mission to Bremen. Some crew members bailed out after the plane was damaged by enemy fire, and the B-17 crash-landed near Bremen, Germany.

On that mission, some of the crew members were wearing their lightweight leather flying jackets under their winter flight suits and heavy jackets. They had the words "Murder Inc." emblazoned in white across the back of the light jackets, and, as Scharff points out, the Germans were quick to exploit this opportunity for their war propaganda machine. The slogan of this B-17 crew probably threw no fear into the hearts of the German people, who saw the photographs of Lt. Ken Williams and his jacket in their newspapers, but it did create an impulse for revenge and more-stringent reactions when other bomber crews were captured.

Back in England, the Eighth Air Force initiated immediate action to ensure that all bombers and all flight jackets were devoid of any inscriptions or paintings considered to be of poor taste, or likely to aid the enemy.

HANNS SCHARFF continues: The same negative impression prevailed in regard to Negroes in Germany. War propaganda dating back further than WWI always pictured black African savages with long knives in their teeth while fighting with the French army. A German mind has a hard time associating a dark man with America. He knows the Redskins, the American Indians, but during WWII and earlier it was not known that America was slowly being populated by blacks through the population explosion and practically unlimited immigration quotas. To the German, a "Neger" could be seen on display only in Circus Hagenbeck's "Wilder Völkerschau," and these blacks came only from the Congo, Nile, and Niger or the African jungle.

Chapter 6: Remarkable! Most Remarkable!

TROUBLESOME FLIGHT JACKET
This photo appeared in German newspapers after USAAF lieutenant Kenneth Williams and his bomber crew were captured. It sent a message not met with approval in Germany.

Early one morning I sauntered out of Auswertestelle West to buy some fresh-baked white rolls at the nearby bakery of Frau Best. She was a tiny, gray-haired woman who, while selling her bread and rolls, generally was mumbling her complaints about the extra-heavy burdens of war, which seemed to always strike heaviest at the families of bread bakers. Sometimes it was this complicated system of ration coupons, sometimes it was the shortage of yeast, or no coal for the fires, or no sleep last night because the RAF night bombers were overhead all night.

"And now this!" she disdainfully sputtered, pointing her trembling hand out the shop's window. "Ugh! How awful! Look at those dreadful savages . . . those horrible black men!"

On the opposite side of the street, the tramcar was disgorging its passengers. Among them were five Negroes and their guards. I had seen many a native in Africa, and I really was not interested in American Negroes since none were pilots, to my knowledge, and I was more interested in Frau Best's bakery goods than her reactions to the blacks.

Behold! I took a peep out the window, and it struck me instantly that the first two Negroes looked like members of a small African tribe whose king was the Paramount Chief Sobhuza and the queen mother was Mshlafagaze II. I had one time enchanted them with some presents at their royal kraal near Mbabane in Swaziland. Could these two really be Swazis? American Negroes did not have

The Interrogator

31st GROUP, USAAF MUSTANGS
These long-range fighters from Italy added to the problems facing the Luftwaffe.

LOCKHEED P-38 "DROOP SNOOT"
A fighter with a Norden-type bombsight in the nose. The Germans needed technical information about this weapon system, so they tasked Oberursel interrogators to obtain it.

Chapter 6: Remarkable! Most Remarkable!

this long typical hair. I tried to picture them in moochies, the warriors in G-strings and armed with assegai and shields.

The other three had South African physiognomies, and their broad noses and thick lips, the shape of their heads, and the peculiar growth of hair meant they could be Zulus. Many a time I have visited Zululand, and for years some of my personal valets had been proud Zulus.

I gathered my rolls, paid the dear lady, and returned to my office. Later on, I looked out my office window and again saw the five Negroes, now being marched into the courtyard. On impulse I leaned out the window and shouted "*Saubona mfondinis!*," which is something like saying "Hello, strangers!" If they had been Americans, I had just made a fool of myself, but they were thunderstruck. They jumped to stiff attention and yelled back at me, "*Nkos Baas!*"

"The great master," as they had called me, walked out of the office quickly and went over to the cooler, where all five had just been led. All five were sitting in one cell on the bed awaiting further processing, and in a moment I found that two were actually Swazis and three were Zulus. I gave each one a package of cigarettes and an extra food ration, and then they told me the simple story of their way to the cross. As lorry drivers of the South African Air Force (SAAF) they had fallen into our hands somewhere in Africa. The Germans sent them from one camp to another and obviously did not know what to do with them. There was no *Mealie Pap* to eat, they complained, and no watermelons to quench their thirst.

"Tell me your names, please," and soon I had a Jim, a George, a Jack, a Peter, and an Abraham. Their native names, though, sounded better to me: N'tabalali, Ololowe, Mbubulu, Ndiamzana, Shlagaanini. George was the only one who had ever worked in a big, white city, in Johannesburg. As a butcher boy he had labored at Rosebank Corner, and I had lived just one block from there, so I told him who I was.

"Oh, Baas! I used to bring your good missus many steaks and sausages. You had a fast white sports car and two big doggies wanting to bite me, and two little masters and many white pidgems in your gaaden. Aha! Take me as your cook boy, Baasie!"

Jim piped up, "Take me as your houseboy, Baas?"

"Me as your gaaden boy," added Jack.

And Peter begged, "I can be your garage boy?"

Amusedly, I turned to the last one and remarked, "All the vacancies are now filled, Abraham, but what about you?"

"Don't let's be enemies anymore, Baas."

"You can't become my boys, and I am sorry it cannot be done. But we will part as friends, and I must leave you now. Before I go, will you sing one of your Zulu songs to me as a farewell?"

"Yes, Baasie," a disappointed George said. "Which one you like?" "Perhaps "Nomashihamba"? No, I think I like to hear "Sponana ndia hamba, sponana e

The Interrogator

"JOLLY ROGER"
This bomber crewman arrived at Oberursel in this jacket. In the background is the cooler. Note barred windows.

bhai." I imagine for the first time ever, in the gloomy silence of a cooler cell, surrounded by Luftwaffe guards, sentries, other prisoners, and German officers, the melodious voices sang their ancient strange tune.

The South African intermezzo was over.

Once more I saw the five little African children being marched past my office one day, late in the afternoon when they were being shipped off to Dulag Luft. "Go in peace!" I shouted from my window, the customary Zulu "Hamba gashle!" "Great Baas!" they called back. "Salla gashle!" "Stay in peace!"

Author comments: Many years have elapsed since this episode, and efforts to contact the participants have come to naught. Perhaps some of these Zulus and Swazis will read this book and recall their part in the life of Hanns Scharff, the Luftwaffe's master interrogator.

German prewar intelligence gathering in the United States was highly successful. The famed "Norden" bombsight, which the USAAF claimed gave American bombers the capability of dropping a bomb into a pickle barrel from any altitude, is a case in point. A German sympathizer working in the Norden plant on Long

Chapter 6: Remarkable! Most Remarkable!

Island City, New York, smuggled the complete drawings out of the factory and gave them to a steward on the German ship *Reliance* in 1938. The steward bandaged an injured leg, hid the drawing in his umbrella, which he used as a cane, and walked calmly through US Customs.

During the war, the Germans heard that the P-38 Lightning was being fitted with a new adaptation of the Norden sight, and the plane would be used as a dive and level bomber. Oberursel's Technical Division searched every P-38 crash for signs of the Norden sight right up to the end of the war. The "Droop Snoot" P-38s that carried the Norden or a radar sight were either completely destroyed while crashing, or they managed to return to their home bases.

7

WORTHY OF IMITATION

Pinch yourself and know how others feel.
—German proverb

A pleasant surprise struck me like a bolt out of the blue one day. Each noon at 1215 hours, all the officers on the staff at Oberursel stood in a semicircle in the main briefing room awaiting the appearance of our commandant. There was a rumor flying about to the effect that he had something important to announce, and the adjutant had hinted to one rumor carrier that it was about me. When that part of the hearsay reached my ears, I hastily began to mentally review all the misdeeds I might have made over the past few days, and could not help but wonder which one had finally caught me up.

After he had gone through the long rigmarole of routine business, he addressed me, and I felt all eyes turn toward me. Unconsciously I tensed at attention while he read from a pink paper of telewritten messages from headquarters in Potsdam.

"INTERROGATION REPORT CIPHER SCHFF / NUMBER 722 REPRESENTATIVE OF DESIRED COMPREHENSIVE AND IMPORTANT INFORMATION STOP EVERY OFFICER HEREBY REQUESTED TO STUDY AFORESAID REPORT AND USE IT AS STANDARD WORTHY OF IMITATION STOP"

"My congratulations!" he added, and conceded to me one of his rare smiles. To be mentioned in dispatches always brings some degree of glory to a soldier. The deputy commander and many others offered their compliments, and the praise was sweet, but yet with it always comes some bitterness as well. That afternoon, Captain Offermann, the security officer, asked my secretary for a copy and commented, "In

Chapter 7: Worthy Of Imitation

MORE NEW ARRIVALS AT OBERURSEL
With the size of the RAF and USAAF bombing raids increasing and fighter escorts rapidly expanding, arrivals at the interrogation center also grew. POWs usually arrived via tram or trolley from Frankfurt am Main.

accordance with the order from headquarters I will read the report, but for the life of me I cannot understand how this man achieved that honor."

Still, not every bullet hits home, as you know, not the security officer's shot or the ones fired at different aims shortly afterward.

All interrogation officers were ordered to attend a lecture being given by two Luftwaffe officers who had been prisoners of the British for some time but had been repatriated to Germany due to very heavy and disabling wounds. The two repatriated officers talked about the grilling they had undergone at the British Interrogation Center in London. For nearly two hours they painted a gruesome picture of such horrible details that everyone present was appalled and felt a strong inclination for revenge. Our suave and persuasive commandant squashed that vengeful mood when making his summary and conclusions of the talks. He warned us not to get carried away with thoughts of retaliation or black-tinted artistry. His warnings kept us on an even keel.

As I walked over to my quarters, I saw some new arrivals standing outside in the blazing sun, and it was a hot day. They were awaiting their turn to be counted and called into the reception barracks. I could see they were quite exhausted. Although my mind was still fresh from the accounts just reiterated by the Luftwaffe men who had been ill treated by the British Intelligence Corps, I stifled an impulse to go on and let these POWs sweat it out. I stopped and looked them over, then said, "Hullo, chums. Sit over there in the shade and take it easy while you are waiting." Their guard smiled his relief at me and moved them into the shadow, where he gave them the command "Rest!"

The Interrogator

Some six months later I learned by fortuitousness that these men had expected to be ill treated by their German captors, even expecting to be beaten, and were grossly surprised and grateful for some little gesture of friendliness that first day at Oberursel.

To my knowledge, no one at Auswertestelle West kicked any of the POWs around or poked at them with bayonets, or even used swear words, not even the lowest ranking of our guards. There was one exception. We had for a while a German lieutenant whose name was Bauer, who seemed to enjoy yelling and cursing a recusant prisoner, but Bauer was equally disliked by officer and soldier, friend or foe. Those who really got kicked around and shouted at were the German privates in this camp by their own truculent sergeant major!

Every now and then, some additional duties would be given to me by the commandant. Frequently I had to escort visitors around the premises, and more often than not these visitors were some of the highly decorated fighter aces of the Luftwaffe. I learned quickly that the greatest attraction to them here in our zoo was the Camp Officer's Reception (COR) room, which, as I said earlier, was like a museum. This was also a place where these big aces could scrounge a souvenir or two from the officer in charge. The biggest desire seemed to be for the silk maps all the POWs carried when captured, and the little compasses used for escapes. Although it was verboten to hand out any of this confiscated material, even to our own combat heroes,

ANTICIPATING THE WORST
Concerned POWs await processing at Auswertestelle West.

Chapter 7: Worthy Of Imitation

I always somehow managed to meet the demand. The more difficult the moonlight requisitioning was, the more the items were appreciated by these fighter aces. They were all a fine lot. I don't believe a one of them suffered from gynephobia, and the silk maps were destined for their girlfriends.

One day the camp was bustling with excitement. I saw the motorcade enter the encampment, bearing well-known squadron standards and bringing a host of Luftwaffe *Kommodoren*, aces, fighter pilots who were real swashbucklers, heroes, and public idols. Two score or more of them! They were to be with us for three days for lectures and tours, and Wild Bill had to come over and run my office since I once more became a sort of cicerone, extraordinary and plenipotentiary.

While I was leading my first group around, Wild Bill intercepted me and told me the commandant had just decreed that I would have to lecture on the subject of 8th and 9th USAAF Fighter Commands for one hour in the officer's briefing room at 1400 hours today! Not much time to get such a briefing ready, so it would have to be "off the cuff," but I knew my job well enough that I never gave it more than a passing thought.

Wild Bill took me aside and whispered, always worried if something out of his rosy and plain world occurred. "Hanns, there are a hell of a lot of "tin-ties" in this big group, and another hell of a lot of reverberation reflectors of political opinion. More brass than you can shake a stick at!"

By "tin-ties" he meant Knight's Crosses, the Ritterkreuz, and by "reverberation reflectors of political opinion," he meant the German Star in Gold, the only decoration a German wears on his right side and the only one with a large, distinct swastika. That was what we called "ground-pounders slang"; just as fighter pilots have their own language, we did too.

I laughed at him. "Bill, don't worry. One listener is the same as all listeners to me, just as I salute everything that moves. You know that!"

"Ja! I know, but you have seen only a small part of this gang. I have a few shots of that superb cognac left over at my room. Let's go over and kill it. It will give us both some courage," he implored.

So we went to his room and killed that bottle, since I began to feel the necessity for a little meditation before talking to the group, and a little fringe benefit of some medication might not hurt. I guess I was always a relaxed speaker, lucky in that sense, since it was not difficult for me to speak about my work at all because I knew what I was talking about. Furthermore, I had made many official speeches in my life, as director of a motorcar concern, addressing a foreign trade commission, praising the ladies' aid society at an important gathering; I had no stage fright at all. The cognac was Three-Star Hennessy, not bad at all, although just a mite too warm to really please my palate.

"Gentlemen!" Colonel Killinger was introducing me to the spectacular crowd. "You will now hear a few words about the enemy's 8th and 9th Air Forces, something about their organization and strategic and tactical tasks." Killinger waved his hand

The Interrogator

in my direction and smiled as if to say, "Okay, buddy, it's all yours, and I hope you have something to say." In reality, he said, "It speaks: Private Hanns Scharff!"

In the very first row I noticed three of the highest awards for bravery, the Knights Cross with Oak Leaf. Next to them sat at least a dozen of the plain Knight's Cross winners, making the atmosphere highly charged. What was my own bright ribbon, of which I was so proud, pinned freshly through my second buttonhole, against such splendor as this? I was not a cockalorum among this gathering of splendid eagles, that was for sure.

My speech covered such subjects as organization of the 8th and 9th Fighter Commands, operations, and tactical approaches. I explained fundamental rules and axioms, the principal circumstances, and the casus belli. I told of conclusions, deductions, decisions, and making full use of my knowledge and experience, and soon I saw audience heads nodding approvingly and heard exclamations of understanding and agreement. My analysis of enemy intentions drew acclaim.

At the final inference, I described the characteristics of the enemy fighter pilot, as well as his behavior and reactions after capture and while in solitary confinement. My audience was gripped! My suggestion that some of them might like to meet a typical American fighter pilot was accepted with eager expectation.

"We have a highly important American fighter group commander in the cooler right now and have just begun interrogating him. He is a West Pointer, a regular Army Air Force man." This heightened their interest, of course. Most of the Luftwaffe fighters in my gallery were wing commanders, full colonels, and so I asked them to select three of their members to join me at the officers' club for tea at 5 o'clock, where they would meet this enemy colonel. I also warned them not to be surprised if I would take the liberty of treating them as bosom buddies in front of my prisoner. A private and *Obersten*, bosom buddies?

This West Point colonel POW lived up to the traditions and esprit de corps we expected from such an officer. Col. Charles W. Stark was devotedly loyal to the USA, correct and alert as all fighter pilots have to be, a refined and polite gentleman meeting even German standards. He was at ease and proved to be a witty and cheerful individual. I know he wondered how a PFC like me could be welcome in the officers' club, and such a personal buddy of three *Obersten*. I think he thought that if I had such a friendly relationship with those colonels, then he would not be overstepping the protocols if he and I had a friendly relationship too.

The situation was just like two good friends in normal peacetime. One would never have guessed that all five of us were not old friends of long ago.

Perhaps it was a little unfair of me to introduce such good-looking, well-dressed, high-spirited officers glittering in the glamour of their decorations, to a POW appearing in the very clothes he was wearing when he was shot down, a jumpsuit type of gabardine coveralls and a pair of heavy flying shoes. He told me later he felt very simple in his clothes among such well-dressed gentlemen. The German aces quickly put him at ease and stressed the equality of rank. Their friendliness was so earnest

Chapter 7: Worthy Of Imitation

"THIS BREAKS MY HEART"
Major Gerald W. Johnson had 17 victories when he was captured by the Germans. When interrogator Scharff showed him the 56th Fighter Group dossier, Johnson was aghast at all the latest information therein. "This breaks my heart!" he muttered.

that the American could not refrain from reciprocation and entered wholeheartedly into friendly banter as only fighter pilots can, regardless of their nationalities.

As it always is when men of the same trade meet, they talked shop. Each trade has its own language, and particularly so the fighter pilots. My four guests were flying with their hands at 30,000 feet, flat on their respective backs, shooting each other down in frontal attacks and in spiraling dogfights, always 60 degrees or more deflection shots hitting the targets. They made terrific zooms and Immelmann turns, negative g, and inverted vertical reversements. The fantastic dives became more and more vertical as the drink took effect and the evening wore on. I was afraid to mention my legerdemain of card tricks and deceptive magic in the face of these absolutely bewitching stories. Sometimes all talked at the same time yet never missed a word that was being said. I was dying to give one of my better toasts but couldn't get a word in edgeways.

All four then fell silent for a few seconds, probably just because they all reached for a cigarette simultaneously. I startled them by jumping to my feet, all looking at me as if I had just ripped my knickers some way or another.

"Friends!" I said quickly. "*Dulce et decorum est pro patria mori!* May I propose a drinking toast to the *fallen* fighter heroes of both sides!" They rose, clinked glasses, and stood a moment in silence. Then they sat, taking up in midsentence right where they had left off. Old friends never need reintroduction, and true friends never need to have their memories refreshed as to what was being discussed when they last parted. These guys never missed a stroke! In fact, I think they gained a couple while toasting the fallen heroes of the air. Hands in air, they were immediately discussing

The Interrogator

VIP CAPTIVE AT OBERURSEL
USAAF colonel Jacob E. Smart was in a bomber of the USAAF 97th Group, flying out of Italy. It was shot down, and due to his rank he was sent to Scharff's office at Oberursel.

tactics of the Me 109 vs. the P-51, the ease with which the greener Luftwaffe pilots were allowed to go after the P-38s to cut their combat teeth. None of us thought of killing a man anymore; it was just the victories of which they boasted.

Comparison of tactics and maneuverability of enemy aircraft with our own interested them greatly. Modest effort on my part kept the conversation going. For two hours I sat and listened, interjecting comment only occasionally. No ventose speakers in this group. No aphasia-affected pilots like the POWs I had been interrogating.

One of the *Kommodoren* smoked big black cigars continually, and now he offered one to the American colonel. "Have a cigar, please!"

"Can I refuse this?" the colonel whispered to me. "I never smoked in my life!"

"No! Absolutely not! You must take it or he will be offended." The colonel took it, lit up, and pretended to enjoy it all the time, although I noted that he was careful not to inhale. Soon the stogie went out.

The Luftwaffe ace with the cigars commented, "I had a tremendous dogfight the other day, colonel. We turned and crisscrossed, looped and rolled, and tried everything to gain the advantage, but finally had to shoot bad snapshots because it was impossible to gain good position. We fired every chance without effect. Then suddenly the American fired a stream of white tracers at me, one passing through my propeller, and those ten or so white tracers reminded me of an intelligence report I had read a couple of days earlier, and I knew that his guns were . . ."

Chapter 7: Worthy Of Imitation

I interrupted him with alacrity. "Of course, you got him, Herr Oberst. To what did that boost your score?"

"As a matter of fact," the gallant fighter retorted as he looked into the smoke curling from his cigar, "I didn't get him. I let him fly home, because I do not shoot at a defenseless man!" The story was true, I found out at a later date from his wingman who had witnessed the aerial joust.

The three *Kommodoren*, Hans Trübenbach of early JG 52 fame, towering Hannes Trautloft of JG 54 "Grünherz," and Josef "Pips" Priller, the diminutive boss of JG 26 "Schlageter," known to the Americans as the "Abbeville Kids" or the "Yellow Nose Boys," finally and reluctantly begged to take leave since they had other programs to attend to that night. They stood shoulder to shoulder in a line, clicked the heels of those long, shiny boots, and smartly saluted the American colonel. Every one of us was sorry the time had passed so quickly.

Our American colonel, Charles W. Stark, shook hands most cordially with one of them, and it was easy to see that he liked that enemy pilot. The moment they left the room, Colonel Stark flung the black cigar, which he had been chewing and not smoking, into the nearest trash bin. A nonsmoker should not begin on a cigar.

Colonel Stark and I fell into silence at our table, both of us lost in our own thoughts. I mused over the fact of how easy it is for a carefully and painfully gathered bit of intelligence to boomerang. The German *Kommodore* awareness that the ten white tracers meant an empty magazine and consequently a defenseless enemy had saved the unknown American pilot's life. Intended to help win the aerial combat, the knowledge had actually preserved the life of the enemy.

The gallant Kommodore Pips Priller had flown up beside the American, waved a comradely salute, and let the enemy fly home. How many more lives would be preserved in this manner, I did not know.

Nor did I know why Colonel Charles W. Stark, our POW of the USAAF, was equally absentminded and lost in thought. Bright and happy just a few moments ago, I thought I could now detect sentimentalism showing through his armor.

Author comments: Colonel Charles W. Stark, USAF, graduated from West Point, Class of '37, and was sent to Randolph and Kelly Fields in Texas for pilot training, graduating with the Class of '38C. The author was a classmate at Randolph and Kelly. A bright and friendly officer, Stark was completely happy to be selected for pursuit training at Kelly and, along with his USMA classmates, advanced rapidly during the early days of WWII from "shavetail" to full colonel. In early 1944 he became commander of the USAAF 79th Fighter Group and took it to Italy.

On Stark's thirty-second combat mission, 5 May 1944, his P-47 fighter was damaged by flak and he was forced to land it in the surf just north of Lido di Roma near Anzio. Within two hours, other American fighters were back at the scene and reported sighting Stark's "Jug" about 10 yards off the beach in shallow water, with many swimmers on and around the aircraft. Secret intelligence reports received later said that flooded territory and demolished bridges had delayed Italian residents from

The Interrogator

COLONEL CHARLES STARK'S ENTRY IN GUEST BOOK
Stark was flying in Italy, but when he went down he was sent to Scharff for interrogation. This was his entry in Hanns Scharff's now-famed guest book.

Chapter 7: Worthy Of Imitation

getting to the plane for approximately one hour, and when they did arrive, the airplane was practically undamaged and the canopy was open, a parachute rested on the wing, and the first-aid kit had been opened. Footprints led from the aircraft across the beach to the fields that lie between beach and inland. Colonel Charles Stark had managed to get away, at least temporarily. Two hours after his landing, German soldiers arrived and fanned out to commence a search for the downed flier.

For two days Stark managed to evade his pursuers, but eventually he was captured just before dawn by an Italian bicycle patrol. Later he was escorted to Oberursel by a Major Doctor Viktor Heisig and two guards from Milan.

At Oberursel, Hanns Scharff had become established as the best interrogator of senior officers, and though Colonel Stark was a 15th Air Force pilot flying out of Italy, "Big Chief" Barth designated Scharff as interrogator. Scharff, showing true adherence to the German custom of great respect for senior military officers, treated the colonel as only some of the outstanding Germans can. Though Stark spent two weeks in solitary confinement at Auswertestelle West, he says the treatment was reasonable at all times.

During the interrogations, Scharff was impressed with Colonel Stark's manners, straightforwardness, military bearing, and personality. He decided to groom Stark for the position of senior Allied officer with station at Dulag Luft, the transient POW camp located at Wetzlar, so he showed the colonel the file he had on the 79th Fighter Group. Stark was amazed and says the data therein was "essentially correct."

"Scharff had us stashed away on the third floor of the hospital at Hohe-Mark in a padded-cell mental ward," Stark writes. This was after his two weeks at Oberursel and after being taken out of solitary confinement. "We had the liberty of walking around the hospital park grounds, if we promised on our officer's word of honor not to try to escape during those walks. All Allied POWs seemed to get excellent treatment at Hohe-Mark, thanks to Dr. Ittershagen and his staff, nothing like what one expected to receive as a POW, and for sure not like many POWs I talked to later. Few of the Germans I came in contact with were the dastardly Nazi types we see portrayed in so many American movies.

"The old Dulag Luft had been bombed out in central Frankfurt, so I went to the new one situated on the Lahn River at Wetzlar, home city of the famed Leica camera. I was the senior Allied officer and had a staff of three officers and thirty-six Allied airmen as permanent party at the Dulag Luft transient center.

"The three Allied officers on my staff were 1st Lt. Gerald G. Gille, my adjutant; Flight Lieutenant Peter W. Gilpin, RAF, our senior briefing officer; and 2nd Lt. Arthur C. Jaros, our mess officer. Warrant Officers Clifford Hooton (our chaplain) and John H. Marini (chief medical orderly) completed the list of officers on the permanent party, the remainder being Allied airmen with ranks from private through technical sergeant.

"I was kept at Wetzlar until April Fools Day 1945, after the American troops came through and liberated us. An American OSS officer, Lt. Commander Robert

The Interrogator

E. Jennings, USN, commandeered a German vehicle about this time and drove T/Sgt. Lee Hughes (he had been in charge of the clothing store in Dulag Luft) and me to the nearest USAAF headquarters.

"Hohe-Mark holds many varied memories for me; I well recall a very homely German medical corporal taking great and very tender care of badly burned Allied airmen, and his tears when those patients were evacuated to the big general hospital at Frankfurt.

"Dr. Ernest W. Ittershagen was a great man and was famous as the understudy of the German surgeon who pioneered the 'pin surgery' for badly fractured bones—stainless-steel pins put in the marrow of bones. Also there was a Dr. Rolf Tomae, who I thought was the same caliber of person as Dr. Ittershagen. Another Luftwaffe officer who struck me as an extremely capable man was Horst Barth, as was the German commander of Dulag Luft, Lt. Col. Otto Becker, and his compound commander, Major Josef Hayden, an Austrian and former Cook's Tour director in Vienna. How they managed to feed, clothe, and house over 2,000 POWs at one time there at Wetzlar is a mystery of super management. Principally they used carefully stored Red Cross supplies and some scarce German food. They had direct and private contact with the Swedish Red Cross officials. We certainly had little complaint on the whole setup. In fact, we understood from a Swiss source that Wetzlar was one of the two best POW camps in all of Germany.

"After all these years I still have contact with Scharff and the interpreter-guard Professor Heinrich Haumann. Haumann could really handle the English language beautifully. Haumann has now retired from the Nürnburg school system and resides in München. I have seen him, Dr. Ittershagen, and Lt. Boninghaus during some of my visits to Europe since the war."

One who has been a prisoner of war does not shed his troubles when he is released from captivity. Indeed, if he happens to have been a senior officer captured by a military-conscious nation such as Germany was in WWII, and because of his rank is given ever-so-slight preferential treatment, he is likely to be accused by his own countrymen and fellow POWs of misconduct as a prisoner.

Colonel Stark was unaware that he was under investigation until 1948, when, as a student at the Air War College at Maxwell Air Force Base in Alabama, he was suddenly removed from the class and assigned as commander of the Maintenance and Supply Group at Maxwell. There were no charges ever made against him, and to this day he does not know who pointed the finger at him and why. At Wetzlar, Stark had his own room, an office, and a small staff, and he escorted German officers when they visited Wetzlar on inspection tours. He was treated as the senior Allied officer by his German captors, and in no way did he collaborate with the enemy.

"Everything I did or didn't do, said or didn't say, under the same circumstances I'd do it again! I ran the Dulag Luft strict and fair, in my opinion, and in the process must have stepped on some opinionated toes. If so, that was just too bad. The overall picture took priority, and I did what I thought best. If it had not been for the dedicated

Chapter 7: Worthy Of Imitation

help I got in 1948 from General Delmar Spivey, General Pete Quesada, General George C. Kenney, Gill Rob Wilson, Hub Zemke, Gabby Gabreski, and others who were personally interested and concerned, the Gods only know what the outcome would have been."

One of those "others" who was interested was Germany's master interrogator, Hanns-Joachim Scharff!

Early in 1948, Scharff was requested by Mr. Noel E. Story of the US Department of Justice to write an affidavit of the activities and conduct of Colonel Charles W. Stark, covering the period while he was at the Luftwaffe interrogation and evaluation center at Oberursel. Scharff complied, and his report was dated 20 May 1948.

According to this report, Scharff saw Stark arrive at Oberursel. He wore no military insignia and carried no luggage. Scharff was assigned to do the interrogation of Stark due to his past experience questioning other senior POWs.

Quoting directly from Scharff's affidavit:

"Colonel Stark behaved, during his stay at Oberursel, as it would be expected of a West Point colonel.

"The treatment of our officer-prisoners was founded upon the traditions, morale, and ethics of the old German officer corps, perhaps a bit romantic for this day and age but which we ourselves lived up to and expected to find reciprocated among the officers of the American Army, and which we sometimes did encounter in such persons as Colonel Stark and some of the other officers.

HOHE-MARK HOSPITAL NEAR OBERURSEL
Hundreds of injured USAAF and RAF airmen were treated here by Dr. Ittershagen. Good food and good care by one of the finest medical doctors made Hohe-Mark a wonderful memory for many POWs.

The Interrogator

"He was a loyal, correct, and alert officer, refined and polite gentleman; at ease a cheerful and witty fellow. On the other hand, I knew he had succeeded in contacting some fellow American officers at the hospital and other places, and that they were forwarding and exchanging information about my own and our camp's activities, and I am sure he never suspected that I knew this and permitted it because it helped to preserve his own morale and that of others. I, of course, knew that if Colonel Stark or any of the others had escaped it would have been very detrimental to our work, and naturally I took very good care that he did not.

"Colonel Stark wrote a postcard to his superior officer, Brigadier General Gordon P. Saville, in Italy that he regretted having fallen into enemy hands, that he was well treated, that he thought the German intelligence was so good they must have a blood and a urine test on every one in the 15th Air Force, and that he was glad, by the way, to learn from enemy intelligence that the general's cold was better.

"As there was not a suitable room in the cooler for Colonel Stark to stay with us for a prolonged period, I suggested that he be moved to a nearby hospital which was under the direction of Doctor med. E. W. Ittershagen, Oberarzt of the Luftwaffe. There he did enjoy better facilities and more freedom. He was allowed to speak to all the hospitalized POWs, including Colonel Jake Smart, Colonel Joe Miller, General Vanaman, AVM Ivelaw-Chapman, Lt. Col. Gabreski, and a South African Air Force officer.

"Colonel Stark was called to the Interrogation Center several times to attend some parties and cinemas (Stark recalls seeing a movie of the 1936 Olympics and

HOHE-MARK STAFF AND POWS
In June 1944 these personnel posed at the hospital. *Standing*: Lt. Bill, Sgt. Donald Ford, Dr. (med). Ittershagen, Horst Barth, Col. Stark, and Sgt. James Shelser. *Seated*: Lt. Del Ray, Sgt. Winter, Sgt. Robert Little.

Chapter 7: Worthy Of Imitation

one showing a USAAF P-47 Thunderbolt on Monte Cassino) to which many other POWs were also invited. My ideas were mainly to make those other POWs feel more at ease through the colonel's presence. Colonel Stark was always eager, at such occasions, to listen to complaints of his fellow POWs and would then do all he could to eliminate such troubles, with my help.

"When the new Dulag Luft, the POW transient and distribution center, was opened at Wetzlar, my CO asked for recommendations for the Senior Allied Officer position there. I suggested Stark, and Captain Barth was ordered to make the necessary arrangements. Stark left, as far as I can recall, about August of 1944 and arrived at Wetzlar the same day."

Apparently, no charges were ever filed against Stark, and the actions taken during the investigation were never explained. Colonel Stark was assigned as commander of the USAF 8th Fighter Wing in Korea and, while there, received the decoration of the Legion of Merit for his outstanding duties while a POW in Germany. When he returned from Korea he commanded the Atomic Storage Depot at Kelly AFB, Texas, and later headed the USAF Ferrying Service worldwide. He retired from the USAF in 1961 and, as this is written, maintains his home in Mexico.

Generalleutnant a.D. Hannes Trautloft, one of the three *Kommodoren* who visited Oberursel and had dinner with Scharff and Colonel Stark, recalls the meeting. He does not recall whether it was he or Kommodore Josef "Pips" Priller who offered Stark the cigar. Trautloft retired from the new Luftwaffe and became director of the civilian airport at Baden-Baden in Germany. He says he loved his job because it kept him up to date with flying, and he got to meet and keep in contact with the younger men who today make up the bulk of aviation's pilots.

Trautloft remembers Stark as stoically relaxed. He enjoyed talking with Stark. He also hopes, since he himself has been a cigar smoker since first learning to fly in 1931, that Colonel Stark has either learned how to smoke them rather than chewing on them or has given them up entirely.

"Colonel Stark was already convinced that the Allies would eventually win the war," comments Trautloft.

Stark enlarges on Trautloft's comment: "Yes, I stated that fact every time I got a chance, and most knowledgeable and practical Luftwaffe officers concurred . . . after being certain they would not be overheard." (Trautloft passed away on 11 January 1995.)

Oberst "Pips" Priller, *Kommodore* of JG 26, was the pilot who waved the American fighter pilot a safe journey home when his ten white tracers announced that the American was out of ammunition. He passed away in 1961. After the war, Priller owned and managed the Riegele Brewery in Augsburg, and his widow Johanna managed it most successfully after Pips's death. Priller's book *Geschichte eines Jagdgeschwaders* ("Story of a fighter wing"; Heidelberg, Germany: Kurt Vowinckel Verlag, 1956) has never been published in English, but it is a classic about the Luftwaffe's 26th Fighter Wing *Schlageter*. Johanna Priller passed away on 17 May

The Interrogator

1990, and son Sebastian Priller now owns and manages the Riegele Brewery in Augsburg.

HANNS SCHARFF continues: I was fortunate during WWII and met many a man of whom it could and should be said, officially mentioned I mean, that his actions merited imitation. I also know that most of them performed their duties in a most outstanding manner without looking for praise. They acted in the pure soldierly sense of doing one's duty.

Opportunities for sudden major decisions and resultant valor presented themselves more often to the leaders of units than to the men. This does not mean the men are less willing or less determined to bear sacrifices. The obligation to show a living example of good behavior and fortitude rests heaviest on the shoulders of an officer.

One of the first Mustang group leaders to be brought to Oberursel was a pitiful sight. Colonel Henry Russell Spicer had taken over the USAAF 357th Fighter Group on 17 February 1944, and 17 March he signed in at Oberursel. He was replaced as commander by Colonel Donald W. Graham on 7 March, so it was obvious that he had been shot down or forced down on the 7th or a day or two earlier.

Although he was known as one of America's toughest fighter pilots and was highly experienced as a pilot, when I first met him he gave the impression that he was an exhausted, ill, and beaten-down man. I immediately asked for medical treatment for him because both of his legs had been badly frozen almost up to his knees.

Colonel Russ Spicer was leading the 357th Fighter Group from his English base into southern France to the region between Cognac and Bergerac, where some of the German secret military installations were located. On the way home, his P-51 Mustang engine began to act up, and it became apparent that he was going to have to abandon the airplane.

Colonel Spicer was well over terra firma and could have landed, but since the Mustang was relatively new in service and perhaps he yet could get home, he nursed his kite along until he reached the English Channel. There his engine gave up the ghost. To make sure we would not recover even a single screw from his fighter, Spicer landed it in the near-freezing waters of the Channel. His three fighter squadrons of the 357th Group, the 362nd, 363rd, and 364th Squadrons, all saw their leader abandon his plane at low altitude and plunge into the chilly brine. "Mayday" was transmitted, the call sign for help, and rescue parties set out from the English as well as the French sides to catch the big fish, but all efforts were in vain. They could not find him.

For three days and three nights, Colonel Spicer fought bravely in his little dinghy, but the breakers kept washing him in toward the French coast, occupied by the Germans. Finally he was so frozen that he had to let the wind and breakers drive him ashore, and he was captured. Lying on the beach of the eastern side of the Cotentin Peninsula, he was picked up by some German soldiers in a state of complete collapse. Slowly the medicos brought him back to life.

Chapter 7: Worthy Of Imitation

DULAG LUFT (WETZLAR) INSPECTION
Once a POW had completed interrogations, he was sent to the transient camp, Dulag Luft at Wetzlar. Here, Luftwaffe major Hayden leads an inspection party. USAAF colonel Charles W. Stark (with wooden stick) was the American commandant.

I liked Russ Spicer and gave him as much freedom as I possibly could, and he took advantage of it. Now and then my telephone would ring, and a very disturbed guard down at the cooler would inform me that the prisoner in number 12 had the audacity to demand the use of the telephone for the purpose of speaking to me. I doubt if this had ever been heard of before in all of German war history.

"Let him speak to me," I would tell the guard, and then in a few moments would come over the line the soft, slow Texan voice of Colonel Spicer, asking for something or another. You would probably call Russ Spicer a "character."

His way of dodging my questions during interrogation struck me as quite amusing, and I admit it was quite effective too. Whenever he did not want to answer a query, he would beg me for the mustache clipper I kept in my desk drawer. He knew where it was and knew I would not refuse him, and as I handed it to him he would walk over to my window so he could see his own reflection and take a long, long time to beautify himself. One cannot talk, can one, when shaving, and it is the same when you are clipping a large mustache.

Spicer made a fool of me, good and solid, teaching me a lesson. At this time I had not had much experience in questioning high rankers and group

The Interrogator

BATTLE OF WITS
Interrogator Scharff (*right*) tried every ploy in an attempt to get POW Stark to divulge any military secrets he might know. Scharff was so impressed with Stark's loyalty and fortitude that he had Stark appointed Allied commander at Wetzlar.

BATTLE OF WITS-II (41 YEARS LATER)
On 23 July 1985 Colonel Stark and interrogator Scharff sat in the same position, only this time they toasted each other and the spirit of friendship; at Los Angeles, California. As Stark wrote in 1944, "YOU HAD YOUR JOB AND I MINE."

Chapter 7: Worthy Of Imitation

commanders. I made the mistake of pulling an old customary gag on him, which was suitable for junior officers who did not yet know too much about higher military spheres.

Right off the bat, I questioned Spicer as to the names of the members of his group, totally unimportant as it was, although I could use them to beef up my burgeoning files. I told him that I knew them already anyway, and to prove it I would say the name of one of his men for every name he would say. I told him that I would believe that he was the man he claimed to be, whose dog tags he wore, if he would name those names. The silly game did not take long because the first thing he said was to ask me if the mustache clipper was handy in my drawer. Then he walked to the window, and I told him who the group executive officer was. He countered by giving me the name of the group medical officer! I told him the name of the group operations officer, and here the list in my possession came to an end but he did not know it, and he gave me the name of the weather forecaster. I switched from group and named a squadron commander. Spicer got busy with the scissors and I waited. One cannot speak while one trims a long mustache. One might cut oneself! After an interminably long pause, Spicer turned to look at me and with a most friendly twinkle in his eyes said:

"Oh, excuse me! Was it my turn?"

I gave up, and he must have felt sorry for me because he declared, "Well, I'll tell you one you haven't got in your book. It's my supply officer. Write his name down, if you wish, since it is hard to spell. First Lieutenant *Krannenshaker*. The other day, just days ago, I asked the fool to fit me with a new parachute, and guess what that ass said!"

"How can I guess?"

"Well, he asked, 'Excuse me, sir, but do you still fly?' Yes, you can put his name right there in your book. I hope it comes in handy!"

The telephone rang, and I was glad to get a break from this character. Wild Bill called and told me he was having a losing battle of wits with a young captain and that Colonel Spicer's name had been used. At this, the young captain became very aroused, wagering that he would answer all questions if he could see this colonel with his own eyes.

"Come on over, Bill, any time you like, and bring your captain along. We shall see."

A son cannot embrace with greater fervor and feeling a father who he was sure had drowned in the cold waters of the English Channel and who was now found, by chance, languishing in the cooler at Oberursel.

Author comment: Colonel Russ Spicer was sent to Stalag Luft I, where he was the senior officer in charge. He got into trouble with the German camp commandant when he made this speech to the POWs at morning roll call one day.

(From the notes of POW Mozart Kaufman, who wrote them from memory just a few minutes after morning call dismissal):

The Interrogator

"Lads, as you can see this isn't going to be a fireside chat. Someone has taken a steel bar off the south latrine door, and the Germans want this returned. They have tried to find it, and I also tried to locate it but have had no success. The Germans have threatened to cut off our coal rations if this bar is not found by 12 o'clock noon. I don't know if this is a threat or not, but we must return the bar to the Germans. Anyone having information is to report to my office after this talk. There will be no disciplinary action taken against anyone.

"Yesterday an officer was put in the cooler for two weeks. He had two counts against him. The first was failure to obey an order from a German officer. That is beside the point. The second was for failure to salute a German officer of lower rank.

"The articles of the Geneva Convention say to salute all officers of equal or higher rank. The Germans in this camp have put out an order that we must salute all German officers, whether of higher, equal, or lower rank. My order to you is to salute all German officers of equal or higher rank only.

"I have noticed that many of you men are becoming too buddy-buddy with the Germans. Remember that we are still at war, and they are still our enemy and are doing everything they can to win this war. Don't let him fool you around this camp."

Spicer went on to make some comments about the Battle of Amheim and some alleged treatment of Allied patients in a hospital. He also mentioned some other alleged atrocities he had heard about from British prisoners at Stalag Luft I. Spicer then turned to the German commandant and other German guards who witnessed his speech to the POWs, and added:

"For your information, these are my own personal opinions, and I am not attempting to incite riot or rebellion. They are my personal opinions and not necessarily the opinions of my men."

Colonel Spicer was promptly thrown into solitary confinement. It was reported that he was court-martialed and sentenced to death. The sentence was not carried out, and he remained in solitary until midnight of 30 April 1945, when the Americans took over the camp.

I, the author, knew Russ Spicer after the war. He was an impressive officer, forceful and correct, and was one of the best leaders I have ever known. Hanns Scharff carried Spicer very high in his estimation of men and always spoke of him as one of the finest of all men. Major General Henry R. Spicer passed away on 4 December 1968.

HANNS SCHARFF continues: The doctor of the POW hospital at Hohe-Mark, Dr. med. Oberarzt E. W. Ittershagen, the friend of the wounded, was fooled by another prisoner in another way. We two were in close fellowship, and there existed between us a mutual attachment based on the same outlook on life, the same likes and dislikes of the problems surrounding us. Above all, we treasured our faraway families most, and both of us were keen to finagle some days furlough whenever we could. Together we invented the most cunning and audacious excuses to justify our request for three-day passes so that we could spend a few happy hours at home.

Chapter 7: Worthy Of Imitation

56th FIGHTER GROUP NOSE ART
A P-47 on the flight line sports this possibly prophetic Donald Duck behind bars at Stalag Luft III.

One excuse worked to perfection. Whenever a transport of recuperated POWs had to be transferred to a different hospital, say to recuperate under the care of an American or British doctor specialist, or some to be repatriated after further examinations, the good doctor and I always managed to get on the German transport staff, he as the medic, I as the interpreter.

The doctor automatically assumed the position of train commander or responsible officer because of his seniority. He had to account for the prompt delivery of all prisoners en route. Now who would ever think of a heavily wounded prisoner wanting or trying to escape from a moving train with locked doors and guards at each end of the car, in the middle of Germany? Unbelievable as it sounds, it happened.

An American POW with a mending spine in a plaster cast jumped from the moving train, unnoticed by guards or other passengers, and tried to effect a getaway. The good doctor probably still has the X-rays showing the spine actually had been broken.

After a day passed, the wounded American was recaught because he had not gotten very far; news of his break went from ear to ear across Germany, the saga of a POW's determination to fulfill his duty, which was to escape at the first fitting occasion.

The Interrogator

Some may argue right here whether I should cite this case under the "remarkables" title, because one could hardly wish to cause other wounded soldiers to believe that such a foolish act, condemned to failure from the beginning, was worthy of imitation.

There is more to this story. This officer had been thrown from an exploding Flying Fortress without his parachute! He fell from 20,000 feet into a forest without losing consciousness and with only his broken back resulting. There were several eyewitnesses, peasants working in the nearby fields, who saw him falling into the birch trees and heavy underbrush. They found him alive and believed in miracles thereafter. The doctor examined him and found only the cracked vertebra, and we were considering sending him home on the repatriation route.

He had used up his quota of luck. But he could not wait and jumped from the train.

Alone, we thought the man with the broken spine deserved much admiration because he expressed something with his desperate undertaking, something that everyone feels who really loves his country.

Article in the *New York Times*, dated 18 August 1955:

IF G.I.'s FAIL TO ESCAPE,
TRY AGAIN, THEY'RE TOLD

Washington, Aug. 17 (UP)—The top-level committee that drafted the new code of conduct for prisoners of war advised captured GI's today never to stop looking for a chance to escape.

"They also serve who only stand and wait," it said. "The Lord helps those who hustle in the meantime!"

We heard of several successful and unsuccessful attempts of the fighter boys to "repatriate" their downed buddies, making daring rescue landings in our midst. Whether their struggles failed or succeeded, we thought we should literally take our hats off to those exceedingly brave men.

Author comments: There were several authentic occasions where the pilot of a fighter plane landed in enemy-held territory in an attempt to pick up the pilot of a downed aircraft. Some were successful, others not. They were all spectacular undertakings, cases of sheer bravery on the part of the pilot flying the rescue plane. One of the most dramatic ended in failure, and both participants paid visits to interrogator Hanns Scharff's "information extraction chair" at Auswertestelle West. Three pilots were actually involved as another fighter pilot landed in an attempt to rescue the other two, but since he was unseen by the unfortunates, he took off and returned safely to England. Here is the story:

Late in September 1944, the 354th Fighter Squadron of the 355th USAAF Fighter Group was over Germany on a fighter sweep. Captain Henry W. Brown was

Chapter 7: Worthy Of Imitation

the leading ace of the group at the time, with 14.20 victories. He was forced to land his ailing fighter in a pasture. The entire 354th Squadron witnessed the forced landing. Squadron commander Major Charles W. Lenfest ordered the rest of the pilots to keep an eye on the sky for German fighters and to circle overhead and keep watch while he landed to pick up Captain Brown. He intended to land, have Brown climb into the cockpit and sit on his lap, and fly the Mustang off to safety after discarding parachutes.

The elements ruled against it. At the end of the landing roll, Lenfest tried to turn the plane around, and one wheel dug into the soft earth of a soggy, muddy irrigation ditch, and Lenfest was unable to power his Mustang out of the mud. The two men were destined for captivity. They set both aircraft afire, waved goodbye to the 354th boys still circling and buzzing overhead like a bunch of hornets, and walked into captivity. Retired colonel Henry W. Brown continues the story:

"After landing, Lenfest got the P-51 stuck in some soft ground and our escape was over. We ran into some woods and tried to hide, but the German forests are so clean a moving person could be seen for miles. While we were trying to hide, the other pilots in the air kept buzzing us, trying to let us know A1 White had landed back in the field to pick us up, but we didn't get the message. All this buzzing alerted the Germans as to which forest we were in, and as soon as the covering aircraft departed, they surrounded our forest, and about four hours later we were under guard in a farmhouse. The farmers were very nice to us, feeding us and making us as comfortable as possible. A young female about twenty came in and spoke to us in English. She repeatedly quizzed us as to whether the USA had been bombed by the Luftwaffe, and we assured her it had not. I'm not sure she or anyone else believed us.

"Late in the afternoon, two German Luftwaffe officers arrived in a car and took us to a nearby railway station, where we were met by four guards and an NCO. They loaded us onto a train and off we went toward Oberursel.

"We were in a large compartment with cushioned couches, and one guard stood near the window and the other near the aisle. The NCO changed the guard every hour, and where the off-duty ones stayed in the car I did not know. There were adjoining latrine facilities, so we had no discomfort except the thought that some trigger-happy American fighter pilot might strafe the train. I worried a lot, since I myself had on several occasions blasted the hell out of German locomotives. They were a lot of fun to shoot, and I still think about it; a P-51 Mustang with six .50-caliber guns, strafing, hair on the back of your neck sticking straight out, all that steam, the boxcars blowing up, the red golf balls of enemy ground fire crisscrossing in front of your windshield. All this was vivid in my mind as I rode toward Oberursel on a train. I was glad our train was not attacked, and later I was glad I had never strafed a German "passenger" train.

"We got off the train in a town near Oberursel and got onto a tram or streetcar. Our guards pushed us to the rear of the car, and the guards were posted. We traveled through the town and could observe the bomb damage. It was bad, but the German

The Interrogator

people had responded well to the situation, and buildings and homes had been cleaned up as best they could be. The bricks and building stones were neatly stacked and the area swept clean. I was very impressed; in October 1944 the German people in this town were not ready to quit, although they had been hit hard.

"While on this streetcar, Lenfest started to cough and sneeze, and I made some caustic comment about the champion of his class at West Point in boxing couldn't cope with the weather on the Continent. We both began to laugh, and the NCO of the guards smartly slapped me on the side of the head with his cap, from which he had not removed his metal buttons and insignia. Needless to say, the blow really got my attention. The NCO reported the incident to Hanns Scharff, who questioned me about it at our first sessions, but he seemed satisfied with my version.

"My stay at Oberursel was for three or four days, as best I can remember. I had a small cell, a bunk, light controlled by the guards outside the cell. There were no windows, and only a tiny peephole in the door. The temperature in the cell was fairly comfortable, and the food was plain but plenty adequate to sustain health. It was lonely in the cell, but I amused myself by walking back and forth, by singing, and by counting the nailheads in the wooden walls.

VIP KOMMODORE VISITS OBERURSEL
Oberst "Pips" Priller of JG 26 visited the interrogation center several times. He became acquainted with an RAF pilot on this visit.

Chapter 7: Worthy Of Imitation

"I remember being interrogated by Hanns on several occasions. He took me for a walk in the woods and in a garden on one occasion. During the interrogations I was offered cigarettes and given coffee and a cookie. His manner was cool, calm, and collected. At first I just gave him the old name, rank, and serial number routine, and he took no offense. He already had all the information he needed about me; all he needed was to confirm and collate it into whatever form he wanted.

"Of course, I had no big secrets to hide. I was only a captain fighter pilot who flew when told to do it by higher authority, and I attempted to destroy as many of the Luftwaffe machines of war as possible. When enemy aircraft were not available as targets, the orders were to hit the deck and shoot targets of opportunity. Hanns knew and understood all this, so there was no reason for him to make a big thing out of the interrogation.

"Had I been on a special type of mission, flying an experimental type of airplane or carrying exotic munitions, I assume I would have been more of a concern to him, and he would have put more pressure on me. However, a lowly captain seldom has the opportunity to have access to strategic information needed by a foreign-enemy government. I was just another fighter pilot whose luck had run out, although US newspapers had written many stories concerning my aerial victories.

"Actually, Lenfest and I were flying the only two Mustangs in the 355th Fighter Group equipped with the new computing gunsights. They may have been the only two computing gunsights in all of 8th Fighter Command, but I am not sure. There in those two burning aircraft was the whole inventory of these new sights, and neither Lenfest nor I spilled the beans to anyone at Oberursel. Maybe they were too badly burned by fire to be recognized by Luftwaffe inspection personnel. When these gunsights arrived at the 355th, they had been accompanied by a British technician and a complete set of metric tooling.

"Exotic ammunition? I had conducted tests on .50-caliber ammunition, which was explosive, but we had used all the test ammo up before this last mission of mine. This ammo was weird stuff, exploding sometimes while still in the ammo can in the plane, or 1 foot from the barrel as it was shot, 1 mile from the barrel, upon impact with the enemy aircraft, and sometimes *after* passing through the enemy plane. We never knew where it was going to explode, so I was glad when it was all used up.

"Hanns Scharff knew everything, it seemed, except the explosive ammunition tests and the new computing gunsights, and I did not tell him about them. We just talked about nonmilitary subjects. He commented on the way the grooves in the screwheads on the telephone were all lined up. He was proud of German workmanship, and rightfully so. He talked of the proposed German process for making clothing from paper, and said it never needed cleaning . . . just wear and discard when soiled.

"One day he brought in a man who said he was a German fighter pilot. I was suspicious and very cautious, so our talk was generalized. If they didn't know by that time that our superior aircraft and larger numbers were winning, it made no sense to question me about it.

The Interrogator

"My treatment at Oberursel can be termed 'nice' when compared to the stories the POWs from Japan, Korea, and Southeast Asia can tell. I saw Lenfest only once during the interrogations and passed another POW I thought I recognized en route to the latrine one day. I believe he was a Medal of Honor–winner bomber pilot.

"After a few days I was sent to Dulag Luft, where we were crowded into a barracks. At long last you could talk to someone other than your interrogator! There also was a group of French POWs there, and they would sing their national anthem for you at the slightest suggestion. My trip on to Stalag Luft III was by train, and it took several days. We were packed into boxcars and were damned miserable from the cold, scant food and the constant fear of being strafed by American fighters.

"Hanns Scharff was a fine officer, and he treated me fairly. He is a cunning devil and could extract a confession of infidelity from a nun. He could have been an injector of sodium pentothal, a sadist armed with an ax handle, or a student of oriental torture, but he was not. He was a professional at his job, with full compassion for his fellow man.

"My mother was living in Washington, DC, when she was notified that I was shot down. She learned about it from a newspaper article caption: 'Zemke is now leading ace in Europe since Henry Brown has been shot down!' She hit the ceiling since she had not received official notification."

Not all attempts to rescue downed fliers in the Lenfest/Brown manner ended in failure. The author is an experienced fighter pilot and knows the sheer guts it takes to land a fighter plane in an unprepared pasture at a speed in excess of 100 miles per hour. In my opinion, this type of rescue act is certainly worthy of the Medal of Honor award in most cases.

One such incident occurred on 18 August 1944, when two other pilots of the 355th Fighter Group successfully pulled it off, Flying a P-51, Capt. Bert W. Marshall Jr. was forced to land gear up 20 miles west of Soissons, France, in a small field. Lt. Royce W. Priest saw Marshall's predicament and unhesitatingly landed beside Marshall's Mustang. Priest jumped out of the cockpit, shucking his parachute and dinghy, and had Marshall climb into the seat. Then Priest climbed in and sat on Marshall's lap and took the airplane off, flying back safely to Steeple Morden in the UK. Deacon Priest was, in my opinion, one who should have been awarded the MOH.

Another incident comes to mind: Major Pierce W. McKennon of the 4th Fighter Group was hit by flak near Prenzlau and bellied his Mustang into a pasture a short time later. Lt. George B. Green sized up the situation and decided there was a chance to rescue McKennon. He landed nearby, sardined both pilots into the cockpit, and flew safely back to Debden, home of the 4th Group. "Bennie" Green was, in my opinion, one who should have been awarded the MOH.

The Luftwaffe also pulled off many such rescues, particularly on the Russian front. They have documented rescues using the Me-109, the FW-190, and the Stuka. Whenever possible, however, the little Fieseler "Storch" was used as the rescue plane, and it made hundreds of such pickups during the course of the war on all fronts.

Chapter 7: Worthy Of Imitation

TRAUTLOFT: KOMMODORE OF JG 54
Oberst Hannes Trautloft was one of the three *Kommodoren* who visited Oberursel and dined with Scharff and USAAF colonel Charles W. Stark.

HANNS SCHARFF continues: One more American flier fell into my hands whom we considered for repatriation. It was, of all good airmen, America's most successful fighter group leader at the time, Colonel Hubert Zemke, who had 17.75 aerial victories against the Luftwaffe. As leader of the 56th Fighter Group, called the "Wolfpack," Hub Zemke had become one of the most famous of the fighter aces in the enemy ranks. We had a file on him, with photographs, and were victims of some consternation when Zemke was transferred from the 56th Group to command the 479th Fighter Group on 12 August 1944. On 30 October, the engine of his Mustang failed and Zemke was forced down in Germany. Later it was determined that his airplane had disintegrated in a thunderstorm. We were delighted to get him. His picture had hung on my wall for several months before his arrival, so I was able to give him a most cordial welcome to Auswertestelle West.

Zemke's personal story in my files begins when he was six years old, a little schoolboy in Missoula, Montana. His schoolmates teased him because of his German parentage, or was it Pennsylvania Dutch? Because of his typical "Hun" name, he was isolated to some extent and became rather embittered, eventually developing into a hater of anything German. Right through his life, one could follow a trend, and the fact lay open, in the files, that he despised anything connected with Germans. Finally, his war records seemed to clinch the trend, and we credited his great aerial combat record to those convictions.

Late one evening early in November 1944, the news reached me that the great "Hun hater" Hub Zemke was over in the cooler, a new arrival. On the turn of my heel, I went over to visit him and pay him my respects.

The Interrogator

One seldom finds a master of two trades, but Zemke was not only a skillful master of combat leadership and fighting, he was also a master of expert fighting in the intellectual field. I was in a squeeze. I was not quite sure whether his reputation was fallacious, but I could not detect any sign of animosity. Yet, perhaps he was trying to mislead me and wished to conceal this embarrassing odium.

I could not help wondering how he would react when I showed him the photos I have of him the next morning. Recently, a captain from his unit had dropped in, and, pointing to a photo on my wall, I said, "Hey! Isn't that a great picture of Zemke?"

The photo showed four men of the 56th Group, and I was pointing to the officer second from the left.

The captain blurted, "Hell, that isn't Zemke, you dodo; that's Dave Schilling!"

We both had a good laugh over that, although this intrepid captain was embarrassed realizing he had identified someone for the enemy. This tactic of mine would not work on Zemke, I am quite sure, and I was also certain it would never work on this particular captain again, either.

I showed Zemke the mournful American newspapers and, conversely, the rejoicing German headlines. To baffle him a little, I had a photograph lying on my desk showing him in the company of five of the 479th Fighter Group pilots at the officers' club at Wattisham in England. It had been taken on 25 October, just five days before he was shot down!

Zemke was a man with outstanding leadership attributes, so I suggested through channels that he be made the senior Allied officer of one of our POW camps, the last one to be set up and called Stalag Luft I, at Barth. It was the camp where most of his fellow officers and members of the 4th and 479th Groups were interned. My respect for this brave man caused me to do whatever favors I could to make his stay with us as comfortable as possible under the circumstances.

When he was released from Auswertestelle West, he was sent to Wetzlar, the distribution center. He was accompanied by a special guard who was an interpreter-sergeant of good education and manners. They took the ordinary train, really a prehistoric commuter train, and while it was steaming through a nice peaceful valley, some American fighter pilots spotted the smoke and steam and initiated an attack. Though it was a passenger train, they clobbered the engine and baggage car first and then, their appetites whetted, decided to shoot up the passenger cars just on the off chance that there might possibly be a German soldier or two on the train.

There were some humble Taunus peasants and tired workers in the compartment with Zemke and his guard. Across from Zemke sat a hausfrau with two pretty little girls. Europe's children, of course, were not yet acquainted with the American GIs' love for kids, and not yet had they tasted American chocolate bars. After a while, and a few moments before the enemy fighters spotted the train, the two little girls had overcome their bashfulness and talked with the man who spoke to them in such odd and funny Deutsch language. He won two hearts at once and then opened his Red Cross travel parcel; there was some chocolate there! It was so sweet; they had

Chapter 7: Worthy Of Imitation

never tasted anything better. The eldest of the pretty blond heads sat beside Zemke, chattering happily about his family and Americans. Suddenly Zemke felt her little fingers digging desperately into his arm in terrible fright!

She, with very keen ears, had heard the first .50-caliber shots fired by the enemy fighters. The train engineer blew the whistle in warning and set the brakes to stop in a mad jerk. Roaring over the treetops and the train were the red-nosed Thunderbolts that Colonel Zemke himself had led into many a battle before being transferred to the Mustangs in the 479th Group.

In that split second, the peaceful tranquility of the autumn afternoon changed. Bombs were detonating, guns firing bullets ripping through the passenger cars, voices screamed, the doors of the compartment were flung open and ripped off their hinges. Window glass flew everywhere. Iron was twisted like straw, and people were lying on the floor, bloodied and moaning. The guard had disappeared.

The colonel sat like a stone, and the little girl's fingers still gripped his arm, but her head was gone, blown off. His uniform was soaked with blood.

Then he jumped into action, since he knew the fighters would be coming back on another pass. In this crazy turmoil, one alone kept calm and collected and went vigorously into action: the prisoner!

The official statement said later that "Colonel Zemke ran into the burning wreckage of the train, in between each firing pass made by the fighters, and dragged several women safely into a nearby wood." The mother and one of the two little daughters were saved.

The German guard had been blown into the river alongside the tracks, and when the ordeal was over he swam back. For the second time I recommended repatriation. Bureaucratic and fatheaded headquarters said they intended to present the War Merit Cross to him instead. He would not have been allowed to accept, since he knew the American rules governing such behavior. Back in England, Zemke had been mentioned in the press many times. He was the one who was worthy of imitation.

AUTHOR COMMENT: Having known Hub Zemke for many years, it was easy to contact him in Oroville, California, and talk him into writing a bit about his interrogations at Oberursel. Since then, Zemke has written two books, *Zemke's Wolfpack* and *Zemke's Stalag*, which give more detail about his WWII experiences. Here is Zemke's story as he gave it to me in 1975:

"On 31 October 1944 I led my last mission with the 479th Fighter Group, escorting B-24 Liberators on a mission to Hamburg. We flew P-51 Mustangs. We were to rendezvous with the bombers over the Zuider Zee, escort them to the target, and stay with them until they coasted out over the Helgoland.

"By the time the 479th reached Holland inbound, we were in and out of broken clouds, with a solid undercast below us. Ahead were multiple layers of clouds, so the group was told to break down into sections of eight fighters and to climb on track to get above the weather. We flew due east, time and distance to the turning point where we would turn north. By now we could no longer keep the bombers in

The Interrogator

"MAY I WEAR YOUR RAINCOAT?"
USAAF colonel Henry Russell Spicer, CO of the 357th Fighter Group, barely survived a dunking in the freezing waters of the English Channel. He was eventually captured and sent to Hohe-Mark hospital in very bad condition. He survived, and when Scharff took him for a walk in the Taunus mountains, Spicer borrowed his raincoat. Cpl. Schwartz and Horst Barth flank Spicer in this photo.

sight, and at 28,000 feet we were still in the clouds. I doubt very much if a single German fighter was launched that day.

"North of Hanover, we took on light ice and were really being bounced around in the turbulence in the clouds when suddenly my instruments tumbled and I found my Mustang was in a tailspin. I cut the throttle back to near idle and don't know how many turns of the spin I had made, but I used opposite rudder and the plane stopped spinning and I was in a vertical dive.

"What happened next will always be a mystery to me. Maybe I yanked back on the stick too hard, putting too many g's on it. I did not black out, though, and I heard a loud report and crack and found myself still strapped in my seat but without my airplane. A rush of air hit me, tearing my helmet, goggles, and oxygen mask off my head. As I fell, I realized I had injured my head and right shoulder in the disintegration. Also, I deduced that the right wing must have torn off the P-51 and split the fuselage, just throwing me out of the cockpit.

Chapter 7: Worthy Of Imitation

"I unbuckled the lap belt and shoulder harness and kicked out of the seat. I could still see nothing because I was in solid cloud and had no idea how far I had fallen or how close I was to the ground, so I desperately grabbed for the D-ring with my uninjured left hand and pulled the rip cord. The chute popped open and arrested my descent rate rather roughly, and anxiously I looked up into the canopy, which I could barely see in the cloud. The silk hemisphere was there, looked OK.

"My descent seemed to take ages, but when I broke out of the cloud I hardly had time to get set. The cloud bases must have been only 400 to 500 feet above the ground. When I hit terra firma, HARRUMPFF! It sounded just like a sack of potatoes hitting the ground after being thrown from a moving truck.

"I think I must have been knocked unconscious for a few moments, since I dreamed I was a drowning swimmer, and I came to find myself clawing at the parachute harness as the chute canopy was still inflated and was dragging me into a marsh. Conscious now, I shed the harness fast and got up and started running for no place in particular.

"Just thought it a good idea to be elsewhere, and I reacted. About 100 yards way I had second thoughts, and I was exhausted. My right knee had shooting pains, and I thought my right arm must be broken.

"I began trembling from shock but soon got this under control, so I hobbled back to my chute, where I cut it up and made a sling for my arm; I also cut a willow stick to be used as a cane. Then I got out my map from my flight suit pocket and found my dime-store escape compass and tried to orient myself. Try that someday! Stand in the middle of a swamp you have never seen before, in a cold, slow sleet and drizzle where there is not a sound to be heard or a thing to be seen in the half-mile visibility. I knew I was north of Hannover and that Belgium and Holland were to the west some unknown number of miles. That was all I seemed to be able to comprehend. I smoked one of my cigarettes, then started walking west.

"My right eye had closed from the wallop I took on the head when the Mustang broke up, and, having fallen in the Luneburg Moors swamps, was one dismal and wet guy. I walked into a small forest area and looked back. No one had seen me, it appeared, so I scraped up some dry wood and built a small fire and rested.

An hour later I began my westerly trek again, and just before dusk I crossed another field and saw two people topping sugar beets. They did not hear or see me coming until I was very close, and the sight of an injured, soaked flier clad in GI pants, flight jacket, and mud must have been startling. I told them in German (from conversation with my parents during my youth and my German courses in the university, I could talk Deutsch) that I was an American flier and I needed help.

"They were an elderly Polish couple, forced laborers, and they both began to shake with fright. The old woman left immediately as fast as she could go, and the old man pleaded with me not to hurt him since he could do nothing to help me. Realizing there would be no help there, I walked on across the field into a forest. An hour later I was cornered by a bunch of farmers and foresters and had to give up.

The Interrogator

"These captors made no attempt to search me, and I was not mishandled, although they were disappointed that I did not have a pistol they could confiscate. One said, in broken English, "For you the war is over!"

"Before long, every man, woman, and dog came to look at the *Terror Flieger*. Then the capturing party took me to a nearby *Gasthaus*, where they let me sit in the kitchen, close to the wood fire. It was nice and warm after a day of near freezing in the sleet. They offered me a bowl of soup, but I was unable to eat.

"Now it was dark, and after two hours three Luftwaffe officers arrived in a small car. They asked me my name, rank, and serial number, nothing else, and then drove me to Fliegerhorst Celle, where they put me in the station jailhouse. They took all my clothing except my undershorts and later that night brought them all back to me clean and dry. I slept on a cot in the cell.

"I don't recall how many days I remained at Celle, perhaps only two. They gave me food morning and evening, but no lunch. Soup and bread was the menu. I concluded this was not the interrogation center, and they were probably waiting for disposition instructions.

"On the second or third evening in my cell at Celle, I was told to get ready to leave. A Luftwaffe officer and an airman took me to a nearby railroad station, where we boarded a passenger train and rode all that night and most of the next day to Frankfurt am Main. We had a compartment to ourselves, we three, and I was not chained or manacled but I was never left alone without a guard. We talked very little, and I shared the sausage and black bread they carried in knapsacks for food.

"At Frankfurt we boarded some junky little street cars, and I was astounded to see all the rubble from Allied bombings as we wended our way to Oberursel. Thousands of workers were cleaning up, and I saw thousands of cannon and panzer tanks loaded on flat cars being shipped from one front to another, I think. This nation was really on a full war economy.

"The rickety street car proceeded through a wooded canyon in the Taunus mountains and finally halted at the gates of Auswertestelle West, the intelligence interrogation center of the Luftwaffe. We walked to a cantonment area fenced in with double-wire fencing, within which stood an array of one-story wooden buildings. At the gate, two uniformed guards checked the orders and credentials of my escorts, then raised the barber pole and allowed us to enter, me with much foreboding.

"Standing with some guards near the doorway of one of the building were two Americans, and I was happy to see I was no longer alone. I was told to join them, which I did silently, without conversation. One does not trust another, even though you may be of the same nationality in conditions such as this. No talk!

"In a few minutes, we three POWs were ordered inside, where we had to disrobe completely, and guards checked every stitch of our clothing, then handed them back to us. Then in walked a young Luftwaffe officer named Walter Hanemann. He looked us over then asked, "Which one is Zemke?"

Chapter 7: Worthy Of Imitation

A VERY BRAVE USAAF PILOT
Major Charles W. Lenfest landed his Mustang in a German pasture in an attempt to rescue his squadron mate Henry W. Brown. P-51 was mired in an irrigation ditch, and both pilots were invited to Scharff's interrogation office.

"My heart sank to the bottoms of my naked feet. I answered quickly, 'I am!,' with much trepidation, but he just sat down on the wooden bench beside me and asked if I was all right, if I had been treated okay. I told him I guessed so, but that I needed to see a doctor about my shoulder and arm. He looked at them, quite professionally, and said a medico would soon see it.

"As soon as I was dressed, I was taken into an adjoining room, where a Red Cross form was produced and Hanemann began to ask questions to fill the squares on the form. After name, rank, and serial number I quit answering, and Hanemann told me that the war was over as far as I was concerned, and that if I did not cooperate there were other methods of getting the information they desired. This was a slight threat with very little emphasis.

"A little while later, another interrogator came in and was introduced as Canadian Wild Bill or some such name. He was an enlisted interrogator, and his command of the English language was much less in quality than I had heard from Hanemann. He gave me the vision of someone who had worked as a logger in the Canadian wilds. His questions were direct and forceful but without finesse.

"That first interrogation lasted only thirty minutes. They wanted me to fill out the Red Cross form and sign it, but I refused, and then they told me it might be a long time before my loved ones in the States knew I was alive, and that held true for my military unit. Too bad.

"'You must be very tired after your ordeal of the past few days, colonel, so we'll show you to your new home.'

The Interrogator

They took me to my solitary cell, escorted by two guards. The cell was small; cot, chair, small table, two windows boarded shut, one single lightbulb encased in a wire cage. There was a small trap door at the bottom of the big door, and later I found out that was the best part of the whole deal. My meals would appear through that little trap door each morning and evening.

"My guards told me to take off my clothes, and they took them with them. I sat down and stared at the ceilings—'So this is it!' After eating some soup and bread and pushing the bowl out through the cat hole, I mentally told myself some of the poems I used to know, whistled and sang some songs, did multiplication tables, and wrapped up in my thin blankets to sleep fitfully through the night.

"At about 9 a.m. the next morning, Lt. Hanemann came into my cell with a guard, who brought my clothes to me. I dressed and was then taken across the hall, where I washed my face and combed my hair. My teeth felt like they were covered with moss by this time, and I had not shaved in five or six days so I was ashamed of my appearance. Hanemann took me to the interrogation room, where, behind his desk, sat Canadian Bill. He indicated I was to sit and then asked if I had spent a comfortable night. I told them okay, but it was cold and I'd had no breakfast. They seemed quite chagrined about that, then offered me a cup of ersatz coffee. Hanemann gave me a cigarette. They expressed much concern about my injured shoulder but did nothing about it, at the time, except talk.

"Then in walked Hanns Scharff! With a big smile on his face and a buoyant bounce to his step, he came straight up to me and introduced himself as Gefreiter

"HA! WE MEET AGAIN!"
American Lenfest (*bearded*) met Scharff again, this time on 26 May 1984 at Phoenix, Arizona.

Chapter 7: Worthy Of Imitation

Scharff. Gefreiter is a private first class, but he acted like he was an officer senior to Hanemann. His next words went something like this: 'Gabby and Spicer certainly will be glad to hear you are safely with us here. Now that you're on our side, all we need is to have Don Blakeslee and Dave Schilling come and join you—then the war will be over!'

"Scharff then turned to Hanemann and smiled, then asked me how I had been treated since arrival at the camp. When I told him I'd had no treatment for my shoulder, the cell had no heat, and there was no breakfast this morning, Scharff acted horrified. 'How can they do this! Idiots are always falling down on details. I'll have to check up on this sorry situation!'

"Scharff impressed me as a real professional. He did most of the talking, carried the conversation along, and interjected considerable humor into the discussion, which helped to relieve the tensions I had. I admit I wondered why this man Scharff dominated the conversation with officers present, since he was only an enlisted man, but it soon was obvious to me that he, not the others, was the master interrogator and was probably used to interrogate all senior officer POWs. A little warning flag went up in my brain, telling me to be on guard with this man above all the others. He reminded me of the typical American insurance salesman who left you with a $10,000 insurance policy after getting his foot in the door.

"Scharff really knew his subject and his interrogation procedures, enjoyed his work, and no doubt was effective. I had the impression that it might even be dangerous just to talk about the weather with him, since he'd probably gain some important or confidential information from it. Though he never seemed to press for information, he'd pop an innocent remark out of the blue, making me think twice. A past master of conversation, a born storyteller, and no doubt a mature philosopher,

"He had made an in-depth study of the organization and operations of the 8th and 9th Air Force Fighter Groups and really knew his subject, including all the latest transfers, scores, names of all the pilots, commanders, stations, and whatnot. He really knew his business.

"Scharff never forced himself upon you; he just seemed to know when to pop in and visit you in your cell. His work load must have been very heavy, but he always found time for you. His memory was phenomenal, and he could recall personal characteristics of POWs who had passed through Oberursel long before my arrival. He studied and maintained his dossiers meticulously and always had one or two key questions to ask you in order to get a discussion going. No coercion at all, just casual conversation with humor and jokes interspersed, sometimes even jokes about the Nazis and their errors.

"He was an internationalist, lived in England and in South Africa, was married to a Scot who had decided, I think, to remain on the Allied side when the war started. Though he never professed that the Germans were losing the war, I sensed the critical losses of the Führer's forces preyed on his mind. I suspect that the Gestapo had ways

The Interrogator

of listening at Oberursel, and he knew it, so he was extremely careful about saying anything that could be taken as disloyal to his country.

"What did he want to know from me? He asked me the policies of Generals Spaatz and Doolittle with reference to Allied strategies. I frankly and honestly told him that I had met these generals only on rare occasions, and that if I had known their plans or strategies I certainly would never have been allowed to fly on combat missions. I told him I had purposely avoided cultivating more than a speaking acquaintance with these gentleman because I knew they would take me out of the cockpit and give me a desk job in some headquarters. Scharff must have believed me because he never mentioned it again.

"One day the guard came to my cell and motioned that I was to follow. To my surprise, he took me out of the building and across an open space to another building just like the 'cooler,' as Scharff called my home for the past week. This was my first trip outside the cooler building, so I studied the center a bit. It was a very simple, hastily constructed series of wooden buildings, all one story high, surrounded by a double barbed-wire fence and some manned observation tower. About five buildings had the windows barricaded, so I knew that was where the POWs were. The buildings with open windows were offices and barracks for the German personnel, no doubt.

"I was taken to Scharff's office. I began to realize that Hub Zemke was something of a curiosity to the Germans because so many people came in to look at me while in my cell and now in Scharff's office. A good-looking German girl secretary, Miss Beck, I think, came in to ask if Scharff or I wanted anything like a cup of tea. I said 'Yes' and she smiled because I understood her request in German. When she left, Scharff was in a jolly mood and opened the conversation, telling me, 'I have something to show you.' All previous interrogations had taken place in the reception room at the cooler or in my cell, so this was a welcome change for me.

"Scharff's office was a modest one, containing two easy chairs, a desk, a table, and some bookshelves. A picture or two adorned the wall. Scharff produced a sizeable photo album, and the first picture was of Dave Schilling, Francis Gabreski, Walker Mahurin, and Hub Zemke working down the perimeter road at Boxted! Scharff commented, 'We don't need to know too much from you to know your organization and reputation, Zemke. Our sources get plenty of information about the 56th.'

"I asked Scharff if he received the *Stars and Stripes*, a military newspaper printed for the US armed forces in England, and he assured me he was a daily subscriber and received each edition three days after it was printed. 'Once in a while we miss a copy, and I hate to miss Terry and the Pirates.' I suspect the German intelligence could get all English newspapers within three days through Portugal.

"Scharff even had a good photo taken inside the officers' mess and bar at Boxted, a recent photo at that, and I thought he must have taken that off some POW, although I don't know how a POW would carry it in his flight suit. 'Now a bit about Zemke!' he said, and he proceeded to read from the dossier he had on the 56th Group,

Chapter 7: Worthy Of Imitation

"BROWN IS DOWN! I'LL PICK HIM UP!"
When Henry Brown landed in German-held territory, Lenfest landed his Mustang beside his but dug a wheel into a muddy ditch. Both became POWS. This is Henry W. Brown.

switching to another dossier on the 479th Fighter Group and beginning where I took command of it after leaving the 56th Wolfpack outfit. He read that I was born in Montana, knew all my education and training dates, and all sorts of trivia about my career. He said I was known as the 'Hun hater.'

"In the course of this interrogation, several visitors dropped in to get a look at Oberst Zemke. They wanted to see this flier, and I guessed it was because Scharff had been telling some of the camp permanent party stories about me, as only Scharff can tell them. The camp commandant, a name like Killinger, came in for a few minutes, as did a civilian named Schmitt who was an SS or a Gestapo man. Later Scharff told me that Herr Schmitt specialized in the interrogation of POWs caught in the French Underground escape system and in the quizzing of enemy spies.

"Scharff told me that he never had to use persuasion of a physical manner to obtain information. He said, 'By using the best psychological approaches of statesmanship and befriending the POW, he could obtain all the necessary information from over 90% of the prisoners.' I think he forgot or did not realize that leaving the heat off in the cells in winter time and forgetting to serve some meals could do wonders to get the POWs to talk too.

"All the first week at Oberursel I complained that my shoulder hurt and kept me from sleeping properly, but they did not take me to see a doctor. I think they hoped it was just a sprain and would clear up soon. Then one afternoon just at dusk, Scharff and Hanemann came to my cell, and Scharff, in his usual casual and disarming manner, said to me, 'If you will promise not to try to escape, your officer's honor, colonel, we

The Interrogator

will take you for a nice walk over to the dispensary at Hohe-Mark.' I agreed eagerly, since I wanted a doctor to look at the arm and I wanted a change of scenery.

"To my surprise, we went out of the center, right through that guarded gate where I had entered about a week earlier, and walked through a forest up toward the Taunus mountains. I think we must have walked 15 or 20 minutes, maybe more or maybe less, and then arrived at a big three-story building among the fir trees. At the big double door, a sister in nun's habit opened the door and bade us welcome. We climbed three flights of stairs, I think, entering an alcove into what looked like reception room. At one side was an operating room, and at the other side was a room with a series of double bunk beds in a large room. Wandering around in that room as well as the reception room were twenty to thirty POWs, some sheathed in bandages, some on crutches, some in wheelchairs.

"The whole place was neat and clean, almost spotless, but it was certainly obvious that the dispensary was very overcrowded. It was warm and comfortable, and most of the POWs were wearing white pajamas or hospital-type robes. There were magazines lying here and there, and I soon heard that the hospital was run by an order of Lutheran sisters. One Luftwaffe doctor, his name was Ernst Ittershagen,

NEXT STOP: OBERURSEL
Lt. Henry W. Brown, 14.2-victory ace of the 355th Fighter Group, chats with Lt. General James H. Doolittle in England shortly before Brown's ill-fated mission, which ended with Brown chatting with master interrogator Hanns Scharff.

Chapter 7: Worthy Of Imitation

was the only medico I ever saw in the place, and he did everything from curing colds to performing surgery. He was obviously the kingpin here, and everyone scurried about to comply with his every wish with smiles on their faces.

"Ittershagen spoke excellent English and conversed genially with all. He seemed completely wrapped up in his medical work and was frank and conscientious, working with tireless interest for medicine. His mannerisms said, 'To hell with the war!' The endless line of patients lined up awaiting his inspection and treatment made me think he had a hopeless task, though. Too many patients! Far too many!

"When I met Doc Ittershagen, he was dressed in air force blue and wore a white smock over it but left it unbuttoned down the front. Scharff told him about my arm, and Doc told me to go into the operating room, strip to the waist. I did, and when he had finished dressing some injured POWs, he came in and looked me over. My right arm was swollen from shoulder to wrist. I could move my fingers, raise my arm to the horizontal position, and he moved it around the shoulder joint. 'At least your arm and shoulder are not broken, and they are not dislocated now. Only a bad bruise, which will be all right in a month or so. Keep exercising it, and if you are lucky you can get some heat treatment on it.' He pointed toward a heat lamp standing in the corner, unused at the moment. Scharff and a POW patient standing by, watching, pulled the lamp to a chair, plugged it in, and I got over an hour of heat treatment.

"This was a lucky break for me, as this hour extended into the POWs' dinner hour. Scharff and I were invited to eat there too! Don't recall the exact menu, but I think it consisted of a stew with generous helpings of meat in it, some vegetables, plenty of black bread and margarine, and a big apple. After the fare served at Auswertestelle West, this was a real banquet!

Scharff and Ittershagen ate right there with us and some other POWs. When we finished, the sisters, with the aid of some ambulatory POWs, pitched in and cleaned the table and turned the room once more into a reception room for the hospital.

"There had been no interrogation by either Scharff or Doc Ittershagen. The diagnosis was minimal but satisfactory, as was the treatment.

"I walked home with Scharff that night with a full belly.

"A couple of days later, Scharff came to my cell again and asked if I would like an encore at Hohe-Mark, including a meal. A fast YES was my answer. When we arrived, Doc Ittershagen was in the midst of changing dressings on some POWs who had bailed out of a burning bomber. Of all wounds I have seen, burns are the most horrible, and since crewmen usually are burned on the hands and face, the exposed parts of the body, they are generally helpless and are even unable to feed themselves in the hospital.

"Doc Ittershagen did not hesitate in calling on anyone nearby to help him. I had a year of experience in a hospital when going to college, so when Ittershagen asked me to give him a hand changing some of the bandages and dressings, I jumped to the task. Since he had no painkilling drugs, some of the wounded really went through some excruciating pain.

The Interrogator

BUT FOR THE GRACE OF THE DEACON...
Bert Marshall (*right*) landed in a German pasture too. Royce W. "Deacon" Priest landed in the same field, threw his parachute to the ground, then, sitting on Marshall's lap, flew the Mustang back to England. Such bravery really should deserve the Medal of Honor! This is a reenactment of the feat.

"Both Scharff and I were pressed into service this evening, and by dinner time we had processed about ten or fifteen burn cases. This time I watched as the ambulatory POWs fed some of the more seriously burned patients. We had a simple but filling meal and listened to Ittershagen tell about the great numbers of injured airmen who passed through his facility with every type of injury known to man. Some cases exceeded his capability to care for them at the small hospital of Hohe-Mark, and these cases were evacuated to a large hospital in Frankfurt.

"Ittershagen implored us to stay a while longer after the meal, since he had another medical case to care for and would need some assistance. I willingly agreed, and Scharff did not object. I was very happy to postpone my return to my solitary cell at Oberursel. The patient in this case was a young airmen whose bomber had been knocked down by flak, and he had taken some shrapnel in the buttocks.

"The Doc needed us, all right, and a couple of other guys too. We had to hold the poor young man's arms and legs while the Doc probed deeply and removed several pieces of deeply embedded flak. He was placed facedown on the operating table, and then Scharff, two other POWs, and I held the airman, and the Doc talked soothingly as he opened the wound. He did not have any painkiller but told the youngster the operation would not take very long. Of course, he had to be sure all the shrapnel was removed to prevent infection, and it took longer than expected. It also took six of us to hold the patient down, the pain was so severe. I have heard screams of pain and seen men violently jerking in pain, but this boy really went through an ordeal, one I won't forget all my life.

"The operation took all of twenty minutes, even though Ittershagen worked

Chapter 7: Worthy Of Imitation

rapidly, talking soothingly to his patient the whole time. As each piece was removed, Doc would drop it in a bedpan, telling the patient he would save the pieces of the 88 mm shell for him to take back to the USA with him when the war was over, 'A memento of your visit to Oberursel,' said Doc Ittershagen.

"Again, I went back to my cell at Auswertestelle West rather late in the night, but I felt that I had done something constructive that day. Much better than sitting and rotting in a cell. Two days later the guards came to my cell and beckoned me to pick up my belongings. One smiled and said, 'auf Wiedersehen!,' so I knew I must be leaving for Wetzlar and Dulag Luft, the distribution center. Scharff came out to see me off and wish me good luck. With two armed guards, I walked to the trolley station at Oberursel and soon was on my way.

"My eight days at Oberursel were over. They had not been harsh days at all, nothing like I had expected them to be. True, it was in isolation with some mild verbal threats. Such things as the lack of heat in the cells, the sand fleas, and the sorry bowls of soup twice each day were expected. After all, the people who held me were the enemy, and it was wartime. I am positive I would not have fared nearly so well in Japanese hands.

"Inconveniences? No shower while there, but I was allowed to shave every day. These were really luxuries I had not expected. The two fine dinners at Hohe-Mark were great, and I doubt if the low-ranking POWs got to partake meals like those were. No doubt Hanns Scharff was behind those little gestures of kindness.

"What did he get out of me? There is no doubt in my mind that he did extract something, but I haven't the slightest idea what. If you talked to him about the weather or anything else, he no doubt got some information or confirmation from it. His technique was psychic, not physical. I had the feeling that he was truly Germany's master interrogator, so my motto was BEWARE!

"I have to smile at Hanns's version of the train strafing by 9th Air Force P-47 Thunderbolts. He is a romanticist! The two little girls in the train compartment where I was with my guard knew I was a POW because the Luftwaffe had painted POW in big, bold letters on my flight jacket. They had also seen me escorted into the coach by armed guards. I did not have a Red Cross parcel with me, as I recall, and I cannot imagine the Germans allowing me such a luxury on a train with civilians when they were on such meager rations themselves.

"I was really amazed to see everyone talking to one another almost as if they were going on a picnic, in contrast to England, where everyone was about as friendly and talkative as two polar icebergs. One could ride an English train for hours and not hear two words spoken.

"Knowing the German language and listening to the talk, it was only natural to smile, and soon I struck up a bit of chatter with the eldest girl. She was utterly amazed that I spoke German and was not the villain she expected. We talked about my little son, her school, her home, and other light matter. Frankly, I really enjoyed talking with her.

The Interrogator

HUB ZEMKE AT BUCHEL AIRBASE IN 1961
Luftwaffe colonel Walter Krupinski, USAF colonel Hub Zemke, Walker "Bud" Mahurin, and Luftwaffe top ace Erich Hartmann spin some yarns in 1961.

"The first pass by a P-47 came out of the blue and scared the living hell out of me. The top of the youngest girl's head had been blown off, splattering me with blood. A soldier across from me doubled over into the aisle, with a bullet through his stomach. A bomb went off nearby, blowing out all the glass windows. Whether my guard was blown out or jumped out, I have forgotten. He fell into a small river beside the tracks and must have swum to the other bank to avoid the next strafing pass by the fighters.

"My first actions were anything but brave. All I could think of was to get under something for protection. I crawled under the wooden seats. Then it dawned on me that this was not the place to be if a second P-47 raked the train. Another did, and another bomb went off very close. People were screaming and the whole situation was one of fear and panic.

"I jumped into the aisle over some bodies and out through a door and outside. If it had not been for a vertical cliff on that side of the train, I'd have been off and running like a deer. Escape was on my mind, but instantly I saw escape was impossible.

"Overhead I could see the P-47s slowly circling in preparation for another bombing-strafing run. I knew they could not hurt me while they were circling; I

Chapter 7: Worthy Of Imitation

quickly decided to run in and get the mother and remaining little daughter from the coach. It took very little bravery to pull them out and make them hide behind the large boulders at the base of the cliff. Several other women and children were also pulled off, and I told them to keep their heads down behind those rocks during each firing pass.

"In the meantime, I saw some German soldiers removing wounded comrades from the coaches.

"Many times since this incident, I have thought of the fine opportunity to escape that I had let slip through my fingers. The strafing lasted about thirty minutes, and complete chaos reigned on the ground, but what the hell! My only thoughts at that moment were to save that mother and her remaining daughter under the most pathetic and morbid circumstances. Destiny deemed it so, I guess.

"I know nothing about the repatriation or the medal Scharff speaks about. He is right that I could not have accepted it anyway. I am completely satisfied that my hide was not etched or tattooed by a .50-caliber bullet or a bomb fragment.

"Later, en route to Stalag Luft I, I went through a daylight bombing raid in the Hannover railroad yards and an RAF Bomber Command raid in Berlin. Needless to say, I was more than delighted to finally walk into the *Stalag Luft* and see so many congenial American faces."

INTERROGATOR'S FAVORITE TRAP
This photo of Zemke, Schilling, Gabreski, and Christensen graced the wall in Hanns Scharff's interrogation room and caused many a laugh when Scharff would point to the wrong pilot and say, "Isn't that a great picture of Zemke?"

SCHARFF'S GUEST BOOK ENTRY BY ZEMKE
Above and opposite: Zemke was considered a VIP (very important prisoner) at Oberursel. He left a big legacy in Germany. He has written two books about his experiences. He passed away on 30 August 1994.

Chapter 7: Worthy Of Imitation

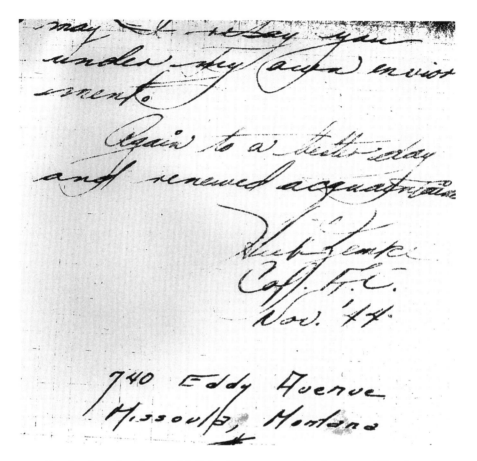

Zemke also takes issue with Scharff's comment that he was a "Hun hater."

"It is true that as a youth I was the brunt of some ridicule and youthful bear-bating, being called a 'Kraut' or a 'Hun' or a 'squarehead' and such things. A few fights resulted, but when I started boxing and football in high school, all that ridicule seemed to come to an end. These early skirmishes only whetted my appetite for competition.

"As a Regular Army Air Corps lieutenant right after the Battle of Britain, I had the opportunity of observing firsthand the aerial combat over Britain and for a short while on the Soviet front in Russia. I came to the firm conclusion that to survive in aerial combat, one was never lenient with the adversary. For certain, he was not easy on you as he shot very hard bullets and played every trap and technique to put a hole in you. This attitude, formed by experience, convinced me one should psyche

The Interrogator

one's self up as much as possible before entering combat or any competition. I later was convinced this applied to any troops under my jurisdiction also.

"Since I was possibly the only member of the 56th Fighter Group to have witnessed the untold destruction of English and Russian forces and facilities by the Nazi Wehrmacht, you can well imagine that I never ceased psyching the 'pink-cheeked' American fighter pilots whom I led. My 'Hate the Hun!' philosophy of leadership certainly seemed to work, since the 56th Group victory rate climbed rapidly.

"The 4th Fighter Group, made up of the old erstwhile Eagle Squadrons from the RAF, was the favored unit by 8th Fighter Command, so the 56th Group really had an uphill battle getting aircraft, supplies, and a satisfactory airfield from which to operate. It was just logical that a balls-out competition developed between us and the 4th Group, and sometimes I wondered if we were fighting the Germans or the 4th Group. This concerned me greatly.

"Back to 'Hun hating,' though. Both my mother and my father were direct immigrants from Germany, and I am and will always remain very proud of my German heritage. In truth, I was not and am not a 'Hun hater,' but in those days of WWII the objective was to shoot down German airplanes, so I just psyched up my boys with the objective. No doubt some of them who preceded me to Oberursel carried the news to Hanns Scharff that I was a 'Hun hater.'"

Colonel Hubert Zemke was an almond rancher, talked very little, worked hard, and was a gentleman in every respect. He was a very brave man, one who was not afraid to walk alone. He was one of the USAAF's finest combat leaders; his 17.75 aerial victories attest to that (Author: Colonel Hubert Zemke passed away on 30 August 1994).

Lt. Gen. Gerald W. Johnson, USAF Retired, recalls an incident at Stalag Luft I at Barth concerning Hub Zemke:

"Hub had the capability of really motivating his men. He wasn't the greatest pilot or the best shot in the air, and I doubt if he has ever admitted that to anyone, but he was a leader of the best form. While we were in Stalag Luft I, there wasn't much for the officers to do, so Hub got the idea he would stage some boxing matches. The Jerries approved, so Hub set it up and said he would be the finalist all-weights champion and would take on any challenger in the camp.

"Well, there is a big army major named Cy Manierre in the camp, and he had done a little fighting himself, is about seven years younger than Hub, and outweighs him by perhaps 50 pounds. Hub had issued the challenge just to get us Kriegies to thinking about something else than the war, but I knew Hub and I knew he had been a Golden Gloves champion at one time, so I thought it might be interesting.

"I lived in the same billet with Cy Manierre and watched him training, jogging, and exercising as much as our meager rations would allow. We set up a ring in one of the compounds, and the Germans allowed all the POWs from the other compound to come over to ours to watch the fight. I think it was the first time all us Kriegies

Chapter 7: Worthy Of Imitation

got together. If Hub did any training before the fight, it sure as hell wasn't obvious.

"It wasn't any Ali-Norton fight for sure, but when they started boxing, Hub displayed his Golden Gloves expertise, and I don't think Manierre ever laid a glove on him. Hub is about Toliver's size (5 feet 8 inches tall, and 145 pounds), and he was under every swing Manierre made. They fought five one-minute rounds, if I recall correctly. Short rounds because all of us were lean and hungry because the rations were short, and they just did not have the stamina to fight longer or more rounds. It was a great fight display by Zemke and no doubt raised his stature in the minds of all the Kriegies, and he was the senior Allied commander."

Hanns Scharff had great respect for the "tough" POWs like Zemke and Stark and many others. It was Scharff who chose Zemke to head Stalag Luft I and Stark to head Dulag Luft because of their personalities and discipline.

8

TO ERR IS HUMAN

A man with a sour face should not open a shop.
—African proverb

HANNS SCHARFF continues: The behavior of fighter pilots in captivity reflected the morale of the fighter units to which they belonged, and it created a manifold pattern of various reputations. With the repeated revelations of personal histories of members of the combat squadrons and the efficacies of their leaders, it was not difficult to sense on our side a spirit of fair play and chivalry in one group, and a more matter-of-fact or even brutal attitude in another.

Reports began to reach us that a number of Luftwaffe fighter pilots who had bailed out of their machines over our own territory had been shot dead in their parachutes by Allied fighters. We at Oberursel were requested to investigate such cases, with the point of view of discovering whether these occurrences were accidental or due to direct orders or perhaps just personal initiative of the pilots concerned. We knew that a fighter pilot who could not shoot and hit another plane in flight might get so frustrated that he would take potshots at a man dangling quite helplessly in a parachute.

Kommodore Pips Priller of JG 26 was particularly incensed when two of his pilots were killed in their chutes, and he called me wishing to know if there was a new policy afoot in the 8th and 9th USAAF Fighter Commands. I tried to cool him down by telling him it had to be just some "buck fever" among new Allied pilots, isolated instances. Then I began to delve deeper into the subject while interrogating American POWs.

I needed to become fully acquainted with the attitude and psychology of our own Luftwaffe fighter pilots if I was going to compare them and eventually judge them against Americans. Therefore, I took every opportunity to interrogate them without their really knowing they were being questioned. I talked to *Kommodoren*,

Chapter 8: To Err Is Human

INCENSED KOMMODORE PRILLER
"Pips" Priller of JG 26 was very angry when Allied fighter pilots began shooting German pilots in their parachutes. He asked Scharff to find out if Allied pilots had been ordered to do it, or if it was just a few renegades. Priller scored 101 victories, survived the war, and died in 1961.

squadron leaders, greenhorns, and any and all fighter pilots of several Luftwaffe units. I soon found out there was a wide spectrum of attitudes that went from the honorable and noble-minded pilot to the careless, evil-spirited, trigger-happy, and detestable scoundrel.

Soon a picture began to form as I talked to both sides, American POWs and Luftwaffe free fighters. The explanations were very strange, and I finally decided that one must have actually gone through the excitement and fear of aerial combat to completely understand the actions some of these men had taken.

"Have you ever shot up a passenger train?" I asked a young German fighter pilot, referring to a sweep he had made over England.

"Sure did," he grinned.

"Did you have orders to do so?"

"No!" he admitted frankly. "I had flown five hours that day and had a couple of noneffective dogfights, saving myself once by diving to safety in a cloud because they were superior to us in numbers. I started home below the clouds, no victory, tired and sorta' beaten, when I came across this train. What do you think that engineer did? He puffed white smoke rings up at me as if he was laughing at me, and he nonchalantly continued his slow way down the tracks. I gave him hell for that. But Mölders gave me hell for it, too, when I landed back home." In my opinion, this young pilot was solely concerned about that impudent engine and gave not a thought to the tragic loss of innocent lives in the passenger cars of that train.

The Interrogator

Later, I escorted some B-17 crews on a trip where they were able to observe the scenes of devastation caused by themselves. Two facts came to light: Beyond a doubt, not one of them ever imagined the misery heaped upon the human beings who were the recipients of their loads of bombs. Second, the bombs were supposed to hit the target, military targets, and when they did it was fine. But when they saw bomb craters 2 or 3 kilometers from the intended target, they became quite gloomy and even sullen. They knew, as I knew, that there is a big distance from that bomb-release switch to the crater in the ground, yet the step from one to the other sometimes is very small and the perspective is easily changed.

Another German pilot told me how he had surprisingly flown over the marketplace in a small French town and fired his guns into it.

"The pots and pans flew everywhere! Never knew those guns could make things jump so high. It was fun! People? Crowds? Oh, I don't know about that, but you should have seen the crockery flying through the air like skeet targets!"

Our German was worried about pots and pans and crockery!

Then I asked an American POW whose combat film we developed, and on it, in two separate instances, we saw him kill a cow in farmers' pastures. "Why did you shoot two harmless cows on your last mission? Do you think you will win the war that way?"

"No!" he laughed, "but they surely do hop funny when you hit 'em . . . and it was a German cow, anyway."

After much study of the varied attitudes, I felt prepared to make the widest possible allowances in my interrogations, except in the cases of deliberate slaughter.

A BOISE BEE AND HIS STINGER
USAAF Duane Beeson from Boise, Idaho, flew with the 4th Fighter Group until he was shot down. When he got to Oberursel he was allowed to send his CO a postcard saying, "paint all the P-47s red."

Chapter 8: To Err Is Human

Fortunately, in my whole career as an interrogator, I ran into only one case of deliberate murder, although I received many complaints and was never surprised to hear Pips Priller lodging another over the phone. He was a most honorable gentleman to the core and took a very dim view of pilots who crossed the line of human decency in honorable combat.

These incidents of shooting parachuting fliers, coupled with some other malevolence reported in army channels, caused rumors to circulate that our German political leaders wanted to break away from the International Geneva Conventions or the Red Cross. Rumors also reached us that the German military leaders were very strongly opposed to such a withdrawal from something that most recognized as a noble two-way street. The first fundamental regulation of that convention is to protect the life of any prisoner of war, and the three following it are derived from the first; namely, to provide the POW with food, clothing, and shelter.

Accordingly, we were horrified when our German radio stations broadcast a statement issued by the civilian Propaganda Ministry, which had no military authority, that all Allied airmen falling into German hands in the future were declared to be "fair game" in the eyes of the populace. The German term was *vogelfrei*—as free as a bird. What did this mean? The civilian population, especially those who had been bearing the brunt of the bombing, were expected to take the law into their own hands in the treatment of Allied aviators before they were turned over to military authorities. In other words, the propaganda machine had tuned its music to hatred and revenge. Oberursel stood fast. Our orders remained the same as before, uninfluenced by any broadcast. We were to fully protect the prisoners.

I recall how one German fighter pilot found himself in a bit of a jam when he bailed out of his Messerschmitt and his chute snagged in a treetop, snubbing him in the air about 15 feet above the ground. Swinging back and forth helplessly, he was horrified to see an angry farmer armed with a scythe and a pitchfork charging toward him with blood in his attitude. The closer the farmer came, the more terrified the German pilot became, because it was obvious this German farmer was going to get some revenge plus do his duty with this American or British enemy. The pilot knew the farmer would never believe a German pilot would lose an air battle and parachute to safety, so it was a grim moment at hand.

"*Ich bin Deutscher!*" the pilot yelled from on high.

"Ja! I'll bet! You are my prisoner, Amerikaner!"

"But I am German! Be careful with that fork, please!"

"Shut up and throw your pistol down or I am going to stick this fork up your . . ."

"*Himmeldonnerwetter! Ich bin Deutscher!*"

"Ja! That's what they all say, you gangster! You can't fool me." It was 12 May 1944, and the Luftwaffe's third-ranking ace, Gunther Rail, came near losing his life on a pitchfork. He had 275 aerial victories at this time.

A new difficulty had arisen as soon as it became known that the American fliers were armed with Colt automatic pistols. That was something new. Did it mean they were going to fight it out on the ground? Who, then, was to shoot first—the pilot descending in his parachute or the waiting trooper on the ground? Would our troops do the sporting thing, knowing the parachutist would start firing as soon as his feet hit the ground, and withhold their fire until he hit the ground? Our civilian populace was unarmed, apart from an occasional pitchfork or scythe, but our rural police all had a Luger in their belongings.

Does a pilot surrender when he abandons his plane? Or does he defend himself? In the parachute or on the ground? The Geneva Convention does not provide an answer to this problem. Even the USAAF group leaders were divided in their opinions of this point, but as it turned out, most of the Allied fliers who took to their chutes did the sensible thing and threw the pistol away as they fell or surrendered it to the first person of authority they met.

A not-so-amusing incident occurred one time, brought about by the casual mannerisms found among American fighter pilots and the .45 Colt automatic. Lt. Colonel Selden R. Edner was a fighter ace with one of the famous Eagle Squadrons and had been brought into the USAAF and assigned to the 4th Fighter Group. Early in March 1944 he made an involuntary landing on the Continent and was captured and brought before an old German garrison colonel.

The Eagle boy, Edner, was a tall and good-looking lad with perfect manners, but he was not fully aware of German Prussian military courtesy and discipline. He was not conscious of the fact that in our old army it was considered an expression of contempt to talk to an older person of authority with one's hands in one's pockets. When Edner slouched "at ease" and put his hands in his pockets, the old colonel roared disgustedly, "Take your hands out of your pockets!!"

Sure! Edner did, but out of habit, after a while as they conversed, the hands slipped back unconsciously into his pockets. Again the old colonel scolded Edner, who complied with alacrity but who forgot again soon, and back the hands went into his pockets.

"I told you to keep your hands out of your pockets!" bellowed the old-fashioned, squareheaded colonel again, his jowls quivering and shaking hitchily.

Lt. Colonel Edner thought to himself, as he removed his hands from his pockets once more, "There's no reason to get so wrought up, you old son of a bitch; I ain't got no 45 in there!"

Interestingly, the two highest-scoring USAAF fighter units, the 4th and the 56th Fighter Groups, enjoyed the best reputations in the minds of our Luftwaffe pilots and in our intelligence circles.

Although they booked over 2,000 victories together and should have been looked upon as a dangerous enemy, they were well liked and respected in the air and on the ground. One could almost tell a member of these two groups by watching their brilliant reactions in the air and their quite polished mannerisms under stress and strain. Our fighters said they had a characteristic quality of fairness in the battles in the air.

Chapter 8: To Err Is Human

13 MONTHS A KRIEGIE
Duane Willard Beeson scored 19.33 aerial victories before it became his turn to visit Auswertestelle West and Hanns Scharff's office. He was shot down on 5 April 1944.

Of course, there were many more such equally well-behaved men in other units, but those of the 4th and 56th exemplified the good soldierly conduct that in turn reflected most favorably the general esprit de corps of their unit as well as their own individual standards.

I could, but I think it unkind and unnecessary, speak about two other USAAF units, both much-younger units, which earned very unfavorable reputations in combat over the Continent. I think they merely reflected the poor guidance and control exhibited by their leadership, but there was a marked difference, very noticeable in the air by our fighters who intercepted them and at Oberursel, where we interrogated them. I suppose it is the same the world over.

One day the 8th and 9th Fighter Commands of the USAAF issued orders releasing their fighters from the close escort of the bombers and from staying above 18,000 feet. Low-level fighter sweeps were now the order of the day. General Doolittle had determined that his fighters were not destroying as many German fighters at those altitudes above 18,000 feet simply because the Germans were not coming up there to fight them, so he told his fighter commands to go get the enemy on the ground.

The Interrogator

That day, all the USAAF groups made an enormous large-scale, low-level attack that covered nearly all of Germany, from the North Sea to the Bavarian Mountains, east of Berlin.

The battle plan had divided Germany into three sectors according to the flying range of the fighters. The Western Zone was covered by Thunderbolt groups. The Middle Zone was covered by the longer-ranged P-38 Lightnings and some Mustangs, and the third or Eastern Zone was covered by Mustangs, which had the longest range. Each zone was divided into about eight squares, and each of these squares was assigned to one specific fighter group. The city of Berlin and its environs were reserved for the fourth group. Targets were mainly air bases, trains, river boats and barges, buses, and other road vehicles . . . anything on wheels that moved.

The 4th, with its sprinkling of ex-Eagle boys, already had some special experiences with Berlin. In a very smart move, they came over this day and attacked the airbases first. How they did it puzzled us. The area was covered with a very thick layer of clouds 600 feet above the ground, yet they let down through that thick deck and broke out exactly over the field. Pilots and observers on the ground were flabbergasted to hear them overhead, then astounded to see them breaking out at exactly the right place to initiate an attack. Within an hour I had received orders from headquarters to interrogate all pilots about this unusual navigation feat. Even worse, it appeared that the red-nosed Mustangs of the 4th had been looking for one particular target on that airfield, had found it, and burned it up. It was Hermann Göring's personal, superdeluxe, fat-catted transport plane, and we heard he was raving mad at having lost his pride and joy. I prepared myself for the arrival of the incoming POWs, which always followed any big Allied operation.

The damage done to Germany that day was very heavy. All over our countryside lay the twisted remains of steam locomotives, and they blocked the railways for a while, irritating the public and the railroad engineers, who, as methodical Germans are inclined to do, wished to be very punctual with their schedules, war or no war. Sunken barges and riverships filled up the Rhine and the canals, "those efficient highways for shipping heavy goods." Smoldering and burned-out airplanes upset operations at the airbases, and flak-tower operators were still shaking in their boots from so many near misses of fighter aircraft diving and firing at them. The American pilots seemed to enjoy shooting up these towers as much as anything else on the ground.

The Americans paid heavily with losses too. Our flak boys put up a lot of lead into the air, and many of the enemy attackers were bound to run into some of it, so many came down for unscheduled landings. Some of the groups lost 20 to 25 percent of their force strength. The 4th Fighter Group alone contributed eight planes to the cause that day, and within a few days seven pilots were admiring the pictures on my walls and desk. They all blamed our new 20 mm flak guns. "Herr Scharff, I'm sorry there will be no Easter holiday for you," my commander's voice told me by

Chapter 8: To Err Is Human

MAJOR WALTER C. BECKHAM: 18 VICTORIES
Beckham was the leading American ace in the European theater of operations (ETO) the day he was shot down by flak. His interrogator, Hanns Scharff, thought he was an extremely intelligent and gutsy opponent.

telephone. "We are being pressed for your report on how they can navigate so well in those fighters, so we need the information as quickly as possible."

As the day's bag of prisoners began to report into Auswertestelle West, I systematically assigned each one to his respective place. Also I queried each one, filling in the squares, and the more I listened, the clearer the picture became. In a few days I had enough information to write a complete history of that big day.

These wild fighter pilots, the Eagle boys or 4th Group boys, are difficult to handle. I sit there and argue for hours with each one, getting a sore throat and dry lips while I could hear the Easter Sunday church bells chiming. Captain Peterson was in my office giving me the name, rank, and serial number routine when he noticed two bottles of blueberry brandy on a shelf behind my desk, almost out of sight. Suddenly he spoke:

"Sir! Is that really brandy in those two bottles?"

We permanent party people at Oberursel had received an extra liquor ration for Easter festivals, and though they were meant for our own private use, who cares at Eastertide? If one's mouth is dry like the African desert or Arizona's sand piles, one must do something about it. I reached back and, taking a bottle, uncorked it and handed Captain Peterson a filled glass.

"By golly! This is good stuff you've got here."

"You like it, eh? It's German. Have another sip, Eagle-boy Peterson; it's an Easter egg."

He laughed. "Thanks! I didn't know you Krauts could make strong liquor."

"Strong? Pshaw! That's like a soft drink! Have another?"

The Interrogator

The liquor loosened his tongue a tiny bit. "Scharff, since you seem to know everything about us, have you talked to Bunte yet?"

"First Lieutenant Bunte of the 4th?"

"That's him! He was my buddy at Debden; stays in your rattle two cells down from mine. I peeked through the hole and saw him going to the showers, but the guard said it was verboten for me to talk to him."

"No, I haven't had time to talk to him, yet. Came in three or four days before you did. Hell, if he's your buddy, shall we invite him to have a nip from the bottle too?"

"Fine! Great! Can I talk to him too? Here in your office?"

Picking up the telephone, I nod my approval.

Bunte is escorted in and in great surprise throws his arms in the air. "So here you are at last, Pete! You sucker, you! Where's the rest of the gang? I hear there's a batch of them coming in."

"Hullo, Bunte," I interject, "we are having a little Easter celebration and libation and thought you might like to join us. I am your interrogator, Hanns Scharff, known as 'Stone Face,' and have not had a chance to meet you before." I saluted him, and he automatically returned the salute, unable to wipe the smile off his face at the sight of Captain Peterson. Then I continued, "Say! We have some more tigers from the 4th over there in the cooler. Want them to share our Easter festivities too?"

"WHAT DID YOU GET FROM ME . . . ?"
Walter Beckham asked that question again when he met Scharff at Phoenix, Arizona, on 26 May 1984. "Zilch!" answered Scharff. Hermann Boschet and Scharff's daughter-in-law Monika Scharff are at right.

Chapter 8: To Err Is Human

"Damn right! I mean, yes sir! Please call them over, Herr Scharff."

"Okay!" another said. "Who are the bastards?"

"Oh, let's see, Captain Van Epps of 334 Squadron and Lt. Williams of 334 too."

When they were ushered in, the real party started. Two bottles of brandy would not last long, but these boys were careful to nurse the supply and share and share alike, true to 4th Group manners. The conversation burgeoned; "Prost!" "Cheers!" . . . "What th'ell happened to you?" . . . "Good stuff, and would you believe it's German?" . . . "War is over for me, maybe for all of us here!" . . . "Hell, I thought I wasn't going to be able to get out!" . . . "How did you get down?" . . . "What did Mansfield do? He was afire . . ." . . . "Do they let our folks know we are alive?" . . . "Sure! If you tell them where to send the radio message." . . . "Cheers!" . . . "Hanns, you got my new Mustang, what more do you want, blood?" . . . "I loved that airplane!" . . . "The Russians call it tough-shitski!" . . . "Hey, gang! Look out the window! Isn't that Clotfelter?" . . . "Jesus Christ! I damn near fell outa' the window!" . . . "Look at his black mouse" . . "Whose mouse? Hey, you wanta bust your tail?"

"Don't lean out so far, ya' damn ninny!" . . . "Hey! Lookit the Clod! . . . He's got a black eye!" . . . "Yeh, some fräulein proba'ly popped him!" . . . "Hi, Clod! Look up here! Come on up to the headquarters of the 4th!" . . . "Okay if he comes up too, Hanns?" . . . "Sure, I'll tell the guard, and maybe I can find some more schnapps while I'm at it."

The noise became so great that I had to call for some semblance of order from the guests, and to the guards to shag Clotfelter up to my office. Shortly afterward, he arrived and then we remembered that two more red-nosed pilots were in the calaboose, Major Mills and Lt. Carr, so we called them out of solitary. Soon our cups were drained to the dregs, and these fighter pilots were looking everywhere to see if I had more hidden away someplace. They were boisterous youth, and through all their talk the fact was accepted that I already knew everything, and they all took it for granted that I had it all down in my book and file on the 4th, the green file folder.

Presently the reception officer on duty called on the phone and told me that he had another fighter boy from the 4th over in another wing. I had forgotten Major Duane W. Beeson, the Boise Bee pilot who had over nineteen aerial victories. A former 71 Squadron Eagle boy with the RAF, Beeson had been clobbered by our flak on 5 April. He stuck to the name, rank, and serial number routine, proving very hard to reach. He took a lot of my time and spent more days in the cooler than normal. I wrote his name on my desk pad as I talked to the reception officer, knowing most of this gang of rowdies in my office was watching as I did. When I finished writing "Major Beeson," the gang erupted into wild cheers.

Good old Bee had been their squadron leader, and they were overjoyed to know he lived through the crash of his plane. We all stuck our heads together and cooked up a suitable welcoming party for Beeson after I called the cooler and

The Interrogator

ordered him to my office. We decided we would all sit in my office very quietly (Impossible! Have you ever tried or even heard of anyone successfully quieting a batch of fighter pilots who haven't had their fill of brandy?), and when the guard opened the door to let Beeson in, we would all give him a rousing cheer. I thought of my schoolboy gags and felt very warm and hospitable inside. Happy.

Knock! Knock! "Come in!" I called, and we all saw the door swing open and Beeson stepped forward smartly to freeze suddenly as he was framed in the doorway. Eyes fixed straight ahead, he stood at rigid attention like a statue. When the shouting from his buddies died down a bit, he saluted me, and our cheers seemed stuck in our throats. I rose from my chair and invited him in.

"Major, come in and say hullo to your buddies!"

Still looking straight ahead, Beeson took one step into the room and stopped.

"I do not know any of these gentlemen!" he snapped.

Pandemonium broke loose.

"Bee! Are you nuts?" they shouted, and when he continued to stare straight at me, they all started talking as one. "Bee! Holy Moses! Don't you remember us anymore . . . after all we've been through together! Don't you see, Bee, this Deutscher has us all taped right there in his book."

"Sorry, gentlemen, I do not know who you are."

His demeanor could not resist change, though, as they all stood and stared in awe at him, no doubt wondering if we Germans had doped Beeson or something. His lips moved slightly and his eyes began to crinkle at the corners. The odds against him were too heavy.

One POW takes it easy, the next takes it hard. Considering the spectrum of human differences in their natures, it was possible for me to still say they were all good men. I spent many hours that night reflecting on that. My report was presented to the commander the next morning, and I am happy to say it received much notice. But the Old Man, when I handed him the report, looked at me very sternly and said, "There was a complaint about you last night, Private Scharff. Some transport officers across from your bay saw how you were celebrating Easter with prisoners of war. They said you all became so merry that one even attempted to jump from your window, and your song 'For He's a Jolly Good Fellow' disturbed the tranquility of Easter for some."

Major Beeson is the officer who wrote a postcard back to his commanding officer in England that tickled my funny bone. The noses on the Mustangs of the 4th Group were painted a brilliant red; that is, the propeller spinner and the leading 12 inches of the engine cowling were painted red. Beeson's card, after I had completed my interrogations with him, said:

COLONEL, THEY KNOW ALL ABOUT US OVER HERE.
PAINT THE ENTIRE PLANE RED! ALL RED!
Bee.

Chapter 8: To Err Is Human

SCRATCH ONE THUNDERBOLT
This is what a P-47 looks like when lying on its back. Pilot walked away unscratched.

Author comment: Major Walter C. Beckham signed out of Oberursel just one day after Lt. Col. Selden Edner and just six days after Colonel Russ Spicer. Beckham's entry in Scharff's logbook reads as follows: "23 March 1944 – Maj. Beckham – Thunderbolt – J584 – USAAF – 351 – 353." J584 was the BUNA case number identifying his airplane, 351 was his fighter squadron, and 353 was his fighter group. Beckham was a triple ace with eighteen aerial victories to his credit when, on 22 February, he abandoned his burning P-47 "Little Demon," parachuting to terra firma and landing in the midst of some unfriendly German civilians who were a mite teed off at all parachutists.

"One of them had a switchblade knife opened, and it is likely I would not have lasted long except for the arrival of police from nearby Opladen. I was kept at the police station until some Luftwaffe people from a base called Ostheim picked me up, I think it was Ostheim that I had strafed. The next morning I was escorted to a train, joining several other captive Luftgangsters, and soon we were off to Oberursel.

"At Oberursel we were jammed into a small room. When my turn came, I was escorted to face an interrogator in another room. He was small, red-faced guy who became infuriated because I stuck to the name–rank–serial number routine. He banged his fist on the wall of his office. Then in walked Hanns Scharff, and the little guy stalked out of the room, stuttering that he was going to turn me over to the Gestapo and . . . "Vot zey vill do mit you!"

"Hanns said hello to me, then stood and watched me, ostensibly waiting for the Gestapo to arrive. If he thought I was frightened, he was absolutely right. Maybe it was just a well-rehearsed act. From then on, Hanns Scharff was my man;

211

The Interrogator

I know nothing about Scharff that makes me think he is great or lousy or whatever, but he always treated me fairly.

"At Auswertestelle West, Oberursel, I almost prayed to go back for more interrogation. At least that gave me a chance to see someone and talk to someone. At least one time, I was treated by Hanns to a tea with some crackers and cheese. It was delicious, and I ate everything on the table, including small crumbs, as fast as I politely could because I was afraid I might get thrown back into my solitary cell upon failure to answer questions.

"The food at Oberursel was reliable. We got a margarine or ersatz-jelly sandwich in the morning and again in the evening. At noon we got a small bowl of weak soup. Every day it was the same; never a change to that menu! I was eternally hungry, like everyone else, even the Germans. I began to do exercises but soon quit because there was not enough food to permit this unnecessary burning of calories. I spent twenty-seven days at Oberursel.

"What did Hanns really want to know from me? I still don't know. I am sure he knew more about everything than I did. Maybe he just fished for confirmation of data he already had, or hoped for a slip of the tongue. He knew the names (in flight order) of all the pilots in my 351st Squadron, and it was a surprise to me because no one who had been shot down earlier could possibly have known this! I knew by heart our lineup, since I was the squadron CO. So did he! He *had* to get this info from someone back in England who had access to our operations office. *He even knew the name of our armament officer's dog!* He knew our squadron intelligence officer's name was Blackie Fuchs, and said he was very sad that he never had a chance of catching any of the USAAF intelligence officers.

"I would decline to answer even his trivial questions, and perhaps he rarely, if ever, got around to asking me what I thought he really wanted to know. I had then a theory that I still hold. I think he really wanted to know whether it was the German long-range or their short-range flak that got me. I got hit high in my dive, so it was the long-range stuff. I was so frightened at the possibility that if I should lie to him about that, he would find out and then get the truth from my weak and hungry attempt to mislead him. I finally did give him a story, saying that nothing hit me, that my engine was overheating even when I coasted out of England and that was why I caught fire over Opladen. I think it was shortly after telling him this little lie that I was allowed to leave that sorry place and sent down to Frankfurt's Dulag Luft.

"I wonder if Scharff considered this to be another victory? He had a false story of how still another Luftgangster had been shot down, or maybe he just didn't care and was just required to get some kind of story. He did suggest several times that I had been accused of strafing civilians. This was not true, and he probably knew it.

"A friend of mine once told me that if he ever saw Hanns Scharff again, he would gladly kill him. I don't know why he says this, since it is not like him at

Chapter 8: To Err Is Human

all, being a cool, kind, nice guy. It was apparent that Scharff was appointed to interrogate the higher-ranking POWs, major and above, probably because he was good at it. Once Hanns brought in about a dozen or so German pilots who had been shot down over England and had been repatriated to Germany. With them was a seventy-three-victory ace who had been highly decorated, Gerhard Michalski. We could have become friends. He asked Scharff if he might have me visit their base as his guest, and Hanns said all right, but it never came off. I harbored silly ideas about stealing a plane and flying back to England.

"I got to Dulag Luft in Frankfurt just in time for it to be bashed by British night bombers, so my first night there was spent in an air raid tunnel; else Pore Daddy would be dead! Our barracks were smashed while we were there. I think one American was killed in this attack the night of 24–25 March. In 1974, I bumped into Lt. Gen. Jerry Johnson (who had seventeen victories too) in the Pentagon. He had gone through the same routine at Oberursel as I had, a month or two later, and he told me Scharff had commented to him that he 'hoped we won't have to do to you what we did to Walter Beckham.'"

Author comment: Walter Beckham had, of course, no way of knowing that an official police report had accompanied him to Oberursel from Opladen, accusing him of having strafed civilians in a small village before he crashed. Interrogator Hanns Scharff had a tedious and time-consuming investigation to make concerning the charge, and nearly four weeks passed before he had enough evidence to clear Beckham. Once such an official accusation was rendered, it had to be officially handled at Auswertestelle West. (Author: Walter C. Beckham passed away on 31 May 1996).

Concerning the 4th Fighter Group dropping down through a low ceiling of clouds directly over the German airbase, Scharff says that Göring was so wrought up that he ordered the interrogation section and the technical section at Auswertestelle West to search for the instrument they used to make the letdown. "How can they find us, coming down through solid clouds in perfect formation? *Find the apparatus!* Find the apparatus!" Observers had noted that the P-51s were being led by a P-38. This was the "Droop Snoot" model, with a radar in the nose in place of the guns.

HANNS SCHARFF continues: A single bad deed by one individual can jeopardize the achievements of many others. The favorable reputation of an entire fighter group can be wiped out by some foolish or unnecessary act of violence by only one of its members. This lapse of common sense actually gives aid to the enemy, who will exploit the misdeed through propaganda and every other means. The guilty conscience alone will perform most of the work advantageous to the inquisitor, but indisputable evidence is even more effective,

As the days passed on, we began to recover more and more gun camera film from crashed American fighters. These films accumulated in our photo department, and occasionally I witnessed an unspeakably ugly scene in them. In one film,

The Interrogator

schoolchildren were shot on a street in front of their homes and schoolhouse. In another, a forester and a peasant in a field were hunted like rabbits until both died after this pilot has made several strafing passes at each of them. In all these cases, the pilot of the plane had been found dead in the wreckage of his fighter, but the gun camera film had been recovered by our intelligence crews, and the film told the story of his last flight. These scenes made me review in my thoughts all those POWs I had met so far, and not one of them could I picture as guilty of any such infamy.

Questions from our headquarters started harassing me to produce admissions of guilt from enemy fliers who could be connected with these so-called atrocities. I had to make the subject a part of my routine interrogations. On the one side, emotionally, I was convinced I had met only honorable enemy pilots, yet on the other side, my cool and logical thinking told me that such villains did exist, and one or more of them surely would turn up sooner or later.

One occurrence caused much discussion during and after the war. The American bomber formations adopted the signal of surrender by dropping the wheels and flaps of their mighty Fortresses, which indicated to our Luftwaffe fighter pilots that the crewmen were either abandoning the aircraft by parachute or wished to be allowed to safely land at the nearest airfield. Upon seeing this surrender signal, our fighters would cease attacking that particular bomber and, sportsmanlike, would often fly alongside the crippled aircraft and exhort the crew to bail out safely, or to escort the plane to an airfield.

In this one case, our fighter leader observed the surrender signal of a bomber of the USAF 100th Bomb Group, and as he flew alongside the bomber, the tail gunner (who may not have gotten the surrender order) cut the Luftwaffe fighter with his twin fifties, killing the German pilot. His enraged buddies immediately reattacked the Fortress, and from that date onward, that Luftwaffe fighter unit made it a point to look for the distinctive markings of the 100th Bomb Group in the huge bomber streams.

Other occurrences bringing ill fame to many American units included the strafing of our Luftwaffe pilots as they hung quite defenseless in their parachutes. Were we naive or were we too gallant and chivalrous to expect aerial jousters to refrain from wanton murder even in wartime?

Consciously I refrained from becoming shyster minded, but I studied each mission closely, sifting every shred of evidence so that not a single dubious character would slip through Oberursel undetected. Sometimes I would indirectly accuse a prisoner of having participated in a deplorable action, but I was never able to prove a single case.

Among the hundreds of fighter pilots flying out of England, I knew of only one who had been involved in a bad show, and he had returned safely home to his base at King's Cliffe. We captured some of his flying mates, and several of them confirmed that his combat films had been shown at squadron briefing. His group

Chapter 8: To Err Is Human

commander had consequently court-martialed him for the act, grounding him for two weeks and fining him a sum of money from his pay. The pilot, a Lt. Dickson (not the officer's real name), was reportedly scolded and shunned by his fellow pilots. When this pilot had allegedly cut down an old woman peasant in a field, he had boasted on his return to his home airfield that he had killed an "enemy."

His name was, naturally, marked in the group file at Oberursel, and I often wonder what would have happened if he had appeared one day at Auswertestelle West as a POW. He probably would have faced a very stiff court-martial, and I may have had a hanging on my conscience to this day. He was never shot down, however, and his less fortunate buddies in the group carried the burden of the bad reputation he had sired. Not that we received them with less amiability, but they suffered heavily under their own bad conscience on behalf of an unworthy squadron mate.

The evildoer's group commander, Colonel Mark Hubbard, eventually fell into our hands. I heaped it all onto his shoulders, and I was deeply moved when I witnessed his complete breakdown in my office. If there can be any blame for not having succeeded in a valiant attempt to adhere to the name, rank, and serial number answers, it should be attributed to the trigger-happy lieutenant under the colonel's jurisdiction.

Colonel Hubbard was truly a superior officer, and I found him prepared to accept full responsibility for the misconduct of a disobedient subordinate. Many days of strenuous essays were necessary to reshape him into a happy man. Since I was once more convinced by him of the USAAF's soldierly standards, I promised

USAAF 20th FIGHTER GROUP CO
Col. Mark E. Hubbard was CO for just 16 days before he bailed out of his P-38 over Germany. Scharff charged him with issuing orders to 20th pilots to shoot parachuting Luftwaffe pilots and having shot a woman worker in a field. Hubbard denied it but apologized for the act of one of his pilots.

The Interrogator

not to let my opinion of the fighter commands be influenced by the bad behavior of a single black sheep. This standpoint enabled me to direct my most upsetting investigation in an unbiased way, and helped me in saving the lives of seven American fighter pilots.

The ancient university town of Greifswald, situated on the Baltic seacoast in northeastern Germany, was hit hard by a strafing Mustang group and Lightning group. With the terrifying sounds of the air raid sirens, the first P-51 fighters appeared flying low over the town, firing into the streets and raising havoc among the fleeing inhabitants. This incident aroused the indignation of Reichsmarschall Göring, and I was informed of his personal concern in the matter. At once I was ordered to report in detail about the activities of fliers taken prisoner after this attack.

The Mustang group, and the P-38 group now branded with ill repute, had about a dozen losses that day. Seven pilots were captured and soon appeared at Auswertestelle West, the remainder of the pilots who were shot down having been killed in the crash of their aircraft. Carefully keeping them apart in their solitary cells in the cooler, I questioned one after another, devoting much time to each individual.

"Captain Garlock," I said to the first one, "without intending to insinuate that you personally participated in this deplorable action, will you describe in detail your part in the fray?"

"PLEASE RETURN THIS TO ITS RIGHTFUL OWNER"
USAF colonel Jack S. Jenkins (*right*) presents the Schwertern award certificate, which Hitler had given to Werner Mölders early in the war, to Adolf Galland, Gerhard Gobert, and Werner Andres. Jenkins had bought the certificate in London in 1945, shortly after graduating from Scharff's school.

216

Chapter 8: To Err Is Human

"Sir," he answered, "I am fully aware of the fact I am involved in an exceedingly serious matter. If my word as an American officer is of any value to you, and it is the only means of proof I can offer, you will recognize my innocence ." His appearance was manly, frank, and without fear. His candid eyes faithful, his speech free and positive. I believed in his complete guiltlessness, and throughout the trying time to come, I thought of him as a responsible and honest officer. There were no hard feelings between us.

The next case, First Lieutenant Tipton, was not so uncomplicated because he contradicted himself several times, and his general behavior made me doubt whether he was telling the truth. Particularly at essential prime points, he always tried to avoid answers by reverting to the name–rank–serial number principle. This approach was abandoned by every one of the Greifswald raiders from the beginning as of no value. They now realized that they were involved in a grave matter.

After considerable, painful questioning, I dictated his story a yarn that gave no indication of a brutal assault on civilians.

"Thank God!" Second Lieutenant Shupe said; "I had to belly in before the dirty work started. I did not fire a single shot on that fateful day, and I would not have shot into the crowded streets anyway."

There was the report on his airplane, and we had his cameras; I looked at the gun films, and indeed his guns had not exposed a single picture. He was in the clear.

Next was First Lieutenant Weisel. A very likeable person, but the boy had the worst record and furnished it himself.

"One of my guns jammed on the way in," he explained, "and all I did was fire some test shots into the ground."

"Into what on the ground where?"

Some small bushes I saw on the outskirts of the town."

"Were there soldiers about or civilians?"

"No, sir, not a soul."

I thought he was trustworthy. He had very convincing manners. He was very worried, as were they all, and the wife of one of them was expecting a baby, and this made these moments even more tense.

The story of the fifth pilot, Lieutenant Rowan, was clear. Flak hit his plane, fired from an antiaircraft wagon that protected the train he had tried to attack. Before he reached Greifswald he had bailed out. The corroboration of his story and the report of the ack-ack unit were faultless.

In the middle of this difficult work I was called to the *Kommandant* to review in detail the proceeding of the case. I stated the facts I had by then ascertained, without adding some of my own impressions or conclusions. He, refraining from any direct reference to the complicated problems, emphasizing every word, presently said in a wise, superior, slightly scornful manner, "Some results of our propaganda have reached me, and I would like for you to think them over."

The Interrogator

He reached for some telegrams and read "Nine prisoners of war in transit to Oberursel were attacked by an angry crowd at the Central Railroad Station in Frankfurt. One of the Luftwaffe guards was stabbed in the back during the scuffle by a Russian civilian. Some of the POWs' boots and leather jackets were taken by the crowd."

"Disgusting!" I said, and he continued:

"Threatening violence of civilians directed against three POWs on a train resulted in the escape of one prisoner. The train had stopped and the guards were occupied warding off onslaughts by angry women."

I began to wonder what it was the *Kommandant* intended to convey to me. He did not explain and merely disclosed bare details of the reactions of our people. Why should he give me this information in such a confidential air?

There was one report that really shocked me. A single American prisoner was led to the burgomaster of a little village along a country road by an auxiliary policeman. They were overtaken by a car, which suddenly stopped in front of them. A uniformed officer of the political corps alighted from the automobile and demanded to know what was going on. The policeman duly reported that he was escorting the prisoner of war to the next sheriff, the burgomaster.

"Step aside!" ordered the officer as he drew his revolver from its holster.

The policeman stepped between the political officer and the prisoner, firmly remarking that it was his duty and his intention to protect his prisoner.

"Have it your own way!" snapped the officer, and without further warning the insane man shot the prisoner at close range, then turned his gun on the policeman, killing them both.

I was speechless and awestruck when the *Kommandant* finished reading that report to me. Then he broke the silence, "You may continue with your good work."

I felt unable to continue my work at that moment, so I left the camp and walked in the woods. When I returned from my solitary sojourn, I had made up my mind that I would resume my interrogations of the captured Greifswald Seven without looking left or right. In my thinking, two wrongs do not make a right, and the outrage committed by some few American pilots should not be attributed to all American pilots, so I had to deal fairly and squarely in this special investigation.

In due course, I completed this investigation, which determined that none of the seven captured pilots could be held responsible for the dreadful deeds perpetrated at Greifswald. Not one of the seven had fired at civilians! Carefully worded, my report would protect them against revenge-minded officials in other headquarters. Relieved, I completed the forms and released all seven to the permanent camp. They left for Dulag Luft the very next morning.

Just before leaving Auswertestelle West, Captain Garlock requested permission to see me once more, and his words of appreciation were to ring in my ears long after he had gone. Almost constantly, our earthly path wound along the precipice of disaster, misery, and death. He and his buddies had known this.

Chapter 8: To Err Is Human

ONE OF THE GREIFSWALD SEVEN
"My name is James Weisel and my serial number is . . . When Scharff visited an ailing Weisel in Bakersfield, California, on 12 December 1977, those were the first words said by Weisel. Weisel called Scharff a few years later, saying, "You saved my life in WWII. Can you do it again?" It was too late.

Four peaceful days followed, and I was able to resume my normal activities. Colonel Jack S. Jenkins, USAAF 55th Fighter Group commander, had come to us as a POW, and I was busy interrogating this interesting flier when I was called by the camp's deputy CO, Major Junge. He was always so friendly and correct, but this time he was strangely distant, nervous, and highly agitated as he informed me about the complete dissatisfaction my report had created at headquarters.

Major Junge criticized me for having released the seven POWs prematurely, and informed me they were being recalled from Dulag Luft. The highest office of the Luftwaffe had ordered a new, more lucid investigation. They also ordered, without explanation, a liaison officer of the Gestapo to Auswertestelle West to participate in the reinvestigation.

This was the first time I was to meet the very loathsome type of Gestapo man of despicable fame. Up until this time, I had met two Gestapo officials and they had been gentlemen, the exception of what we had commonly imagined they would be.

The usual custom would have been to invite Gestapo liaison officer Gail to my office, to discuss with him the intended procedure to be used, before calling in the prisoners. For some reason, it was not practical to do so in this instance,

The Interrogator

and therefore I learned during the pervicacious questioning just what his intentions were. His objective was clearly the conviction of these seven fighter pilots whether they were guilty or not. I could only sense this in the beginning, as the cases were heard, but soon I was fully conscious of the danger facing the Greifswald Seven.

They also sensed the gravity of the situation. They did not know that every move they made was being watched and that we heard every word they spoke day and night. I listened to the unsteady voice of Weisel reading from his Bible to his comrades, one night after we had released them from solitary so we could listen to them talk together.

"Pilate sayeth unto Him, what is Truth?"

Crucify? But Pilate found no fault at all!

"Have you any notion why all of you have been returned to this camp?" I asked this question at the first session. I was standing behind my desk, and Gestapo officer Gail was by my side. Before us stood, in a half circle, Weisel, Garlock, Michaely, Rowan, Tipton, Shupe, and Bernstein. (Author: Four of the seven names are correct, the other three uncertain at this writing. Scharff's records and memory have been unable to recall the exact seven. Another POW, Bert Shepard, recalls that only five pilots were under suspicion.)

"No!" replied Lt. Tipton, speaking for all. "We know it must be very grave and about Greifswald. Why are we back here?"

I looked serious, no doubt. "I will be frank with you. Headquarters is not satisfied with my previous investigation. It must be done over again, I expect you to give me the whole truth even if you missed or omitted any details in the first sessions I had with you. Yes, this is a very grave situation, gentlemen, involving the murder of noncombatants, women who were sadistically strafed, and the highest headquarters will be watching this inquiry. Do you understand that you can save yourselves only by telling me the whole truth?"

After a long silence, Captain Garlock spoke, "Are you handling this inquiry, sir, or is it this other gentleman beside you who is in charge?"

"I am handling it, Hauptmann, but you may reject me as your interrogator if you wish, and another will be assigned. If you keep me, then you must regard me as your advocate, not as a persecutor or prosecutor. What is your desire?"

In unison, the seven men indicated they wanted me to act as their advocate. "All right, so be it. I want to make it clear that your stories did not satisfy my superiors. I am compelled to question you again. Herr Gail, the liaison officer of the Criminal Division of Gestapo headquarters, has been assigned to sit in. I implicitly believed your stories, and they checked out true. However, now we must hear them all over again, and I am hoping that perhaps we can find a missing link or uncover new evidence one way or the other. Furthermore, we have just identified the crashed fighters that participated in the Greifswald raids that day, and two of them may supply more raw data to us that may prove of use in the case. Now, Lt. Weisel, will you start by telling us your story from beginning to end again, please?"

Chapter 8: To Err Is Human

"Yes, sir!" Weisel spoke strongly, then suddenly began to stammer.

"I will . . . well, sir, I am sorry . . . I mean . . . well, there was something else, you see."

My heart sunk. Good God! What was he about to say? Weisel had turned pale as the blood seemed to drain from his face.

"All right, Lt. Weisel," I said almost sternly, "tell us all about it. Leave nothing out."

"It's like this, sir. My story is correct just as I told you before, except I forgot to tell you something."

The eyes of his six buddies stared at him in bewilderment, and the tight lips of the Gestapo man Gail twirled a match between his lips. Gail was a headhunter type, and I was fearful of his reaction.

"What, Weisel?"

"I . . . I fired a few test shots into the main street of Greifswald!"

"What did you say? You did? Are you crazy?"

"Remember I told you the test burst was into a clump of bushes on the outskirts of town? That's true, but I held the trigger down a little too long, and with the speed of my P-38 the bullet trail went into town, and I saw the bullets hit the stairway of a big yellow building on the main square. It looked like the city hall building or some such thing. There was no one near." White as a sheet, he leaned against the wall for support, "I should have told you, but my life did not depend on it then."

Gail had heard enough and jumped to his feet, shouting, "Look at the guilt written all over that bastard's face!"

"Just a minute, please," I said trying to maintain my lithoid mannerisms. "Let's find out first what really happened before we declare anyone guilty. This is a serious matter."

Gail turned on me like an imperator, "We have found out enough! You need not find out anymore from this dirty swine who has admitted enough already!"

"Lieutenant Weisel, did you or did you not hit anyone, shoot a civilian when your bullets flew into the town?"

"Hanns, so help me God, my bullets hit no one, and so I did not kill a civilian!" Inwardly, I relaxed. "All right, I am prepared to accept that for the moment, but you know there was panic at Greifswald, and many people were running through those streets. Could you possibly and accidentally have hit a single person there?"

"No, I am positive I did not hit a soul. The stairs on that city building were empty. There was no one near them at all."

"Okay, we can check that. Every point made here must be checked. If it is true, then it's a good point for you, Weisel."

Gail gnashed his teeth and stamped on the floor, then shook his fist. "What? Why the hell did this gangster forget to tell you about this in the first place? Guilty! That's why. He's guilty! Look at him!"

The Interrogator

The seven prisoners knew they had met their Armageddon, and they cooperated fully with me while I very carefully and conscientiously worked on each case. Garlock's story was as straight as ever. So was Rowan's and Michaely's. Tipton again contradicted himself and sent the Gestapo man into another frenzy of wild accusations, which took all of my knowledge of psychology to counteract. Then Bernstein and young Shupe changed their statements, and I, already being in a rather awkward position, began to experience doubts anew. No one had lied to me the first time, but they had just failed to recall everything and were now bringing up new details of the attack.

When they had come back to Oberursel from Dulag Luft, I had told them that we were overcrowded in the cooler and that they would all have to stay together in one special large cell. Actually, I wanted them together so that they could discuss their plight with each other, and I could have my listeners record every word that was picked up by the microphone that was hidden in their big cell.

That night they threw at each other every wild accusation they could think of. Every human instinct came to light, and all the traits of the lower animal contained in man were revealed. Suspicion, egoism, greediness, gullibility, intrigue, viciousness. Mitigating these negative qualities was the outstanding superior quality of giving comfort and encouragement to each other. This came to light with Weisel's reading of the verses of St. John.

The grilling continued, and I called them into my office one by one. I had their names listed on an official-looking piece of paper lying on my desk, where

NEW SHOES—NEW BLISTERS
RAF warrant officer Slowey was shot down over Germany. Slowey had lost his shoes when he parachuted from his Spitfire and was captured by Germans. His captors gave him a pair of high-top boots, but they wore blisters on his calves. Passing by, Hanns Scharff loaned him his pocketknife to cut the boots. Slowey was suspicious of Scharff.

222

Chapter 8: To Err Is Human

their prying eyes could see it and they might read it upside down. If they hadn't that capability before, they certainly developed it during the inquiries. Tipton's and Weisel's names I had underlined with red pencils; Shupe's and Bernstein's were marked with large Xs. I knew the habits of POWs very well and merely wanted to arouse their curiosity, and the markings meant nothing whatsoever. They took the bait, and each time a man returned to the communal cell, a new storm broke loose, especially against the marked men. Actually, though, I learned not one thing from all this eavesdropping. They were going in circles and so was I. Not one shred of solid evidence could be produced against them.

Having again convinced myself of everyone's innocence, I wrote out a new report. Fourteen wearisome nights I worked on this treatise, meanwhile trying to attend to my routine duties as well as possible during the daytime. I felt like a defense lawyer submitting his final writ to an unsympathetic judge and jury. This report, I knew, must not bear the flavor of an actual plea for the defense. I reversed Marc Anthony's funeral oration by emphasizing not the honorable qualities of the seven who stood accused, but the dishonorable or questionable qualities of each. At the same time I stated the extenuating circumstances for their conduct, which offset their guilt, a circumlocution, if you will.

Every day I visited the prisoners, moving them once more into separate rooms in an effort to give them an extra measure of comfort. Still, their morale sank rapidly, and they appeared to be suffering from hypopraxia. The longer they had to wait, the more listless and depressed they became. As I passed their windows going to and from lunch or dinner, they would call down to me: "Hullo! Hanns! How goes't today? Any news? Do we have a chance?" Their faces were pale and carried worry lines, and their anxious eyes followed my footsteps. I did what I could to give them comfort and confidence.

Suddenly a break came in the case! I could not tell them, since it may have come too late. Gun camera film from one of the crashed 355th Mustangs was finally recovered, and it showed four German women in the middle of a small country road being mercilessly and needlessly mowed down by the Mustang's .50-caliber machine guns. Now we knew we had the guilty party, and he was found dead in the cockpit of the American fighter plane. The Greifswald Seven were innocent! I hastily wrote an addendum to my last report, enclosed prints of the combat film, and forwarded it to headquarters posthaste. Then I prayed that innocent soldiers would not be stood before a firing squad before those red-tape artists at headquarters had time to digest this conclusive new evidence. The gun camera film was evidence enough.

A week went by. I was becoming very apprehensive, and the seven whose lives were at stake were filled with anguish and despair. They visibly lost all faith and became frightfully apathetic. Göring's headquarters was taking their own sweet time swallowing my presentation. Then one night, it was half past one in the morning and I had just fallen asleep after insomniac hours; the charge of

The Interrogator

FAVOR FOR AN OLD ACQUAINTANCE
Prior to WWII, Hanns Scharff had rescued a rally driver named Etienne Rocher who had stalled in the middle of a river in South Africa. Rocher joined the South African Air Force and was shot down and came to Oberursel. POW Rocher told interrogator Scharff he would like to ride on a sled before going to Stalag Luft. Scharff arranged it.

quarters rousted me out of bed to answer the telephone. Major Junge, our deputy commander, his voice much less indignant this time, was on the line.

"Gefreiter Scharff? I have just received a priority message concerning the Greifswald bunch. Very important! Come to my private quarters immediately!"

My heart was thumping as I stumbled through the night, trying to read into the sound of his voice what I wanted to hear. When I entered his quarters he jumped to his feet and grabbed my hand and vigorously shook it. With a big smile on his face and forgetting military protocol, the major addressed me happily: "Herr Scharff! The Reichsmarschall decided this afternoon that Captain Garlock . . . the Greifswald Seven . . . should be regarded as honorable combat soldiers and should proceed to a permanent camp!"

I tossed down the wine he was pouring for me, overjoyed by this development. Then I begged permission to go tell the POWs. Dark and silent lay the long cooler building, since everyone must be asleep. There was a slight mist falling, but I was so exuberant over having won justice in the name of humanity that it might as well have been a sunny midday. Wake up, boys! Good news!

The reactions of the Greifswald Seven were something to behold. All had been expecting execution, I am sure, and the way they took the news will be one

Chapter 8: To Err Is Human

of my everlasting memories. The first one embraced me unabashedly and broke into tears on my shoulder, just as my little son had done once when he realized he had just safely passed through a serious surgical operation. I consoled this American POW as best I could.

The second one, however, just opened his weary eyes, closed them as he turned his face to the wall, and ordered me to get out of his cell and leave him alone. He did not want to be bothered and I could go to hell; I decided this was no time to try to change his apomictic mind.

Number three was speechless! He paced back and forth beside his cot in the small cell, punching and shoving me gently each time he passed. His beaming face is etched in my memories forever.

The fourth one surprised me by delivering a solemn speech. With eloquent phrases he conveyed his gratitude. Visibly moved, he suddenly bent down and extracted a 1-inch cigarette butt from a secret hiding place in his bunk and ceremoniously presented it to me. "Sir, may I present my most treasured possession to you as a token of my appreciation? I have saved this for this occasion, for better or for worse. It's all I have."

Number five took the news calmly, untouched by emotion, as if it were just a matter of logic. Not a ventose person, this.

The sixth man acted as I expected he would. He chatted excitedly, began to sing, and when I crept from his cell a few moments later, his songs had turned into near-hysterical laughter as tears of joy streamed down his face.

Number seven was awestruck. Then he asked me to sit by his side on the cot, and he reached for his Bible. His hands shook and he spoke hesitatingly as he ran his fingers along the lines:

"Verily, verily, I say unto you, that ye shall weep and lament, but the world shall rejoice: and ye shall be sorrowful, but your sorrow shall be turned into joy." First Lieutenant Weisel had just reaffirmed his faith in God.

Author comments: Hanns Scharff considers the Greifswald Seven incident as the most difficult and perplexing yet the most rewarding of episodes in his entire career as an interrogator. The controversial seven were as good as dead when they returned to Auswertestelle West, the prejudgment of guilt already obvious in the demeanor of the Gestapo representative. Scharff knew there would not be much time to build up a defense for the hapless American fighter pilots. Some gun camera film had been destroyed when the planes burned; some of the film was still good, yet he had been unable to tie the damning portion of film to an aircraft flown by one of the seven accused. Finally the technical men at Auswertestelle West were able to positively identify the plane number to which the film had belonged, thereby exonerating the Greifswald Seven.

The seven stars of this cliffhanger scenario all survived the war. If they could be contacted and would give their views of the incident in its entirety, it could be a most interesting story of considerable length.

The Interrogator

IT IS A SMALL WORLD! A few weeks after the Greifswald Seven story was written into this manuscript, Judy Barras, a correspondent for the *Bakersfield Californian* newspaper, wrote a feature story about Hanns Scharff as an ex-interrogator and now a mosaic artist. Her story was published in the Bakersfield paper issued on 26 November 1977, and it produced a call from Lt. James Weisel, one of the seven, who lived in Bakersfield.

Scharff and the author visited Weisel in his home on 12 December 1977. Weisel, a victim of Parkinson's disease, lived alone with a beautiful dog and his memories, which he thought must be fast fading. However, the sight of Hanns Scharff and the warm reunion brought memories back to Weisel beyond belief. Speech difficulties attendant to Parkinson's disease prevented Weisel from expressing those memories as they flooded back into his mind, but he talked as much and as fast as he could. The author asked him, "Who was your flight commander the day you were shot down?" Weisel, without any hesitation whatsoever, commented: "My name is James Weisel, my rank is first lieutenant, and my serial number is . . . ! He had not forgotten the three replies to all interrogations.

Weisel stated he knew, as did the other POWs involved, that their lives hung by a thread during Scharff's questioning. He also said, "I did not blame the Germans at all for being very angry over the Greifswald incident. After all, when a fighter pilot strafes four women in a field, that's murder. I saw the film from the gun camera, and you could see the tracers from the machine guns as the pilot walked the rudders to correct his aim and mow them down. I knew I was innocent, and the others claimed they were, too, but how could we prove our innocence other than to trust in our German interrogator, Hanns Scharff."

James Weisel remembered that there were *nine* pilots involved instead of the seven as recalled by Scharff. "When we were at Wetzlar at Dulag Luft and were expecting to go on to Stalag Luft III, someone culled us out of the waiting POWs and marched us outside to a waiting bus. Also waiting there were nine German guards, each one carrying one of those burp-type machine guns. When we saw that, we knew the fat was in the fire again."

When asked about his experience with Hanns Scharff's interrogations when first reporting to Oberursel, Weisel said the first problem was establishing his identity as an American soldier. "I gave him my name, rank, and serial number and nothing else until he told me what happened to spies who could not convince him they were soldiers, not spies. Scharff said he knew I was a 55th boy, but I could prove it by giving him the names of some of my squadron mates whom he already knew. I refused, so then Scharff said, 'Okay, I'll give you some nicknames and you tell me the last names. If you can do that, I'll believe you are who you claim to be.' Then Scharff said, 'Spider!' Before I knew what I was doing, I retorted, 'Oh! You mean Spider Webb!' Scharff laughed and nodded affirmatively, and my identity was now established in his mind."

Chapter 8: To Err Is Human

THUNDERBOLT P-47
Republic Aviation Co. built the warhorse fighter for the USAAF. With its big R-2800 engine, it was able to carry a large array of weapons, including these ten high-velocity aircraft rockets (HVAR), eight .50-caliber machine guns, and external fuel tanks. It was extremely effective against ground or air targets.

The author mentioned a name, hoping to draw more from Weisel. "Do you know Art Thorsen?" Weisel responded, "Wheels-up Thorsen! He landed a T-6 wheels up because the warning horn was so loud he could not hear the tower telling him to go around."

Former 1st Lt. James H. Weisel was a religious man, warmhearted and friendly, and when he threw his arms around his wartime interrogator Hanns Scharff when we first appeared on 12 December 1977, we knew the tone this interview was going to take. We knew Weisel was genuinely happy to see Scharff, and we soon learned Weisel knew that Scharff had saved his life with that eloquently appealed case back in 1944. When we departed following lunch in Bakersfield, Weisel once more hugged Hanns Scharff and expressed his extreme pleasure over this dramatic reunion. Alas, Jim Weisel passed away in 1984.

SHOOTING AT PARACHUTING AIRMEN

The Germans and the British carefully avoided strafing of parachuting air crews throughout the war, just as they carefully avoided strafing of women and children on the ground. Abandoning an airplane in flight was considered a sign of surrender, and most fighter pilots stood aside and watched, hoping the parachuters would safely make it to the ground. There were hundreds of instances where wounded bomber crewmen were pushed out of American bombers because they needed

The Interrogator

immediate medical attention and would not live through the next four hours for the long flight back to England.

After the United States entered the war, top American military commanders rationalized that German fighter pilots who parachuted from damaged aircraft would probably be back flying another fighter the next day. A verbal order was issued in 1944 that erased the last fragment of gallantry from aerial combat over Europe. American fighter pilots were encouraged to shoot Germans in their parachutes. At least 99 percent refused to do it!

9

UNWEPT, UNHONORED, UNSUNG

Fool me once, shame on you! Fool me twice, shame on me.
—Chinese proverb

Psychological warfare is an ancient tree that grows on the battlefield as well as on fertile homeland fields. Roots spreading into every imaginable cranny, branches overshadowing every military development, psywar is the other side of total war. In the form of mass suggestion used on warring peoples, it is total war of the mind, reaching every individual in some way. Great strategists have been the foremost employers of psychological warfare. Sulla, Hannibal, Frederick the Great, Napoleon, Wellington, and Lee, among others, performed miracles by exploiting the common mind.

WWI and WWII featured sizable endeavors and achievements in this particular field, and in all future wars they will continue to play a highly important part and should not be underestimated as ideologies become increasingly opposed. Varied organizations are set up on each side to produce and harvest the psywar crop. Military intelligence is one of these institutions, and it resembles a gigantic oak tree.

Standing at the trunk of this tree is the man upon whose shoulders rest tremendous responsibilities. This prolific harvester is the man who gathers information from the enemy by way of interrogation of captured prisoners of war. His gleanings reach the highest branches of the tree, the top councils of war and government, and become the basis for far-reaching decisions. The interrogator, therefore, must possess, together with many other qualities, a good knowledge of psychology. He must know how to apply its methodology as well as how to test, analyze, and judge.

Whether we want it this way or not, the interrogator is the man who has to exploit the facts of feeling, will, and intellect. He is the evaluator of the whole tangle of thoughts, memories, emotions, desires, fancies, feelings, resolves, and aspirations, all that make up the reasoning and actions of men. In the case of

The Interrogator

interrogation of a POW, this material is confined to the experience of the single individual, the universe of mind being open to but one. To each man his own!

Apart from the immense armies of honorable soldiers, apart from infiltrators, disguised agents, spies, and counterintelligence men, none of whom would betray their country if captured, there are some other types we must mention. These are the numerous species of traitors, deserters, confidence men, stool pigeons, informers, collaborators, and Zoes. These auxiliaries come from two sources; they are recruited from the enemy as well as from your own ranks, and they are generally embittered people. Last but not least is the most despicable character of all, the *double agent*, the double-crosser who tries to work for both sides. His road is usually steep, dangerous, and strewn with mighty boulders. Factors usually leading an honorable man into such a life are greed, dissatisfaction, love, selfishness, fear, racial-religious-political considerations, ambition, and pure downright stupidity.

The sly fox, from whom an interrogator obtains little or no results, is the one who is intelligent but tries to play dumb; the stupid ass who tries to play clever is exactly the type the inquisitor looks forward to meeting.

Only one double-agent type came through my office at Oberursel, to my knowledge. His case was to have far-reaching effects upon the rest of my life, for it was his trial in the United States in 1948 that took me to America, and I decided to stay there the rest of my life.

USAAF lieutenant Monti, whom I shall call by his nickname, "Monti," was captured at the Vienna airport. When he arrived at Oberursel he wrote two words across the face of his questionnaire: LANDED DELIBERATELY!

This bold, young lieutenant had been in a USAAF unit stationed in India and had gone absent without leave (AWOL), hitchhiking aboard military aircraft all the way to North Africa. Somehow he managed to work his way up to Sicily and to Naples, Italy, where he reportedly managed to become a flight test pilot for another USAAF unit. He took off one day from there in one of the latest models of the Lockheed P-38 Lightning, ostensibly on a test hop. Monti kept going and landed at Vienna, turning the plane over to the Luftwaffe there. Then he volunteered to help Germany in its fight against Russia!

My friend Walter Hanemann, who headed up the southern fighter section just as I handled the northern section at Oberursel, signs Monti in because he came up from Italy. Walter came to me that evening and told me that he had a new case likely to become a "sticky wicket." There was considerable doubt that this pilot was really the traitor he was purporting to be. I was asked to come have a look at this strange and rare bird. We had to find out if this Monti might not have been sent over to us deliberately and therefore was actually an intelligence agent, his new P-38 notwithstanding. This looked like an interesting change of pace to me.

"Glad to meet you, Lieutenant; you were lucky you were not shot down by our flak boys. They are very good, there, and have one of the best tally sheets of all. Very accurate, you know."

Chapter 9: Unwept, Unhonored, Unsung

	NAME	RANK	POW NO.	SERIAL NO.	DUTIES
	CAMP STAFF				
1.	Stark, Charles W.	Colonel	1	O-20839	Sr. Allied Off.
2.	Gille, Gerald G.	1st Lt.	2	O-676373	Adj.
3.	Gilpin, Peter Wm.	Flt/Lt	4	124402	Sr. Br. Off.
4.	Jaros, Arthur C.	2nd Lt.	39	O-718324	Mess Off.
5.	Hooton, Clifford	W/O	11	963846	Chaplain
6.	Birtwell, Fred	Sgt.	7	2209632	Camp Sgt.
7.	Marini, John H.	W/O	9	R-162818	Chf. Med. Ord.
8.	Trail, John B.	Pvt.	26	7392264	Med. Ord.
9.	Reeves, Albert H.	L/Cpl.	31	6405303	" "
10.	Hill, Edward	Sgt.	9730	3443476	Hygiene
11.	McGowran, David P.	L/Cpl.	30	97000995	"
12.	Lyne, Albert W.G.	Sgt.	3104	531766	Chf. Cook
13.	Stewart, Robert C.	S/Sgt.	14	13087773	Kitchen
14.	Hammond, Fredrick W.	Sgt.	6	1287893	"
15.	Quick, Ernest E.	"	10	1605066	"
16.	Wilkinson, Ben	"	8	1594094	"
17.	Griffiths, Edward J.	L/Cpl.	35	1557805	"
18.	Lodge, Leslie K.	Pvt.	25	14549712	"
19.	Lamb, Albert	"	36	14200540	"
20.	Webster, Lawrence W.	"	37	14292508	"
21.	Martin, Douglas	Sgt.	3026	1114056	Mess Hall
22.	Whitlock, Clarence G.	S/Sgt.	5	19059787	B'rks Chf.
23.	Hetherington, John	Sgt.	32	L-1092	"
24.	Cooper, Fredrick S.	"	13	1586856	"
25.	Grainger, James	Pvt.	21	4928955	"
26.	Hughes, Lee	T/Sgt.	29	36382232	Cloth. Stores
27.	Eidmans, Gordon H.	L/Cpl.	9728	6846611	" "
28.	Webb, Gilbert F.	Pvt.	9716	5248672	" "
29.	Woodward, Harold T.	"	23	5334821	Carpenter
30.	Hard, J. Z.	Pfc.	22	3804,8651	Gardener
31.	Beaver, Arthur W.	Pvt.	24	14318890	Stf. Bks. Ord.
32.	Law, Charles T.	Spr.	34	4504398	Off. Batman
33.	Dillon, James D.	Pvt.	28	B-132067	Artist
34.	Moffatt, George H.	"	27	D-138185	Groc. Stores
35.	Miller, Harold S.	Cpl.	15	G-24083	Works Detail
36.	Mearow, Douglas T.	Pvt.	16	B-131751	" "
37.	Waddell, Don O.	"	17	B-135431	" "
38.	Dumphy, Clyde L.	"	18	F-56432	" "
39.	Dumas, Jean B.	"	19	D-106002	" "
40.	Summerhays, Wilfred J.	"	33	M-104461	" "

DULAG LUFT (TRANSIENT CAMP) STAFF ROSTER
Scharff arranged for Col. Charles W. Stark to be the senior Allied commandant at Wetzlar. This is a rare copy of the late 1944 staff.

"Yes, I was afraid of that, but I evaded them by flying out over the Adriatic beyond the range of their guns, then directly across to Vienna, where I think only a few shots were fired before I was on the ground."

"So you knew your way quite well."

"No, not well. I just flew north, and when I saw an airbase I landed there."

"Nicely done! But why did you do it?"

"I wanted to help you people in a good cause. I wanted to fight the Bolsheviks, not the Germans."

"Good! Excellent! . . . But your own people might take a very dim view of your actions. They might not approve of it at all."

The Interrogator

"I know, and I will not fight against the Americans. In fact, I will not undertake anything detrimental to the interests of the USA."

"But Lieutenant! The Russians are your country's allies, now."

"That won't last long. You'll see."

"How do you think you can help us? Do you want to take a gun and shoot Russians?"

"That is up to you how I do it."

He is just a youngster, tall and dark haired, brilliant teeth, good looking, a little clumsy, but not the least shy or embarrassed. He is not a good speaker, but he does emanate a certain impression of purity. This external show of sincerity means to me that we will probably have our hands full really determining whether this guy is a double agent or not.

"As you might expect, we have some captured OSS men here undergoing interrogation. Perhaps you would like to meet them, Lieutenant?"

"Fa' Christ's sake, no! I want nothing to do with those types!"

"Well, surely you discussed your plan with others? A girlfriend or maybe some buddies?"

"Yes, I have. Personal friends of mine with the same convictions. They really ought to come in too, if I am successful."

"The same convictions against communism, you mean?"

"Yes, plus a friendly leaning toward Germans."

"And toward America?"

"We'd rather die than fight or betray our own people."

Monti is firm and frank. He tells us about his education, his military career, his family background, his devotion to church. He asks no special treatment as regards quarters, food, or other facilities.

"Don't you think you will be regarded very unfavorably by your military authorities?"

"Possibly. But sooner or later they will realize that I do in my own way the best I can for my country, admittedly ahead of time. Eventually America will realize that Russia is the real enemy and Germany is our ally. That's inevitable, but my way is the right way."

"Lieutenant, how do you expect us to trust you?"

"Didn't I bring you a new fighter plane?"

"Yes, you did, but that could have been done to fool us. After all, we now possess a number of flyable Lightnings, and your people know all about that. Your intelligence people know it."

"I told you I have nothing whatsoever to do with intelligence."

"How can you convince us of that, Lieutenant?"

"Give me the chance I ask for. Let me fight against the Soviets."

The chance Monti asked for was given to him, but it led him along a winding way to the Propaganda Ministry in Berlin, to the German shortwave overseas

Chapter 9: Unwept, Unhonored, Unsung

broadcast station, where he was reported to have transmitted adverse propaganda to the American troops. We later heard he did not work out well there, perhaps due to his reluctance to talk against America. Next he went into the German SS brigades in a German lieutenant's uniform, the leader of the American contingent of the German Foreign Legionnaires, who had been without an officer until his arrival. Yes, there were Foreign Legionnaires fighting for Germany on the German side in WWII. Besides the famed Vlasov army of Russians, which everyone has heard about, there were also contingents of English, Americans, Belgians, Norwegians, French, Spanish, and others.

Lieutenant Monti, however, did not ever take up the gun and shoot at the Ivans or anyone else. After some time in Germany, he wanted to be allowed to make his way back to Italy to see his old and waning grandmother there, but army headquarters did not want him to leave the country.

Author comments: Two years after WWII had ended, Hanns Scharff was living at Treisberg in the Taunus mountains near Usingen and Oberursel. In April 1948, two Americans from the US Army headquarters at Frankfurt am Main called upon Scharff and questioned him concerning the interrogation of Lt. Martin J. Monti, asking him to make an official statement about the incident. They also asked Scharff if he would be willing to travel to the USA to testify in the trial for treason that faced Lt. Monti.

Scharff's statement, dated 8 April 1948, is quoted verbatim:

"In accordance with the request of Mr. Noel Story and 1st Lt. Moller, H.Q. Frankfurt, I hereby state the following facts concerning Lt. Monti, to the best of my knowledge.

"THAT WAS THE KIND OF HUMAN BEING SCHARFF WAS!"
Lieut. Jack LaGrange (USAAF), a 78th Fighter Group pilot, fell into Scharff's hands. "Scharff listened to my story about my very ill mother and sent a radio message to her that I was alive and okay but a POW." LaGrange is shown here as a brigadier general in the Nevada National Guard.

The Interrogator

"MY OWN GUNS ALMOST KILLED ME!"
Gerald W. Johnson (now lieutenant general, ret.) landed his P-47 wheels up in a German pasture. He set it afire and ran . . . right out in front of the guns, which started firing, just missing him. In October 1986, Johnson and Scharff met again in Los Angeles. Johnson had 17 victories when he was downed.

"In my capacity as interrogation officer at the former Luftwaffe Intelligence Center Auswertestelle West at Oberursel during the years 1943–1945, I was in charge of all captured fighter pilots who served in the 8th and 9th Fighter Commands, 8th and 9th USAAF, for the sole purpose of conducting their military interrogation (with the exception of Col. Stark, who came from the 12th USAAF).

"All interrogations concerning captured fighter pilots who served in the 12th and 15th USAAF were conducted by Mr. Walter Hanemann, interrogation officer at Auswertestelle West.

"Mr. Hanemann and I worked together in close cooperation. We exchanged experiences in our routine work, general and particular questions, personal views, and such almost daily. It often so happened that Mr. Hanemann participated, upon my request, in interrogations I conducted, or vice versa I took part in Mr. Hanemann's interrogations.

"In the latter part of 1944, approximately end of October or the beginning of November, Mr. Hanemann told me of a very unusual case he was handling at the time, namely that of an American fighter pilot who had 'landed deliberately' behind the German lines 'to help Germany in its fight against Russia.' He asked me to come to his office to meet the man. When I entered the room sometime later, Mr. Hanemann introduced me to 2nd Lt. Monti, with the actual words 'Hanns, meet Lt. Monti, the man who wants to help us.' The usual exchange of courtesies followed, and I noticed the questionnaire on Mr. Hanemann's desk, bearing the prisoner's names; on the bottom was his signature, and written in ordinary handwriting right cross the page, from the left lower corner to the right upper edge . . .

Chapter 9: Unwept, Unhonored, Unsung

LANDED DELIBERATELY. These words were penciled, I believe, in red. I took this page into my hands and studied it closely. None of the questions were answered except the first three, namely *rank, name,* and *serial number.*

"After that followed a general conversation as to what type of airplane he had flown, where he landed, and finally as to his motive for landing deliberately behind German lines. Lt. Monti stated he strongly believed in the cause of the German people fighting Bolshevism, that he would not mind rendering the Germans his help. He stated further that he would not like to fight against his own country nor do anything against the interests of his own people, yet he had decided to fight Communism in the belief he would be doing his best. The USA and Germany, he said, should fight side by side.

"Such ideas, openly expressed, were quite common amongst Allied prisoners and gave no reason for surprise. The outstanding fact in Lt. Monti's case was that he followed his political convictions so completely that he *went* over to the enemy.

"The last I heard of Lt. Monti was a few days later, when Hanemann told me Bonninghaus had taken charge of the prisoner."

signed . . . *Hanns J. Scharff,* 8/4/48.

Lt. Monti had returned to the United States in 1946 after having been court-martialed on a minor charge. After remission of the sentence, he had been allowed to enlist in the US Air Force as a private. He advanced to the rank of sergeant in due course and was discharged from the service at Mitchel Field, Long Island, New York, in January 1948.

The day of his discharge from the service, Lt. Monti was arrested by the FBI and was subsequently tried in the courts of the Brooklyn Federal Court. Upon the advice of his attorneys, Lloyd Paul Stryker and Harold Shapero, Monti's parents encouraged him to plead guilty, and Judge Robert A. Inch fined him $10,000 and sentenced him to twenty-five years in prison.

Monti's propaganda broadcasts from Germany were made under the alias or radio signature of "Martin Wiethaupt." He maintained steadfastly, during his trial, that he had no intentions whatsoever to harm the United States in any manner, but that he felt it was his duty to warn the people in America about the Russians and communism. In the light of the behavior of the Soviet Union after the war, there are those who believe Lt. Monti was ahead of the times. Regardless, his method of expressing his belief was a treasonable action.

Edward Sittler, a German American who lived in Germany during WWII and made broadcasts on the radio of newsworthy items, worked with Monti on occasion. In an affidavit he made for Mr. Woerheide in 1949, he described Lt. Monti as follows: "His father's family was of Italian (Swiss) origin . . . it would be a grievous mistake to say that he wanted America to lose the war. He wanted Communism to lose the war . . . America he regarded as misguided and would see the light once the Russians had been defeated . . . If ever there was a 'son of the church' he was it."

The Interrogator

Author Toliver has obtained a copy of General Court-Martial Orders Number 118, issued by Headquarters, Mediterranean theater of operations, United States Army, AP0512, dated 18 September 1945. They were obtained from Carlos Herrera of Santa Maria, California. Order 118 includes the attachments outlining the charges and the outcome.

Lt. Monti told the court a completely different story than that which actually occurred. He claimed that he was shot down by flak near Milano, whereas German records show that he landed deliberately at Vienna and handed the airplane over to German authorities there. The court-martial papers show that Lt. Monti went AWOL on 2 October 1944, while stationed in the 126th Replacement Battalion at Karachi, India. He hitchhiked via C-46 transport plane to Italy, with stops at Abadan, Cairo, Tripoli, and eventually Foggia. At Foggia, he tried to join the 82nd Fighter Group, but the commanding officer refused to take him. Monti claimed he was then flown by a friend, Lt. Marvin E. Andrews, to Naples in a piggyback, two-place P-38.

Near Naples, at Pomigliano aerodrome, the 354th Air Service Group was responsible for the erection of newly arrived P-38 aircraft for delivery to various fighter units when needed. On the tarmac, Monti saw a new F-5E standing ready for flight. The F-5E was a reconnaissance version of the P-38. This was F-5E (a P-38L-1-LO), serial number AAF 44-23275. According to the testimony of Monti before the court, he reported to the officer on duty that he had been sent there by the 82nd Fighter Group to test-fly and accept the airplane. The officer said he did not have the authority to let him fly the airplane, and sent Monti away to find the commander. Instead, Monti talked a British supply unit into letting him borrow a parachute, then climbed into the plane and took off. The date was 13 October 1944.

According to the court-martial report, Lt. Monti claimed he flew north-northwest and while passing over Milano was hit by flak, losing one or both engines. He hit the silk and claimed he was immediately captured by some Italian civilians and turned over to some German soldiers. His first and only combat sortie, if you can call it that, was over.

In due course, Monti was first interrogated by the Germans at Verona, Italy, about 62 miles (100 km) west of Vienna and 93 miles (150 km) east of Milano. This was deemed a strange case by the Germans, because in actuality, Lt. Monti had flown almost directly to Vienna, landed deliberately, and turned the new airplane over to the Germans. The court-martial did not know this in 1945, since they only had Monti's newly minted story to go on.

The interrogator at Verona sent Monti by train to Oberursel, where he met Walter Hanemann and Hanns Scharff. In January 1945, Monti was sent on to the Dulag Luft and from there to Sagan and Stalag Luft III. He was sent to another stalag near Munich after only a week at Stalag Luft III. When the train arrived at his new prison, Monti gave his guards the slip, remained on the train, and disembarked at a small village southeast of Munich. For the next few weeks he worked

Chapter 9: Unwept, Unhonored, Unsung

HOW FAR ARE WE FROM HOME?
POWs erected a signpost at the Dulag Luft at Wetzlar, which gives the mileage to various cities. Allied camp commander Col. Charlie Stark is seated. Standing under signs is Arthur C. Jaros, and at far right is one of the Luftwaffe officials.

his way south and went over Brenner Pass and back to Milano, where he turned himself in to the US Fifth Army, claiming to be an evader.

On 14 May 1945 the military police picked him up in the Red Cross Club in Bari, and he was headed for a court-martial charged with desertion. He talked his way into getting the charge reduced to AWOL and misappropriation of military property. Found "guilty," he was dismissed from the service, was ordered to forfeit all pay and allowances, and was to be confined at hard labor for fifteen years.

In October 1945, Lt. Monti's sentence had been commuted, he was given an honorable discharge from the service, and he was permitted to reenlist as a non-commissioned officer in the USAAF. The wheels of justice were turning slowly, though, and the true story began to emerge. Lt. Monti had landed deliberately at Vienna, and on 26 January 1948 he was arrested and charged with treason. Found guilty of this charge, Sgt. Monti (ex-Lt. Monti) was sentenced to twenty-five years' imprisonment and fined $10,000. Scharff and other witnesses were brought to the United States to testify in this trial.

Quoting from the minutes of his treason trial, Monti admits he landed deliberately:

"Q: At the time you landed the plane, was the plane intact?

"A: Yes, it was intact.

The Interrogator

"Q: Did you have gas?

"A: Yes.

"Q: Were you then immediately taken into custody by members of the German armed forces?

"A: Yes."

So, from 1945 until the treason trial in 1948, the full story of Monti was not publicized. How many years of the twenty-five-year sentence were actually served is not available to the writer.

HANNS SCHARFF's story continues: Another such incident occurred later on. An American bomber boy dropped in and would have been handled routinely, but he sent word through the cooler guards that he desired to speak to an interrogation officer. The *Abwehr* officer, a combination between a counterintelligence officer and a security officer, one Hauptmann Offermann, was delighted to hear of the enthusiastic intentions of the American POW. Fight the Bolsheviks!

That's exactly what he said he would like to do, if only he wasn't on the wrong side; if only he wasn't locked up in the cooler! After all, his parents came from good old Dutch stock. The name "van Düren" proves that. Of course, if there was a way, or a way could be found . . . well, he'd gladly take a crack at the bastards. Perhaps he could even join up with the SS?

A highly interesting character, the combined security-and-counterintelligence officer decided, and he took Johnnie van Düren out of the cooler. Good lad . . . he wants to fight against the Soviets. Very decent sort of fellow . . . at least one of them sees the danger of the Red menace. He should have some extra food rations, since it might boost his morale a bit. Sardines, corned beef, biscuits, cheese . . . all in tins!

At night, Johnnie was confined to his cell in the cooler, but during the day he had permission to go freely about the camp and worked in the little carpenter shop we had on-base. Our security officer had taken a hand in the testing procedure, which was to test the reliability of the POW concerned.

There are, perhaps, more and perhaps better methods of going about the selection of a Zoe (stool pigeon): other decoys or lures than tinned foods, and freedom to work with tools. There is a criterion called TIME, and another called QUESTIONING OF HIS PALS, both of utmost importance.

Others include covert observation of his activities, secret search of the locales frequented by the prisoner, how he acts and talks under the influence of alcohol, frequent changes in his domicile, information from planted informers, and kindred checks. Constant personal contact is maintained whether he knows it or not.

"Well, now, how about this SS assignment, Johnnie? It's been approved and you'll soon be in our Foreign Legion. How does that grab you?" our combined security-counterintelligence man asked him one morning. No doubt he was wishing about fifty more Johnnie van Dürens would come over to the German side too. Good material, this!

Chapter 9: Unwept, Unhonored, Unsung

"Fantastic! How did you do it? Can't wait to get out of sleeping in this damn cooler anymore and feel like a man doing a man's job again." Van Düren was obviously pleased. He would soon be on his way, and he looked to the west at the threatening clouds on the horizon.

The weather front passed through Oberursel that night. Thunder and lightning and very strong winds rattled the window shutters of the cooler and made the wooden beams in the roof creak. It was such a thunderstorm that it was a wonder the roofs did not get blown away. Everyone stayed inside, and even the guard sentries huddled in their posts. The noisy watchdogs, who hate to get wet, were chained by their wardens in their own little hutches or doghouses. The wind made so much racket that it was impossible to hear any suspicious noises most of the night. In this pitch-dark blackout with its horizontal driving rain, nobody at all noticed a darker shadow in the night tiptoeing away. Nobody.

Nobody! The storm had passed by dawn, leaving everything dripping and a little debris around camp, also revealing something else that caught the attention of a startled guard. A 20-by-20-inch hole had been cut in the wall of A-wing of the cooler! What in the world could have caused that? Where's Johnnie van Düren?

The hole was just a few inches above the floor, behind the cot in Johnnie's cell. The electric lightbulb in his cell was missing, too, and on the little table lay a note that said

"Just gone to see my girl."

DON'T FENCE ME IN!
POWs at Dulag Luft seldom lost their sense of humor. Seven are recognizable: Art Jaros, C. G. Whitlock, Hal Woodward, Gerald Gille, Fred Cooper, and Ernest Quick.

The Interrogator

Later it was rumored, not without some confirmation, that Johnnie had been one of the smartest agents the enemy had sent over to us in an attempt to get an idea of how our intelligence center worked. We also heard that our security officer received a postcard one day, with a London postmark, telling him how happy Johnnie was to get back to England. Our security officer continued to grieve that Johnnie had not joined the SS Foreign Legion after he had been so kind to him. To this day, I think he is the only man who still believes his friend's real name was Johnnie van Düren.

Canadian Wild Bill stuck his head in my doorway and, grinning from one ear to another, asked me whether I knew the difference between an optimist and a pessimist. I was at my desk in conversation with a POW who later would have the chance to become one of my most valuable silent informers.

Bill did not wait for my reply but went on: "The German optimist says, 'We are definitely going to lose this goddamn war!'"

"And the pessimist . . . ?" I queried.

"The pessimist says, 'Yes, yes, of course, but when? When?'"

My prisoner laughed as heartily as we did, but his eyes asked silently how we could dare to tell such jokes in Naziland. Sensing an opening for my work with him, I told one of my own jokes.

"Have you heard this one? A big, hearty storm trooper, in long boots and brown shirt, stood in front of a blackboard reading the party newspaper pinned there. Above the blackboard was a poster that said, 'The Jews Are Our Misfortune.' Coming up behind the Brownshirt was a little man with thick glasses, a shortsighted Jew, trying to read the news. 'Pardon, please. Wat is written?' The storm trooper looked down at him and replied in a rather harsh voice: "It says *The Jews are our misfortune!*" Excitedly, the little man turned and walked away, muttering, "*Hoffentlich! Hoffentlich!* Let's hope so!"

My session with this POW turned into a joke session as we each told and laughed at them. Then the POW spoke up, puzzled:

"I always understood the Nazis would put you in jail or a concentration camp if you make fun of Hitler's regime."

"Pshaw!" said Bill, "they can build the walls around those places as high as they wish . . . if we want to badly enough, we can get in!"

From that day on, I had a very friendly association with that particular POW, and it lasted until just before the end of the war. Though he did not know it, he became one of my most active silent informers, and I doubt if he ever did realize his important function. It was easy for me to find a plausible excuse for his permanent stay at Oberursel, particularly since he more or less asked to be kept there. Frequently he told me the daily prisoner gossip, all the latest news from the other side that came in via the newly arrived prisoners. He even told me about the attempts of some of the POWs to organize a little intelligence activity within our camp.

Chapter 9: Unwept, Unhonored, Unsung

He told me the opinions the prisoners had of my colleagues and myself, and I learned from him the names of certain prisoners who had managed to smuggle escape compasses past our searchers. Naturally I took no actions against them. I even knew of a planned escape, and I did not plan to prevent it because I was afraid I would destroy something much more valuable: his confidence in me. Luckily, the escape attempt did not come off. I could influence other POWs through him, and I constantly received up-to-date information from him, all given in good faith and mostly while he was under the influence of liquor, which he liked very much since he was an alcoholic. I based many auspicious reports on information gathered from him. Not a minute was he really aware of the services he rendered to me, and it was many months after our first meeting that he confided in me that our silly jokes of the first day had won his confidence.

What else, I often asked myself, must I do to serve my country?

Stool pigeons flew into our dove cote from all countries. Everyone wanted to know what was going on inside Germany. They seemed to think the place to start was in our intelligence collection center, Oberursel. These agents and XX agents, double agents, were coming and going just like in a house where the servants are frequently changed.

We had our own stool pigeons, too, and would occasionally make use of our own permanent-party officers. They would change from their blue-gray Luftwaffe uniform to the USAAF olive drab or to RAF dark blue as the necessity arose. It was, sometimes, quite difficult to recognize one's own pal when he was all made up as an enemy POW, slightly wounded perhaps, with a bandaged arm or hand, not too well shaven, sullenly chewing gum. An armed German guard, not knowing he was escorting one of his own men, would bring him into the compound barracks where the rooms were already filled with other POWs. There, until assigned to solitary cells in the cooler, they had ample time to chat with each other. They also gathered there while awaiting transport to Dulag Luft before going on to permanent camp, *Stalag Luft*.

Just what kind or type of a heart beat under that uniform sitting right next to you was impossible to know.

Canadian Bill was having a running argument with one of the reception officers at the cooler, accusing the man of out-of-place ambitiousness in respect to several overly long periods of prisoner interrogations. How easy it was to deceive a man, and Wild Bill decided to pull an April Fool's joke on him to teach him a lesson. Bill transformed himself into an American staff sergeant Nelson, just after returning from a three-day pass. Complete with dog tags, family photographs, escape compass, an old plaster bandage over his left eye, untidy hair, dirty fingernails, and three-day stubble of beard, Bill arrived and was clapped into A-16 in the cooler.

The next morning, Wild Bill's assigned interrogator in the bomber section looked over the roster of new arrivals and went to see Sgt. Nelson. When he left our building, eight of us who were in on the joke rushed to the listening post and

The Interrogator

tuned in on A-16. In a few moments we heard voices as guard and the interrogator approached the cell, heard the screeching noise of the lock being turned and the door being swung open, the rustling of the straw mattress as Nelson sat up. "Good morning," we heard the reception officer say. Wild Bill answered with an inarticulate grunt. "I am the reception officer and I have to ask you some questions so that we can fill out this form. Another dreadful groan from Bill. He was laying it on rather thick. "Are you sick?"

"No! But I hate this goddamn bed!"

"So? Well, now, what is your name?"

"Because it's so damn hard I never slept a wink!"

"Oh? Now, what did you say your name was?"

"Staff Sergeant Nelson . . . number 3241656."

"Nelson! Nelson? There was once a very famous admiral . . ."

"And a goddamn Limey he was too."

"Oh! I beg your pardon. Of course, you are an American. I did not intend to hurt your feelings. Are you 8th or 9th Air Force?"

"Now, now. Name, rank, and serial number is all you get, you know!"

"Ja, ja, I know, but you must tell me a bit more for this form."

"Nope!" with finality. We listeners guffawed merrily.

"Would you care for a cigarette, Sergeant Nelson?"

Certainly he would. We knew our friend Wild Bill, and that he would take every cigarette the man had, but there was only one. He could not be bribed with one lousy cigarette, and he remained silent and gave only name, rank, and serial number.

Alas. Everyone knows how these things turn out. The Wild Bill was too clever for the reception officer, who sent the guard for a new package of cigarettes, and then Nelson had to tell him this and that. Wild Bill liked to talk. While we sat laughing in our hideout, Bill unfolded one of the most dramatic and terrifying battle yarns of the war. All names and data were pure invention, a pack of lies!

At lunchtime we had our proof. Bill entered the mess hall clean shaven, ostensibly just returned from a wonderful three-day pass with his girl, and sat down opposite the reception officer who had just spent some morning hours with him in cell A-16. He chatted with Bill, and it did not occur to him that he was talking to Nelson again. None of us, carefully watching the two, gave the secret away, and it was never discovered. It was a valuable lesson even to us who had been interested observers.

The receptions officer's report on Sgt. Nelson read:

"Chain smoker, very talkative, gives out any information desired but is limited by stupidity!"

Not all plans based on false pretense were without danger. In one scene it ended with complete failure. The escape route of Allied soldiers, known as the French Underground, had to be checked quite frequently. In this instance, two of our men disguised themselves much like Wild Bill had done, and set out on their

Chapter 9: Unwept, Unhonored, Unsung

A FRUITLESS SEARCH FOR THIS ONE
USAAF captain Fletcher E. Adams, nine-victory ace, was shot down on 30 May 1944 but was not found in his crashed Mustang, yet he was not captured so did not show up at Oberursel, and he did not return after the war.

ANOTHER AMERICAN PILOT NOT ON SCHARFF'S LIST
Thomas F. "Jeeter" Neal of the 355th USAAF Group had several aerial victories when he disappeared over Germany on 20 April 1944. He too failed to arrive at Oberursel.

tasks, a dangerous trek since, pretending to be downed fliers, they had to run the risk of being regarded as escapists by our own people should they fall into German hands. They were therefore without any assistance from us once they had left the enclosure.

Contact with the underground was quickly established, and our boys soon found themselves being shipped around the various underground stops, seeing and learning a lot. When they reached Belgium, their cover was accidentally blown. Their true identity was discovered by the famous Madame Direkteur of the mysterious spy and underground headquarters in Brussels, to which they had advanced. All they could do then was to run for their lives!

Author comments: Let us be clear here that the reception officers were not interrogators at Oberursel. They were responsible for receiving the new POWs as they arrived at Auswertestelle West, searching them and "signing them in." They had a questionnaire on which they were to list name, rank, and serial number, and the POW was supposed to go on to the interrogators for further questioning. As in all governments, these receptionists had a tendency to become overzealous and on occasion tried to get much more information from the POWs. This is the reason that Canadian Wild Bill, an interrogator, was miffed at one of the receptionists and pulled the little trick on him.

The French Underground served a busy and useful purpose for the Allied side and managed to safely return hundreds of Allied crews. Likewise, hundreds were caught, and most of these soon found themselves at Oberursel.

One who did not manage to make contact with the underground was Major (now Lt. Gen., Retired) Gerald W. Johnson of the USAF. Johnson was the commander of the 63rd Squadron of the 56th Fighter Group at the time of his last flight over Europe in WWII. Here is his story:

"The morning of March 27 was not much different from any other day. James Cagney and his group of entertainers had been with us the night before at our Halesworth, England, base, so it had been a late night. But it didn't take much encouragement to have a late night in those days. My main interest was getting this day's mission finished and getting back to the date I had that night with one of the cute entertainers. Anyway, we were up early, as usual, and reported to the briefing room. Before the briefing was finished, we were placed in standby due to weather. Later, the mission was scrubbed, but we were still on standby. Most of us had changed from our flying gear when suddenly it was on again, and with a relatively short time to take off. Since it was going to be a milk run anyway, I didn't bother to change back completely into my combat gear and was wearing English street boots.

"We were flying split groups at this time, forty-eight aircraft plus spares, but in two sections of twenty-four each with about thirty minutes between sections. Bud Mahurin was my operations officer, and he was leading the first section. I was leading the second section and took off twenty-eight minutes behind Bud.

Chapter 9: Unwept, Unhonored, Unsung

"We were on a bomber escort mission to Bordeaux, France. Shortly after making landfall I could hear Bud's section involved in combat, and very soon I knew from the comments I was hearing that Bud was down. This really upset me for two reasons: (1) I was wondering what could have happened, because Bud had been in all kinds of trouble before and somehow got home, and (2) I doubted this mission was really important enough to cost us one of our leading aces and a really great guy. I was determined to repay the bastards and, hopefully, that day.

"The bomber escort was a milk run—no action—so on the way home we dropped down to lower altitude, looking for anything on the ground to shoot up.

"Needless to say, we soon found a target, and on my third pass I was clobbered—there I was, practically on top of the trees with an engine just barely alive, with no altitude and very little air speed. There was nothing to do but ride it in through the tree tops. Just as I started to mush through the tops of the trees, there suddenly was a plowed field, fairly smooth, in front of me.

"The aircraft was still intact after the crash landing, so I climbed out of my parachute, left it in the cockpit, pulled the ripcord, and kicked the primer pump so gasoline was dripping in the cockpit, and then applied my trusty Zippo. A good fire was started. By that time there were several Frenchmen around. I thought they would help, so I gave them my gloves, jacket, and lighter but reluctantly threw my almost 100-mission leather helmet into the fire. Despite my gifts, the French would not help, saying Germans were all around and very close.

"Since our intelligence people always said to get as far from the crash as soon as possible, I started for the woods about a mile away. The ground was somewhat rolling, the aircraft was burning furiously, and apparently I was just about directly in front of it, when suddenly there was a burst of machine gun fire that swooshed over barely above my head. I hit the dirt and was trying to dig in when I suddenly realized that those were .50-caliber guns that had fired, and the Germans had none. So I knew it was my guns firing the remaining ammunition from wires being shorted. As I raised up to have a look, I saw Frenchmen running from the burning aircraft and realized how nearly I had come to being killed by my own guns.

"Despite my best efforts to evade, in less than two hours I was a prisoner of the Germans. I still remember so well one of their first remarks in guttural English: 'Ver you de var is over!' I never accepted that statement. After capture, I was told that they searched those areas they believed a downed airman had had time to reach, and kept expanding their circle until he was captured. I would have been better off to have stayed well hidden in close proximity to the burning aircraft, at least until after dark."

Author: Jerry Johnson, with sixteen aerial victories, was shot down by flak on 27 March 1944. After some sessions with Hanns Scharff at Oberursel, he was sent on to the Dulag Luft on 19 April.

HANNS SCHARFF continues: Volker von Collande, the progressive German playwright, actor, producer, and film director, had fallen in disgrace with Goebbels

The Interrogator

SURPRISED INTERROGATOR AT OBERURSEL
Ulrich Haussmann was in the Bomber Branch at Oberursel. He was shocked when two USAAF POWs whom he had seen at Oberursel were brought before him at Mainburg, disguised as French laborers. They had escaped late in the war, and they talked Haussmann into surrendering to Patton's forces. They were Donald Hillman and Henry L. Mills.

for being "too realistic in his pictures and in the utterings of his players," so he was banned from filming for three years. He was soon drafted into the Luftwaffe and set to filming again on behalf of the Luftwaffe, over which the propaganda minister had no jurisdiction.

One day he arrived in our camp accompanied by a staff captain from headquarters. He was to study our operation very closely so that he could produce a series of lecture films about Luftwaffe intelligence. After having made the rounds, Collande came to my office to watch my efforts to extract some information from a particularly difficult POW, efforts that might mean using a stool pigeon of some type.

During an ordinary and routine interrogation, I had run into two of the biggest secrets of the Allied air forces in some time. Nothing like "Vendetta" or "Ironside" or "Royal Flush," but something more interesting to my side of the war effort: "Fido" and "Pluto."

Fido was a code name the Allies used, and it meant Fog Investigation and Dispersal Operation. Sometimes England was covered with such intense fog that it was impossible to recover aircraft at any of the airfields, and the loss of hundreds of combat and transport aircraft, often with their crews, sometimes exceeded the loss of aircraft to German action. Therefore, it behooved the RAF and the Americans to develop some manner of temporarily dispersing the heavy fog at an airfield long enough to get some airplanes safely on the ground.

We at the intelligence center knew that Fido was being tested at either Woodbridge or Bentwaters air bases on the east coast of England, but we needed drawings and technical information of this new landing aid.

Chapter 9: Unwept, Unhonored, Unsung

Pluto was a code word for Pipe Line under the Ocean, an Allied plan to lay a large pipeline across the English Channel bottom to carry fuel to the troops and panzers after the invasion of the Continent. We needed drawings and pump station information about Pluto.

My prisoner made a slip about Fido and Pluto in the questioning and realized he had made the slip, so he clammed up. I could not get another word out of him. So great was my determination to get this information that I considered employing a professional hypnotist, but I was informed that all earlier experiments with hypnosis had failed.

Injections of any type were verboten, in spite of the fact that most Allied POWs thought they were going to be used in such experiments. Only once had it been tried, and that ended in complete failure due to the moral strength of the prisoner.

My tool, I decided, would have to be a confidence man, one whom I had very carefully trained and used before. He had not once disappointed me, even though I had once told him that I harbored great contempt for such skulduggery. He was of English extraction and complained:

"Nine years of unhappiness made a man hater out of me. The people of my own country did me grievous harm, and now I am happy to take my bloody revenge. There is no such thing as a nation or a people anymore. How can they fight each other as peoples? We are all the same human beings, some good and some bad. We are in this war because England and Poland wanted it!"

His confused statements made me think of him as a fanatical individual with distorted ideals, or perhaps a poacher on morals. Although useful to me once or twice, he was unworthy of consideration.

This character, we had decided, should be woven into the background of Collande's moving picture, sort of as a warning to the trainees who would see the film. All we had to do was to copy every phase from actual life.

Step by step, the Zoe lured his innocent victim into discussions on the primary subject. Deeper and deeper he penetrated into the mystery, and greater and more profound became his satisfaction. Under the pretense of having been mistreated by the Oberursel interrogators in particular, he won the sympathy of his new buddy. Our stool pigeon, or Zoe, had promoted himself to an imagined higher rank so that it seemed to have more authority when he asked the questions in utter confidence. Also the mask of love and loyalty and devotion to duty and country gained more confidence. He fostered friendship by sharing Red Cross food and rations. His provocative manners toward the guards seemed to eliminate all suspicion. Reliance was achieved by boasting, and he won further dependence by some cunning manipulations that secured some tobacco from one of the night guards. Trust grew when he told of his own struggles with the interrogation officer, and soon he had the POW ready to say he would never yield to the enemy.

Last, our Zoe had some technical knowledge, and this gave him reason to create opportunities for lengthy conversation about the Pluto and Fido secrets.

The Interrogator

Good bait catches fine fish, since the days of yore, and it was inevitable in this instance too.

Collande portrayed this loathsome figure in a gripping scene and with this act was able to teach interrogators what to expect. It also taught our soldiers what to expect and how to resist if they were captured. I was able to write comprehensive reports on Fido and Pluto that were of great interest to our headquarters, who were girding for the coming invasion by the Allies.

I remember a cartoon in a prominent German newspaper that showed how the enemy imagined everybody in Germany was supervised. In an airplane sat the pilot, while standing behind him with a gun pressed against the pilot's back stood a supervisor. This supervisor was supervised by a super-supervisor holding a gun to the supervisor's back, and so on, until the plane was five times longer.

The average German laughed at this cartoon, although there must be some truth in it, and even if he himself was completely free from supervision. I was one of those average Germans. Ours was, nevertheless, a military camp, and there was just this type of supervision. Even the American army has a system of loyalty checks on every soldier, and there certainly was no reason a German Luftwaffe camp should not have theirs. Traitors are always in one's midst, and the very nature of our business made it important that loyalty checks be made regularly. Rumors and hearsay labeled several of our officers as informers, and whether they were mere tattlers, scandal mongers, or official informers I must leave undecided.

A German deserter in US uniform? A spy? A double-crosser? Yes, that also came to pass at Oberursel. I heard excited arguing in Canadian Bill's office and went over to see what was happening. A young flier in American uniform was standing there in front of Bill.

"I have to hand you over to the provost marshal," Bill told his prisoner decisively. A twenty-one-year-old Luftwaffe corporal had deserted to the Americans only to be captured shortly afterward by German panzers. He confessed to volunteering his services to the enemy in an attempt to avoid common POW status. He wanted to have it both ways; leave the losing side and stay in freedom on the other.

The corporal had picked up an American uniform. He knew enough English to fill out the questionnaires they gave him, thinking he was one of the hundreds of survivors of decimated combat units, and he went to work at an advanced 9th USAAF airbase. That's where he was when he saw trouble coming as the panzers captured the base.

Convinced of the lad's sincerity, Bill was about to release him when a small discrepancy unmasked the boy. Herr Gomman's files noted that his age and his serial number did not ring true! The whole tissue of lies came to light! The youngster's doom was near.

Action and antidote, success or frustration; one relieved another. Spy or counterspy, agent or counteragent, confidence man, traitor, informer, deserter. They came and they went!!

Chapter 9: Unwept, Unhonored, Unsung

"CANADIAN WILD BILL" ENGLEHARDT
"Wild Bill" was Scharff's assistant interrogator. He was very proud of his years in Canada before WWII. His Canadian accent is well remembered by POWs whom he interrogated.

For him no minstrel raptures swell!

Author comments: There never is such a thing as an ideal place to interrupt a good story. Apropos here, however, is another story to help us keep the man Hanns Scharff in complete perspective.

Brigadier General Jack LaGrange Jr., on duty in 1978 with the Nevada Air National Guard, was a young first lieutenant flying with the 83rd Fighter Squadron, 78th Fighter Group, when he was shot down in October 1944. Here is his recollection of the incident and his eventual interrogation at Auswertestelle West:

"Odd as it may seem, after thirty-two years I certainly do remember Hanns Scharff. He was the first German officer that acted like a human being instead of a tin god, as all other Germans I had met up to this time acted. Also, he treated me like an officer and a gentleman, not like a diseased animal.

"Let's begin at the beginning though. I was strafing an airfield that was loaded with Ju-88 aircraft. The flak was extremely heavy, a fact not reported by our intelligence people at the morning briefing, and when I saw how heavy the defense was, I made my runs at full bore, water injection and all. About halfway through my run, I realized I was hearing some sort of odd noise, so I sneaked a peek at my instruments and saw that the supercharger on the P&W R-2800 engine was running wild. Finishing that strafing run with a last few shots at a flak emplacement, I zoomed away and looked in the cockpit again to see my oil pressure was at ZERO and the cylinder head temperature up in the red. In seconds, the engine froze, and when that prop stopped suddenly, my P-47 flipped over onto its back. I continued the snap roll back to upright position and saw a big pasture over on the right. Not having enough altitude to parachute, I made a belly landing in the field.

"This all happened so fast that I did not have a chance to radio to my flight that I was going in, so no one knew whether I had gone straight into the ground or crashed into a wooded area or just what. When the Thunderbolt slid to a halt, I crawled out onto the wing and punched the destruct button to blow up my plane. Then I started running toward the nearest grove of trees. Tearing around the first line of trees in true Jesse Owens style, I ran headlong into two German officers out for a Sunday morning stroll. My running days were over for a while!

"Naturally, they were Luftwaffe officers from the base I had just strafed, so in a very short while I was standing rather erectly at attention in front of the base commander, who was understandably quite unhappy about all his burned Ju-88s. After some twenty minutes or so of most unpleasant abuse verbally, he smiled and offered me a cup of coffee. Then he relieved me of my freshly saddle-soaped leather flying jacket and my nice cowboy boots. Then he informed me that I was a good shot because I had burned six of his Ju-88s on that one run.

"That night, they drove me with a guard to the train for the trip to Dulag Luft. The train traveled right down the middle of Happy Valley, and naturally the RAF was bombing all along there as they did every night. There were a few very close misses, and I didn't get much sleep that night. Twenty-four hours later I was sent on to Oberursel.

"The most important thing that happened to me at Oberursel was the fact that Hanns Scharff cared enough to listen to the most important problem I was having at the time. Since none of my squadron mates knew whether I was dead or alive, and knowing the physical condition of my mother back in the States, I feared she would die if the US government sent her a message saying I was missing in action, or killed in action. Hanns listened to my worries about that and astounded me when he sympathetically said he would get word via radio to her that I was alive and well and a POW. AND HE DID JUST THAT! That was the kind of human being he was and no doubt still is."

10

EHR, LEHR, WEHR

Let your hook be always cast; in the pool where you least expect it, there will always be a fish! —Ovid

The further my activity as an interrogation officer (*Vernehmungsoffizier*) drew nearer its conclusion, the more I became convinced that the continuous rich results of my formal questioning sessions could not be explained by my methods alone. *None of the hundreds of flying officers I had questioned had been able to withstand my particular art of deception.* I knew the situation would remain the same in the future. At the same time, no cause existed for complaints against the prisoners themselves, because they would have had to be extraordinary humans had they not finally answered my questions. I thought I should search deeper for the real reasons for my success. I therefore welcomed the occasion to talk about this phenomenon when the opportunity arose.

"Hullo!" he said, as if no world of more than twenty years lay between us. "Here I am again. I was bombed out in Frankfurt and now live here in your neighborhood. I have heard about you and hope I may, as your old teacher, disturb you and learn a little bit about your highly interesting work?"

Indeed, there he was again, my old tutor who had given me much sound advice for my winding path of life.

"Excuse me, please," he asked in his old-fashioned high style accompanied with a little bow, "if I have my breakfast here? I am terribly hungry and can listen while I eat." With that he produced two apples from his pocket, put them carefully on my desk, cut each one with his pocketknife, and began to eat slowly bit by bit. I asked Miss Beck to bring us some coffee.

"Please tell me about your function here, Hanns," he begged, "that is if you are permitted to tell your secrets to a civilian who fought honorably in World War I."

"Of course. No problem. I interrogate prisoners of war."

The Interrogator

"That is clear. Do you obtain any results?"

"Oh, yes! From everybody."

"Everybody? How can you explain that?"

"Yes, they all tell me, sooner or later, all they know about the military part of their lives. Perhaps it is method, on one side, that gets them to talk, and unfulfillable demand on the other." I then give him the general lecture that I usually give to visiting VIPs. He listens intently.

"Do you think it is possible that equal conditions prevail over on the enemy side?" the old pedagogue wants to know.

"We accept it as a fact, Herr Gottschow," I said categorically. "Our boys are treated extremely well in America, and we know they will tell what they know too. We often hear our men are coddled in the USA."

Gottschow looks at me pensively, his palms together with his index fingers pressing slightly upward on his nose. "If I understand you, no prisoner is guilty even if he oversteps his orders that he is to remain silent. Doesn't that mean he becomes a traitor?"

"Indiscreet, but certainly not traitorous. If one has not been a POW, how can one understand and correctly judge a POW? Beyond the obvious cases of treason, one should not be inclined to feel bitterness toward a prisoner who has succumbed to persuasions and talked too much. No one should direct criticism toward these young men who, for reasons quite beyond the understanding of someone not placed in a similar position, might have been unconsciously indiscreet but certainly in no way were traitors. There is a vast difference. Most prisoners of war do not know any military secrets, anyway."

Herr Gottschow shook his head doubtfully. "I would imagine there are countless variations in any sequence of happenings, just as I have found in my classes. Does that not reflect upon your results? Surely there are differences of character and temperament to cope with, and circumstances of a varied nature?"

"Naturally, sir. Each case is different. Nevertheless, certain fundamental rules of conduct are usually observed. To my knowledge, no American pilot has talked to me through fear or through any ignoble hope of bettering his conditions as a prisoner."

"So? But is it not true that a prisoner is more reluctant to talk if things are going well for his side?"

"Victory does boost the morale of soldiers whether they are free or fettered. However, here in this prison atmosphere it loses most of its influence. Lately I have noticed a new attitude among the newly arrived prisoners. They rationalize their talking by saying, 'What does it really matter what I tell you and what you already know? As long as we are winning the war anyway.' They know we are unable to stop their advance, and some like to impress us with the answers to our questions."

"Would it be the same with our own troops if we were enjoying big military successes?"

Chapter 10: Ehr, Lehr, Wehr

P-47 THUNDERBOLTS ESCORT B-24s
Eighth Air Force bomber crews were always happy to see USAAF fighters nearby . . . but not TOO close. These are P-47s from the 62nd Squadron, 56th Fighter Group.

"Definitely! That point was proven during the successes in our campaigns against Poland, Norway, France, and Africa."

"Hmmmm. Do you believe that your knowledge and the work of this institution will have any influence on the fortune of war?"

"Professor, you have not changed a bit. You get right down to the meat of the problem. We here at Oberursel are the eyes and ears of our higher headquarters. We do the groundwork, the spadework, and they do the planning. Göring recently said that we are the best and most reliable source of information he has. We may not be able to sway the scale, but we are indispensable."

"How can one prevent prisoners from passing on information and disclosing secrets to the enemy?"

"Sorry, my friend, I cannot offer you any surefire solution. The less a man knows, of course, the better for his country if he becomes a captive; the better he understands how to play a delaying game during interrogation, the more credit is due him. The most difficult POW I meet is the one who is friendly and willing to talk, but who convinces me that he cannot answer my questions simply because he does not know the answers. I guess the intelligence schools have no choice but to teach them to tell only their name, ranks, and serial numbers."

My learned master of science frowns and cogitates deeply. "There are three other virtues, Hanns, the three I have often praised in my lectures as man's highest qualities: *Ehr, Lehr, Wehr.*"

The Interrogator

"How well I remember! *Ehr, Lehr, Wehr, kein Mann braucht mehr!*" This old proverb says that no man need have greater assets than *Ehr, Lehr,* and *Wehr.*

Ehr means more than just honor; it stands for reputation, rank, praise, and glory, or the total moral and social value.

Lehr reflects education and knowledge, the refinement of heart and mind that is acquired by time of learning, system of instruction, theory, and science.

Wehr adds the mental and moral virtues, the physical strength and the morale. *Wehr* means valor, defense, resistance, weapon, and armor.

The visit from my old tutor was a great inspiration. He provoked new thinking on my part, causing me to clearly delineate my objectives as an interrogator.

"Lead me to this 'Stone Face Scharff'" were the words of the American leading fighter ace Gabreski as Wild Bill brought him to my office. Gabreski's luck had given out, and at last he had fallen into our hands.

"What is your impression of America's top-scoring fighter ace?" was the question constantly put to me as the news of his capture spread through our center. What does Lt. Col. Francis S. Gabreski look like? What does he say? How are his manners? Is he really a tough guy as we had so often heard from his erstwhile squadron mates?

My *Kommandant* wanted to know, the German fighter pilots wanted to know, the newspapers, even the office girls were eager to get a glance at him. Berlin and Paris headquarters were overly curious. We had caught a big fish and everyone seemed to know it, which meant that perhaps our own security net needed tightening.

LOADING THE STINGERS
The 56th Group armorers loading .50-caliber ammunition into the gun bays of Francis S. Gabreski's P-47.

Chapter 10: Ehr, Lehr, Wehr

"Gabby! So glad you came! I've been waiting for you for a long time." Of course I knew how this most famous of American aces looked, because I had his portrait hanging on the wall of my office for several months before he so kindly dropped by. Now, there he stood before me, the man with the eagle eyes, the gallant duelist . . . Gabreski!

About 5 feet, 7 inches tall, muscular, well built, Gabby impressed me as a proud and determined officer. On guard in his utterings, always a little smile on his face, he spoke clearly and the twinkle in his eyes seemed to be saying, "Sorry, I couldn't evade your invitation."

I had carefully studied his military and private background, and I had a quite up-to-date account of his twenty-eight aerial victories. He personally had been identified as the pilot who had downed some of our best fighter pilots. Prominent American newspapers had run articles about him, and I had these in my hand when he arrived. I also knew that he had set out on his last combat sortie determined to get two more and bring his total to thirty victories so that he could take the record home as a wedding gift to his fiancée, Kay, whom he was to marry while on leave following this mission. But it was not to be!

The Pratt & Whitney R-2800 engine on his Thunderbolt, one of the most reliable airplane engines made during the war, succumbed to some foreign-object damage, and he had had to crash-land near one of our airbases. His squadron buddies had seen him land and escape from the scene. Official news of his missing-in-action status was withheld from publication in order not to jeopardize the possibility that he might evade capture. He made a valiant try. Even five days of dreadful hunger endured by Gabreski were eventually in vain. He was caught.

"We must do something about your little Kay," I told him. "She will be notified you are MIA and will cry her eyes out."

As a good soldier, Gabreski rejected my proposal to send out a radio message. Much later I learned how much he would have liked to comfort his family by sending some news that he was all right, yet he stayed adamant. A few days later I showed him copies of the American newspapers, some with Kay's picture, which reported how she had put her trousseau away and said "all we can do is pray." On that day I sent out the radio message to tell her Gabby was safe and well as a POW in Germany. He had still refused his consent, so I sent it on my own initiative.

Gabreski was so cautious in his interrogation sessions that I tried to loosen him up a bit by involving him in a rather silly argument. One of the American newspaper clippings referred to him as Lt. Col. Francis E. Gabreski, from Oil City, Pennsylvania, and it said he was from Colonel Hubert Zemke's "Wolfpack" outfit. I noticed the mistake of saying his middle initial was *E* instead of *S*, so made a point of it.

"Colonel, you are trying to put a fast one over on me? I don't know whether you are the real Gabby or not. Look here . . . see for yourself. You are called Francis E. Gabreski in your newspapers, and surely they know you very well . . .

The Interrogator

but you state you are Francis S. Gabreski. Perhaps you are really "E" and the brother of the famous one, the "S" Gabreski?"

"I am Francis S. Gabreski!"

"Jawohl! And who is Francis E. Gabreski?"

Heated debate followed. My lithoid countenance, which had earned me the nickname of Stone Face, did not betray me. Gabby thought I was serious about this. Could there be brothers of similar names? Of course! Not too long ago a pilot came through our center who begged to be sent to Stalag Luft III in Sagan because his elder brother was already there. Should his younger brother show up at Oberursel, too, would I see to it that he also went to Stalag Luft III?

"Gabby, surely you know them since they were in a Polish fighter squadron in the RAF."

"Yes, certainly I know them," he said almost angrily, "but their first names are all different."

"True! True! Now Gabby, it is a possibility for two first names to be identical. Look, I have three sons called Hanns-F. Scharff, Hanns-C. Scharff, and Hanns-C. Scharff. Would you mind if I show you their pictures?"

"I don't mind."

"This is Hanns-Felix, this one is Hanns-Christian, and this one Hanns-Claudius . . ."

"Nice boys, Hanns."

EAGLES WITH CLIPPED WINGS
Sunning at poolside, courtesy of Hanns Scharff, are NCO Schroder of the Luftwaffe, Francis S. Gabreski, top USAAF ace with 28 victories but now a POW, and Kenneth G. Smith.

Chapter 10: Ehr, Lehr, Wehr

TWO DOWN AND ONE WENT HOME
The 56th Group top aces shortly before disaster struck. Robert S. Johnson (27 victories plus one unconfirmed) came home to the USA unscathed, but Hubert Zemke (*center*) tore the wings off his fighter in a thunderstorm and was captured, and Walker "Bud" Mahurin parachuted but managed to evade capture.

The Interrogator

"Thank you. Would you like to see my two girls? Here they are. Rydell here is my daughter and Margaret is my wife."

"Pretty girls too. Handsome family, Hanns."

"Have you a brother who is the big ace Francis E.?"

"Doggone it! I am Francis S. Gabreski. There is no E. Gabreski!"

The argument started all over again. I could just see him thinking, "This bloody stupid Kraut, another blockhead!" Meanwhile, I was thinking, "He is really tops! He lives up to his billings!" I then decided to take him over to the beautifully laid-out swimming pool in the municipality of Oberursel. It was in a nice big park surrounded by trees, lots of nice green grass, and the sun and the pretty girls were out in force. Besides Gabreski, Captain K. J. Smith of the 335th Squadron, 4th Fighter Group, went along, as did noncommissioned officer Schroder from our Luftwaffe complement at Oberursel. We had a lot of fun that afternoon and almost forgot there was a war going on. The townspeople were unaware that the man wearing the bandage on his face, Capt. Smith, who had recently had some skin transplanted on his face at Hohe-Mark, and the hawk-nosed Gabreski were two famous enemy fighters sitting peacefully in their midst.

I tried all the tricks I could think of, and all the surprises, but Gabreski didn't take the bait. I even provided him with an extra-nice room in the hospital—soft bed and a couch, bath, hot and cold water, books, cigarettes, radio music—and how do I find him one day?

Armed with a huge broom, he is up sweeping the floor of the rooms where the wounded prisoners were lying.

Next I tried to tire him out by taking him for a long walk up the Herzberg mountain. No use! I was the one who got the blisters on my feet.

"Let's take a car," I suggested, "and drive through the forest to Baron von Opel's hunting lodge. The baron is a personal friend of mine, a great sportsman, and he will be pleased to meet the USAAF hero. There are many deer, Canadian wapiti, and some moose there too. The big house is a very cultured resort with numerous trophies and antique weapons on the walls, cozy rooms, and exquisite wines. This lodge is a home any man of taste will enjoy." Gabby looked interested.

We drank lots of wine. Gabby could take a lot more than I. His intelligence people had trained him right, too, since he kept his mouth shut whenever I tried to lure him into volunteering some information. Friendly, sociable, relaxed, humorous, and quick witted, but not one word more than what I knew already. When we got back to Hohe-Mark, I took him to his room because I was responsible for his safety and his return to the hospital. I was so tired that I felt I could not walk from the garage where I should park the car to my own barracks, so I just curled up on a cot in his room.

When I was later asked what was the most striking feature of America's best tough fighter boy, I just said the deepest impression was what he said when he got

Chapter 10: Ehr, Lehr, Wehr

ANOTHER PHOTO ON SCHARFF'S WALL
Just a few days after this photo was taken in England, this copy appeared on Scharff's wall at Oberursel. The German spy system was working too well, and the photo upset new 56th Group arrivals. *Top row*: Walter V. Cook and David C. Schilling. *Foreground*: Francis S. Gabreski, Robert S. Johnson, Walker M. Mahurin, and Robert M. Landry.

ready to turn out the light that night. He asked me for permission to say his evening prayer! There he knelt, faithful and devotional, a pure and clear heart his armor.

Author comments: Gabreski retired as a full colonel from the USAF in 1967. He worked in the aviation industry for several years and then became president of the Long Island Railroad. He had scored twenty-eight aerial victories in the skies over Europe in WWII, the top American ace in the ETO. He then flew F-86 Sabres in the Korean War and scored 6.5 victories, giving him a total of 34.5. He is the top living American ace, and only two other American fighter pilots exceeded his score: Richard Ira Bong had forty kills in the Pacific theater of operations (PTO), and Major Thomas B. McGuire had thirty-eight, so they ranked one-two. McGuire lost his life in combat during the war, and Dick Bong lost his life in the crash of a P-80 jet fighter on 7 August 1945 at Burbank, California. US Navy captain David McCampbell is next in line with thirty-four aerial victories, also in the PTO.

Gabreski, in a letter to the author concerning Hanns Scharff, wrote the following:

"I came in contact with Hanns Scharff the latter part of July 1944 after running my P-47 into the ground while strafing some bombers parked on a German airfield in the Ruhr Valley. Leaving my wrecked plane, I evaded for five days and was

The Interrogator

finally picked up by some civilians who turned me into the Wehrmacht, who in turn delivered me over to the Luftwaffe. Soon I was reporting in at Oberursel, the Interrogation Center.

"A guard took me from my solitary cell to Scharff's office, and he greeted me with pleasant enthusiasm, extending his hand to shake mine. He stated that he had waited a long time for my arrival, and now it was a great day to be able to meet me in person. He asked, politely, for me to have a seat and to make myself comfortable as 'the war is now over for you!'

"After some generalities, he said, 'We will get to know each other better in the next few days, Gabreski. Now there is very little that you can tell us that we don't already know. Say! Do you recognize those chaps in the picture on the wall?'

"I was flabbergasted! How could he have such a recent photo? It was one taken of me and several other aces such as Bob Johnson, Bud Mahurin, Dave Schilling, Fred Christensen, James C. Stewart, and a couple others, just after we landed following one of our most successful missions less than a week earlier.

"My amazement was not lost on Germany's master interrogator, and he chuckled. 'Now Gabby (his easy-going, friendly manner almost made me overlook his familiarity of using my nickname, and although I was not sure of his rank, I thought he was not dressed like an officer), you can already see that we know a great deal about you, perhaps even more than you had thought. You can also believe me when I say that we even know how you spent your evenings in England, your railroad trips into London, all of that. We do have excellent intelligence contacts in the U.K., and they keep all you very important pilot aces under observation. Oh! By the way, we had your friend Jerry Johnson here just a month ago. He almost got killed by his own guns when he ran out in front of his burning plane!

OLD FRIENDS MEET AGAIN
In 1948 the US Justice Department brought Hanns Scharff to America to testify in the trial of an American flier. Scharff took the opportunity to call on ex-POW Francis Gabreski, who lived on Long Island, New York.

Chapter 10: Ehr, Lehr, Wehr

Nice guy, that one. He's gone on to one of the Stalag Lufts now, and perhaps you'll be joining him there soon. Boy! Was he one surprised cookie when he heard about all the detailed data we have on him in our folders here! Johnson just commented, "this breaks my heart!"'

"Scharff was not pushy or arrogant at all, just talked as if we were passing the time of day. So far he had not asked me for a single answer to his questions. Leisurely he continued, 'Too bad that you decided to fly that one more mission which was to be your last . . . and it was just that. Well . . . Kismet! But since you are here, now, and we know your organization, your 56th Group, we also know that a number of our own aces would like very much to meet the American top ace, so I'll make the arrangements. No doubt you fighters will find a lot of common ground to plow.' (I do not recall ever meeting any of the Luftwaffe fighter aces, though).

"Hanns rambled on: 'Do you know Jake Smart? What a great guy he is! We took him over to Eschborn to meet our fighter boys and even let him sit in the cockpit of a 109. And do you know General Vanaman? He came to visit us too. Did you know that he was the American Air Attaché at the American Embassy in Berlin before the war? He personally knows many of our big fighter aces and other dignitaries and has been able to meet several of them since he left us. Oh, yes, Gabby. They move you fellows around so much over there in England. I need some information to fill out this form . . . are you or were you still with the 61st Fighter Squadron on your last flight?'

'Sir, you said you know everything about me, so why do you ask me such a silly question when you already know the answer? Now all I can give you is my name, my rank, and my ser— . . .'

"He never hesitated . . . 'Ach! Gabby! Excuse me. You are just like all the others who pass through here. You just won't believe that we have most of the answers, but please realize that I am your interrogator and I must confirm that you are whom you claim to be. We cannot have any spy get through here dressed in USAAF uniform and claiming to be Gabreski. Please?'

'Sorry, but my name is Francis S. Gabreski; rank is Lieut. Colonel, and my serial number is 0-406131.'

"Scharff always played the part of a gentleman, and he pursued his job as an inquisitor in a wholly professional manner, but he never did force an issue. I can recall, after one of our lengthy interrogation sessions, that I asked him if it would be possible for me to go to a Catholic church some Sunday. Without hesitation, he nodded yes, and the very next Sunday the two of us went to a cathedral in Frankfurt/Main, where I participated in a Mass with many Catholic Germans who, I am sure, never realized an American prisoner of war sat in their midst.

"Upon my departure from Auswertestelle West there at Oberursel, en route to Dulag Luft, the distribution center, and eventually on to Stalag Luft I southwest of Barth, Hanns Scharff made it a point to come see me and about twenty other Kriegies off to our new home, our *Heim ins Reich*. As a most touching parting gesture, Scharff brought along and presented to me a small box filled with buttered rolls! This was the kindest farewell gift anyone could give a hungry Kriegie. The goodies were enjoyed by all of us, and that Hanns Scharff will always be remembered as a *GOOD GUY!*"

HANNS SCHARFF continues: In the course of the war, numerous Very Important Persons passed through the camp (*VIP in this case could mean Very Important Prisoner). The first had been England's famous legless ace, Wing Commander Douglas Bader. We had caught another famous RAF ace, too, and an air commodore, a USAAF brigadier general, a colonel from General Arnold's staff, a staff captain from Eisenhower's headquarters, a well-known colonel from the 8th USAAF Bomber Command, and now we had the most successful USAAF fighter group's leader, Colonel Hubert Zemke.

Perhaps the singly most important individual captured, in the views of the Luftwaffe and possibly so in the eyes of the entire German war machine, was the USAAF general Vanaman. Before the war, Vanaman had been the air attaché at the US Embassy in Berlin, and he had known all our top-ranking personalities of political, military, and industrial circles.

The general wanted to fly a combat mission so badly that he was allowed to go on one and was shot down over France, in one of the "invincible" Flying Fortresses. In his head, at the time, he was carrying the plan and details of the pending "D-day" invasion. Why he assumed this risk, or why his superiors in the USAAF let him go over enemy territory, will forever be a mystery to me. Apart from his capture and the possibility that he might let slip certain elements of this vital Allied secret while being interrogated, his death alone could well have been a big misfortune for the success of the invasion. Unhappily, this was one case where we did not have the slightest suspicion that he carried within him the details of this cardinal point, and had we had this knowledge, it could have resulted in prolongation of the war.

Several years after the war I discussed interrogation procedures with American authorities. I learned that General Vanaman's capture caused great consternation in American commands and that General Eisenhower said he would have preferred Vanaman had not survived rather than falling into our hands as a POW. I can state categorically that if our intelligence had outgeneraled the general, it would have been one of the biggest accomplishments of the war. We passed this man through Auswertestelle West unsuspected and unchallenged, and to this day he is happy to say how courteous and proper was the treatment he received as a POW.

Another captured officer of high rank was not so lucky. Accidentally, he professed his knowledge of the affixed D-day timing, even though he knew that was the main question in our minds.

An old custom of the people around Frankfurt is to hike on the trails leading up the Taunus mountains. Germans love to hike, and they take their rucksacks, guitars, etc., ride the streetcars to the terminus at Hohe-Mark, and head up the trails toward Feldberg. On Saturday, literally masses of hikers hit these trails.

Chapter 10: Ehr, Lehr, Wehr

EVADEE
Twentieth Group pilot Jack Ilfrey went down in June 1944 but successfully evaded capture, returning to England dressed like this.

A Saturday late in May, an interrogator took this POW for a stroll, no prying or evil intentions in mind at all, and when they crossed the main trail and had to pick their way through the mountain-bound weekenders, our interrogator exclaimed, "Well! The invasion has started!" The double meaning was unintentional, merely light talk. The prisoner of war, knowing the Allied invasion was imminent and fully expecting his escort to ply him with questions on the stroll, snapped back without thinking, "WHAT! Already? A whole week early?" Great astonishment on both sides!

The highest-ranking officer of the wounded POWs at Hohe-Mark hospital was an RAF air commodore. The Gestapo had caught him in France after he had evaded them for six weeks and, since he was dressed in civilian clothing, treated him very roughly until his military status was confirmed. When his airplane crashed, he had dislocated his shoulder and literally torn his left arm out of its socket. He did not get proper medical attention, and he arrived at our hospital in a bad state. His arm was merely skin and bone hanging uselessly at his side. Our marvelous doctor was shocked.

"Commodore Chapman, if you will put yourself completely in my care and do exactly as I say, though you will suffer a lot, I know I can save that arm. In fact, when you leave my care you will salute me by scratching your back between your shoulders with that hand. It will take time and surgery. Shall I proceed?" (*Air Commodore Ivelaw-Chapman nodded and, in time, was recuperating under the combined efforts of Doctor Ittershagen and the choice supplies received from the Red Cross. After he had gone through the most-intricate and advanced surgical

The Interrogator

OUT OF THE COOLER FOR A FEW HOURS
Scharff enjoyed taking some special POWS for a walk in the Taunus mountains. It helped him get their confidence in him. Gestapo-Paris Schmitt, POW Charles Stark, Horst Barth, Gestapo-Oberursel Schmidt, and POW Joseph Miller are happy, but this was about two hours before the "gravy" incident.

AU JOUR LE JOUR
It was just such incidents as this that endeared POW Stark to the Germans. On an outing to Saalburg Castle, Stark took two sticks to emulate a bow and arrow and imitated early inhabitants protecting the castle.

Chapter 10: Ehr, Lehr, Wehr

operations with full willpower and self-discipline, he slowly regained the full use of his arm. Just as the wizard Ittershagen had said, he saved the arm, and it took a long time. Air Commodore Ronald Ivelaw-Chapman was promoted to air vice-marshal at the end of the war and subsequently promoted again to the rank of air chief-marshal. He has also been knighted.)

For more than a year, the air commodore could be seen walking about with his damaged arm in a weird contraption that held his arm extended at shoulder height and out to the left front. In the area under the cast, Chapman had made use of the wire slots by stashing his cards, cigarettes, pipe, tobacco, pencil, and paper in them so that he could reach them with his free hand. He never allowed anybody to assist him, not while dressing, eating, shaving, or playing cards. He would fill his pipe with one hand and play his daily gin rummy or solitaire without help.

Once a month the German paymaster would appear and pay him as well as all the other POWs, who were paid the equivalent of a German soldier's pay according to rank. The air commodore did not know what to do with the Reichsmarks, because there was nothing to buy, and since we could not stand to let all that money lie around, we often got up a bridge or poker party. On occasion, Ittershagen and I also played, and we often lost our own pay.

That was how Ivelaw-Chapman beat me! In fact, it shows how an enemy prisoner could defend himself at Hohe-Mark. Though it hurts to tell, I must divulge how the RAF beat the Luftwaffe on the ground, armed with but five playing cards.

Four players, a USAAF captain who had been wounded in the thigh, Doctor Ittershagen, the air commodore, and I were sitting in the dispensary around an improvised card table. We were using Chinese mah-jongg stones as chips and were playing with the customary fifty-two-card deck without the jokers, as I recall the game.

For an hour or longer, Fortuna could not make up her mind which one of us to favor. Then I was dealt "Pat," four nines and a jack, and I was surprised to see the dealer, the captain, open with a high bet of ten marks. That surprise was topped immediately when the good doctor spoke up, "I'll meet that and double it, if you please," and he threw four chips onto the table.

"So will I," said Cmdr. Chapman dispassionately.

Naturally, this type of betting suited me because I had four nines, so when it was my turn I raised the pot another 20 RM. As the betting went around again, with each player staying, everyone met the bet, and there was over 200 RM in that pot. I knew I was going to get well from a previous betting round. I was confident, but then I began to wonder if someone else might have four of a kind higher than my nines when I heard how many cards they each wanted to draw.

"How many cards, Doc?" asked the captain.

"Pray for one, sir."

The commander put two cards down facedown and drew two. I asked for one, discarding my jack, to sort of conceal my holdings. The dealer drew two for himself. I gathered from all this that my real opponent was the doctor, and instead of getting the money from the Americans, I'd most likely be getting Luftwaffe pay away from my friend Ittershagen.

The captain, original opener, started the betting again with 20 marks. The doctor called; the commodore raised the bet to 40. These cats were playing right into my hands! "Stone Face" Scharff found it hard to suppress a smile, but I managed to do so and casually raised the bet to 80 RM. The captain called tremulously, and the doctor did also. With discouraging self-assurance, the commodore again hiked the bet, raising it to 160 RM, and looked at me questioningly.

I was, naturally, a bit surprised because I knew he had drawn two cards, and it had to be something to beat my four nines, but there was no hesitation on my part.

"There is your 160, and I am kicking it another 160," I say as I pushed in a stack of chips.

"Well," mused the commodore, "let's see now. It costs me 160 more to call, there it is, and here is 320 more to keep things rolling."

I intended to meet his bet by calling, but I knew the old commodore to be a bluffer on occasion, having caught him more than once with nothing more in his hand than a measly pair. "Okay, sir, I will meet that and kick it again—here is 1,280 marks more."

"Hanns, I'll see you," he said quite simply, "but before I show you my hand, I am calling because you cannot beat me. I have the hand of a lifetime." He turned over a royal flush in clubs!! I quit breathing for a few moments!

We all stared at it unbelievingly. It was almost as big a thrill to see one as to draw one. Finally I got my breath back as I watched him rake in the biggest pot I have ever seen!

"But you drew two cards," I said, very puzzled.

"Yes," and his eyes twinkled, "inside and outside, the queen and the ten. It was too one-sided for a friendly game, Hanns, and I feel guilty about it."

Doc Ittershagen laughed heartily. "That's the first time I have ever held a full house and didn't mind losing. I only paid 80 marks to see a real sideshow."

"A most extraordinary game!" the commodore added. "A full house, four of a kind, and a royal flush all in one play. Probably never see it again."

However, the air commodore did see it again. At least I hope he did. About two years later, following my own capture and subsequent release from captivity after my own sufferings and recovery in a hospital, I entrusted Frankfurt's post office with a valuable parcel. It contained ten playing cards mounted under glass, neatly framed, and it would be a credit to the wall of a gentleman's study; five cards in a semicircle, showing an ace-high royal flush in clubs. The lower half consisted of four nines and a jack, similarly arranged. Between the two hands were engraved the names of four poker players—an Englishman, an American, and two Germans; the date, 9 February 1945; and the amount of the pot, 1,680 US dollars. I hope he got the memento. My gift to Air Commodore Ivelaw-Chapman

Chapter 10: Ehr, Lehr, Wehr

PERSONALITY AND BATTLE OF WITS
POW Charles W. Stark and Gestapo liaison officer at Oberursel, Walter Schmidt, at the Opel hunting lodge near Oberursel. Stark's open and friendly, well-disciplined manners won the praise of Schmidt, who was then able to use his influence on behalf of the beleaguered POWs.

was a token of the three virtues, apart from which no man need possess more: *Ehr, Lehr, Wehr*!

Author comments: Air Commodore Ronald Ivelaw-Chapman underwent two operations at Oberursel with Dr. med. Ittershagen presiding. When he appeared at Oberursel, the commodore's arm hung uselessly at his side and was nothing but skin and bone, and the dislocated bone was visible through the skin. Ittershagen responded to the challenge, and in a few months the patient began exercising the arm in accordance with the good doctor's instructions. Chapman lifted small weights, marking on the wall how high he could lift them. Every time he managed to lift them a little higher, a new mark was proudly put on the wall.

Months passed before he could lift his arm straight out from his shoulder, but Ivelaw-Chapman withstood the pain and did it. By December he was nearly recovered and early in 1945 was so confident that he went skiing and broke the arm again! This time he did not jerk the arm out of the socket, and the arm was healed in just two more months.

Promoted to air vice-marshal at the end of the war, Ivelaw-Chapman testified for the defense before a war crimes tribunal at Wuppertal, where ex-Kommadant Killinger was on trial. Some RAF ex-POWs had made the charge that upon arrival at Oberursel during the conflict, they had been stripped, thoroughly searched,

The Interrogator

required to answer questions in violation of the Geneva Rules, and asked to complete a trick Red Cross questionnaire that would have revealed their unit designation and location and the type of aircraft they flew. One RAF crewman, a man named Lang according to reports, claimed that when he refused to give more than his name, rank, and serial number, his captors had put him in solitary confinement and turned the heat up so high in his cell that he divested himself of all clothing and lay flat on the floor with his nose near the slight opening at the bottom of the door. He claimed inhumane treatment.

Air Vice-Marshal Ivelaw-Chapman voluntarily testified at the Wuppertal trials on behalf of the defendants, Lt. Col. Killinger, Major Heinz Junge, Major Otto Böhringer, Lt. Heinrich Eberhardt, and Lt. Gustav Bauer-Schlichtegroll. Ivelaw-Chapman testified that he had been shot down in May 1944 and evaded capture for some days. He was later captured wearing civilian clothing by the Gestapo, who used every form of third-degree coercion in an attempt to make him talk about the help he had received from the French Resistance movement. Later he was sent on to Oberursel.

Lt. Col. Erich Killinger and the other defendants, according to Air Vice Marshal Ivelaw-Chapman's testimony at Wuppertal, were very concerned over his physical condition and took immediate action to have him taken to the hospital at Hohe-Mark. There he underwent protracted treatment. Meanwhile, Killinger and Doctor Ittershagen requested permission from higher headquarters to transfer their patient to a bigger and better hospital, where more facilities would be available.

THE GRAVY EPISODE CAME VERY SOON
Gestapo Schmidt and Col. Charlie Stark laughed and ate well at Opel's hunting lodge. Schmidt took it good-naturedly when Stark spilled gravy all over him.

Chapter 10: Ehr, Lehr, Wehr

GENTLEMEN OPPONENTS
Chief of the fighter interrogators Horst Barth and fighter leader Colonel Charlie Stark take a break and pose for Hanns Scharff's camera. Barth said, "I have never met an opponent with more aplomb, resolve, and a better sense of fair play," Stark said, "Barth is one of the finest men I have met on this side of the line. A gentleman through and through."

Ivelaw-Chapman's testimony at Wuppertal failed to persuade the tribunal, however, and the defendants, who actually had made the lot of the Allied POWs much more comfortable than would generally be the case of any prisoner, were declared guilty and sentenced to five years' imprisonment. It must be pointed out here that the American government did not participate in the Wuppertal trials, even though many times more Americans passed through the center of Auswertestelle West than did British.

Though Air Vice-Marshal Ivelaw-Chapman was unable to dissuade the tribunal, he nevertheless eventually prevailed upon British authorities in Germany, and the sentences imposed by the court were reduced. Sir Ronald Ivelaw-Chapman later was promoted to air chief-marshal and was knighted. He has written a book, with Anne Baker, titled *Wings over Kabul*. His book tells the story of the evacuation of civilians by air from the capital of Afghanistan during the civil war in 1929. Ivelaw-Chapman played a leading role in the first air rescue, under extremely difficult conditions.

In a letter to the author dated 22 March 1977, Sir Ronald Ivelaw-Chapman, CBE, DFC, AFC, and erstwhile bomber group commander, wrote:

"Hanns Scharff did not interrogate me at Oberursel, as far as I remember, since he was the fighter interrogator and I came from the bombers. I was dealt with by Karl Schmidt-Luders and Wiebach. As to my treatment at Hohe-Mark hospital, I

The Interrogator

cannot do better than refer you to the evidence I gave *for the defense* in 1945 at a war criminal trial at Wuppertal, in which the accused included Erich Killinger, the former Commandant of Dulag Luft. My evidence is fully and faithfully recorded in a book entitled *War Criminal Trials—Vol. IX—Dulag Luft Trial*, edited by Eric Cuddon and published in 1952 by William Hodges of London and Edinburgh. From this evidence I think you will gather how well I was treated, especially medically, whilst I was at Hohe-Mark. Maybe the Luftwaffe wanted in some way to compensate for the rather rough handling I had previously suffered from the Gestapo *before it was established that I really was a military POW* and was then passed on to the Luftwaffe Interrogation Center at Oberursel [emphasis added].

"Concerning Scharff's poker-hand plaque: actually his kind thought misfired, as the parcel never reached me. This is the first time I have heard of this generous gesture on Hanns Scharff's part and now, 32 years later I offer him my sincere thanks." /s/ R. Ivelaw-Chapman

HANNS SCHARFF continues: How an American colonel took revenge on the Gestapo was perhaps the best-known incident throughout the Luftwaffe and the prisoner-of-war camps. It all started when one of the Gestapo officials in Paris came to Auswertestelle West to discuss the fundamentals of processing individuals disguised as civilians who fell into German hands. Most of these "civilians" came

GERMAN HONOR GUARD AT POW FUNERAL
Captain Wallace N. Emmer of Omaha, Nebraska, was hospitalized after flak knocked his Mustang down. He died later of myocarditis while in a *Stalag Luft*. This 14-victory American ace was interred at Wetzlar cemetery.

Chapter 10: Ehr, Lehr, Wehr

from northern France, Belgium, and some from southern France and Spain. American and British evadees habitually shed their uniforms and donned civilian garb in their attempt to escape back to England. Once captured, however, they wanted military identity. No lengthy interrogation, it was agreed, should be conducted in France, since it would merely have delayed our work. Prisoners should be sent on to Oberursel as soon as possible.

Major Junge, our deputy commander, invited the Gestapo man and several of us to tea at the officers' club that afternoon, and we had no sooner sat down at the big, round table when the Gestapo chief asked Major Junge, "Sir, I understand that you had a miraculous escape from death when your airplane crashed and sank in the South China Sea. Would you be so kind as to tell me all about it?"

"I must have narrated that story at least nine thousand, six hundred and fifty-four times," replied our chief with an obliging smile. "However, I don't mind if it is not boring to you."

All of us except the Gestapo man had heard the story many times, but we all politely pretended great interest in hearing it again.

He began: "Back in 1938 we were attempting to break the record from Berlin to Tokyo, and we had made wonderful progress with our Heinkel from Berlin to Karachi. We were well ahead of our schedule and were confident we would easily break the speed record. My copilots were Flight Captains Hencke and Morreau, both of whom were killed later in aircraft accidents. In what must be the most God-forsaken part of the world, out over the South China Sea, we ran into trouble. One engine failed. As we had to increase power on the remaining engine to stay in the air, we must have demanded too much of the power plant. It quit too! We alighted on the sea, and though we were able to perch on the wings for a few minutes, the plane began to sink and we had to set sail in our dinghy. From there we watched the Heinkel disappear below the waves. When the first engine had failed, we had sent out a radio report which was followed by several SOS signals when we knew we would have to ditch the airplane. We had a faint hope someone would hear us and come to our rescue."

"Well, you were saved, I am glad to see," observed the Gestapo man with courtly attention.

"Yes, that's true. We despaired of ever being found because we were off the shipping lanes and we had no food or water. Just when all seemed lost, we were rescued by an American Air Corps pilot. He was stationed in the Philippine Islands, and the USAAC radio had picked up our SOS. A Captain Joe Miller stationed there thought he knew exactly where we would be, so he asked for permission to go have a look, and he found us. The rest is not much of a story. We went home on the German Lloyd steamer *Potsdam*, rather discouraged but grateful to that nice fellow, the American Miller."

"Pardon me," interjected the Gestapo man, "we have a civilian in our prison in Paris by the name of Joseph or Joe A. Miller. He was an American military pilot

The Interrogator

at one time and claims to be an American colonel now. Could you describe this man?"

"Yes, of course. I will never forget that face. First of all, he has a remarkably strong chin . . ."

"That's the man!! We have him!"

Colonel Miller's bomber had exploded over France. He landed by parachute, evading capture with great skill and luck, finally arriving at the Spanish border dressed as a French civilian. Approaching the little town of Perpignan, which seemed to him to be the right gate to freedom, it was still too light, so he decided to remain hidden a while longer. While he was awaiting full darkness, he was discovered by a German border patrol.

French civilian Miller, actually Colonel Miller, was transferred to a Paris prison by the Gestapo. His cellmates were suspected spies, burglars, draft dodgers, common criminals, house thieves, and the like. Miller, being a quick learner, rapidly picked up their peculiar language and their tricks of the trade.

Unexpectedly, one day, the fruit of his good deed in the South China Sea several years earlier had ripened, A special guard awakened him, asked him how he would like to travel and see a bit of Germany, then escorted him to Oberursel, to the man who remembered his face and the strong chin so well, Major Junge.

Those stormy days in France were followed by warm and friendly weeks of affection in Oberursel. Junge instructed us there was to be no cooler for Miller, and he went straight to a nice room in the Hohe-Mark hospital. There was to be no interrogation. In the midst of total war, here was true manly fidelity. Throughout the time the steadfast friends Junge and Miller spent together, now, only one difference of opinion occurred between them, and this was settled by a wager. Miller bet the war would be over before the nearing 1944 yuletide, and Major Junge maintained it would be after the New Year festivities.

One of my fighter-colonels*, meanwhile, happened to occupy the room next to the one of the lifesaver at Hohe-Mark hospital, and for company's sake they asked to be allowed to move together. (* Author: Colonel Stark was being trained to take over as senior Allied officer at Dulag Luft, the transient camp.)

This was approved. One day I suggested a weekend excursion into the woods. My fighter boy, however, was not very fond of hiking, and he rather preferred a drive around the countryside. Besides, he now had a roomy, Miller, and did not wish to leave his friend alone, so I happily invited Miller as well. Then I had to find a car. My eye had caressed that big, black, beautiful Mercedes-Benz Continental cabriolet that belonged to the Gestapo official Walther Schmidt, and thinking it would not hurt to ask, I suggested he lend it to me for this jaunt.

"Certainly," he said, "you take my car with my chauffeur. Since you say you are going to entertain Colonel Miller, and, in my opinion, the Gestapo owes him some consideration for those uncomfortable days in Paris*, it occurs to me that I myself would be extremely pleased to receive an invitation to go too (* Author:

Chapter 10: Ehr, Lehr, Wehr

LUFTWAFFE CORPORAL WITH TWO VIP POWS
Gefreiter Scharff stands behind USAAF colonel Charles Stark and South African captain B. W. H. Fergus. Scharff was seldom required to wear a uniform. Though just a corporal, Scharff was believed to be a high-ranking officer by most POWs.

POWs captured in civilian clothing were usually interrogated by Gestapo, personnel whose interrogation methods were known to be harsh.).

"Likewise, I would be pleased if I could bring my adjutant along."

There I was! A Mercedes-Benz, a chauffeur, a Gestapo man and his adjutant, and two American colonel POWs. All I had planned was a nice, quiet walk in the woods! I quickly called my boss, Captain Horst Barth, told him of the developments, and invited him to accompany us. Barth accepted, and now we were ready to go.

I decided to drive my guests to an old Roman castle, the Saalburg, built under Emperor Hadrian roughly two thousand years ago. Just like ordinary peacetime tourists, we looked at everything of interest and wandered for hours through the vast ruins of this ancient stronghold.

"How about some chow?" I was suddenly asked by my hungry prisoners. I must have looked perplexed for having forgotten to provide food, because the Gestapo chief, who had uttered hardly a sound the entire trip, now came forward with the suggestion that he would arrange everything in a nearby roadside inn.

"I regard it as a favor to be of some help," he said.

I still wonder whether he pointed a couple of six-shooters at the poor innkeeper,

The Interrogator

SENIOR ALLIED OFFICER AT DULAG LUFT
USAAF colonel Stark was a West Point graduate, class of '37, and was CO of the 79th Fighter Group in Italy when he was forced to land his P-47 on a beach and was captured. Here he is starting out on a trip to the Taunus with Scharff.

or perhaps he exempted him from punishment for black marketing. Whatever, the result was that we had, to quote my prisoner-guests, "the finest steaks since we left America!" Altogether we had a most enjoyable dinner after a marvelous afternoon at the Saalburg Castle.

The POWs crammed and wolfed the food down, filling their hollow legs, so to speak, and it was not enough. I asked my guests how they were doing, and they replied frankly that they could do with some more. I summoned the innkeeper, and he just shrugged his shoulders and shook his head. "Sorry, gentlemen, no more. That was the last I had."

"Well, never mind about the steaks," I said, "you must have something else?" "Oh, mein Herr, if you would be content with some more fried potatoes and some gravy left over from the steaks? Nice, juicy gravy?"

We were content.

With the nice potatoes and gravy came disaster!

Nobody could really explain, afterward, just how it happened. Colonel Miller had taken a helping and passed it on to the Gestapo chief, sitting on his right. For unaccountable reasons, the huge bowl of gravy started wobbling and dancing on its saucer just after the Gestapo man took it into his hands. He and Colonel Miller must have tried to steady it and, in doing so, tipped it with such force that the entire gravy bowl flipped onto its side, and a huge wave of gravy flew over the chasm onto the Gestapo, splashing over him from head to foot!

His hair was full of gravy, and gravy dripped from his eyebrows. Also from his nose and his chin. His collar, tie, shirt, jacket, trousers, and shoes all got their

Chapter 10: Ehr, Lehr, Wehr

share of the grease. What a commotion! Everyone jumped up to help, suppressing laughter as best as one could, until my witty and naughty fighter ace colonel commented that he had watched how Colonel Miller, with malice aforethought, had given the bowl a cunning twist as he handed it over. We all burst into laughter at the slapstick comedy, except the Gestapo chief, and even he joined our laughter when he finally got it all off as best he could. It reminded me of a statement made by some famous American to the effect that "everything is funny as long as it is happening to someone else."

Although the insinuation of the fighter colonel was entirely untrue, and even the victim accepted the outcome as a joke, the story spread throughout the POW camps and the Luftwaffe. As such things usually do, the story got a little better each telling and no doubt was a gross exaggeration in a very short span of time. The last version I heard was how an American colonel picked up a big bowl of soup at a formal dinner party and poured its contents, in cold blood, over the head of France's top Gestapo ruler.

Until the end of the war, the Gestapo man had the nickname "Gravy," and the story will remain for all time, when former POWs spin their yarns, as the tale of the revenge of an American colonel on the Gestapo.

How quickly things changed. Less than a year later, Colonel Miller was free and his protector in Germany, Major Junge, was in prison. The major was a lonely man there, and he lived for one thing alone, the arrival of mail from South America. Across the South Atlantic Ocean, his family had lived there during the war years, and now they waited for his return home. One day he received a letter from his wife:

"A former prisoner of yours," it said, "who once saved your life in the South Seas, sent us some money. He said it was to pay an old debt that he has owed you for many years. He also said he wished this dreadful war had ended before Christmas. How nice of him to say so because that was exactly our prayers too."

As it is everywhere, Christmas comes but once each year. However, to lonely people, Christmas always takes on a very special meaning, and the POWs, locked up and faraway from their loved ones, especially look forward to the day. All Germans alike are much devoted to Christmas too.

I went to the hospital to celebrate with the wounded POWs in a peaceful and quiet manner because my thoughts, too, were faraway with my wife and children. Each POW at Hohe-Mark had received a bottle of red wine as a present from the *Kommandant* and a plate full of German cookies, the old-fashioned kind, made by the sisters.

Members of the Allied permanent staff had distributed extra rations to the POWs and had decorated a big Christmas tree with candles. I had brought from my home some champagne and some trinkets and gifts such as a cigarette lighter, a Meissen ashtray, a little silver beaker, a leather dice box, and a chess set.

Christmas night, all of the disabled, who were permitted to walk about, assembled at the meeting hall and were sitting around a long, T-shaped table listening

The Interrogator

to the traditional German Christmas carols being sung by the Sisters of Mercy. Doors to the wards were left open for the benefit of the wounded who could not get out of their beds.

There had been some difficulty in arranging this touching scene. Ridiculous as it seemed, orders were orders! The rule was that *no prisoner should be brought in contact with women*, so we were compelled to hide the group of singing sisters behind a drapery or curtain so the POWs could not see them and visa versa.

The opening ceremonies of the festivities ended with the sisters singing "Silent Night," followed by the senior Allied officer standing and delivering a well-spoken and solemn message that left not a man untouched. The prisoners were practically alone for the first time since capture, I mean unattended by Germans while they were in a group, because the three Germans present were practically unnoticeable in the crowd: Ittershagen, Barth, and myself.

When the speech ended, not a POW lifted his glass, although they each held a glass of wine in their hand. I saw the air commodore, who was the senior Allied officer, lean over and whisper in Ittershagen's ear. The doctor stood where I could see he was signaling for me to follow him, and then he signaled Barth the same message. We followed him to his private room, where he closed the door behind us, filled three glasses with wine, and said, "Listen, you two fools. Do you know why I asked you to leave and come here for a drink?"

"No," we admitted frankly, "is something wrong?"

"Yes! They cannot propose the proper toasts in our presence. Though we have to disregard orders and leave them alone, they will not drink until we leave. At this moment the commodore is proposing his toasts: 'Gentlemen! To the King! To the President!'"

DOWNED B-17 BOMBER
Luftwaffe personnel from Oberursel inspect this American bomber from the 339th Squadron, 96th Bomb Group, stationed at Snetterton Heath, England. The 96th had the second highest MIA loss record in the 8th Air Force.

Chapter 10: Ehr, Lehr, Wehr

UNUSUAL OUTING
American POWs (*hatless*) Stark, and Col. Joe Miller visited the scene of the crash as guests of Hanns Scharff. *Left to right*: Horst Barth, Hanns Scharff, Stark, Miller, and Gestapo Schmitt.

With that, he passed each of us our glass and, with a sour face, continued, "So what the hell is left for us to say but Heil Hitler!"

Although Germany was at war and most of the men we associated with at Auswertestelle West were our enemies, they were so much like us that it was easy to find one admiring this one or that one as a potential friend rather than just an acquaintance. The empathy we felt for these men, these POWs, was not mine alone but was the way nearly everyone felt. I would like to give you an example.

Hundreds of injured POWs passed through Ittershagen's hospital, and he saved many a life, many a limb. In three cases he lost the battle for survival. Death was stronger. Two pilots had received such horrid wounds that they collapsed and died after seemingly getting well on the road to recovery. Internal injuries were just too severe. A third POW fought a lonesome, hopeless struggle for weeks and weeks and lost the battle just before the end of the war. He was too ill to repatriate, too ill to move before death took him.

The Interrogator

I had known him for several months, lying in the basement ward for internal diseases in a huge Frankfurt hospital. The boy, away from home, lonely, in strange surroundings, could not be helped. Every day he looked paler and thinner.

One day I took another POW down to the big Frankfurt hospital from Oberursel and met this young man again, and since I had to take the man to Frankfurt for treatment two or three times each week, I would drop in on the sick one and try to cheer him up.

Then, after weeks of such visits, he called me close to his bed and said calmly and seriously, "I know that I am going to die, Hanns. I will never get to see my home again. For months I have not seen the sky, the sun, the trees, clouds, or the stars. If I could get out of here, if I could be someplace where I can see in the distance toward my homeland, I would feel much nearer the ones I love. Then when my time comes, I would feel at peace with the world. Do you think?"

The ambulance took him very carefully from Frankfurt to Oberursel to the beautiful park of Hohe-Mark. Doctor Ittershagen put him in a bed next to a west window overlooking some of the park. No one but God could help this poor young officer. There is no defense against death.

At Wetzlar cemetery, his American pallbearers let him down slowly into his grave. A chaplain, Allied officers, and German officers alike paid homage and last respects. Ten Luftwaffe soldiers fired rifles in volley over his grave; The Salute of Honor. *Kein Mann braucht mehr.*

11

LOVE'S LABOR LOST

A soft answer turneth away wrath, but grievous words stir up anger.
—Old Testament

If my reader could now lean back in his chair at this moment, take his glasses off for a while, and perhaps take a few puffs from his pipe; if he would close his eyes and imagine for an instant that it was his task to select a staff of interrogators for some hypothetical work, he would give himself time to understand the qualities of the man he is seeking. There are effective procedures that can be taught and acquired by learning, and there are virtues, natural gifts, that cannot be attained by education, origin and background, tradition and social standing; qualities that cannot be learned have to be considered.

The capacities to be gained by teaching divide into two main categories: special knowledge—special experiences, and general education. Special knowledge is composed of the ability to speak, write, and understand a foreign language, to know foreign countries and their peoples, the art of writing, of memorizing, and the training in any special subject, as, for instance, aeronautics. General education is of equal importance, the fount of good conduct, tact, diligence, elocution, judgment, quick apprehension and observation, systematical industriousness. Of the natural gifts we demand in our search for an interrogator are ambition, uprightness, and conscientiousness, next to a natural ingratiating demeanor. Last but not least, an implicit loyalty is indispensable. I leave it to your discernment to rule whether a soldier's loyal feeling toward his country is a learnable or a natural virtue. In the Wehrmacht, soldiers, particularly officers, were examined by an act of judgment quite often similar to the American army's so-called "loyalty" tests.

At Oberursel we were often required to discuss very strange business propositions with prisoners, and our loyalty to Germany had to be beyond doubt. As an example, I became a witness to an exceedingly touchy and notable case shortly

The Interrogator

before the attempted assassination of Hitler. A high-ranking officer from an air force headquarters was captured. There was some doubt whether he let himself be captured or if he was a bona fide victim of flak or our fighters. Almost immediately upon arriving at Auswertestelle West, he made overtures about contacting the initiators of the 20 July 1944 assassination attempt. He might easily have met one of the men he wished to find had he not been too impulsive and imprudent. The interrogator he broached the subject to was unsympathetic and very loyal, and his efforts were stalled. Patience might have helped, and he eventually would have known which man to approach.

It was at this time that we became aware of the fact that ties existed between this association and the enemy. Absurdly, we found out through the enemy from the other side what was going on among our own people. We had some false alarms too. One USAAF captain was brought in under suspicion. He had been found wandering around in Normandy, alone and faraway from his base. He was unarmed.

The captain was brought to me, and I carefully checked him out: his training, serial number, career background, and unit. I was finally satisfied when he convinced me his intentions had been harmless. The man really had been looking for souvenirs in the empty battlefield: a bayonet, a German helmet, or, if he was really lucky, a Luger. He was among the German frontline troops when he looked up from his leisurely search for war booty. Surprise!

It was leisure time for the alert pilots at the German base Eger in Czechoslovakia, and two Luftwaffe leutnants were resting in deck chairs near their ready-to-go fighters. They were basking in the sun, which warmed happily on them occasionally as the pretty cumulus clouds passed overhead. Suddenly came the sound of wind rushing over the wings of an airplane overhead, although the warning siren had not sounded. An RAF Lancaster, with engines idling, burst through the broken deck of clouds, leveled out, and, as power came onto the engines, circled the base, obviously looking it over. It was unusual for a big bomber to be out alone like this, and the RAF preferred to fly in darkness, anyway. What . . . ? It put the wind up everyone on the ground.

A sergeant, lolling in another chair nearby, one of the alert pilots, jumped from his chair and screamed, "They'll be smashing us to pieces! Get to the shelter!"

The senior leutnant called him back. "Don't be an ass! Don't sweat it! See, down comes the landing gear; they want to land here. Shoot green! SHOOT GREEN!" His voice reached the man with the Very pistol, who immediately fired a green flare into the air, the aviator's signal that landing is approved.

The Lancaster made a beautiful landing and taxied to the parking ramp. As the crew emerged from the bowels of the aircraft, the senior lieutenant met them with drawn pistol. Surprise!

"Sir, would you mind restarting your engines, two of them, and taxi that big bus into that hangar over there, the one where the doors are just being opened?"

Chapter 11: Love's Labor Lost

"Sure thing!" The RAF pilot was a gentleman and did exactly as the man with the gun directed him to do. Our Luftwaffe leutnant was so proud of his booty that he personally escorted the RAF crew to us at Oberursel.

The bomber interrogation section was overloaded with American crews, since there had been a big action a few days earlier and some thirty crews arrived almost at the same time. I was pressed into service, and this RAF crew was one of the few bomber interrogations I did. Because of the unusual circumstances of the Lancaster browsing around in our sky in daylight and the voluntary landing of the pilot, I was very skeptical of what might be behind this insidious performance. Were they spies or agents putting themselves into our hands for a reason?

"What in the deuce were you doing?" I asked the pilot.

"I'm frightfully sorry to upset you, old chap. My bloody navigator kept giving me the headings while on top of the soup, and he must have been out of his mind. We finally saw the ground through the first hole we have seen in the clouds for six hours, and there was your pretty base. Looked just like ours, you know. And here we were doing our best to fly these inert cement bombs round and round for six hours on a petrol consumption test, thinking we were just over Essex. Quite a surprise to see Jerries when we got out. Quite!"

"Frightfully sorry, too, old chap."

Four new-looking Mustangs came snarling around one of our bases one day too. Dropping their gear, they made the break from formation and set up a landing pattern. This time the German flak units were in the mind that they wanted some more silhouettes to paint on their guns and mess hall wall, so they opened up with 20 mm and even larger flak guns. No green flare this time.

"Auf Wiedersehen!" cracked the American leader as he tucked his gear back up and buzzed away, having decided he would go somewhere to land where they would welcome him instead of making it hot for him.

An additional supply of four more nice Mustangs would have been a welcome addition and fine gift to the "Flying Circus Rosarius," our Luftwaffe's training, evaluation, and experimental squadron that was exclusively equipped with captured enemy aircraft. This unit had Mustangs, Thunderbolts, Lightnings, Spitfires, Tempests, Mosquitos, Marauders, Havocs, B-17 Fortresses, Liberators, Lancasters, and other such foreign curiosities. Still, I thought a brand-new Mustang quadriga would have pleased the director.

Not all was lost, though. The planes had come so low, before tucking their landing gears up and scatting away, that their squadron letters and markings had been clearly observed. Whenever we received a new POW from that squadron and group, they simply loved to hear my story of our flak gunners' *Love's Labor Lost.*

Author comments: Fritz Schröter, fifty-victory Luftwaffe ace of WWII, tells a similar story. After the Allies had captured southern Italy, Schröter was ordered to fly a four-plane *Schwarm* of fighters on a mission against Allied bombers but was to land at another forward base for refueling and rearming the planes.

The Interrogator

The melee with the bombers and Allied fighters was hot and heavy, and his flight consumed more fuel than planned since they could not break off the combat until the American fighters ran low on fuel and turned back toward their own bases. Schröter then led his *Schwarm* to the forward base and landed as quickly as possible. He wanted to be serviced with alacrity so they would not be caught on the ground by the enemy.

Rolling to the flight line out of a fast taxi run, Schröter was shocked out of his helmet to see American troops with machine guns and rifles suddenly appear from behind the sandbags of the revetments. An officer with drawn pistol beckoned for Schröter and his cohorts to cut the engines and peacefully dismount. It was too late to make a break for it and try to take off again, and the Americans were very careful to stand at the side of the fighters, not in front of the cannon. Schröter shrugged his shoulders, smiled wanly, and beckoned his other pilots to comply with the enemy orders. He spent the remainder of the war as a POW.

However, Luftwaffe headquarters was not through with the case. Incensed at the ease with which the enemy had obtained four nearly new Focke-Wulf fighters, they ordered General Wolfrum von Richthofen to take disciplinary action. Schröter was tried in absentia by a court-martial board, found guilty of gross negligence and carelessness, and sentenced to die by firing squad. Of course, the sentence could not be carried out as long as Fritz Schröter was in an American POW camp, and it was reasonable to assume that the Americans would not put him before a firing squad just because the Germans had sentenced him to die. In fact, had the Americans known of the trial and its outcome, they most likely would have increased his rations for the duration.

SCHARFF continues: Another case in which I became involved also had an element of dubious oddity. An elderly and very serious colonel was brought to me for interrogation and investigation. According to his statement, he came from SHAEF, the Supreme Headquarters Allied Expeditionary Force, and when I first met him I could see that this one had deeper potential and was not to be the usual interrogation of a junior officer who knew no secrets.

First of all, I disbelieved his capture was accidental or genuine.

My nature was not to trust or believe an enemy who drives straight to our lines in his car. I had to be cautious with his explanation that he had lost his way. On the other hand, I had to take into account that he surrendered to us without a fight, and with him he had a briefcase chock-full of enemy secret material. *Top secret!*

After a short interrogation, it was agreed that the plans he carried concerning a peace treaty between the Allies on the western front and Germany, if they were generally acceptable to us at Oberursel, should be regarded as the basis for immediate negotiations between the military leaders concerned, without regard to the present government stipulations.

It was further agreed that this courier officer would bind himself, upon his word of honor, to personally submit the German proposals to the Allied Supreme

Chapter 11: Love's Labor Lost

Command; regardless of the outcome, this officer would return to Germany voluntarily.

After deliberations with the *Kommandant*, I dispatched a copy of the agreement through ordinary Luftwaffe channels. To be certain it did reach our topmost level, I sent a second copy through another army liaison office. By utilizing a certain jealousy between two organization, I assured myself that each party would work on the plan quickly and neither would dare to ignore it.

My last sentence in the letter of transmittal reads "For security sake and expediency, a second copy has been dispatched through another organization." No doubt all who read it understood its meaning.

"You are wanted by the legal officer," my friend Walter Hanemann said. He was sitting on my desk in my office, awaiting my return from lunch. Canadian Wild Bill and Captain Horst Barth were there too. Bill looked worried, Barth was biting his finger nails, and Walter knitted his brow.

At lunch, I had had another of my usual slightly hostile encounters with the security officer Offermann. I wondered if his constant harassment stemmed from a personality conflict or from his shrewd, pointed concept of loyalty and duty. But why the legal officer?

"We don't know, but you are to report to him right away."

The next hour was the most upsetting and discouraging of my life as a soldier. Major Sandel had always been friendly toward me, and when I reported, he offered me a chair and a cigarette and started talking about a film I had presented a few days before at the officers' club. I had shown movies of my life in Africa, scenes from the bush and veld, with wild animals, motorcar races, family pictures, sailplane training, and native war dances. My friends, some ladies, deputy commander Major Junge, and a few officers of the permanent staff and a few invited POWs had thoroughly enjoyed it.

Major Sandel then broached the real subject. Never had it been a secret that my wife was British born, or that some of her relatives were fighting for England against the Germans in Africa. It was not an uncommon happening in Auswertestelle West because all of us were bilingual and had lived or traveled in foreign countries. I had never made a secret of my Anglophilic feelings.

"Herr Scharff, what connections did your wife have in Berlin to influence your transfer from the panzer grenadiers to the interpreter?"

"Now look here, Major, sir, that is long past and absolutely irrelevant. The fact is I did not want to go to Russia, and she did not want me to go either. The fact she is very pretty was in her favor, too, and without any connections whatsoever, or any influence other than a lot of nerve, she went to the headquarters without my knowledge. There she happened to meet a general officer who listened to her story and who fully understood her dismay. He was a smart and competent man in my opinion. He decided to put the right man in the right place."

The Interrogator

LATE ARRIVAL
USAAF colonel Sydney S. Woods had two victories in the Pacific theater, then scored five more over Europe with the 4th Fighter Group. He was shot down by flak near Prague on 16 April 1945. He arrived at Oberursel just at the time that Scharff was being troubled by the Postel accusations.

"It is remarkable, though," the major said, almost musing to himself, "how the intelligentsia of the Germans living abroad managed to pool themselves in those interpreters' units."

"But sir, is that not understandable? Who else would know those foreign languages well enough, other than a few college professors who teach the English language? Surely it is important that an interrogator know the language extremely well, or vital data would be lost in semantics."

"Yes, true! But at the same time, these English influences can so easily become detrimental to our cause. Is it possible that those interpreter companies were purposely created and held in the background for eventual collaboration with the enemy by those revolutionists of the 20th of July?"

"Sir, will you permit me to ask the question straight? Do you have any doubt whatsoever of my loyalty to my country?"

Major Sandel did not give me a straight answer. He got up and paced around his office, very slowly, then halted in front of me and put one hand on my shoulder. "I have my own ideas about you, but it is not I who doubts your stainless respectability. The Gestapo has furnished me with an official charge sheet . . ."

"On what grounds?" I answered in my shock.

"This goes back over a year. You were sent away to another camp for twenty days, where you were covertly observed. Actually, it was the same charge then, accusing you of being an enemy spy, but we were able to repudiate it at that time. You may have known you were being . . . ?"

"No, sir, I did not!"

Chapter 11: Love's Labor Lost

"Well, this same charge has been urgently repeated, and I have been appointed to investigate it."

"Please, sir, tell me who has denounced me, and perhaps I can . . ."

"That, I am afraid, I cannot do, since I am not permitted such a disclosure. But now tell me more about yourself; how was it that you were transferred from the interpreters company to this interrogation center?"

"Very simple, sir. Wiesbaden Army XII Headquarters selected me."

"Well, how did you happen to get into the Wiesbaden headquarters?"

"Also simple, sir. I chanced to meet an old World War I friend of my father. This man was a retired *Oberst*, and he wanted to help me since he was a friend of long standing with our family. Postel was his name."

"Are you certain that they were very good friends of yours?"

"Beyond the slightest doubt, sir."

"Oh? I want to read something to you that might help you understand. For a number of years the German government has been popularizing the slogan *Der grosste Lump im ganzen Land, das ist der Denunziant*. Well, my opinion is that regardless of the form of government, the lowest scoundrel in the whole country is the denunciator."

"Sir! You don't mean that my own friends . . . ?"

Standing there by his desk, Major Sandel looked again at the accusing, damaging document, then placed it down, faceup on his desk. "I am not at liberty to tell you anything about it." With that, he walked over and stared out the window for a long time.

I leaned slowly forward in my chair and felt my blood rising while my eyes read the accusation. Clearly I could read it:

"My deceased husband," the document read, "having been a close friend of the father of this man Hanns Scharff, thus was persuaded to lend his help and his influence for the furtherance of a spy's aims. Afterward, his conscience gave him no rest right up to the end of his life, and it was his last will, and my wish, that this man be rendered innocuous in the interest of Germany."

The signature was POSTEL!

This scene had gone full circle.

I rose from my chair, nearly blind with indignation. The major turned and came over to where I was standing.

"Well?"

I replied, trying to control my inner self as best I could, "Sir, it would be below my dignity to defend myself." I saluted Major Sandel, turned on my heel, and left the room.

I do not remember walking over to my office, but there I found the latest news release on my desk. General Patton's Third Army's spearheads had crossed the Rhine River. Was this the real beginning of the end? There were my two faithful buddies awaiting my return, anxiously, and they could see I was very upset. I

The Interrogator

begged that they leave me alone with my thoughts. They reluctantly left, and I locked my door and sat in my room with my preoccupations. Wild Bill, Otto Engelhardt, and Hanemann were perplexed as they left.

My boyhood and youth had been filled with war. My father had not returned from the front, but he had done his duty with dedication and unquestionable loyalty. Over there was the picture of an Englishman, my father-in-law, who had done the same duty. My family, my home, England, Germany, peace, war, happiness, sorrow, misfortune. Now this!! Suddenly I thought that intelligence work had now become superfluous. In my mind I could see that every soldier must eventually take his rifle and fight his last battle. I resigned myself to facing the Soviets at last.

The telephone rang. Shall I answer it? It rang again, as if it was urgent. Here I wished to be alone with my depression, but my reflexes acted without thought and I reached for the receiver. The legal officer was on the other end, and I heard his voice speaking as if I were in a trance: "Obergefreiter Scharff, I thought I should inform you immediately that my investigation of your case has been completed, and *the charges against you have been dropped!* It is believed you were the victim of a foul and erroneous denunciation. I know that you will suffer greatly from the shock of a betrayed friendship, because I know you as a warm and conscientious man. But, please, *don't let this break your heart!*"

12

END OF THE RAINBOW

> *"When I get home, I'm going to build a house!"*
> *Chorus: "BOOOOU"*
> *"A whore house!"*
> *Chorus: "Hoorayyy!!"*
> *"No women!"*
> *Chorus: "BOOOO!"*
> *"Just 18-year-old girls!"*
> *Chorus: "Hoorrayyy!!!"*
> *"Going to fence it in!"*
> *Chorus: "BOOOOO!"*
> *"A fence 3 inches high"*
> *Chorus: "Hoorrayyy!"*
> —Stalag Luft I, anonymous

Author comments: Scharff's first-person account ended here. Luftwaffe headquarters became nervous about the approach of the American armies and decided to disperse the intelligence operation from Oberursel. Scharff became a member of a team composed of Captain Tobler, three sergeants, including Dr. Nagel, and two secretaries, with Major Waldschmidt as team chief. They were ordered to proceed to Weimar. Scharff said "goodbye" to the POWs. Air Commodore Ivelaw-Chapman, curious as always, asked Hanns Scharff if it wasn't dangerous, even impossible, to travel on highways and railways now, since transient POWs had said the German transportation system had been bombed into oblivion. Scharff assured him there was no problem, but the commodore still could not understand how Hanns could travel 350 miles to Berlin to visit his family over the weekend and still be back to work on time Monday morning. "This forthcoming journey must be impossible!"

The train trip to Weimar was practically uneventful, and within hours after arrival the new interrogation center was in full operation.

The Interrogator

In three days, twenty-nine POWs, of which twenty-eight were American pilots, were interrogated and being held in the makeshift cooler at Nohra airbase. Patton's American panzer spearheads were getting closer every day, making Nohra an untenable base for intelligence operations. Major Waldschmidt made arrangements to move them all to Altenburg. How to get there was a problem until the major discovered he could borrow a brand-new Mercedes fire truck, providing he would leave it at Bad Suiza railhead. There they would catch a train to Weissenfels and on to Leipzig, where they were to change trains and proceed on to Altenburg.

They did not want to leave their twenty-nine prisoners behind at Nohra, so they hooked a flatbed wagon on behind the Mercedes fire engine and had the POWs lie down on that. There were no armed guards to go along, so the POWs were unguarded.

The soldier who drove the fire engine had never driven a diesel-powered truck before, and perhaps had never driven any truck before, and after a few minutes of near-nervous prostration, Hanns asked the major if he couldn't do the driving since he had had experience with such vehicles. The switch in drivers was made instantly.

Keeping a sharp eye out for enemy strafers, Hanns drove over hill and dale "with élan!," as Waldschmidt puts it, perhaps a bit too fast for the twenty-nine POWs hanging onto the trailer for dear life, but they soon arrived safely at the railhead, where they were to hand over the big red Mercedes.

At Bad Suiza was also located Stalag Luft 9C, which was for French POWs only, and most of the prisoners held there had been POWs since 1940. When the gang on the fire engine arrived, they tried to turn the twenty-nine POWs over to the commandant, who refused to take them.

Major Waldschmidt futilely negotiated with the camp commander while Scharff was guarding his POWs. Walking past them were the French officers, wearing full regalia including medals, pompously parading back and forth for nonexertive exercise. Scharff could only shake his head and wonder what the Americans were thinking of this ridiculous show.

The twenty-ninth POW in Scharff's ensemble, the Free French prisoner, called something over to one of the officers. In a few minutes a French POW orderly appeared and approached Scharff, saying, "Request permission to bring cigarettes to the prisoner." Scharff nodded his approval. The orderly had a covered tray loaded with packages of cigarettes, which he offered only to the Free French POW in the column. The POW stuffed them all in his pants pockets and jacket pockets and inside his shirt. Some of the American POWs held their hands out but were rebuffed as both Frenchmen ignored their pleas.

One of the Americans was a strapping six-footer with muscles to match. He moved over beside the French POW and, towering over him, lowered his head and looked straight into the Frenchman's eyes for a few moments. Then he straightened up and yelled across the fence to some of the French officers who were strutting past with swagger sticks under their arms: "Hey! Hey you! Look here!"

Chapter 12: End Of The Rainbow

MAJOR WALDSCHMIDT, BOMBER CREW INTERROGATOR
He was a professor of Indiology at Göttingen University before the war and became one of the best of the Bomber Section interrogators at Oberursel.

The French officers stopped and looked questioningly at this Yank ruffian. The American knew he had their attention and pointed down at the Free French man and the orderly, then in his best high-school French called out, "He's a queer! He's a queer!"

The little cigarette-laden POW got the drift. He immediately began handing out a package of cigarettes to each American POW.

The Auswertestelle West personnel could see that they would not get food or help here at Stalag Luft 9C, so they prepared to move on. Just at the moment of departure, Scharff heard someone call his name. He turned to see a familiar figure running toward him.

"Hanns Scharff! What are you doing here?" It was South African doctor B. W. H. Fergus, who had been one of the POW medics at Hohe-Mark for some time before being sent on to a camp in need of a doctor. "I am the camp doctor here. Are you having a problem?"

In moments the standoffish attitude of the camp changed to one of warm hospitality. Food was arranged, more cigarettes appeared, and cognac came from the camp *Kommandant*, along with an apology and an offer to take the twenty-nine prisoners after all. All too soon the pleasantries were over, and the Oberursel crowd had to be off to the Bad Suiza railhead, which was a kilometer away in the center of the town. One major (Waldschmidt), one captain, three sergeants, one corporal (Obergefreiter Scharff), two secretaries (Miss Beck and Miss Bollinger), and a nondescript driver who did not know how to handle a fire truck mounted their steed, hauling their inventory with them: two typewriters, a Cardex file, several file cabinets filled with folders and papers, squadron histories, BUNA data, and a suitcase filled with the personal belongings of American fliers who had been killed in crashes of their aircraft. All that, along with the personal suitcases of the nine men aboard the fire truck, made up the payload as they whizzed along to town with Scharff driving with élan again.

The train left Bad Suiza at sundown, making stops at Bad Kosen, Naumburg, Weissenfels, Bad Dürrenberg, and Ehrenberg, finally arriving at Leipzig about midnight. The train puffed in on track 1 of the largest railway station in the world.

The train to Altenburg was due to leave in less than thirty minutes.

They all knew that meant the train would leave whether everybody and everything was aboard or not, and it was leaving from track 36, the last track on the far side of the stations. The harried seven looked at the tremendous pile of baggage and knew they would have to make several trips to get it all over to 36. They would never meet train departure schedule. What to do?

Off to one side of the platform was a small motor-powered baggage cart. Hanns Scharff had some experience with these contraptions while working in his grandfather's textile mills in Greiz, so he quickly commandeered the vehicle, and it was loaded in a matter of moments. If the twenty-nine POWs had still been with them to act as baggage handlers, they could have made the train easily. Reduced to only seven, the load was far too much to hand carry. The baggage cart solved the problem.

Hanns drove the vehicle, with some occupants riding, others walking alongside, in on track 1 to the main platform, then across all tracks to track 36, then turned out on 36, where their train sat puffing steam with the engineer sitting stolidly in his cab looking at his watch. Only two minutes to go, and in two minutes he would go, come hell or high water, war or no war, loading passengers or not.

As Hanns drove the heavily loaded vehicle toward the first car at top speed, the platform suddenly caved in with a crash, and the vehicle fell 20 feet into a bomb crater. Scharff and the other riders barely had time to leap clear of the plunging cart, and all stood stunned looking down the cavernous hole at their belongings.

The engineer tooted his whistle, and the train jerked as it made its first move to take up the slack in the car connectors. Scharff was the only happy one in the group. He was delighted to be rid of all those files. Gleefully he called to everyone to make a run for the train. One after another, the seven jumped onto the moving train, and only Waldschmidt looked back at the cloud of dust still rising from the hole in the platform on track 36. Some had been carrying suitcases and other luggage, and they were the only ones who saved a thing from the debacle.

Though Altenburg is only about 40 klicks* south of Leipzig, train travel was slow this night (* klicks = GI slang for kilometer). Earlier bombing raids had damaged the roadbed. Dawn was breaking when the exhausted seven dismounted from the train at Altenburg. The morning was quiet, but in the distance could be

Chapter 12: End Of The Rainbow

heard the rolling thunder of artillery . . . Russian artillery. When they left Weimar they had clearly heard heavy guns firing from and against the advancing Americans and British, who had already captured Kassel just 68 miles (110 km) west of Weimar and had advanced to within 12 miles (20 km) of Weimar with their leading armored units. Hanns had looked at nearby Mount Ettersberg, a 1,568-foot foothill 3 miles (5 km) west of Nohra airbase as they left the day before, half expecting to see American tanks perched there. Now, at Altenburg as a new day dawned, Scharff could hear the rumble of Soviet heavy artillery. He wondered if it wouldn't have been a hell of a lot better to have stayed at Weimar.

Duty was duty, and the interrogation center had to be set up and in operation as soon as possible. There were and are those who criticize the Germans for resisting to the very last moment, saying that it was obvious the game was up by the middle of February. Some may have recognized that fact, but to most German soldiers, steeped in the German traditions of discipline, duty, and God, the game was never up. To these men and women of the intelligence center, the game was *never* up, and they continued functioning up until the very last moments.

The Luftwaffe at Altenburg was getting nervous about the proximity of the Soviets. Major Waldschmidt thought the two girls, secretaries Beck and Bollinger, should be evacuated westward immediately.

"Herr Scharff, these two young ladies must not fall into the hands of the Russians. Do you have any suggestions?"

"Yes, sir. I have friends in Gera, and my family lives in Greiz. One or the other would be safe for them."

"Good! What about transport?"

"I'll find a way to get them there, sir."

Scharff's grandfather, Christian Jahn, owned textile mills at Greiz, and in Gera lived one of the directors of the Botany Worsted-Wool Mills of Gera and Passaic, New Jersey, USA. The Gera-based director was William Wilfing from Connecticut, now living in Gera. Scharff would take the two secretaries to him because they would enjoy some protection from the US government due to Wilfing's US citizenship.

Commandeering a car, Scharff drove the two women to Wilfing's villa, where Mr. Wilfing personally welcomed them. Mrs. Wilfing pleaded with Hanns to remain at Gera with them and forgo returning to his unit at Altenburg. In the distance the sirens could be heard announcing the arrival of American armored units in the outskirts of Gera. Scharff was adamant; he had to return to his post of duty. Others were counting on him.

"Herr Scharff!" Miss Bollinger countered, "Lt. Bruno Tgarth gave me some presigned blank army release forms. It is a legal signature. I can fill one out for you, and you are officially out!" Again Hanns declined, and in the middle of the Gera alarm, Scharff drove back, arriving at Altenburg to find the airbase afire.

The Interrogator

Major Waldschmidt and Captain Tobler were already gone, and the three sergeants, Nagel, Wolf, and Wolff, were soon found, awaiting Scharff's return. Before them stood this huge, empty air base with supply buildings filled with goods. The four men immediately set about replenishing their own supplies, appropriating new uniforms, sidearms, blankets, and a new full-length greatcoat for each. They were outfitted better than ever before.

No sense staying around the base risking capture by the Russians, so they departed toward Gera and Greiz, hoping for the best. General Patton's spearhead tanks were already traveling on the autobahn between Gera and Chemnitz, making travel by vehicle out of the question for the four men. They departed Altenburg on foot, without breakfast. Within a few kilometers, hunger pains drove them to search for food. Along the road they spotted several large milk cans in front of a farmhouse, so Hanns advanced cautiously and met an old man who emerged from the house as Scharff approached.

"*Tag!* I am old man Schnabel. What may I do for you?" the old man inquired.

"Sir, we are very hungry soldiers, and would it be all right if we took a drink of milk from one of those milk cans?"

"Of course! Help yourself. Be my guest."

"Thank you so much, my friend. It's nice of you to be so kind to four hungry German soldiers."

"What? *German* soldiers! I thought you were American officers! Be off with you! Get off this property immediately!"

Scharff recalls that this incident was the first time he had a bad feeling about what the future held in store for him.

Two hours later, still hungry, the foursome approached the small village of Schmölln. It was occupied by American troops. Before surrendering to a party of Patton's tankers, Scharff decided he would change into civilian clothing, leave the other three men, and make his way back to Greiz. He crossed the autobahn through an underpass but had traveled only a kilometer or so when an American squad captured him and took him to a post where several other Germans were being held.

The Americans did not know Scharff could understand English, and when the squad leader said, "Check them over closely. The ones in uniform are no trouble, but that guy in civvies has a military passport so he may be a spy. If so, we have orders to execute him," Scharff needed no further prompting. The squad men were not near their rifles, and Scharff was off running at full speed for a nearby forest. Bullets tore into the trees but not into Scharff. He quickly made his way back to the spot where he had buried his Luftwaffe uniform and put it on again. Then he ran back through the underpass and caught the three sergeants, his buddies, just before they entered Schmölln to surrender.

"The city of button factories," as Schmölln is known in Germany, was home for the four only a short time. A US Army truck drove up to the spot where they

Chapter 12: End Of The Rainbow

were being held prisoner, and an officer ordered them to leave all luggage on the ground, and they were to get aboard the truck. Scharff, however, was concerned about the suitcase Sergeant Wolff was carrying, so he spoke to the officer, "Sir, that suitcase contains personal articles removed from American fliers who were killed in aircraft crashes. The suitcase must be kept secure until it can be delivered to the Red Cross."

"DEAD GUYS! What dead guys? American fliers?" He was incensed.

"Well, sir, the bodies of Americans found in their crashed aircraft were carefully searched and their belongings tagged and cataloged for return to the next of kin. Our unit was in charge of that."

"Oh! Okay. We'll take care that you see the Red Cross." The sergeant and his buddies were suspicious of Scharff and "the dead guys." Scharff had not yet heard that the American forces had uncovered evidence of the extermination camps. All American troops seemed to take it for granted that the entire German populace had known of these camps and had approved the actions being taken there. The attitude of his captors served to warn Scharff and his friends that the slightest slip of the tongue could cause great grief here at Schmölln.

The four Germans were ordered onto trucks and driven westward past Weimar again, through Erfurt, Eisenach, Bad Hersfeld, Alsfeld, and Bad Homburg; within a few kilometers of Oberursel and Hohe-Mark; to Frankfurt am Main; and across the Rhine River to a vineyard near Bad Kreuznach. There they were thrust into an open-air camp for POWs, which contained at least 10,000 prisoners, *packed so closely together they could not lie down* on the muddy ground. No food that evening, and since they had been forced to leave their bedrolls and overcoats outside the enclosure, their only warmth in the sleet was their own bodies crowded next to each other. By midnight, as the temperature dropped below freezing, the tired, hungry, and wet POWs started singing and rocking back and forth in unison. By morning, many of them were dead.

The US Army was not equipped to feed and house so many POWs. More camps were formed adjacent to this one, but no shelter in any of them. All were overcrowded. Four days of torture by hunger and the elements passed before Scharff tasted food again, and that was a tin of whole tomatoes given to a group of POWs. They sliced the tomatoes with a razor blade, and each man got a very thin slice.

German POWs began to die from exposure to the freezing nights, starvation, dysentery, and any number of other diseases that accompany malnutrition and lack of proper and sufficient clothing. However, because of Scharff's linguistic abilities, Lt. Holzman from Portland, Oregon, pressed him into service as a translator. One of his jobs every morning was to accompany Holzman and a Sergeant Francis on a tour of the camp to mark the bodies of the POWs who had died during the night. An X was marked on the forehead of more than 100 a day!

Hanns came across his cousin Oskar Feustel by chance, in the same camp. They embraced, and Hanns, who was now enjoying slightly preferential treatment

The Interrogator

"BRIEFCASE KING" OSKAR FEUSTAL
A born optimist, Oskar would make the bright side of the darkest hour miraculously appear. When a Nazi official overheard him make a joke about Hitler, he was dispatched to the Russian front with the notation on his records "Never to return." Just a few weeks later he suddenly appeared at the Scharff home unscathed. This photo was taken in 1975.

and improved conditions due to appointment as translator/interpreter, offered to make his cousin one of the interpreters in the camp too. Cousin Oskar's English left much to be desired, but he knew a joke in English about a big elephant and a little elephant, and he told it so well that the lieutenant approved the appointment. *Vetter* Oskar became assistant translator under Hanns Scharff.

Though Scharff was an interpreter, the position did not exist on the US Army's Tables of Organization, so he was officially assigned to duties in the motor pool under the jurisdiction of Sergeant Francis, who hailed from the Arkansas Ozark Mountain area. This sergeant was neither ambitious nor overly intelligent, and his vocabulary was limited. He probably knew at least a hundred four-letter words but most of the time used only one of them. His conversation was "#@!% this and #@!% that," to such an extent that the Germans all called him "#@!% Francis." One morning Sergeant Francis called Hanns into his office at the motor pool, and this incident took place:

"Hey, you bastard Kraut, my mama used to make the best #@!% cup of cocoa in the Ozarks. None of these mothers in the US Army know #@!% from shinola about making cocoa. Do you know how to make some?"

"Sir! I have been doing nothing but making good cocoa all my life down in the Transvaal."

"Okay, get your #@!% ass down into that cellar over there, and you'll find some #@!% bags of sugar there. Bring one up and make me a #@!% cup of cocoa. Here is the #@!% cocoa." With that he took his feet off his desk and, opening a lower drawer, produced a can of Hershey's cocoa.

Chapter 12: End Of The Rainbow

Needless to say, Sergeant Francis had improved the language of the interpreters almost instantly by teaching them how the " #@ \% trucks in the #@!% motor pool had to get some #@!% service pretty #@ 1% fast," so Hanns understood his instructions concerning the cocoa as well as any teenager today.

Obergefreiter Scharff saluted smartly, clicking his heels in a maneuver Sergeant Francis really enjoyed, turned on his heel, and proceeded to the basement as ordered. It was flooded with about 3 feet of water! The 100-pound sacks of sugar were, fortunately, stacked above the waterline. Scharff waded over to the pile, and when he tried to shoulder a bag of it, it was much heavier than he expected, and it slipped KERSPLASH into the water. He returned to the sergeant and embarrassedly told him what had happened.

"That's okay, Kraut! Go back and get another #@!% bag!"

Hanns enjoys telling the story of how it took him 200 #@!% pounds of sugar to make one #@!% cup of cocoa for his first American boss. He also likes to tell about the suitcase filled with the personal belongings of dead American airmen.

When he and his three companions departed Schmölln aboard the US Army truck as POWs, the suitcase accompanied them because Patton's advance forces thought the situation could be handled best at Bad Kreuznach, where a main Red Cross contingent was supposedly functioning. Upon arrival at Bad Kreuznach, Scharff had spoken to the first American GI he met at the gate, saying, "I wish to see your commanding officer. I have here . . ."

The American soldier would not let him finish, "You have no wishes here, you understand? You're a goddamn POW now, you son of a bitch, and don't you forget it!"

"Yes, sir!" replied Hanns, saluting and standing very stiffly. "I have here a suitcase filled with the personal belongings of American airmen who were killed when their planes crashed. These items were brought to us for safe keeping at our intelligence . . ."

"Oho! One of those G-2 guys, eh? You bet your socks I'll take you to the Old Man. I'm warning you, though, he's a tough bastard, and you'd better not be pulling anything funny. Come on!"

"We have orders," said Lieutenant Colonel Holzman in a rather loud voice after Scharff had been marched with his bag into his office, "not to fraternize with the enemy. You are the first one I am going to fraternize with!" With that, he stood up and shook Hanns Scharff's hand.

"Now, you look a bit shopworn. What can I do for you? First off, though, I want you to go over to that building over there and get yourself a complete new uniform. Now, what's in the bag?"

Scharff was taken to the supply shed, where he was outfitted with winter clothing, but no overcoat. He did get a Russian fur cap like the Soviet Cossacks wear, and he successfully implored the colonel into letting him have similar caps for his three mates, Nagel, Wolf, and Wolff. The caps caused much concern among

The Interrogator

some of the American soldiers, especially the officers, who took a dim view of Germans wearing Russian hats. Since Scharff and his three friends wore the red armbands of interpreters and they had the approval of the camp CO, nothing could be done to prevent them from wearing the odd apparel.

Sergeant Francis from the Ozarks soon depended on Scharff for nearly every action he took. Interpreter became foreman, and one day Hanns made a suggestion that gave Francis's ego a good boost. "Sir, it's not right that these German POWs do not salute you when you make the rounds of the camp. All should salute!"

That suited the sergeant to a tee. "Okay, Scharff, you issue the #@ !% order."

"Yes, sir. Another thing: You should not have to carry that rifle when we look over the camp. Down in the Transvaal, the boss always has a gun bearer. May I humbly suggest that Oskar be your gun bearer? This will give you the dignity you deserve."

"Issue the #@!% orders, *Obergefreiter*!"

When the next rounds of the camp were made, the new orders created quite a stir; Germans stood and saluted with broad smiles on their faces as the remarkable entourage passed them. In the lead was Ozark Sergeant Francis, followed by gun bearer Briefcase Oskar three paces behind. Another three paces back, chin high, walked translator extraordinaire Hanns-Joachim Scharff, wearing a high, black-silk top hat with a long-stemmed poppy stuck in the hatband.

THE INHUMANITY OF WAR
The war was over, and the British and Americans established outdoor POW camps for millions of German prisoners. Instead of sending them home to help the country recover, they were literally starved to death or died of exposure to the elements. This is a photo of just one of the camps, taken months after the surrender.

Chapter 12: End Of The Rainbow

HELLHOLE OF BAD KREUZNACH
This rare photo is one of the few ever made inside an Allied POW camp. An unidentified American sits at the left (he allowed the photo to be taken). Next is Oskar Feustal, and Hanns Scharff is second from the right. In order to starve and mistreat German POWs legally, the Allies reclassified them as Disarmed Enemy Personnel and no longer eligible for treatment under the Geneva Convention Rules.

The flower flopped comically each step Scharff took.

Actually, there was so little to laugh about at Bad Kreuznach that the prisoners developed a unique sense of humor and forgiveness. How cold, tired, and hungry men could laugh at all was almost unbelievable under these circumstances. The customs and manners of the American captors both astounded and amused them, but most of all, the Germans were happy to see that Americans were so much like Germans after all. Not so with the Soviets!

Regardless, savagery lurks just below the surface in the most civilized of men. Under American jurisdiction the prison camps at Bad Kreuznach soon became known as the Hell Hole of Bad Kreuznach!

Within a few days, the camps along the Nahe riverbanks seemed numberless, one camp after another, each swelling to contain 100,000 to 120,000 German POWs. Approximately one million captive soldiers were incarcerated there, all without shelter, clothing other than what they had on their backs, and blankets or sufficient food. The POWs were seemingly intentionally placed on starvation rations, and men who had weighed approximately 180 pounds were soon down to 100-pound walking skeletons.

The serious historian must open new avenues of investigation in his quest for details, and this book has now revealed an event that occurred at war's end. This unsavory discovery really is not new, since many Americans, British, French, and others knew about it. Several million Germans knew about it also, but seldom has it been mentioned by either side. The losing side, the Germans, have preferred to overlook those dark days and forget about it. The Allies, of course, would like it forgotten, for it appears the Allies lowered themselves to the level of the savage in perpetrating this misdeed.

Human nature's natural tendency is to point the finger at "the other guy" and accuse *him* of being cruel and inhumane, a savage or a sadist, a murderer or a torturer, meanwhile viewing one's self as lily white, innocent, perhaps the protector of human rights. Uncommon it is to ever hear an American or a Britisher or a Frenchman admit that it would be possible in any way for their country to resort to the lowest form of human behavior in the treatment of prisoners of war. Revenge or retaliation, according to the civilized person, is the way of the savages, the barbaric underdeveloped races on this earth.

As Hanns Scharff has often said, *"The civilized handle the savage in a civilized manner; the savage handles the civilized his own way."* That axiom is true, in general, but not in all cases. The Japanese are just 100 years past the feudal age, and their barbarism burst through again in World War II. America celebrated its bicentennial year as a nation in 1976, but WWII and Vietnam unmasked the all-too-often cruel and savage impulses that lie just behind our civilized outer facade.

All America, and perhaps the world, knows of the black eye we earned in Vietnam. My Lai is an example. Few know of the Hell Hole of Bad Kreuznach of WWII! Bad Kreuznach was not the only POW camp for Germans to feel the lash of retribution and revenge.

This book is not the right place to explore the Hell Hole and the terrible events that occurred there, so that shall be left to other historians. We will merely touch on a few details herein, since space is insufficient to do complete justice to the subject. To quote Chaucer: "Vengeance is not cured by another vengeance, nor a wrong by another wrong."

The Geneva Convention Rules, it appears, to which the Allies were all signators, apparently were thrown out the window as regards treatment of the German POWs. As Allied armies began to overrun Germany in early 1945, it came to light in concrete evidence that camps such as Belzec, Auschwitz, Treblinka, and Dachau were indeed concentration and extermination camps. Indignation rose to white heat, and the Allies let anger overpower reason. In that moment of victory, the victor's decision makers turned their heads and allowed one criminal act to be avenged by a similar act; that two wrongs do make a right after all. Was this Allied action a policy? If it was actually a policy, historians will probably have to wait until the year 2045 for the exact answer, since records classified "TOP SECRET" with the notation "100 YEARS" will not be released until that time.

As the captured German soldiers arrived at Bad Kreuznach, they were required to leave all overcoats and blankets at the gate. "Don't worry," the camp guards told them, "you'll be issued new coats and blankets inside!" But they were not! Little did they know that it was the beginning of a program to get even with the German people for allowing their leaders to persecute people. On a cold, rainy night with sleet falling occasionally, the German POWs were packed into such small enclosures

Chapter 12: End Of The Rainbow

that they could neither sit nor lie down, no shelter and no food. For hours the men stood, and about midnight they began to sway back and forth in an attempt to keep from freezing, singing songs as they suffered through the night. By dawn, scores of the men had perished. It was nearly a week before most of the prisoners tasted food. The wounded, sick, and weak perished at an alarming rate.

During that first week of incarceration, the sick POWs began to fall, some to die lying in the mud, many trampled almost to death. Dragging the dead out of the enclosure was almost impossible, and it was a full week before any semblance of humane treatment manifested itself at Bad Kreuznach.

One might rationalize that such treatment of POWs was justified because the great influx of prisoners the first few days and weeks after cessation of hostilities found the Allies unprepared to cope with the gigantic logistics problem. How, then, does one explain that the POWs in the Hell Hole of Bad Kreuznach still were without shelters a full year later? The Allies stained their honor while savoring the wine of victory. (For further details on the treatment of Germans after the war, see *Other Losses*, by James Bacque.)

Major General Richard Steinbach, US Army, Retired, has written his memoirs, as yet unpublished, and has granted the author permission to quote a few passages concerning treatment of the Germans during this time period. Steinbach, then a colonel and chief of staff of the Army's VI Corps, commanded by General Morris, was based at Esslingen, Hesse, which is 124 miles (200 km) southeast of Bad Kreuznach and about 6 miles (10 km) southeast of Stuttgart. The VI Corps, now that the war was over, was charged with the responsibility of policing a part of

COLONEL RICHARD STEINBACH, US ARMY
Steinbach, shown here while he was in the Korean War, was chief of staff of the VI Corps in Europe after WWII. He was stunned to discover that German POWs had been reclassified as Disarmed Enemy Personnel and were literally and systematically starved and frozen to death by the Allies.

The Interrogator

defeated Germany, overseeing the return of displaced persons (DPs), and trying to keep the victorious Allies from getting into too much mischief. Steinbach observes that the "German men and women were out in the streets salvaging bricks and stone from their houses. In France the men stood looking at the rubble, and in Italy they were not even looking at the rubble."

The usual troubles of administering military troops who have too much idle time and too much authority under prevalent conditions took most of VI Corps attention, but other situations arose that were just as important. Here we pick up General Steinbach's story:

"We also had trouble with displaced persons. These were the people the Germans had been using as slave laborers. Their living areas were filthy, and they existed like animals. We put all the DPs into German army barracks, generally three-storied brick buildings. When we put them in, the buildings had been in order with windows in, plumbing working, all neat and clean. When I inspected one DP camp a week later, I found they had ripped up the wooden parquet floors to use as firewood even though there was firewood piled at the end of each barracks. They had even removed the glass window panes to sell on the black market. Worst of all, they defecated in the hallways even though there were two latrines on each floor of all the barracks! A man named Wise, spiritual head of a congregation, came and complained bitterly to General Eisenhower about how badly we were treating the DPs, so we took him around and showed him how they were acting. He just made all kinds of excuses for them, none of which were valid. If they thought they were getting even with the Germans by destroying their own living area, it certainly was not an intelligent move.

"Another problem arose. The first trains endeavoring to transport Russian DPs back to Russia reported large numbers of DPs were committing suicide. Even more were jumping off the trains. It seemed that some Russians would rather die than return to Russia. (Author: Subsequent reports indicate the USSR sent nearly all returned POWs to Siberian penal colonies.)

"Some broke the windows in the train and cut their throats with the glass. President Roosevelt had promised Stalin they would be returned, and the Allies were living up to that promise.

"Our intelligence section tried to keep track of incidents and rumors among the German population. One persistent rumor concerned the way Germans were being treated in our POW and internee camps. We heard some were committing suicide, many were starving to death, men were going crazy because they had nothing to do, clothing was woefully inadequate, and many other such terrible things.

"We heard that conditions in the Heilbronn POW camp, located 80 km [50 miles] north of Stuttgart, were unbearable, and the weather had turned extremely cold. These German soldiers had entered the POW camp with only their individual field equipment, shelter halves, and blankets. They had arrived in May and June, were marched into an open field, and were told to establish camp. Now, in October, the weather was rainy

Chapter 12: End Of The Rainbow

and freezing. They dug caves and holes in the ground, living like rats and trying to keep warm. We had been directed to operate in accordance with the Morgenthau Plan, and according to it we could feed the POWs and the internees food only from the German economy. The German economy could produce only enough food for a small percentage of the Germans in the US Zone, and without supplemental rations and more water, these men were on the road to starvation. Those in the internee camps were housed in barracks and fared much better than the POWs who were living in the open fields with only a shelter half for protection from the elements.

"One day we received an order to take over responsibility for the camps in our area of occupation. I went to General Burris, who had become commander when General Morris returned to the States, and told him we had inherited a job from Seventh Army that they must have found too hot to handle. I suggested that we make an immediate inspection of the camps.

"The first camp I visited was an internee camp containing ex-members of the Nazi Party who had held high party positions. Some were suspected of war crimes; others were to be witnesses. These men had lost much weight, some were suffering from tuberculosis, and some were slowly losing their minds. I had the camp's German doctor accompany me on this inspection, as well as the American army's camp commander and his German counterpart. The barracks rooms were clean and neat, as was the rest of the premises. The rooms, however, were grossly overcrowded. Four-man rooms had eighteen to twenty bunks in them, all occupied.

"The food allotment provided these men only 1,000 calories per day, and it requires about 1,700 calories to sustain life over a period of time. This was one of the points of the Morgenthau Plan. (Author: It should be noted that the German soldiers were not eligible for the Red Cross assistance and packages because the Allies reclassified them from POW to Disarmed Enemy Forces [DEF]. Red Cross packages, in plentiful supply, were sent back to Switzerland or to the USA unopened. Henry Morgenthau [1891–1967] was US secretary of the Treasury from 1934 to 1944. He oversaw the freezing of Japanese assets in the USA, and his Plan for Germany was to transform it into a strictly agrarian nation.)

"I was amazed and furious. Starving men who also had no reading material were forced into idleness and treated inhumanely and were 'stir crazy.' Was this the American way to treat these people? I directed the US camp commander to draw supplementary rations from the railhead, enough to bring the calorie intake up to normal levels. Also, he was to start an arts-and-crafts program immediately, in order to keep the internees busy. I suggested he ask the Germans in the surrounding area to donate books and art supplies to the camp. I instructed him to have the men write letters home asking for winter clothing and to set up a system for receiving and inspecting the packages. I advised him that I would be back again the next week, and I wanted to see a big improvement. I also talked to the US officials charged with investigation of these internees, and urged them to speed up their queries and to try to release many of these men quickly if their records were clean. Reducing the

The Interrogator

population of the camp would help a lot.

"Next, I inspected several other camps and found the same terrible conditions in every one. I ordered the same remedial actions there too. Something must be very wrong when a great nation such as ours can allow one bitter man in a high political station to cause a situation like this. Returning to headquarters, I met with General Burris, who had been inspecting other camps. He had found identical conditions and said the German POW camps were something beyond his comprehension. He had, on the spot, directed tentage and lumber for tent floors be supplied immediately so that these poor souls could be decently housed.

"The 7th Army then set up impossible goals, directing us to have all POWs under canvas in two weeks. Our corps engineer set up a sawmill in each camp and put the men to work on shifts twenty-four hours a day. Within a month we had a model camp set up, and the effect on the inmates, as well as on the surrounding population, was remarkable. All sorts of items began to arrive at the camp, including clothing, books, magazines, art supplies, and art craft. The VI Corps area of responsibility reversed the inhumane treatment immediately."

It is sad that the Hell Hole of Bad Kreuznach, just 124 miles northeast, did not have a US Army colonel of Richard Steinbach's fortitude, drive, and stature. Steinbach and General Burris refused to follow the precise instructions sent down by Secretary Henry Morgenthau Jr.* for the care and feeding of the defeated Germans. Blind obedience to superiors was not their cup of tea (* US secretary of the Treasury, 1934–1945).

Hanns Scharff survived the rigors of Kreuznach, but hundreds of others did not. Seventy-two days after his admission to this inhumane dungeon, a traumatic event hidden under sheep's clothing occurred. Guards passed the word through the camp that all POWs whose homes were in Thuringia and Saxony were to assemble at the main entrance. There they were informed that the Allies had decided to release them from captivity, but they would have to be transported to the vicinity of their homes before the release took effect. Excited men were packed into railroad freight and flatcars, and trainload after trainload puffed eastward. The POWs were not informed that this seemingly magnanimous gesture was made to reduce the population of the Hell Hole and, further, that they were being sent to the Soviet Zone of Occupation, where the Russians would be responsible for them.

The train reached Weimar, where Hanns Scharff and several others were placed aboard a truck and driven to Hermsdorf, a small village about 9 miles (15 km) west of Gera. There, Hanns was told to dismount and make his own way home. Well! It appeared that the Americans were going to make the Russians find the Germans; at least the Germans were not being taken under guard to them. Hanns happily started the nearly 19-mile (30 km) walk to Greiz, his home. Although elated at being completely free once more, he was uneasy about his future.

An exhausted and hungry Hanns Scharff finally trudged through the gate of the family villa at Greiz late that evening. The family valet met him at the gate, happily

Chapter 12: End Of The Rainbow

welcoming him back, but setting the stage for the bad news Hanns was sure would come.

"Welcome back, Herr Hanns! Your family, all except your mother and your brother Eberhardt, have fled. They are gone!"

"Gone? What do you mean? Why have they fled?"

"The Russians are coming! Soon!" He went on to explain it was rumored the Soviets were taking over all of Berlin, Thuringia, and Saxony in the next day or two. "You must go too, Herr Hanns, because you were a soldier and they will send you to Siberia!"

Too tired to comprehend everything that was happening, Hanns refused to run, and, after a hearty meal, crept into bed and slept the sleep of the dead. At dawn he awakened to the voice and shaking of his brother Eberhardt.

"Hanns! Wake up, Hanns! Listen! During the night the last Americans left Greiz, and some Russian forces are already on the outskirts of town. They'll be here at the villa later this morning. What are you going to do? I did not fight against them, but you did."

A friend soon arrived and offered to drive Hanns and Eberhardt to Hof in Franconia, but after weighing the possibility that it might put the friend in great danger, the Scharffs rejected the offer. About nine o'clock the friend, who had driven to the city hall, returned and told them it was imperative that they both get out of Thuringia as soon as possible because the Soviets were in possession of a roster of all capitalists from Greiz and they were on that list, scheduled for trial by a Soviet military court immediately.

"Your factory and your villa are to be seized by the Russians!"

While they were planning the next move, an American Jeep drove up the villa driveway. In it was an American friend of Eberhardt's, an army captain named Fletcher.

"Eberhardt! Sergeant Fox and I have driven all night to get you Scharffs out of this part of Germany. The Russians are to occupy all of eastern Germany, including Thuringia, and they must not get their hands on you. We leave in ten minutes. I'll take you to the new western zone." This gesture by an American indicates the respect and esteem many Americans held for the Scharff brothers.

In minutes, Hanns, brother Eberhardt, and Eberhardt's wife, Hildegard, were in the Jeep with Captain Fletcher and Sergeant Fox, speeding their way toward freedom. The captain took them to the village of Helmbrechts, 12 miles (20 km) southwest of Hof, where an old friend of the Scharff family resided.

The Schetlich family welcomed them and fed them a meal of fresh tomatoes. They slept there overnight, and as they were preparing to leave the next morning, up drove Scharff's cousin "Briefcase" Oskar Feustel, the erstwhile gun bearer of Bad Kreuznach.

"Briefcase King" was a nickname cousin Oskar had earned early in life by always having a leather briefcase in his possession, and it stuck with him. He had found at his home his almost new Mercedes-Benz automobile. When he heard the

The Interrogator

Soviets had been handed the plums of Berlin, Saxony, and Thuringia by the western Allies, he raced to Greiz, only to be informed the Scharffs had already fled to Helmbrechts. He sped westward to join forces with them there. Briefcase King Oskar Feustel and his Mercedes were a godsend to the Scharff brothers.

At first, the group thought of going south toward Munich, but Briefcase Oskar made the best suggestion. "You know, I recall an old proverb that went like this: 'The safest place to live is to sleep under the guns of the enemy!' What say we get jobs as translators for the Americans? I heard they are in Hof."

"Agreed!" chimed the Scharffs. They all drove to Hof, where it was easy to locate the American Counter Intelligence Corps (CIC) offices, and asked for jobs. To their surprise, they were accepted immediately. Scharff jokes: "CIC means Christ, I'm confused!"

Hanns Scharff had two bosses at Hof. They were Harry Toombs of New York City and Ralph May of Denver, Colorado. After a lengthy talk with Hanns, Harry Toombs invited him to dinner. "We have orders there is to be no fraternization here. Recognizing that you are a true gentleman, however, you are my guest at my table, Mr. Scharff." A lasting friendship began between the two men; Hanns Scharff

BRIEFCASE KING OSKAR FEUSTAL
A firm believer in Shakespeare's dictum that "a merry heart goes all the day," Scharff's cousin Oskar maintained a happy, jocular spirit, even after 72 days in the Hell Hole of Bad Kreuznach. He was leading an orchestra in Munich when this photo was taken in 1970. He died on 19 September 1992.

Chapter 12: End Of The Rainbow

stipulated one caveat in his agreement with the CIC. He would translate anything, but he would not furnish any information concerning his countrymen that would cause them to be arrested. His new superiors agreed.

Scharff was in his element once more at Hof, which is located about 93 miles (150 km) north of Regensburg and 155 miles (250 km) north of Munich. All the good things in life, such as good food and excellent living conditions, including good shelter, were there. All too soon the CIC unit was ordered to move to Schlüchtern, a village some 15 miles (24 km) southwest of Bad Hersfeld on the main highway to Frankfurt am Main, and the Scharffs went with the move. This too proved to have a short life, and the CIC operation was closed down. Toombs and May returned to the United States.

Hanns Scharff could not stay at Schlüchtern, since he had not been there long enough to establish residency. He could not return to Greiz, either, which had now become Russian-controlled East Germany, so he claimed residency in the state of Hesse, choosing to live in a small village, Treisberg im Taunus, near Usingen, a few miles north of Oberursel. However, this idyllic country life lasted less than a year. His WWII experiences at Oberursel were to have a major effect on his future. The US Department of Justice located him at Treisberg and ordered him to the USA to testify in the upcoming trial of an American pilot who defected to the Germans during the war. This was the delayed hearing of American lieutenant Martin J. Monti, a USAAF pilot who had flown a late-model P-38 Lightning from Italy to Vienna, Austria, late in 1944, now charged with overt acts, including treason, being an enemy propaganda agent, and theft of a US government airplane.

Awaiting the Monti trial, Hanns Scharff was invited by the US Air Force to lecture senior officers at the Pentagon on the provocative subject of POW interrogations. Following these talks, he was asked to remain in the States, possibly to testify in another trial, so Scharff accepted more lecturing requests. When the potential trials were dropped, Secretary of the Air Force Stuart Symington offered to send Scharff to South Africa so that he could visit his family, providing Hanns would promise to return. In May 1949, Hanns was flown aboard Military Air Transport Service from Washington, DC, to England and via South African Airlines to Johannesburg.

South Africa was bad news for Scharff. His wife wanted a divorce. Hanns returned to the United States just three months after he had flown away, arriving this time determined to make his home in the United States. He submitted a request accordingly, and it was soon approved. In the meantime, Scharff made speeches about wartime interrogations before gatherings in Chicago and New York.

His first gainful employment was in Chicago, working for a toy manufacturer and later for a construction company. He lived in Chicago for one year, then moved to New York City, where he opened his own business as a mosaic artist. Three years later, in 1954, the US Immigration and Naturalization Service (INS) discovered that the Department of Justice had illegally allowed him to remain in the United States.

The Interrogator

The INS contacted him and arranged it so that he would leave the States by going to Cuba. Upon arrival there, he would contact the US Embassy for further instructions, which would take him to Miami, Florida, where he would enter the US officially and legally. This was done, and Scharff soon became a naturalized American citizen.

Hanns-Joachim Scharff's divorce was finalized in 1957, and later that same year he married Martha Meyers of St. Louis, Missouri. They produced a son and named him John Robert Scharff. This marriage resulted in a divorce in 1961. Less than a year later, Hanns married the baroness Sabine von Danckelman, who was then living in Las Vegas, Nevada.

Hanns Scharff had never seen his son John until an odd happenstance in 1984. Invited to make a speech at a convention in Las Vegas, Scharff enlisted the services of Brigadier Jack LaGrange to introduce him on the stage. The night before the speech, LaGrange stopped in the bar of the hotel and happened to sit next to a strapping young man who had lost a leg in a motorcycle accident at Point Mugu, California. In the conversation, LaGrange told his new acquaintance that he was going to introduce the speaker. When asked who the speaker was to be, LaGrange mentioned Hanns Scharff's name.

"He is my father!"

LaGrange almost fell off his chair because he was certain Scharff had only three sons and a daughter. More conversation followed, then LaGrange rushed back up to Scharff's room and told him John was there. A mini family reunion followed, and John was eagerly accepted into the Scharff family fold, meeting his three half brothers within a few days.

Another who came to America, as a visiting professor at New York University in 1966, was Dr. Bert Nagel, who had been a sergeant at Auswertestelle West and was well known there as "the wizard of BUNA" (*Beute- und Nachrichten-Auswertung*). Hanns Scharff tabs him as one of Germany's leading scholars in literature. He is the man who quoted Hamlet every time he found, among the confiscated POW property, photographs of a prisoner in civilian clothes. Nagel was the man who could tell the unit and operating base of a POW merely by studying the photo.

Bert Nagel was born in Karlsruhe in 1907. After attending the normal schools there, he proceeded to study literature, history, and philosophy at the University of Heidelberg, receiving his PhD in 1929. For a period of time he did linguistic and literature studies in London. His professional goal was to become a university professor.

The Nazi Party, however, soon controlled Germany and its universities, and when Nagel applied for an academic position he was highly appreciated as a scholar but nevertheless rejected because he "was not active enough politically." Therefore he could not launch his career as a university professor until 1949.

Bert Nagel was drafted into the Wehrmacht in 1939 and eventually found himself assigned to a medical corps, where his duty was extremely difficult and depressing. He had to work with men who had been severely wounded during the course of the war. In 1943, because of his knowledge of French and English, he maneuvered a

Chapter 12: End Of The Rainbow

TWO OLD FRIENDS AT TEHACHAPI LOOP
Prof. Dr. Bert Nagel, of the BUNA Department at Oberursel, and Hanns Scharff watch as a train crosses over itself at the famous Tehachapi Loop in California in 1977. Nagel was professor of Germanic studies at several branches of the University of California in the 1970s.

transfer from the medical corps to the interpreters school Dolmetscher Kompanie VI, located at Bonn-Hangelar (Interpreter Company VI came under the jurisdiction of the 6th Army).

There he exchanged his lapels with the blue colors of the medicos for the red lapels of a Luftwaffe flak unit. The flak assignment was merely a holding post while awaiting the beginning of the next class at interpreters school.

Usually, in the enlisted ranks of the Luftwaffe, a man could be promoted only when he was transferred from one position or station to another. Dr. Nagel was promoted from *Gefreiter* (Pfc.) to *Unteroffizier* (NCO) when he left the medics for the flak unit. He was promoted to *Wachtmeister* (equivalent to sergeant) when transferred to Auswertestelle West. By preference, he did not apply for officer's training school.

Hanns Scharff had progressed from panzer grenadier to *Gefreiter*, then to *Obergefreiter* (corporal). He, too, had chosen not to attend officer's training school.

All military personnel had to carry an identification book or passport. This booklet carried an entry signifying the bearer's linguistic capability. Naturally, nearly every soldier checked "English" whether he knew any English or not, so Wehrmacht headquarters devised a system of testing to determine the true qualifications of each man. This test established nine levels of capability, divided into three main categories:

Category 1. slight knowledge of a language
Category 2. translator
Category 3. interpreter (*Dolmetscher*)

The Interrogator

Each of the three categories contained three levels of accomplishment, so if a person started at the bottom in the lowest category, he would have nine examinations before reaching the top or interpreter level. Those who reached the top level were issued a red certificate, which was then carried in the military passport. Hanns Scharff and Sgt. Nagel were proud bearers of the red certificate.

Nagel was attached to Dolmetscher Kompanie VI at Bonn-Hangelar from April through August 1943, then reassigned to Oberursel, where he was placed in charge of BUNA. There one of the Camp Officer, Reception (COR) men, Sgt. Bartus, collected all the booty taken from pilots or recovered from enemy aircraft, tagged it, and turned it over to Nagel for evaluation. The pilot's wristwatches were confiscated and the POW was given a hand receipt signed by an NCO named Göring. Later, it turned out that many of the POWs refused to surrender the receipt because they thought it was worth more than the watch. "See here? I have Göring's signature. Worth a lot more than my watch!"

A gifted, dramatic speaker, Sgt. Bert Nagel tells a story about one of his findings while studying a map taken from a crashed American bomber. He noticed lightly penciled dots and numbers leading from England's coast to a turning point, thence to Frankfurt and back to England via another route. Since no big raids had been made on Frankfurt for some time, this must be the plans for a new raid coming up soon. Nagel notified the proper commands, and three days later the raid did take place. The Luftwaffe *Jagdfliegern* were ready for them that day and shot down many Fortresses and fighters. The USAAF 20th Fighter Group, flying out of Kings Cliffe, contributed no fewer than eight of its planes that day, and four of the 20th pilots paid visits to Auswertestelle West.

Nagel's ability to recognize the unit and operating base of an American POW almost at a glance at his "escape photo" was a major contribution to the Oberursel interrogators. It made it possible to confuse the interrogatee. When the interrogator told the POW that he already knew his unit and base identity, the captive was usually so awed that he would be easily induced into giving out other seemingly unimportant information.

Sgt. Nagel knew the various interrogators well and was able to form an opinion of the degree of effectiveness of each of them. "I read the reports each interrogator wrote and in this way knew which ones were best. Scharff was unbeatable! Not all of our interrogators were first class, and their reports proved it."

Nagel, Scharff, and others at Oberursel deplored the actions of one of the interrogators, who insisted on using bullying tactics and coercion, yelling, browbeating, foul language, and threats. In Nagel's words, "This interrogator never hurt a prisoner physically, as far as I knew, although we heard that he had turned the heat up high or shut it off in the cells in the cooler. He embarrassed the rest of us. In fact, I felt that he ruined our reputations on more than one occasion. Not one of us liked this officer at all."

Chapter 12: End Of The Rainbow

"Allegedly, this particular unpopular interrogator was related to the German consul in Paris who was murdered by Greenspan before the war, and some of us suspected he was bitter toward the English and Americans for this reason, although it could also just have been his natural personality. In Scharff's opinion, one of the worst characteristics an interrogator could have would be a bitterness toward the prisoners he interrogates. His nasty aggressions cause the POW to clam up, and nothing is gained."

Bert Nagel was one of the three sergeants who went to Altenburg, Schmölln, and Bad Kreuznach with Hanns Scharff. To this day he remembers with heartfelt sincerity a gesture of great friendship and concern by Hanns Scharff while at Bad Kreuznach. Nagel had become gravely ill and was on the edge of death; he had resigned himself to being counted among the hundreds dying daily in the camp from hunger, illness, and exposure. One of the camp's German doctors saw him lying in the mud, noticed he had an eye condition, which the doctor knew how to treat, and ordered him carried into the hospital shack. The camp hospital was a wooden shack big enough for approximately twenty beds crowded closely together. There the doctor worked over the near cadaverous body of Nagel and nursed him back toward recovery.

Food in the hospital was slightly better than it was for the average POWs in the camp, but this was not known outside the hospital. Hanns Scharff came one day to visit his friend, patient Nagel, bringing him his entire day's food ration. Nagel will never forget this sacrifice on the part of his old friend Obergefreiter Scharff.

Recovered sufficiently to become ambulatory, Nagel plotted to stay at the hospital as a translator. His previous experience as a medical orderly helped, and he was appointed to the job of making the entries in the patients' records. No longer did he have to spend his days and nights exposed to the elements outside. He soon became acquainted with the staff at Bad Kreuznach and recalls the names of several of them for the author. Oberstleutnant Eschwege was the senior German officer in command; American doctors Major Schwartz and Captain Benkendorf worked with a German doctor, Adolph. They tried to care for 115,000 German POWs.

"Food quantity and quality in the camp," states Professor Nagel, "had improved by late July 1945, but the luxury was short lived. Administrative control of the Bad Kreuznach camp complex was turned over to the French in August. This was a catastrophe for the German POWs. Repressions began anew, but one should, I suppose, take into consideration that the French themselves were suffering from acute hunger. True, some Frenchmen may have wanted revenge, remembering that the Germans had invaded France five years earlier. The POWs at Bad Kreusnach were not responsible for that invasion, but people have to suffer for the crimes of others. That is the general rule worldwide, and we humans seem unable to change that."

While Dr. Nagel was desperately ill in the Bad Kreusnach hospital shack, a German "Gray Lady" (Red Cross volunteer) from the village adopted him, bringing extra food, books, and papers for him to read, and even reading to him when his

The Interrogator

eyes would fail him. Nagel has never forgotten this extreme sacrifice and kindness on her part. When he had recuperated enough to walk around a bit, he wrote a note to his wife and surreptitiously threw it over the fence in the dark of night. He had not asked the Gray Lady to carry the note out of the camp, because the situation was so tense at that time that it might have endangered her own freedom.

Some passersby, apparently, picked up the note and passed it from hand to hand until it finally reached Frau Nagel in Heidelberg. After an exciting chain of events, she managed to get to Bad Kreuznach for her only visit with Bert during his year in the prison camp. Nagel heard she had arrived in the village and was able to wheedle a "Certificate to Leave Camp" from the hospital commander, and the two were reunited in the home of a friend in the town.

In 1946, just after one year in the camp, the French released him to go home. Nagel was still in poor health and convinced the French that he was a liability to them and that he would get better medical treatment, or die, at his home. When he departed the camp, he estimated some 80,000 POWs languished there.

After recuperation at home, the professor resumed his quest for a university chair. In 1949 he started teaching at the University of Heidelberg and other nearby universities. In 1966 he was invited, as a distinguished visiting professor, to New York University. He enjoyed this duty, and it led to other invitations from American universities. The University of California brought him to their Irvine branch, where he has been their professor of Germanic studies.

What does he consider the most unusual thing about the war?

"There were so many amazing, hilarious, and fascinating events in our lives during the war that it is hard to single out any one as the most unusual. The fire truck episode, the close call at Altenburg, many at Bad Kreuznach, but an amusing one comes to mind just now:

"An RAF pilot, fluent in the German language, was shot down and managed to evade capture. He very bravely walked into the city of Köln after a bombing attack, in full uniform with his RAF wings and rank insignia in full view, and thought it would be best if he kept out of sight until dark, so he walked up to the ticket window of a movie theater. The girl behind the window looked at him questioningly.

"'One please,' and when she hesitated, he continued, 'Surely you know who I am?'

"'Oh! Yes, certainly! You are a *Reichsarbeitsdienstführer*!'* she replied as she read the RAF letters on his uniform (* *Reichsarbeitsdienstführer* = Reich labor service leader).

"The bold flier's freedom was short lived. His uniform finally gave him away, and he soon arrived at Oberursel. Perhaps this could only have happened in Germany!" Well, there is some doubt that it could only happen in Germany. Many German POWs interned in Canada managed to escape and make their way into the USA. Many were never caught again, and some disappeared into America

Chapter 12: End Of The Rainbow

and have never resurfaced. No doubt they are still living in the USA, and not all of them under assumed names.

Where was the Red Cross after WWII when the German POWs were starving in Allied POW camps? Now it is known that the Allies reclassified German soldiers from POW to "Disarmed Enemy Forces" (DEF), thereby removing them from the protection of the Geneva Convention Rules! This kept the Red Cross from delivering parcels to the POWs even though they had warehouses full of them. Thousands of tons of food parcels were returned to Switzerland and the United States. In addition, the German population was put on rations that were really starvation rations. Here is the CHRISTMAS 1947 RATION ALLOTMENT:

Per Month   Per Day

1.1 QT. / 1 L SKIM MILK   .06 PT. / .035 QT.
4.6 OZ. / 130 G FAT .15 OZ. / 4.3 G
 2.2 OZ. / 62.5 G CHEESE or COTTAGE CHEESE   .07 OZ. / 2.0 G
14 OZ. / 400 G MEAT   .46 OZ. / 13 G
17.5 OZ. / 500 G SUGAR or MARMALADE   .60 OZ. / 17 G
17.5 OZ. / 500 G FISH   .60 OZ. / 17 G
280 OZ. / 8000 G BREAD   9.35 OZ. / 267 G
440 OZ. / 1250 G NOODLES/OATMEAL 1   .44 OZ. / 41 G
280 OZ. / 8000 G POTATOES   9.35 OZ. / 267 G
20 CIGARETTES (WOMEN 10)
(Hopes to increase daily calories to 1800 in 1948 looks very dim) Standard letter weighs 1 OZ., 1 G = 0.035 OZ.

Needless to say, the population of Germany was made up of very thin people by 1948.

So it came about that Hanns Scharff became the master interrogator of the American fighter pilots. Soon after becoming a full-fledged interrogator, Scharff's superiors recognized he was perhaps the most effective and intelligent man on the staff. His dignified, friendly, and completely organized approach to the task coupled with his studious and thorough preparation for each interrogation impressed Killinger, Junge, and "Big chief" Barth to the extent that he was given the extra-sensitive duties of interrogating the more senior POWs as they came to Oberursel, even though they may not HAVE come from 8th or 9th Air Force fighters, but from Italy and sometimes even from bomber groups. Whenever one of the interrogators ran across a tough nut to crack, so to speak, they sought out Hanns Scharff, whose magic in the battle of wits always seemed to turn the tide of events. His thoroughness worked both ways. Not only did it get the information the Germans needed, but it also saved many a POW from being handed over to the Gestapo. The fact that he could soon determine the Group and Squadron

The Interrogator

SCHARFF AND AMERICAN FRIENDS, 8 JULY 1991
A luncheon at the Los Angeles Hilton Hotel brought Scharff and friends together again. Present were Francis S. Gabreski, Scharff, James L. Brooks, Walker M. Mahurin, Robert M. DeHaven, and Raymond F. Toliver.

TUSTIN, CALIFORNIA, 2 NOVEMBER 1991
Hanns Scharff (*center*) met with Luftwaffe ace Walter Schuck (206 victories) and Kurt Schulze (who flew with Schuck in Norway) at an art gallery in Tustin.

Chapter 12: End Of The Rainbow

MOSAIC ARTWORK BY SCHARFF AT DISNEY WORLD
Hanns Scharff became noted internationally for his mosaic creations after WWII. This one can be seen at the Cinderella Castle in Orlando, Florida.

a POW came from, even though the POW refused steadfastly to cooperate, kept many a prisoner in civilian clothes out of the clutches of the Gestapo. Hanns's success at wringing information out of every POW became the talk of the Luftwaffe. That information may not have seemed important to the POW concerned, but it was another piece in the mosaic Scharff was constructing for the benefit of the Luftwaffe.

Hanns-Joachim Scharff has become one of the foremost mosaic artists in America, and perhaps in the world. He began a mosaic business in 1950 in New York City, making tabletops that were sold by Neiman-Marcus and other major stores. The Scharffs were separated, and his wife, shortly after war's end, had taken the three sons and daughter back to South Africa. As the three sons became of age, they elected to move to America and joined their father. Today, two sons live in the Los Angeles area, and the third on the East Coast. The fourth son lives in St. Louis.

The Interrogator

ANOTHER VIEW OF SCHARFF's MOSAICS
Cinderella losing her slipper is depicted in this mosaic by Hanns Scharff. It is located in the castle at Disney World.

Hanns Scharff celebrated his seventieth birthday in December 1977, but the man shows no signs of slowing down the pace of his life. His mosaics are famous, now, and visitors to Disney World in Florida can view his work in Cinderella's Castle, where there are five huge glass mosaics, each one 15 feet tall and 10 feet wide in the form of arches. At least 400 colors are visible in each one. Other examples of his work and craftsmanship may be seen in the fountains in the Los Angeles City Hall mall; at the University of Utah, St. George, Utah; and in numerous homes in Hollywood and other cities throughout the United States.

Yes, Hanns-Joachim Scharff, gentleman extraordinaire, has established his third career and found his calling once more. It is the opinion of this author that Hanns-Joachim Scharff, ex-merchant, ex-interrogator, now mosaic-artist supreme, would find his calling at any endeavor he would ever care to undertake. He is that kind of a man!

EPILOGUE

Dear Reader: Up to this point I have tried to lead you through the complicated spiderweb of a military intelligence center. You have seen and heard what happened to American fighter pilots who fell into the enemy's hands. You have also been told what I did when I was obliged to fight for my country. But now I want to take you away from that scene and transport you across the years following WWII.

In 1943 I had made a deal with my friend Walter Hanemann. His home had been in Rochester, New York, and his wife and daughter were Americans. My permanent home for more than ten years had been Johannesburg, and my wife was English and our children were considered South African or British subjects. I was very reluctant to work to the detriment of my former host country, and so was Walter's feeling about America. As a result, we two agreed that he should tackle the POWs of the South African Air Force and I would take on the POWs from the United States. That is how I became the specialist of the Eighth and Ninth USAAF fighter commands.

In 1948 I received an invitation from the US Department of Justice to come to Washington, DC. The treason trial of Lt. Martin Monti was in preparation by the special assistant to the attorney general, Mr. Victor C. Woerheide, and I was asked to be one of the thirteen witnesses before the grand jury in Brooklyn, New York.

At the same time, another trial, called Chandler and Day, was being prepared against American journalists of the Berlin press corps who had stayed in Berlin when war was declared. Moreover, the Department of Justice intended to investigate my work as a Luftwaffe interrogator and any possible collaboration with American POWs. This all took place during the atmosphere of hysteria surrounding

The Interrogator

SCHARFF'S 75th BIRTHDAY
On 16 December 1982, Francis S. Gabreski and his son, then Major Don Gabreski, flanked Scharff to toast another successful milestone in the interrogator's life. The party was held in the beautiful home and garden of Howard and Esperanza Troller in Glendale, California.

such topics as the Whitaker Chambers–Alger Hiss conspiracy. My request of Mr. Woerheide to contact the Air Force Intelligence Department at the Pentagon was granted, and I fell into the hands of Colonel Robert Work. Not only was he able to establish with me the fact that there had been no collaboration or treachery, but to have the secretary of the Air Force decide to return me to my home and my family in South Africa.

Spare me now, dear Reader, to describe my downfall! I found a broken home and a broken family. Again I was disillusioned, sick at heart, and penniless. To stay in South Africa was now impossible, but where to start a new life?? Right then I decided to go back to America, work hard there, and start a new life. Everything else was lost.

I began a new life in 1950 in New York City. My formal training in Germany had been that of a textile designer, which, as I soon found out, is very closely related to the skill used by the famous ancient mosaic artists. I had developed the ability of doing mosaic pieces for friends and family before the war. After getting started in New York, praiseworthy newspaper write-ups helped me become well known, and my business started to grow. I was established in America.

In parallel with these events I surprisingly found that there were also newspaper articles about me on a different subject. Harrison E. Salisbury wrote in the *New York Times* (18 August 1955), "History Relates POW's Hard Lot." In this story he

Epilogue

describes in detail my successful work as an interrogator during WWII, and the conclusions drawn from the investigation by a special committee of the air force.

Then my former enemies became my friends!

One of the first was also the highest in rank: General James H. Doolittle. He invited me most graciously to a luncheon at Rockefeller Center, together with his wartime G2 Colonel Edmundson. We compared notes, and I think I impressed both of them with my knowledge of their secret wartime headquarters and organizational setup. From memory I drew with a pencil on the white tablecloth the diagram of the Eighth Air Force organizational structure, and the general laughed bitterly when I thanked him for having helped me with those "escape photos" each captured airman was required to carry.

After that, many publications began to appear. Most significant were the *Argosy* magazine (May 1950) article titled "Without Torture"; Rita Rooney wrote in *Parade* magazine (October 1968) an article titled "The German Who Quizzed Downed U.S. Pilots"; and the story that changed my life again was written by Royal D. Frey, who was then a curator at the Air Force Museum in Dayton, Ohio. It was titled "The Luftwaffe's Master Interrogator." The author Ray Toliver mentioned this occurrence in the preface of this book.

After the first printing of this book in 1978, many former interrogatees began to contact me, and I was really touched by their most cordial manners and sincerity. There was top gun "Gabby" Gabreski, truly gracious and now a good friend. Long ago he had been my guest at Oberursel. Thirty-eight years later he was again my "guest of honor," but this time it was at my seventy-fifth birthday party at the home of the Howard Trollers in Glendale, California.

Hospitable Hub Zemke of the 56th Fighter Group invited me to his home in Oroville, California. There in his garden I admired a huge persimmon tree covered with ripe fruit. I had never seen one before, and he was so amused that from then on he sent me for every Christmas what he calls a "Red Cross Parcel" containing these delicacies.

My "perfect gentleman" prisoner, West Pointer Charles W. Stark, re-created with me, after forty-one years, the toast shown in one of the pictures in this book, but this time we fortified ourselves with snifters filled with Armagnac!

At another event, an invitation from the US Army brought Ray Toliver, Charlie Stark, and me back to the scene of my wartime activities, Oberursel, Germany. Colonel Robert H. Pratt, CO of the U.S. Army 4th Transportation Command, based at Camp King, Oberursel, Germany, invited us to come to Germany and visit his unit, which was at the same place our interrogation center was during WWII. It was an honor to be feted so royally by US Army men, who were hungry for information about the wartime activities that took place there at their station. It was mid-August 1986.

Following the ceremonies at Oberursel, where hundreds of German civilians mingled with US Army personnel, we three drove to Wetzlar and searched for and

The Interrogator

found the remnants of the old Dulag Luft, the transient center where Stark had been senior Allied officer. After forty-two years, only a few foundations could be found amid the growing brush and trees.

Where have all the soldiers gone? Here is one touching example:

BERT SHEPARD, ex-POW, COMMENTS: "I am delighted to have this opportunity to express my deep appreciation for the excellent medical care I received while a German POW. I also wish to thank Hanns Scharff for interceding on behalf of five or six P-38 pilots by rescuing them from the Gestapo and most likely execution.

"I was shot down by flak on 21 May 1944 while strafing a German airfield near Ludwigslust. I was about 20 feet above the ground when my right foot was shattered and I was hit in the chin. I hit the ground flat at 380 mph! When I woke up a few days later, my right leg had been amputated 11 inches below the knee, and part of my skull (2 square inches) above my right eye had been removed. Seven weeks later I was discharged from the Ludwigslust hospital and delivered to Oberursel and the Hohe-Mark hospital.

"It was at Hohe-Mark that I met Hanns Scharff and Dr. Ittershagen and learned that several P-38 pilots from my 55th Fighter Group were shot down the same day that I had gone down. None, though, had been injured. That day some P-38s from another group had strafed and killed some civilians at Greifenwald, so it was only natural that these pilots were wanted by the Gestapo to be tried as war criminals.

"Lt. James Weisel was one of the five. Jim and I had gone through pilot training and had shipped overseas together. During interrogation, Scharff became convinced that these five had not been the guilty culprits. Hanns did not want to see innocent pilots convicted and die for something they did not do, so he reported to Reichsmarschall Göring that they were innocent soldiers. Göring ordered the five treated as POWs and removed them from Gestapo control. Hanns Scharff went far beyond the call of duty to save these pilots.

"Dr. Ittershagen was a tall, handsome man who spoke English with a sort of Oxford accent. He was one of the four doctors who developed and were authorized to use the Küntscher pin for setting badly broken bones. He would invite me into his office and show me X-rays before the pin was inserted, after it was inserted, and after the pin was removed, leaving a perfect fusion of the broken bone. He was using the Küntscher pin as needed on Allied POWs, and the pin is now used worldwide.

"I also met Captain Ken Smith from Boise, Idaho. He had flown with the RAF 355th Eagle Squadron before joining the USAAF in England. Shot down, his face was badly burned, and he was terribly worried about the disfiguration and the reaction of Irene, his recent bride waiting for him in Scotland. Ittershagen and Scharff arranged for Smith to make trips into Frankfurt to a Dr. Dennecke, a plastic surgeon. I think Hanns Scharff paid all costs for this treatment out of his own pocket.

Epilogue

SPEECH AT AIR FORCE MUSEUM, DAYTON, OHIO
Hanns Scharff was invited to speak to a full house at the museum at Wright Field, Ohio on 5 May 1979. Royal D. Frey (*left*) was one of the POWs interrogated by Scharff and was now one of the curators at the museum. Francis S. Gabreski and Ray Toliver are at the right.

"I and many other badly wounded POWs were sent to Meiningen. There, a Canadian doctor, Don Erry, a fellow POW, made me an artificial leg. I had been a minor-league baseball pitcher before the war, and so I began throwing, pivoting, and running on my new leg. I was repatriated to the USA in February 1945 aboard the *Gripsholm* in a prisoner exchange, and Walter Reed Hospital made me a new leg. Four days later I joined the Washington Senators and played professional baseball the next two years.

"Years later I visited Jim Weisel in Bakersfield, California. He was a very special type of person, saw only the good in everyone, was very honest and loyal, and was proud to have worn the uniform and fight for his country. The Bible was his favorite book, and if you had to share anything with him, he would always make sure you got the biggest piece.

"Weisel's wife had died, his children grown, and Jim was alone and suffering from Parkinson's disease. We talked about how we were shot down, prison camp, and he stressed how worried he and the other guys were when the Gestapo tried to take them over. He also told me how Hanns Scharff had saved their lives. Scharff and Toliver had visited him for a nice reunion.

The Interrogator

"Years later, Weisel's health had deteriorated so much that he was on his death bed. Jim Jr. and sister Patti were searching for something they could do for their dad the last hours of his life, when Patti mentioned Scharff's name. Jim's eyes lit up and his face came to life. Jim Jr. called Hanns's home, but Hanns was in New York for three days. The doctor did not believe Weisel would live that long, but he did. His faith in God and his desire to see Scharff once more pulled him through a few more days. As soon as Scharff arrived home, he rushed to Bakersfield.

"It was a silent but emotional meeting. Jim couldn't talk, so they just squeezed each other's hands to express their respect for each other. Jim died shortly after Hanns left. "To prolong life is to save life," just the same as "to hasten death is to cause death." If Jim Weisel could talk to us once more, I think he would say Hanns Scharff saved his life not once but twice. We all thank Hanns Scharff for giving Jim Weisel the will to live a few more days and make it possible for Jim to pay his silent and deep respects to a man he dearly loved.

Bert Shepard
Hesperia, California

HANNS SCHARFF continues: There were many private reunions and organizational meetings with former POWs all across the USA, among them the Generals LaGrange, Smart, Gerald Johnson, and again Jimmy Doolittle.

Even in South Africa, former opponents remembered me kindly. My son Hanns-Claudius had to go there on a business trip, and I told him to look for a character named Assad Assad in the Johannesburg telephone book. He did. It was there; he called. The response was overwhelmingly friendly: "Where are you? I pick you up right away! My whole family is grateful for the treatment I received from your father in 1944 when he sent to my worried mother a telegram from Portugal in which he told her I was safe and well." The whole family appeared that night, and the father of the family retold the story in front of my son and produced the original telegram as proof and as a precious heirloom.

Much later I was honored to receive from the government of South Africa the medal of Grand Officer in the Order of Spes Bona (Good Hope), which cited humane treatment of white and black soldiers taken prisoner by Germany in World War II.

Author comments: There were also some reunions at organized conventions of ex-POWs. Hanns Scharff and I were invited by retired general Delmar T. Spivey, ex-POW himself, to address the Stalag Luft III reunion to be held at the Bismarck Hotel in Chicago, Illinois, in mid-April 1983. The dinner hour was seven p.m., and we were standing on a mezzanine overlooking a tremendous convention room filled with about 2,000 reunionees. It was about an hour before dinnertime.

"They're all big guys, bomber guys, not fighter types," commented Scharff.

"Yep!" I answered, "but I do see some hands waving around down there in the middle. They have to be fighters!"

Epilogue

ACES, GENERALS, AND THE INTERROGATOR
On 17 October 1980, Wilbur Bettis, owner of the noted gourmet restaurant Nieuport 17 located in Santa Ana, California, hosted a banquet honoring interrogator Scharff. Among those present were aces James L. Brooks and Robert M. DeHaven, General James H. Doolittle, Hanns Scharff, and General Curtis LeMay.

Scharff stared for a moment, then nodded, satisfied he would not be speaking to an all-bomber crowd. He said he wanted to go up to the hotel room to rest for a while so would meet me at the elevators in the lobby about seven. After he left, I made my way down to the hall and through the crowd, looking for fighter pilots. Soon I found them. Introducing myself, I ventured to ask them if they had been interrogated at Auswertestelle West, Oberursel, and if so, did they recall who interrogated them. One spoke up quickly, saying that yes, he did, and he was the scion of the Sharp Pencil Company, and if he ever met him again he'd kill the son of a bitch! "Why?" I asked, somewhat taken aback.

"Because the SOB kept me in solitary for two months!"

I remarked that I couldn't understand that because the Geneva Convention Rules expressly stipulate that a POW cannot be kept in solitary confinement during interrogations longer than four weeks, twenty-eight days. "Well, maybe it was only four weeks, but it sure as hell seemed like eight weeks to me!"

"And how about you?" I asked the other fighter boy.

"Same guy, only his name is actually Scharff, not Sharp, and he was 100 percent gentleman with me. I was really impressed with his knowledge of our fighter unit. In fact he knew more about the personnel than I did."

After a few seconds of mulling this state of affairs over in my mind, I asked them if they'd like to meet Scharff again, since he now lives in the USA.

The Interrogator

"Yeah, maybe I would see him if he ever came to Knoxville. Maybe I wouldn't, too!"

The other fighter boy was different. Sure, he'd really like to see Scharff again. It would be a pleasure after all these years.

"Well, he is right here tonight and will be making the speech after dinner." Looking at my watch, I saw it was nearly seven o'clock, and I must get to the foyer to meet Scharff at the elevators. "Come with me, if you wish, and I will introduce you to him . . . again!"

We wended our way through the crowd and stood waiting where we could see all the elevators. "He will be coming down on one of those lifts any minute now." Almost as if acting on signal, one of the doors opened, and there was Hanns Scharff. Seeing me, he waved his hand and started toward us. When he was about 20 feet away, he stopped, stared intently at the two fighter boys, then exclaimed, "Hey! You were in the 364th! And so were you!"

With mouths wide open in awe and amazement, both quickly rushed to Scharff. Grabbing his hand, hugging him, and then patting him on the top of his head, the guy who wanted to "kill the SOB" was now all smiles.

"You SOB Scharff, you haven't changed a bit! Maybe you've lost a little bit more hair!"

These two 364th fighters were self-appointed escorts for Scharff the rest of the time we were in Chicago, proudly introducing him to anyone who would stand still long enough to hear their stories. Needless to say, Hanns Scharff was an attraction at that Stalag Luft III reunion. It was sad, though, that the famous and well-liked General Delmar T. Spivey was not there. He had passed away just a few months before the reunion.

HANNS SCHARFF continues: At another convention of ex-POWs in Roanoke, Virginia, I told the audience of my identification trick using my phony "Colonel Bullshit" dog tags. When I started home, they paid my expenses by check . . . made out to Colonel Bullshit. When I got back to Los Angeles and deposited the check at the Bank of America, the pretty lady teller looked at me with quibbling eyes.

Colonel Toliver and I, as a team, delivered many a speech, and I, now close to being eighty-five years of age, look back on my life with a sense of content fulfillment. I did not seek any reward. But there came one, much later, no doubt the highest any man can strive for. Colonel Work, from the Pentagon, sent me the revised manual on the "Conduct of Prisoners of War" as had been ordered by President Eisenhower, who had recognized that the "Rank, Name, and Number" rule does not work. Colonel Work's inscription on the title page reads: "This country owes you a lot of thanks!"

I feel it is not so.

It is the other way around.

I am the one who owes this country!

Epilogue

POSTSCRIPT: Hanns-Joachim Scharff passed away on 10 September 1992, just three weeks before his eighty-fifth birthday. A true gentleman, a man worthy of emulation, has passed on to a better world.

APPENDIX

The following are reproductions of pages from Hanns Scharff's logbook, showing POWs who went through his office from January through December 1944. Not all of the POWs interrogated by Scharff were entered.

Appendix

FIGHTER-INTERROGATIONS

1944						(F)Sqn.	Gp.
JAN.							
6.	1st.Lt.	RABIE	Spitfire	ME 109	SAAF	4.	7.(?)
9.	2nd Lt.	LARSON	Lightning	J 390	USAAF	343.	55.G.
12.	1st.Lt.	WESTPHALL	Thunderbolt	J 255	"	357.	355.
25.	2nd Lt.	HINDERSINN	"	J 470	"	83.	78.
FEBR.							
7.	2nd Lt.	GREENUP	Lightning	KSUJ 688	"	49.	14.
10.	1st.Lt.	CONROY	Thunderbolt	J 454	"	359.	356.
13.	F/O.	McCALL	Spitfire	KSEJ 721	TAF.	225.	324 W.
13.	F/O.	DITZEL	Beaufighter	" 722	RAF 600.NF.	—	
16.	2nd Lt.	MEAD	Thunderbolt	J 488	USAAF	335.	4.
22.	2nd Lt.	KREBS	Mustang	J 520	"	355.	354.
23.	1st.Lt.	BALLEW	Thunderbolt	J 515	"	325.	4.
24.	Lt.Col.	ROBBS	Marauder	KSE 720	SAAF	24.Sqn.	3.W.
25.	1st.Lt.	MATTIE	Mustang	J 586	USAAF	353.	354.
MÄRZ.							
6.	W/C	LOUDON	Spitfire	KSE J 810	TAF	—	324 W.
6.	1st.Lt.	VAN WART	Spitfire XI	J 634	USAAF	27.PRU	Ph.
7.	2nd Lt.	JOHNSON	Lightning	KUJ 670	"	77.	20.
8.	2nd Lt.	PFEIFFER	"	647	"	55.	20.
9.	1st.Lt.	BOTHA	Spitfire	KSE J 729	TAF	111.	324.
10.	2nd Lt.	ROUGEAU	Thunderbolt	KUJ 622	USAAF	62.	56.
12.	2nd Lt.	MARCOTTE	"	663	"	63.	56.

März						(F)Sqn.	(F)Gp
14.	2nd Lt.	CONNER	Lightning	J.777	USAAF	97.	82.
14.	2nd Lt.	BROCK	"	J.665	"	383.	364.
15.	Maj.	NELANDER	Thunderbolt	J.646	"	377.	362.
k 17.	Col.	SPICER	Mustang	J.651	"	—	357.
22.	Lt. Col.	EDNER	"	J.660	"	—	4.
23.	Maj.	BECKHAM	Thunderbolt	J.584	"	351.	353.
23.	1st Lt.	LANE	Mustang	J.615	"	356.	354.
23.	1st Lt.	TALLMAN	Lightning	J.688	"	385.	364.
23.	2nd Lt.	TURNER	"	J.697	"	385.	364.
23.	1st Lt.	COLTMAN	"	J.747	"	384.	364.
23.	2nd Lt.	WESTMORE	"	J.748	"	384.	364.
23.	1st Lt.	SOOMAN	Mustang	J.709	"	336.	4.
31.	Maj.	MILLS	"	J.667	"	334.	4.
31.	Lt. Col.	HUBBARD	Lightning	J.707	"	—	20.
31.	2nd Lt.	RICCI	Mustang	J.718	"	353.	354.
April							
2.	1st Lt.	CARVER	Mustang	J.691	"	358.	355.
5.	Cpt.	PORTER	Thunderbolt	J.715	"	367.	356.
6.	1st Lt.	JOHNSTON	Mustang	J.752	"	357.	355.
13. k	1st Lt.	BUNTE	"	J.770	"	334.	4.
13.	1st Lt.	CARR	"	J.772	"	334.	4.
13.	Maj.	BEESON	"	J.778	"	334.	4.

Appendix

April						(F) Sqn.	(F) Gp.
16.	Cpt.	PETERSON	Mustang	J 140A	USAAF	336.	4
16.	1st Lt.	CLOTFELTER	"	J 754	"	335.	4
16.	1st Lt.	WILLIAMS	"	J 734	"	334.	4
16.	Cpt.	VAN EPPS	"	J 799	"	334.	4
16.	1st Lt.	POMPETTI	Thunderbolt	J 700	"	84.	78.
16.	Cpt.	JOHNSTON	Mustang	J 819	"	354.	355.
16.	2nd Lt.	REEDY	"	J 800	"	357.	355.
16.	1st Lt.	GRAY	"	J 814	"	364.	357.
16.	1st Lt.	HALL	"	J 833	"	356.	354.
19.	Maj.	JOHNSON	Thunderbolt	J 753	"	63.	56.
19.	2nd Lt.	DUNLAP	"	J 816	"	370.	359.
22.	1st Lt.	PINO	"	J 805	"	368.	359.
	1st Lt.	McCOLLOUGH	"		"	360.	356.
23.	1st Lt.	KENNEY	MUSTANG	J 849	"	358.	355.
23.	2nd Lt.	McCASLAND	"	J 850	"	357.	356.
23.	Cpt.	PARKER	Thunderbolt	J 817	"	360.	356.
25.	Maj.	CARPENTER	Mustang	J 865	"	335.	4
25.	Cpt.	CARE	"	J 834	"	334.	4
25.4	Cpt.	WYNN	"	J 855	"	334.	4
30.	1st Lt.	YOCHIM	Thunderbolt	J 798	"	328.	362.
30.	Lt. Col.	RICHMOND	"	J 873	"	486.	352.
28.	2nd Lt.	PLANCK	Mustang	J 857	"	356.	364.

The Interrogator

Date	Rank	Name	Aircraft	Serial	Unit	(+)Sn.	(+)Grp.
April 30.	2nd Lt.	POSTLE	Mustang	KUJ 847	USAAF	364	357
Mai 2.	1st Lt.	FORBES	Thunderbolt	101-791	"	389	366
4.	2nd Lt	Kaczynski	Thunderbolt	" 896	"	367	356
4.	1st Lt.	Hinman	Mustang	" 936	"	369	357
4.	2nd Lt.	Parnell	" "	o.V.	"	353	354
4.	"	Roberts	Thunderb.	o.V.	"	86	98
5.	Col.	Malmstrom	"	2895	"	—	356
11.	2nd Lt	Scarbrough	Mustang	o.V.	"	355	"
14.	1st Lt.	STEINCAMP	Lightning	KUJ 1052	"	385	364
"	Cpt.	SPRADLIN	"	" 1016	"	384	364
"	1st Lt.	BOSWORTH	"	" 1029	"	383	364
14.	2nd Lt.	McCARTY	"	" 952	"	79	20
16.	Cpt	HEWETT	Thunderbolt	" 1004	"	367	356
16.	1st Lt.	BOULET	Mustang	" 939	"	354	355
20.	2nd Lt.	BORSHEIM	Thunderbolt	KS2J 1205	"	85	79
24.	2nd Lt.	BENSON	Mustang	J 1054	"	380	363
"	2nd Lt.	BRUCE	"	J 1055	"	380	363
"	2nd Lt.	BARLOW	"	J 887	"	380	363
25.	Cpt.	TAYLOR	Thunderbolt	J 1065	"	—	405
"	"	MOSSE	Mustang	o.V.	"	368	359
27.	1st Lt.	PROKO	Lightning	J 1070	"	13.PRO	7.PRG

Appendix

May/June						(F)Gr.	(E)Gr.
31.	F/O	BAILLIE	Typhoon	183 to 33	RAF Rhod.	266	20
31.	Sgt.	McMURDON	"	1045	"	266	20
	Lt. Col.	"JONSIE" SZANIAWSKI	Mustang	KH 1106	USAAF	357	355
	1st Lt.	LUKSIC	"	1187	"	487	352
	2nd Lt.	HANNON	"	1189	"	487	362
	1st Lt.	McCONNEL	"	O.V.	"	358	355
2.	"	WEISEL	Lightning	J 1133	"	343	55
2.	Cpt.	GARLOCK	"	1188	"	338	55
2.	1st Lt.	TIPTON	"	1184	"	38	55
2.	1st Lt.	ROWAN	Thunderbolt	1137	"	350	353
2.	2nd Lt.	SHUPE	Mustang	1135	"	370	359
2.	2nd Lt.	ANDERSON	Thunderbolt	1100	"	360	356
	1st Lt.	KOCZAK	"	1145	"	360	356
1.	1st Lt.	MASLOW	Mustang	1068	"	370	359
1.	1st Lt.	SMITH	"	J.1195	"	381	363
2.	2nd Lt.	MULVEY	"	J.1122	"	503	339
3.	Cpt.	TUCHEIM	Thunderbolt	1267	"	83	78
4.	1st Lt.	RAFALOVITCH	Mustang		"	334	4
5.	2nd Lt.	DICKSON	Thunderbolt	KH 1236	"	377	362
6.	1st Lt.	ADAMS	"	1177	"	377	362
6.	2nd Lt.	CHAPLIN	Lightning	J.1240	"	385	364
"	"	WITTGREVE	"	J.1271	"	385	364

The Interrogator

Juni						Sqn.	Gr.
7.	1st Lt.	ALEXANDER	Mustang	4567 1302	USAAF	2.	52.
7.	Cpt.	MILLIKAN	"	1280	"	336.	4.
16.	Cpt.	SMITH, KT	"	37727	"	335.	4.
"	Lt.Col.	PIPER	Thunderbolt		"	63	56
9.	2nd Lt.	YOUNG	Mustang	401 1218	"	336	4.
"	"	SPEER	"	" 1274	"	334.	4.
"	1st Lt.	SCHULTZ	Lightning	J 1181	"	401	370
"	Col.	JENKINS	"	1840	"	—	55
10.	2nd Lt.	McDONALD	Thunderbolt	J 1240	"	350.	353
"	"	JOHNSON	"	J 1092	"	63	56.
12.	Cpt.	COON	Lightning	401 1166	"	77.	20.
"	1st Lt.	FURR	Mustang	J 1322	"	328.	362.
"	"	BROWNING	"	J 1309	"	354.	355.
13.	2nd Lt.	KARIVA	Thunderbolt	J 1363	"	360.	356.
"	"	DOUGLASS	Mustang	J 1350.	"	357.	355.
2.	Lt.Col.	CLARK	"	J 1186	"	—	354.
7.	1st Lt.	MICHAELY	"	J 1137	"	363.	357.
16.	2nd Lt.	DOESCHER	Thunderbolt	401 1282	"	395.	368.
18.	1st Lt.	PRICE	"	J 1224	"	494.	48.
22.	2nd Lt.	HILL	Mustang	2x	"	380.	363.
25.	1/Lt.	Wicker	Lightning	1324	"	22. TRG	7
"	2nd Lt.	HILL	Mustang	1407	"	380.	363

Appendix

Date		Name	Aircraft	Serial		Sqn.	Grp.
Juni							
26.	1st Lt	HAIRSTON	Lightning	J 1416	USAAF	77.	20.
"	"	PORTER	"	1473	"	343	55.
"	"	GREENAMYRE	"	1475	"	38	55.
Juli							
1.	Col.	STARK	Thunderbolt	KSU J. 1127	"	—	79.
3	Maj.	GOODSON	Mustang		"	336	4.
"	1st Lt.	BOLT	Thunderbolt	J 7A	"	379.	362.
4	2nd Lt.	KNOX	Lightning	J 1193	"	429.	474.
"	"	LAROCHELLE	Thunderbolt	79 A	"	404	371.
7.	Lt. Col.	TYRRELL	MUSTANG	1447	"	368.	369.
"	Cpt.	BUTLER	Lightning	1479	"	435.	479.
11.	Cpt.	BENNETT	Dakota-C47	A.	"	(TC) 32.	314.
"	2nd Lt.	WARK	Thunderbolt	J 17A	"	386	365.
"	"	MARCINKIEWICZ	Mustang		"	368.	359.
"	"	KORINEK	Lightning		"	338.	55.
14	"	DIXON	Mustang	KUJ 1572	"	357	365.
15.	"	OHLIGSCHLAGER	Lightning	KUJ 1437	"	434	479.
16.	"	HALL	"	494	"	360.	356
"	"	HASS		J 1622	"	434	479
"	Maj.	EDWARDS	Mustang	J 1633	"	—	4
17.	1st Lt.	NESSELBUSH	Lightning	J 1444	"	436.	479.
"	"	TUCKER	"	J 1519	"	434	479.

331

The Interrogator

					Sqn.	Gp.
Juli						
27.	1st Lt.	WILSON	Mustang	KU7 1652 USAAF	328	352
29.	1st Lt.	BLOUNT	"	1436 "	338	55
"	1st Lt.	SCHWAB	"	J 471 "	354	355
31.	1st Lt.	HUNSBERGER	Thunderbolt	"	412	373
Aug.						
2.	Cpt.	MARINI	Thunderbolt	J 444 "	397	368
3.	1st Lt.	BULLARD	Mustang	J 454 "	382	363
"	2nd Lt.	RHODES	"	KU1 1763 "	38	55
"	"	EWERT	"	1661 "	375	367
"	1st Lt.	GOODMAN	Spitfire	o.V. SAAF	247	237
"	Maj.	LUNDQUIST	Mustang	(D) 148 USAAF	486	352
"	1st Lt.	ROBBINS	Thunderbolt	J 1595 "	396	368
4.	2nd Lt.	HANRAHAN	Mustang	J 1625 "	335	4
7.	1st Lt.	RISTAU	"	"	15	67
"	2nd Lt.	ROBINSON	Thunderbolt	J 1664 "	360	356
"	Maj.	CORTNER	"	"	23	36
8.	2nd Lt.	STRONG	Mustang	o.V. "	505	339
"	1st Lt.	POTOCHNIK	"	1867 "	383	364
"	"	MACDERMOTT	"	1754 "	383	364
"	2nd Lt.	JOHANSON	"	?		
9.	"	CARTER	"	J 1759 "	362	357
"	Cpt.	TURNER	Thunderbolt	J 1804 "	389	366

Appendix

Date		Name	Aircraft			Sqn.	Gp.
Aug.							
9.	2nd Lt.	DAVIS	Mustang	KH 1452	USAAF	374.	367.
10.	Maj.	BARLOW	Typhoon	J 591	SAAF	182.	124.
"	Cpt.	LOWMAN	Thunderbolt		USAAF	365.	358.
15.	Maj.	KELLER	Lightning	J 1910	"	434.	479.
17.	Cpt.	CLARK	Thunderbolt	J 1847	"	82.	118.
17.	Maj.	ELLEDGE	Thunderb.		"	506.	404.
"	1 Lt.	Tiorle	Mustang		"	343.	55.
"	2nd Lt.	DIFFENBAUGH	"	J 1877	"	383.	364.
25.	Maj.	SMITH	"		"	334.	4.
"	Cpt.	NURTZ	"		"	354.	355.
"	2nd Lt.	SHAW	"		"	505.	339.
27.	Cpt.	GODFREY	"	J 1992	"	336.	4.
"	2nd Lt.	ACHEN	"	J 1951	"	384.	4.
"	"	PISKLAK	Thunderbolt	J 1944	"	412.	373.
28.	"	CHERRY	Mustang	J 1915	"	368.	359.
"	1st Lt.	BURKHARD					
Sept.							
1.	Cpt.	RYAN	Thunderbolt J		"	410.	373.
2.	1st Lt.	DOERING	Mustang J		"	77.	20.
"	Col.	WILSON	"		"	-	20.
5.	Lt. Col.	GABRESKI	Thunderbolt		"	-	56.
6.	1st Lt.	MILLS	Lightning		"	429.	474.

				Sqn	Gp
Se/ptbr.					
10.	2nd Lt. UNDERWOOD (FUSTING)	Mustang	USAAF	334	4
"	" SANDLER				
"	" RUDKIN			334	4
"	" WESTBROOKE			10	50
"	" FUENFSTUECK	Mustang J 2004	"	486	352
"	1st Lt. ESKRIDGE	"	"	338	55
11.	Cpt. HUTCHINSON	B26 KE 1591	SAAF	12	3.W
14.	2nd Lt. MOORE	Mustang	USAAF	505	339
"	" MULL	"	"	343	55
30.	1st Lt. VINYARD	Mosquito KU	RC "	654	25 R
"	1st Lt. O'MARA	" Nav.	"	"	"
"	Maj. LENFEST	MUSTANG	"	354	355
"	Cpt. BROWN	"	"	354	355
Oktober					
19.	1st Lt. LAGRANGE	Thunderbolt J 2284	USAAF	83	78
21.	Maj. CHENEY	MUSTANG	"	376	361
"	1st Lt. KOSLOSKI	"	"	384	364
"	" CROUCH	"	"	385	364
30.	Cpt. MUELLER	MUSTANG	"	350	363
30.	2nd Lt. KING	Lightning	"	401	370
37.	Cpt. SILVERNAIL	./.	"	11.A.Com.Sqn	
"	Cpl. LIBERTY	./.	"	"	"

Appendix

November					Sqn.	Gp.
1.	2nd Lt.	SMOLEN	MUSTANG	USAAF	109	67
3.	"	BRIDGEMAN	LIGHTNING	"	394	367
5.	1st Lt.	HOLMES	MUSTANG J13D	"	434	479
11.	"	WALSH	"	—	334	
14.	Col.	ZEMKE	"	"	—	479
16.	1st Lt.	SMITH	"	"	435	479
"	"	HULL	"	"	354	355
"	2nd Lt.	WOOLARD	"	"	354	355
"	2nd Lt.	GREENE	" J 2391	"	107	67
22	"	POOLE	"	"	355	354
"	"	LEYMEISTER	LIGHTNING	"	485	370
"	"	LUND	Thunderbolt	"	390	366
23.	1st Lt.	QUIST	Mustang J 2445	"	336	4
December:						
2.	CPT.	HICKEY	Thunderbolt	"	82	78
3.	1st Lt.	GASTON	Mustang J	"	385	364
3.	"	RIVERS	" J	"	385	364
9	2nd Lt.	BRETHEN	Thunderbolt	"	81	50
20.	"	HOOD	MUSTANG J 2564	"	374	361
26.	1st Lt.	GORE	Thunderbolt	"	81	50
"	2nd Lt.	CAIN	MUSTANG	"	505	339
30.	"	DEMMON	Thunderbolt	"	391	366

1944				Sqn.	Grp.
Dec. 30	Lt. Col	HARBECON	USAAF	—	362
"	1st Lt	LOCK	"	5	239
"	2nd Lt	FOSTER	"	378	362
"	1st Lt	ALLEN	"	384	364

Appendix

NEW YORK TIMES
AUGUST 18, 1955.

HISTORY RELATES P.O.W.'S HARD LOT

Since Bible Days Prisoners Have Suffered and Died in Enemy's Hands

By HARRISON E. SALISBURY
Special to The New York Times.

WASHINGTON, Aug. 17—The history of prisoners of war is a history of death, deprivation, suffering and torture.

In Bible days prisoners were butchered on the spot. The Romans tortured them to death for public amusement. Medieval knights preferred quick death in battle to a lingering one in "durance vile." George III ordered every American who rose in rebellion against him hanged until dead if caught.

The name of Andersonville, the great Confederate prisoners' camp, is still synonymous with horror.

Only in comparatively recent times—the report of the Secretary of Defense's Advisory Committee on Prisoners of War makes clear today—have humanitarian concepts of treatment for men taken captive in battle begun to win acceptance.

Code Often Ignored

The idea of a modern code for the protection of prisoners of war was born during the first "modern" conflict, the American Civil War. These concepts are still far more honored in the breach than in observance, the advisory committee made plain.

And even as concepts of law and regulations for protecting the rights of prisoners have begun to win international approval, new threats are emerging — threats of psychological attacks on prisoner morale, new scientific techniques for extracting military information and skilled methods seeking to induce prisoners to change allegiances.

So far as Communist methods of proselyting prisoners are concerned, the committee offered a strong and positive answer:

"The way to combat such a subject as communism is not to hide it or hide from it. The way to combat it is to explode it. Americans have the means at hand—the Bill of Rights. Or call it democracy or republican government, or the American way.

"Armed with a knowledge of American principles — and a knowledge of the enemy's—the American fighting man possesses a sword and shield which cannot be wrested from him in combat or in captivity."

The committee found that the history of hardship and peril for the prisoner was as old as the history of warfare itself. In the earliest times there was no prisoner problem simply because there were no prisoners. Warriors fought to death. Victors took no prisoners.

Chivalry Helped

The rise of Christian civilization brought about some amelioration, the committee reported. While warfare remained cruel, the chivalric codes of knighthood, closely connected with the Christian Crusades, began to develop.

"The ideal—the Golden Rule was there," the committee reported. "It was threatened by intolerant ideologies and the fanaticism which fosters atrocities. The Islamic conquests were savagery untrammeled. Woe to the unbelievers captured by the stepsons of Abu Bekr. But even as it clashed with the sword the scimitar acquired tempering. Possessed of his own code, the Moslem warrior could appreciate gallantry."

The first rules regarding the terrogation of prisoners, the committee reported, were developed from the codes of knighthood. In the Seventeenth Century the concept of the prisoner as being in the custody of the sovereign or state rather than the individual who personally captured him began to evolve.

But the prisoners' plight was still most unhappy—and often tragic during the days of the American Revolution. The British were under orders to treat all rebelling Americans as war criminals subject to hanging on capture.

The conditions under which the British held American prisoners during the Revolutionary War probably have never been equaled in the annals of American warfare, according to the report.

The committee quoted an account of the British prisoner ships in New York Harbor. "There is nothing in history to excel the barbarities there inflicted. Twelve thousand (American prisoners) suffered death * * * on board the filthy and malignant ships. The scenes enacted in these prisoners almost exceed belief."

Worst Hulk Was Here

The worst of the ships was Old Jersey, anchored in Wallabout Bay, Brooklyn. The bed of the bay was covered with the skeletons of the dead, thrown overside after they expired in captivity.

The Revolutionary War also saw the birth of the tradition that an American prisoner does not meekly accept captivity. Capt. Gustavus Conyngham, with a group of American seamen succeeded in tunneling their way out of the heavily guarded "Old Mill" British prison at Plymouth and escaping despite their legirons and handcuffs.

Prisoners fared little better during the war between North and South.

"Prison camps were harsh," the committee reported. "In Southern camps, particularly Andersonville and Florence, men suffered greatly from malnutrition and lack of medication. The Union prison on Johnson's Island in Lake Erie was a bleak Alcatraz, and Union stockades at Point Lookout on the Potomac were described as hell holes."

But it was this conflict that gave birth to the modern movement for protection of prisoners and codification of their rights and privileges.

Because of widespread public indignation over the treatment of prisoners, President Abraham Lincoln in 1863 requested Prof. Francis Lieber to prepare a set of rules on prisoners of war.

The Lieber code is believed to be the first comprehensive system ever promulgated by a Government for the treatment of prisoners. It established that prisoners might not be treated as bandits, could not be punished as public enemies nor made victims of revenge, suffering or disgrace.

Rules Were Harsh

Prisoners remained responsible for crimes committed before their capture. They were to be regarded as prisoners of the Government and not of their captor. They were to be subject to confinement and might be shot in the course of an escape attempt but might not be punished if recaptured. They were, however, subject to prison rules—harsh in those times.

Civil War prisoners were sometimes chained together, placed in brutal irons or "bagged" by means of a suffocating canvas sack tied over their heads.

Simultaneous with evolution of the Lieber code the Swiss philanthropist Henri Dunant was working toward the creation of the International Red Cross which the United States joined in 1882.

It was through these efforts that the Brussels and The Hague conferences on prisoners of war were developed. These led eventually to The Hague conventions of 1899 and 1907 and ultimately to the Geneva conventions of 1929 and 1949.

Meantime, new prisoner-of-war techniques were developing. In World War I the Germans evolved pioneer methods of psychological warfare. They set up "political camps" at Limburg and Zossen, primarily designed to work on Irish prisoners and lure them, if possible, into Irish units which would fight against the English. Only a handful of Irish were recruited in the effort.

World War II spread the horrors of prisoner atrocity to civilians in large numbers, through the practices of both Nazis and Japanese.

But one of the most striking developments was the refinement in psychological treatment of prisoners of war developed by the Germans.

One of the most skilled practitioners of this art, the committee found, was one Hanns Joachim Scharff who carried out interrogations for the German Air Force at Auswerestelle West, Oberursel, Germany.

All captured airmen except Russians were brought to this center.

Scharff was one of the principal interrogating officers for American prisoners. He questioned some 500 American fighter pilots and from all but a handful extracted the information he desired.

After the war he was brought to the United States to explain his methods. They combined psychology and an excellent cross-reference file. Scharff used a "soft" technique with prisoners offering them cigarettes, easy chairs, putting them at their ease with small talk.

When the prisoner declined to give information as was almost always the case, he adjourned the proceedings briefly while he consulted amazingly elaborate files.

The files usually contained details concerning the airman's comrades and sometimes information on his own background. Armed with these facts Scharff seldom had difficulty in persuading the prisoner that he knew so much already that no useful point was served by holding back further minor details.

"In the war there were many Scharffs," the committee reported. "The prisoners in an interrogation center is a fly in a web. The enemy has all the say. At the end of World War II the consensus of the experts was this: It is virtually impossible for anyone to resist a determined interrogator.

"But the experts came up with another consensus: Although a determined interrogator cannot be resisted, he may be evaded by the prisoner. The prisoner may dodge loaded questions."

So far as Communist methods are concerned the committee reported that those displayed in World War II by the Soviets and by the Chinese Communists during their war with Nationalists were "nothing more than a high-gear recruiting campaign."

"Boiled down," said the committee, "it amounted to advertising."

"The war for the minds of men is a war of wits," the committee concluded, "It will not be lost by the serviceman who is equipped with the necessary education."

That is what I drew onto the table cloth:

VIII Fighter Command: Gen. Kepner
                                  Gen. Griswold.

  65 (F) Wing – Gen. Anton
  Groups: 4 – 56 – 355 – 356 – 479

  66 (F) Wing: Gen. Woodbury
  Groups: 55 – 78 – 339 – 353 – 357

  67 (F) Wing: Gen. Anderson
  Groups: 20 – 352 – 359 – 361 – 364

VIII Rec.: Col. Roosevelt
  Group: 802 Rec – 7 PR.

GLOSSARY

Abschusskartei: List of shot-down aircraft
Abwehr: Defense
ace: Pilot with five or more aerial victories
auf Wiedersehen: Goodbye; au revoir; so long
Auswertestelle West: Intelligence and evaluation center–West
Bahnhof: Railway station
Beute- und Nachrichten-Auswertung: Booty (captured material) and information evaluation
Blitzkrieg: Lightning warfare
Booty: Captured or confiscated enemy material
BUNA: *Beute- und Nachrichten-Auswertung* (*see above*)
CIC: American Counter Intelligence Corps
cooler: Jailhouse
COR: Camp officer–Reception; the reception office
D-day: The day the Allied invasion of Europe started
DMZ: Demilitarized zone
dog tags: Metal tags hung on a metal chain around the neck of all American soldiers. Name, rank, serial number, and blood type indicated on the tags.
Dolmetscher Kompanie: Interpreters company
D-ring: The handle or ring a parachuting man must grasp and pull, thereby pulling the rip cord, which activates his parachute
Dulag Luft: Luftwaffe transient POW camp. Dulag is short for the word *Durchgangslager*
D.v.D.: *Dolmetscher vom Dienst*: Translator on duty

The Interrogator

Eagle Squadron: One of three fighter squadrons in the Royal Air Force (RAF), composed of American volunteer pilots
Eeldberg: Mountain peak in the Taunus range
Ehr, Lehr, Wehr: Honor, Study, Armor
ersatz: substitute; unnatural foods
Feldwebel: German military rank equivalent to the American sergeant rank
Fido: Fog Investigation and Dispersal Operation
fighter ace: Fighter pilot with five or more aerial victories in aerial combat
flak: in German, *Flieger Abwehr Kanone*; antiaircraft cannon
Flieger: pilot, airman, aviator
force majeure: Overpowering force; an act of God
Fortress: The Boeing B-17, a four-engined American bomber
Gefreiter: German rank equivalent to America's private 1st class
Gestapo: Popular name for the German state secret police, Geheime Staatspolizei
Hande Hoch: Hands up!
Hals und Beinbruch: Humorous "good luck" or "all the best," though it actually is "break your neck and bones." German fighter pilots thought it bad luck to wish another pilot good luck just before a flight, since the opposite usually happened.
hari-kiri: Japanese ritual of suicide by cutting the belly with a sharp knife; self-disembowelment. Also *seppuku*.
Hauptmann: German rank of captain
He-111: A twin-engined bomber manufactured by Heinkel
Heim ins Reich: Home into Germany
Hohe-Mark: Small village in the high forest near Oberursel
Jafü: *Jagdfliegerführer*: A fighter leader. Usually the commander of a fighter division or several wings.
Jagdgeschwader: A Luftwaffe fighter wing; i.e., JG 26, JG 27, etc.
Jawohl: Yes
jibaku: Japanese, meaning "self-destruct" or "self-blast"; suicide rather than capture or surrender
Katschmarek, Kaczmarek, or *Katzmarek*: Wingman or the number two man in a flight of two fighters
Kdr. I.R. 364: Kommodore Infantry Regiment 364
Kein Mann braucht mehr: No man needs more
klicks: Slang for kilometers
Kommodore: The commander of a military unit such as a fighter wing; commander of a squadron is a *Staffel-Kapitan*.
Kriegsgefanger: Prisoner of war (POW)
Kriegies: Slang for prisoners
Lagezimmer: Situation room or briefing room
Liberator: American consolidated B-24 bomber, four engine
Luftwaffe: German air force

Glossary

mayday: Universal radio call of distress on voice frequency. On CW frequencies, the SOS signal is used; i.e., ... - ... (in Morse code, ... is S; - - is O, ... is S).

Me-109: Messerschmitt 109 single-engine fighter. Original versions were called Bf-109, up to the D model.

Mustang: North American Aviation Co. P-51, single-engine fighter airplane

Oberarzt: The head physician of a hospital or clinic

Obergefreiter: Corporal or leading aircraftsman rank (military)

Oberstleutnant: Lieutenant colonel

Oberleutnant: First lieutenant

Oberst: Military rank of colonel

Panzergrenadier: Infantryman assigned to an armored unit

Pinetree: Code name for an Allied communications center in England during WWII

Pluto: Code word for "Pipe Line under the Ocean"

POW: Prisoner of war

R-2800 engine: An aircraft engine manufactured in America by Pratt & Whitney. Used on the P-47 Thunderbolt fighter and Martin B-26 Marauder bomber, among others.

Rotte: German for a two-ship formation of aircraft. Sometimes called a *Kette*, especially when the two craft are jets. Two *Rotten* or *Ketten* are a *Schwarm*.

rpm: Revolutions per minute

Schwarm: A four-ship flight of airplanes (German)

SNAFU: GI slang meaning "situation normal, all fouled up"

SS: Schutz Staffel or Defense Corps. A special police corps founded by Hitler's orders in 1925.

Stalag Luft: Short for German *Stammlager*, a prisoner-of-war camp under Luftwaffe control. It means permanent camp.

Thunderbolt: The Republic Aviation Corp. single-engine fighter, the P-47. It was often called the "Jug."

tracer bullets: A bullet containing a pyrotechnic mixture that is ignited by the powder in the cartridge in order that the pilot can visibly see the trajectory of the bullet

V-1650 engine: An in-line, liquid-cooled engine used in the P-51 Mustang fighter. Manufactured by Rolls-Royce in England and by Packard in the USA.

Verboten: forbidden; prohibited

Vernehmungsoffizier: Interpreter or interrogation officer

Verstehen: Understand, comprehend, know

Vetter: Cousin

Wache: Guard

Wehrmacht: Unified German armed forces

Y-Kompanie: Intelligence-gathering communications company. The Germans called it "H-Kompanie," short for Horch. American services called it "Y Service," a code name for radio intercept service.

INDEX

4th Fighter Group, 111, 127, 178, 198, 202, 201, 206, 213, 284
8th Air Force, 125
8th Fighter Command, 96, 127, 177, 198
8th Fighter Wing, 167
9th Air Force, 132, 194, 242, 311
9th Tactical Air Force, 127
20th Fighter Group, 135, 138, 308
48th Fighter Group, 125
55th Fighter Squadron, 138
56th Fighter Group, 159, 179, 198, 244, 317
65th Fighter Wing, 66, 127
78th Fighter Group, 102, 249
79th Fighter Group, 161
82nd Fighter Group, 236
100th Bomb Group, 214
354th Air Service Group, 236
354th Fighter Squadron, 175
355th Fighter Group, 66, 78
357th Fighter Group, 168, 182
361st Fighter Group, 68
474th Fighter Group, 134
479th Fighter Group, 179, 180, 182, 189

Abwehr, 238
Adams, Fletcher E., 243
Andres, Werner, 216
Andrews, Marvin E., 236
Auschwitz, 298
Auswertestelle West, 16, 93, 132, 156
Auton, Jesse, 92, 119, 127

Bacque, James, 299
Bader, Douglas, 16, 45, 46, 47, 262
Barras, Judy, 226
Barth, Horst, 32, 35, 36, 37, 41, 42, 48, 95, 109, 140, 164, 166, 264, 273, 283
Battle of Britain, 16, 198
Bauer-Schlichtegroll, Gustav, 268
Becker, Otto, 164
Beckham, Walter C., 207, 208, 211, 213
Beeson, Duane W., 119, 202, 209
Belzec, 298
Bettis, Wilbur, 321

Index

Biehler, Frau, 64, 95
Birch, Deryck, 99, 104, 111
Blair, Charlie, 97
Blakeslee, Don, 119, 122, 127, 187
Bohner, Professor, 54
Böhringer, Otto, 72, 268
Bong, Dick, 259
Boschet, Hermann, 208
Brooks, James L., 312, 321
Brown, Curly, 95
Brown, Henry W., 67, 106, 175, 185, 189, 190
Buchenwald, 112

Care, Raymond C., 111
Carson, Kit, 98
Chambers, Whitaker, 315
Christensen, Fred, 260
Collande, Volker von, 245
Conger, Paul A., 136
Cook, Walter V., 259
Cooper, Bill, 95
Cooper, Fred, 239

Dachau, 298
Danckelman, Baron Eberhard von, 32
Danckelman, Baroness Sabine von, 306
Day, George E. "Bud", 115, 116
DeHaven, Robert M., 312, 321
Dolmetscher Kompanie Nr., XII 22
Dolmetscher Kompanien, 17
Doolittle, James H., 66, 92, 95, 127, 190, 317, 321
Dulag Luft, 16, 37, 146, 164
Düren, Johnnie van, 238

Eagle Squadron, 87, 89, 127, 198, 204, 318
Eberhardt, Heinrich, 268
Edison, Harry T., 125
Edner, Selden R., 204, 211
Eisenhower, Dwight D., 86, 117, 118

Emmer, Wallace N., 270
Erry, Don, 318
Esch, Herr Major von der, 66

Feustel, Oskar, 293
Fokker, Anthony, 148
Ford, Donald, 166
Foreign Legion, 233
French Underground, 189
Frey, Royal D., 5, 132, 135, 139, 317, 319
Fuchs, Blackie, 212

Gabreski, Don, 316
Gabreski, Francis S., 131, 134, 165, 188, 254, 256, 259, 261, 312, 316, 319
Galland, Adolf, 39, 42, 45, 50, 60, 216
Geneva Convention, 93, 112, 204
Gentile, Don, 119, 127
Gentle, Ernest, 6
German Foreign Office, 142
Gestapo 48, 52, 59, 72, 90, 112, 189, 219, 222, 263, 268, 272, 313, 318
Gibson, Squadron Leader, 66
Gille, Gerald, 239
Gille, Gerald G., 163
Gilpin, Peter W., 163
Gobert, Gerhard, 216
Godfrey, John T., 111
Göring, Hermann, 42, 50, 58, 206
Graham, Donald W., 98, 168
Green, George B., 178

Hanemann, Walter, 143, 230, 234, 236, 283, 315
Hartmann, Erich, 194
Hartwell, Norris E., 124
Haumann, Heinrich, 164
Haussmann, Ulrich, 246
Hayden, Josef, 164
Heisig, Viktor, 163
Hillman, Donald, 246

The Interrogator

Hilton, James, 94
Hiss, Alger, 315
Hommes Forty, 20
Hooton, Clifford, 163
Hubbard, Mark, 215
Huth, Oberst, 45

Ilfrey, Jack, 263
Inch, Robert A., 235
International Red Cross, 90
Ittershagen, E. W., 166, 172
Ittershagen, Oberarzt, 104
Ivelaw-Chapman, Marshal, 104
Ivelaw-Chapman, Ronald, 265, 267

Jagdgeschwader, 53 36
Jahn, Christian, 18, 291
Jaros, Arthur C., 163, 237, 239
Jenkins, Jack S., 216, 219
Jennings, Robert E., 164
JG 26, 161, 167, 176, 200
JG 52, 161
JG 54, 161, 179
Johnson, Gerald W., 6, 159, 198, 234, 244
Johnson, Robert S., 257, 259
Junge, Heinz, 52, 72, 268

Kaltenhauser, Corporal, 77
Kaufman, Mozart, 125, 130, 172
Kenney, George C., 165
Killinger, Erich, 17, 72, 121, 157, 268
Knight's Cross, 157
Krupinski, Walter, 194

Lagezimmer, 56
LaGrange, Jack, 233, 249
Landry, Robert M., 259
Lawson, George A., 124
Ledebur, Herr von, 24
LeMay, Curtis, 321
Lenfest, Charles W., 175, 185

Little, Robert, 166
Loock, Philippe, 143

Madame Direkteur, 244
Mahurin, Walker "Bud", 188, 194, 257, 312
Malmstrom, Einar, 31, 36
Manierre, Cy, 199
Marini, John H., 163
Marshall, Bert W., 178, 192
McCampbell, David, 259
McGuire, Thomas B., 259
McKennon, Pierce W., 178
Meyers, Martha, 306
Michalski, Gerhard, 213
Miller, Joe A., 166, 264, 271
Mills, Henry L., 119, 246
Mölders, Werner, 216
Monti, Martin, 315
Morgenthau, Henry, 301, 302
Murder Inc., 74, 148, 151

Nagel, Bert, 55, 136, 306, 308
Neal, Thomas F. "Jeeter", 243
"Norden" bombsight, 152

Offermann, Captain, 53, 72
Opel, Georg von, 143
Owens, Jesse, 107

Peterson A1, 96, 107
Plack, Werner, 140, 141, 142
Pompetti, Peter E., 102, 108
Postel, George Wilhelm, 24
Pratt, Robert H., 317
Price, Richard, Jr., 57
Priest, Royce W. "Deacon", 178, 192
Priller, Johanna, 168
Priller, Josef "Pips", 161, 167

Quesada, Pete, 165
Quick, Ernest, 239

Index

Rail, Gunther, 203
Raphael, Jack, 122
Red-Nosed Boys, 127
Richthofen, Baron Manfred von, 82, 136
Richthofen, Wolfrum von, 282
Rickenbacker, Eddie, 135
Rocher, Etienne, 224
Rooney, Rita, 317
Roosevelt, Elliott, 124, 125

Salisbury, Arthur G., 96
Salisbury, Harrison E., 316
Saunders, Homer L., 124
Saville, Gordon P., 166
Scharff, Hanns-Hermann, 18, 22
Scharff, Monika, 208
Scharff, Robert, 306
Schilling, David C., 92, 180, 187, 188, 259
Schmidt, Generalmajor, 121
Schmidt, Walther, 267, 272
Schröter, Fritz, 281, 282
Schuck, Walter, 312
Schulze, Kurt, 312
Schwartz, "Blackie", 32
Seifert, Johannes, 46
Shapero, Harold, 235
Shelser, James, 166
Shepard, Bert, 220
Shoop, Clarence A., 124
Silvernail, L. A., 126, 129, 132
Smart, Jacob E., 160, 166
Smith, Kenneth G., 89, 256, 258, 318
Spaatz, Tooey, 92
Spicer, Russ, 168, 171, 211
Spivey, Delmar T., 165, 320, 322
Stalag Luft, 16, 147
Stark, Charles W., 158, 161, 231, 264, 317
Steinbach, Richard, 299, 302
Stewart, Everett, 57, 75

Stewart, James C., 260
Stoertebecker, Klaus, 39
Stokes, Claude, 81, 83
Story, Noel, 233
Story, Noel E., 165
Stryker, Lloyd Paul, 235
Sublette, John L., 92
Swedish Red Cross, 164
Szaniawski, Jonesy, 78, 88

Terror Flieger, 184
Tgarth, Bruno, 291
Thorsen, Art, 227
Thurman, Wayne E., 125
Toliver, Ray, 41, 312, 317, 319
Tomae, Rolf, 164
Toombs, Harry, 304
Trautloft, Hannes, 167, 179
Treblinka, 298
Troller, Howard, 317
Trübenbach, Hans, 161

USO, 141

Vernehmungsoffizier, 37

Weisel, James, 219, 226, 318
Whitlock, C. G., 239
Wilfing, William, 291
Williams, Kenneth, 149
Wilson, Cy, 133, 134
Wilson, Gill Rob, 165
Winchell, Walter, 140
Woerheide, Victor C., 315
Woods, Sydney S., 284
Woodward, Hal, 239
Work, Robert, 316
Zemke, Hubert, 92, 165, 179, 194, 198, 255, 262

Also from the publisher

FIGHTER ACES OF THE LUFTWAFFE
Raymond F. Toliver & Trevor J. Constable

Size: 8 1/2" x 11" over 600 photographs
352 pages, hard cover
ISBN: 0-88740-909-1 $49.95

**THE RAGGED IRREGULARS
The 91st Bomb Group in World War II**
Marion Havelaar

Size: 8 1/2" x 11" over 300 photos
288 pages, hard cover
ISBN: 0-88740-810-9 $45.00

**HERKY!
The Memoirs of a Checkertail Ace**
Herschel H. Green

Size: 8 1/2" x 11" over 150 b/w photographs
192 pages, hard cover
ISBN: 0-7643-0073-3 $45.00

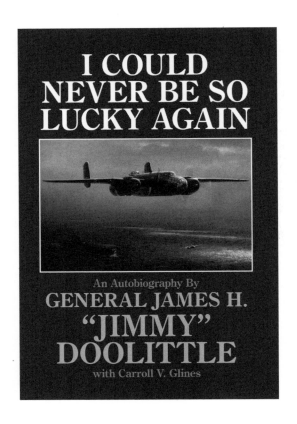

I COULD NEVER BE SO LUCKY AGAIN
An Autobiography of James H. "Jimmy" Doolittle
with Carroll V. Glines

Size: 6" x 9" 48 pages of photographs
622 pages, hard cover
ISBN: 978-0-88740-737-6 $29.99